OFFICE PROCEDURES

Related titles in the series

OFFICE PROCEDURES

Geoffrey Whitehead, BSc. (Econ.)

MADE SIMPLE
BOOKS

Made Simple
An imprint of Butterworth-Heinemann Ltd
Linacre House, Jordan Hill, Oxford OX2 8DP

ℛ A member of the Reed Elsevier group

OXFORD   LONDON   BOSTON
MUNICH   NEW DELHI   SINGAPORE   SYDNEY
TOKYO   TORONTO   WELLINGTON

First published 1994

British Library Cataloguing in Publication Data
Whitehead, Geoffrey
    Office Procedures. –
    I. Title
    651

ISBN 0 7506 0869 2

Printed and bound in Great Britain by
Clays, St Ives plc

Contents

Preface

Office Procedures Made Simple provides a sound background in office procedures for all those who propose to work or are working in a business environment anywhere in the world. It meets the syllabus requirements of the UK National Vocational Qualification in Office Procedures, Levels 1 and 2, and equivalent syllabuses in other countries where the language of instruction is English. It is a successor to the highly successful text *Office Practice Made Simple*, which sold over half a million copies.

It is intended both as a classroom text around which full-time or part-time courses can be built, and as a self-study manual for those seeking to improve their educational standing in the 'office procedures' field by private study. It is also of use as a general reference book for those returning to clerical, secretarial and book-keeping roles after some time in other occupations.

In writing this book I am indebted to many helpful people who have responded to my requests to firms and companies for assistance with photographs, background material, etc. It has been impossible to include them all, and I must apologize for any disappointment. I trust that my admonitions to students who eventually take employment in this field to keep in touch with the trade press will enable all firms to bring their products to the attention of interested parties. I am most grateful for the generous assistance given. At the same time the views expressed in this book are my own, and the featuring of particular products cannot be deemed to be the responsibility of any firm or company.

GEOFFREY WHITEHEAD

Acknowledgements

Blakeley Business Forms
British Olivetti Ltd
British Telecom
Business Equipment Digest
Croner Publications Ltd
Data Card (UK) Ltd
Department of Trade and Industry
Evrite Ltd
Formecon Services Ltd
IBM (UK) Ltd
International Time Recording Co Ltd
K + N International (Office Systems) Ltd
Kalamazoo Ltd
MFI Ltd
Neat Ideas
Olympia (UK) Ltd
Pitney Bowes Ltd
Reliance Systems Ltd
Silver Reed Business Machines Ltd
Twinlock Ltd
George Vyner Ltd, Huddersfield
Wilson and Whitworth Ltd
F.W. Woolworth PLC

1 The office as the centre of business activity

1.1 The place of the office in organizations

The 'world of work' is a huge collection of organizations of every type and size. Some businesses are 'sole trader' enterprises, where one individual (male or female) has complete control of the organization. Others are huge organizations with hundreds of thousands of employees. In the United Kingdom the Civil Service has over half a million employees, working in hundreds of different 'ministries' with branches and departments in every part of the land. The biggest organization ever in the United Kingdom was the British Transport Commission, set up in 1947. It had 943 000 employees. It was so big, and so difficult to run, that in 1953 Parliament decided to break it up into more manageable pieces.

Every organization is controlled from a nerve centre called 'the office'. If it is a large organization it may have many offices, and the most important one will be called the 'head office'. If it is a tiny organization, run by a sole trader, the 'office' may be just a single desk, with a chair and a telephone. Figure 1.1 shows a compact piece of furniture called a 'home office'. It has a desk, a place for a typewriter or a personal computer (PC), some drawers, shelves, filing places to keep important records, etc., etc. The ends fold in at the end of the day and hide everything from view.

The lucky sole trader, working from home, has everything necessary in the 'Home Office'. He/she gets up in the morning, makes a cup of tea, opens the 'office' and starts work. No commuting, no bad weather to worry about, no driving and no delay. From such a tiny office the sole trader plays his/her part in organizing the production, distribution and sale of whatever goods form the stock-in-trade of the business, or provides the services he/she offers to the world at large.

What part does the office play in the business activities of production, distribution and exchange of goods and services? The original meaning of the word 'office' was 'piece of kindness, or service to one's fellow men'. Today it is used more often to describe a room, or building, where clerical processes are carried out to start, develop and control the many activities of a business. There are head offices, branch offices, factory offices, cost offices, transport offices, sales offices and many more. They vary from the magnificent 'boardroom'

Figure 1.1 A compact home office (reproduced by courtesy of MFI Ltd)

of an international company to the single unit of furniture called a 'home office' shown in Figure 1.1.

Every single organization has at its very centre the office which gives life to the whole organization. Not a wheel turns until the orders go out from head office, or branch office, or the departmental office. It is in the office that projects are conceived, plans made, prototypes devised and arrangements for practice runs are made. An office is not therefore a dull and lifeless place. It is more exciting than the busiest transport depot, the most exposed North Sea oil rig, the deepest gold mine and the remotest space station. They can carry out only what the office has planned and authorized.

1.2 The functions of the office

The functions of the office include the following:

(*a*) The starting of any enterprise by the issue of instructions to departments to proceed with projects.

(*b*) Devising report and feedback systems so that the progress of projects, sales, etc., can be followed and if necessary stimulated by whatever action seems necessary. **Control activities** are an essential feature of office activities.

(*c*) The supervision of money flows to ensure that funds are available to meet expenditure at all times.

(*d*) Routine administration matters; the recruitment and payment of staff, the ordering of equipment and materials and the safeguarding of assets once they have been purchased.

(*e*) Receiving and collecting information in various formats, sorting and processing it if necessary, either manually or with the help of mechanical or computerized equipment, and passing it on to interested parties who need to be kept informed.

(*f*) The keeping of all essential documents in good order (filed and indexed) so that they are available when required.

(*g*) Ensuring that all the requirements of both statutes (Acts of Parliament) and local bye-laws are kept. Such laws and bye-laws may relate to a wide variety of matters − the safety of products manufactured; the use of poisonous or dangerous materials; health and safety at work; the reporting of accidents; the racial and sexual balance in an office, factory or depot; the licensing of vehicles; the inspection of goods, etc.

(*h*) Above all the office, in every aspect of its work, is concerned with **information**, with obtaining and collecting information, sorting, arranging and interpreting it, supplying it to management when required and preserving it for as long as it is useful in promoting the enterprise concerned. The office maintains communications between departments and with outside firms and government agencies.

(*i*) Finally, and a point that may not occur to younger readers, there is a general duty on all office staff to safeguard and preserve the assets of a business. The term 'assets' may be applied to everything that a business owns − from the paper clips to the heaviest machinery. However, the term is usually reserved for those items that are used in the business long-term (longer than one year). Thus land and buildings, furniture and fittings, office equipment, plant and machinery and motor vehicles are all assets of the business. We must take care of them if the business is to remain efficient and prosperous.

Considering some of these aspects in more detail we may list the activities discussed below.

(a) Receiving and collecting information in various formats

(i) *Many firms receive orders over the telephone.* If the order is from a regular customer there is no problem. For example, a café might phone through a daily order for milk, yoghurts, soft drinks, pastries, cream, etc.

If the order is from an unknown customer, we may want to take a credit card number. Students ordering textbooks often pay in this way. Before sending off the book, the publisher phones the credit card company's telephone number and is given payment at once for the item.

(ii) *Many firms receive information by fax.* Fax is short for facsimile copier, a copier that receives letters, pictures and diagrams over the telephone wires. At each end of the telephone network is a transceiver (a machine that can both transmit and receive). At the transmitting end the letter or picture is passed into the machine and scanned by an electric eye. The eye reads the quality of the light at every point on the paper and transmits it as a message along the line. At the receiving end these messages are turned back into an exact copy of the document.

A clerk at the receiving end takes the FAX from the machine and passes it to the appropriate person. Orders go to the order clerk for processing and eventual dispatch, proofs of advertising copy go to the sales department for checking, etc.

(iii) *Complaints by letter.* Another format for information is the ordinary letter, postcard, completed questionnaire, etc., arriving by post. Taking complaints as an example, these are sent to the public relations department, where they will be considered and a suitable reply prepared. We often collate the statistics about complaints – to see if the same complaint occurs regularly. Steps will then be taken to correct the fault. One ferry company began to receive reports that its paper cups were littering the beaches all along the South Coast. On investigation it found that a lazy steward was throwing the cups overboard instead of filling the trash sacks. Unfortunately the cups were almost unsinkable. The solution was to lay down firm rules about the trash.

(b) Sorting and processing the information

Almost all information has to have some action taken. An order has to be passed to an order clerk, who will check the availability of stock to fulfil the order, price it and send it to an invoice typist, who will type the necessary invoice. We must now send a copy to the customer, pass further copies to the 'order pickers' in the stores, who will pick out the items and send them to the dispatch department, etc.

Mark Twain, the American humorist, wrote in one of his letters home from Nevada where he was working in a government office, 'Our motto is – Never put off until tomorrow what you can put off until the day after tomorrow'. This is not an idea that will appeal to office managers. Many firms respond by return of post to correspondents. Some firms pride themselves on fulfilling orders the same day as they are received. In the latest e-mail systems (where memos are sent electronically) if you receive a memo from someone addressed to you, all you need to do is tell the machine to reverse the orders — the receiver becomes the sender and the sender becomes the receiver — key in your reply and off it goes. It takes about 6 seconds only, even if it has to cross the Atlantic with your memo.

(c) Communicating information

(i) *Start-up activities*. No business activity starts of its own accord. Someone has to show enterprise, and we usually use the term 'entrepreneur' for this individual. In a large organization we may have many entrepreneurs but for each project there is a single individual — the team leader — who becomes the entrepreneur for the project. He/she starts with a problem and finishes with a solution. It may be 'How can we use the principle of jet propulsion to fly an aeroplane?' It may be 'How can we use the waste product from the manufacture of our copper boilers?' Eventually the solution will be found and the production line, or the sales drive, or the activity required will be planned, prepared for and finally started. The office will be involved with every aspect — appointing staff, finding the necessary finance, authorizing the purchase of stocks and supplies and, finally, giving the go-ahead. Nothing moves until head office says 'Go!'

(ii) *Passing information down the chain of command*. In a large company decisions are made at the top level of the organization, by the board of directors, but they often have to be carried out lower down, at the 'grass roots' level. The key link between the board and the workforce is the managing director; it is up to the managing director to make sure that the board's decisions are conveyed to the lower ranks in some way. He/she may delegate the job to departmental managers, or may have notices drawn up and sent to all staff, but somehow the decisions must be conveyed to everyone who needs to know. The person who can truthfully say 'They never tell me anything!' is being placed in a very unfair position. Staff at lower levels soon lose morale if they are treated with indifference.

Figure 1.2 shows a simple chart of a large company and the various tiers of responsibility. Each department has some useful function to perform, and such a company is said to be organized 'along functional lines'.

1.3 A public sector organization

Public sector organizations, such as the Department of Trade and Industry (shown in Figure 1.3), are naturally very complex. The chart in Figure 1.3 was produced by the Department shortly after a

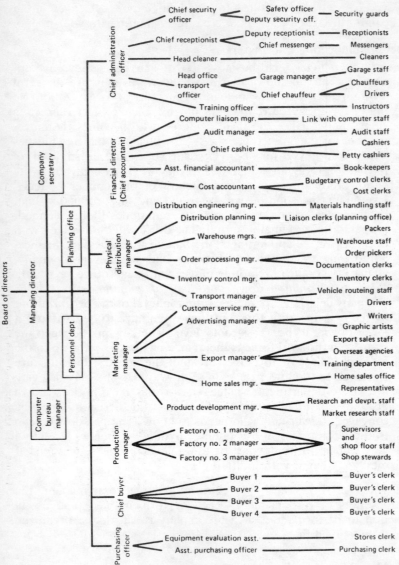

Figure 1.2 A typical business organization along functional lines

The Department of Trade and Industry

President of the Board of Trade

Minister for Trade | Minister for Industry | Minister for Energy | Parliamentary Under-Secretary for Technology | Parliamentary Under-Secretary for Corporate Affairs | Parliamentary Under-Secretary for Consumer Affairs and Small Firms

Permanent Secretary

British Overseas Trade Board (BOTB)

Deputy Secretary for Trade Policy and Export Promotion
- Europe
- International Trade Policy
- Projects & Export Policy
- Overseas Trade (Three Divisions)
- Joint directorate

Deputy Secretary for Industry 1
- Textiles & Retailing
- Telecommunications & Posts
- Nat. Phys. Laboratory
- Warren Spring Laboratory
- Laboratory of the Government Chemist
- National Engineering Laboratory
- Weights & Measures
- Radio Communications

Deputy Secretary for Industry 2
- Chemicals & Biotechnology
- Steel, metals and Minerals
- Vehicles
- Aerospace
- Electronics & Electrical Engineering
- Mechanical Engineering

Deputy Secretary for Science & Technology
- Research & Technology
- Information and Manufacturing Technologies
- Environment
- British National Space Centre
- Patent Office

Deputy Secretary for Energy
- Industrial Competitiveness
- Coal
- Electricity
- Atomic Energy
- Oil & Gas
- Offshore supplies
- International Energy Unit

Deputy Secretary for Regional Affairs & Small Firms
- Small firms
- Enterprise Initiative
- 8 Regional offices

Deputy Secretary for Corporate & Consumer affairs
- Competition Policy
- Deregulation
- Consumer Affairs
- Insurance
- Companies
- Insolvency Service Agency
- Companies House Agency

The Solicitor
- Investigations
- Four Divisions of legal advisers

Deputy Secretary for Establishment & Finance
- Finance and Resource Management
- Personnel
- Services
- Information
- Economics & Statistics
- Internal audit
- Accounts

Figure 1.3 Organization of a public sector department (August 1992)

major reorganization in 1992, in which the Department absorbed a number of divisions from the Department of Energy and also the Small Firms Division from the Department of Employment. The chart is largely self-explanatory, showing the various divisions of work covered and giving some idea of the variety of civil servants employed. The reader might be amused to know that when this Department was first started in Victorian times the person in charge of it was called the President of the Board of Trade (the title has recently been restored), and the entire staff consisted of the president and one clerk. At that time the whole of the government's revenue consisted of £69 million, whereas today it is over £240000 million. There are many offices in the government departments today, and the whole nation is much richer than in Queen Victoria's time but it does take a lot of organizing to keep the country prosperous. One Victorian prime minister said, 'The chief business of government departments is the saving of candle-ends'. Today the chief business of government departments is to keep the nation prosperous.

One difficulty about understanding what offices do is that they serve the 'world of work', which we are all bound to enter as soon as we complete our education. We cannot understand what offices do unless we have a fairly clear picture of the world of work, and the many organizations mankind has developed to provide the prosperity we all desire. The world of work is described later in this chapter.

1.4 The office junior

When children left school at 12 or 14, it was common for such young people to take posts as office juniors. Naturally their level of ability was fairly low — we would regard them today as being in the position of completing their education at work, just as today pupils in their final school years take a week or two away from school for 'work experience'. Today those who stay on at school until 16, or go to college until 18 or even older, have already acquired many office skills and may hope to go straight into departments such as the accounts department, the general administration department, sales department, etc. It remains a fact that there are many junior posts in offices today. Such posts are considered in some detail in Chapter 2. Here it is only worth making this point — do not despise the post of office junior. It is a vital job in any organization and has the following advantages:

- It is a post where you can meet and get to know everybody.
- Almost any type of work can be offered you, and you therefore find which jobs suit you and which you thoroughly dislike.
- You will also find which jobs offer the best careers for the future, and you can follow up those that appeal to you.

- Your level of ability is not high, so that if you do make a mess of a particular job, no real blame will attach to you — while your numerous successes in particular activities will be noted and will reflect on you with credit.
- The work is companionable. Often good friendships made at this level are helpful in later life. Perfect marriages may be made in heaven, but perfectly satisfactory ones start every day in the routine hurly-burly of office life.

1.5 Points to think about and discuss

(*a*) Discuss which of the following offices would be the best place to work in:

   (i) A sales office in a mail order house.
  (ii) A solicitor's office.
 (iii) A buying department for a fashion house.
 (iv) A coroner's office.

(*b*) A young female office worker has the following complaints:

   (i) Much of the work is boring and repetitive.
  (ii) The workplace is poorly designed, cramped and largely unventilated, and she has an old, uncomfortable chair.
 (iii) Although she has now worked for 3 months no one has discussed her career structure with her or given any advice about promotion prospects.

Discuss what she should do to remedy these complaints.

1.6 Rapid revision — office activities

In this book each chapter ends with a test-yourself section, which acts both as a chapter summary and a revision test. Cover the page with a sheet of plain paper and uncover the first question. Try to answer it from your knowledge of the chapter. Lower the paper and read the answer to question 1. Then read question 2 and try to answer it. (This test appears on page 10.)

1.7 The nature of the 'world of work'

We live in a world where everyone 'wants' things. Babies cry for milk, warmth and protection. Teenagers demand trendy clothes, the latest 'hit' records, driving licences and interesting textbooks. Old-age pensioners 'want' tasty food, television sets, geriatric wards and pain-killing drugs. It is the working world that supplies these things, satisfying the wants of millions of people by the production of goods and services. An endless flood of cornflakes, biscuits, loaves of

Answers	Questions
–	1 What is an office?
1 It is the nerve centre of a business from which orders flow out to all sectors of a firm or company.	2 What is a 'home office'?
2 A neatly organized piece of furniture from which a sole trader, operating from his/her own home, can run his/her enterprise.	3 What do we call a person who shows enterprise?
3 An entrepreneur.	4 What is a boardroom?
4 It is the room in the head office of a company where the board of directors meets to conduct its board meetings.	5 What are the functions of the office?
5 (i) To start activities by giving orders. (ii) To devise report and feedback procedures and thus establish control. (iii) To supervise money flows and ensure funds are always available. (iv) To keep routine activities (paying staff, cleaning, canteens, etc.) going. (v) To receive, collate and process information and pass it to those interested. (vi) To file and keep records of every sort. (vii) To ensure compliance with statutes and bye-laws. (viii) To safeguard the assets of the business.	6 What does it mean when we say a business is organized along functional lines?
6 It means the activities of the business are carried out by departments, each of which is charged with some important function.	7 List some of these functions.
7 Buying, selling, manufacturing, accounting, dispatch, transporting, research, marketing, etc.	8 What are the main activities of government departments, such as the Department of Trade and Industry?
8 (a) They seek to encourage activity that will be of benefit to the nation and its citizens (b) They seek to control harmful activities such as those with adverse effects on the environment, or unfair practices of various sorts.	9 Who is in charge of a government department?
9 A minister (who may be a member of the Cabinet) and a Permanent Secretary, who is the senior official appointed to carry out the Minister's programme.	10 Go over the page again until you are sure of all the answers.

bread, clothing, footwear, furniture and other goods pours from the production lines to be packaged, boxed, warehoused, transported and delivered to customers in every corner of the globe. Other businesses are at work providing services. Electricity generating stations are busy day and night generating power for homes, factories and transport systems. Surgeons are on duty round the clock for emergency cases. Soldiers guard our frontiers because we 'want' peace. Police patrol our streets to bring security.

All this activity can be described in five words: enterprise, production, distribution, marketing and consumption. Someone has to set up a basic organization for each good or service required. These people who show enterprise (they are called *entrepreneurs*, a word of French origin which means 'those who undertake a task') begin to produce the goods or services we all require. Then they have to be distributed (if they are goods) or we have to *move* to them if they are services (like hospital or dental services). At some point we buy the goods, or pay for the services. This is the marketing activity, where buyers and sellers are in contact to exchange goods and services for money, known as 'the price'. Then we enjoy them, which is called 'consumption'. Of course, the word 'consumption' in general use means 'to eat' and we certainly do eat many of the goods we buy, but consumers also consume the clothes they wear, the cars they drive, the shelter they live in, etc. A complete picture of the whole process requires only two more words: 'wants' to describe the causes of this immense hive of activity, and 'satisfactions' to describe the results it achieves. The pattern of the entire working world can therefore be described in brief as:

'WANTS' → ENTERPRISE → PRODUCTION →
DISTRIBUTION → MARKETING → CONSUMPTION →
SATISFACTION (and back to WANTS again for another cycle).

Of course, as soon as we have consumed one meal, we start to think about the next, and the whole process has to start all over again. There is therefore an endless cycle of production, consumption; production, consumption; production, consumption. This cycle is shown in Figure 1.4.

1.8   Why are organizations formed?

Organizations are formed to provide the goods and services mankind needs. Some of the things we need do not spring to mind straight away. Unlike food, water, clothing and shelter, which we need every day of our lives, we only get born once, we only die once, and most people only get married once. The maternity services that help us into the world, the registrar or other appointed person who

Figure 1.4 The cycle of business activity

marries us and the undertakers who lay us finally to rest are not the sort of organizations we need every day.

Although few of us ever go to court, the legal services are there for those who require them; if we travel abroad, the passport office will help us make the necessary arrangements; while the Inland Revenue Department collects taxes from the rich to help the poor, like some modern Robin Hood. We don't think how important this is until we strike hard times and turn to our well-organized Department of Health and Social Security for assistance. What a relief it is then to find that they have money available; shelter for the homeless; food for the hungry; wheelchairs for the disabled, etc.

If we list therefore the various reasons why organizations come into existence we find the following main causes:

(*a*) The production of goods for personal consumption (consumer goods).

(*b*) The production of capital assets (often called producer goods), such as factories, tools, machinery, office equipment, heavy motor vehicles, etc., to help the production process.

(*c*) The provision of personal services, such as education, medical and dental care, hairdressing, entertainment, etc.

(*d*) The provision of commercial services, such as banking, insurance, transport and communication.

(*e*) The provision of protective services, including defence, police, fire and rescue services.

(*f*) To legislate: parliament and local government bodies.

(*g*) The provision of administrative services, such as taxation, Customs and Excise, social security, licensing and control services of all sorts.

(*h*) To administer justice; the courts' system and the prison and related services.

We should note, though, that there is a limit to the wealth that can be created, and therefore each of the types of organization listed above must operate as efficiently as possible. *In our economic activities the aim is to create the greatest output of useful goods and services from the smallest possible input of resources, for resources are scarce and we try to avoid wasting them.*

1.9 The private and public sectors of the economy

In all countries some degree of private enterprise is found and some measure of public enterprise is bound to exist too. These two sections of the economy are usually called 'sectors', or parts of a circle. The whole wealth of goods and services of our nation is looked upon as a large round cake, cut into two large portions, one part produced by the **private sector** (business firms) and the other part produced by the **public sector** (local and central government departments).

In a mixed economy like the United Kingdom, then, we have a complex pattern of organizations producing the goods and services we need. The pattern is constantly changing but in general the production of goods and commercial services tends to be performed by *private sector business organizations*, though some goods (like coal) and some services (like hospital services, electrical power from atomic energy and education) are mainly produced by nationalized industries (i.e. *the public sector*). In recent years many industries formerly run as nationalized industries have been privatized (sold off to private buyers). However, for *Office Procedures*, we need not consider the merits or demerits of the two types of organization.

Organizations range from one-person businesses (sole traders) to huge organizations with thousands of employees. If we list the types of organization in the United Kingdom, we find them to consist of three main types: private-enterprise units, non-profit-making units such as clubs and co-operative societies, and public enterprises. The list is as follows:

Private enterprises
  Sole traders
  Partnerships
  Limited partnerships
  Private limited companies
  Public limited companies
  Holding companies (a more advanced type of public company)

Non-profit-making units
  Clubs of many types
  Co-operative societies

Public enterprises
  Autonomous corporations
  Quasi-autonomous non-governmental organizations (Quangos)
  Nationalized undertakings
  Local government departments
  Central government departments

These are the organizations in which we all work. We may set up a business of our own, and become a sole trader. There are more than 1 million sole traders in the United Kingdom. We may take employment with a large company. There are about 2 500 really large companies, some of them so large that they handle every year more wealth than whole nations (such as developing countries in Africa or Asia). We may join an autonomous corporation, like the Port of London Authority, or work for a government department, like the Department of the Environment. Whether we choose the private sector or the public sector we shall be providing the goods and services needed, and in return we shall receive a share of the nation's output, so that we are fed, clothed, sheltered, educated, entertained, cured when we are ill and finally buried when we die.

In the mixed economy the pattern of business organizations is therefore as follows:

(*a*) A very large number of small business units, mainly organized as sole trader or partnership enterprises. Frequently they will have employees, but not many, the sole trader or partners playing a leading role and making the crucial business decisions. A great many of these small firms are organized as private limited companies. This has certain advantages which are explained later (see Figure 1.6) but they do not have to be large firms and many of them are only £100 companies. (This means that the authorized capital subscribed by the owners is only £100, so clearly they are only small organizations). A 1970 inquiry into the needs of small firms (the Bolton

Report) found that there were $1\frac{1}{4}$ million of them in the United Kingdom of which about $\frac{1}{2}$ million were private companies. In manufacturing 94 per cent of firms were small (with an average of 25 employees) and in retailing 96 per cent of firms were small, with turnover at that time of less than £1000 per week. Today this average turnover would be about £4000 per week. These small firms fill the gaps between the very large firms and the huge nationalized organizations. They supply local, or specialized, services in a very wide range of industries.

(*b*) The second major group of business units is the group of large, private enterprises, limited liability companies who form the backbone of the nation's industrial and commercial power. They are not very numerous; there are, for example, only about 2500 **public limited companies**. The name 'public' company is applied to companies whose shares are quoted on the Stock Exchange, and may be sold to the general public. All such public issues have to be made in such a way that they observe the strict rules of the Stock Exchange and comply with the requirements of the Companies Acts, 1985–9. Although these companies are not very numerous, most of them are very large. Many have over £500000000 capital, which contrasts greatly with the £100 companies so common in the unquoted companies mentioned in (*a*) above. In fact, the Bolton Report already referred to showed that in manufacturing the 94 per cent of small firms only did 16 per cent of the work carried out by the industry. In retailing, 96 per cent of the firms were small but they had between them only 32 per cent of the turnover. Large firms did 84 per cent of manufacturing, 68 per cent of retail trade, 73 per cent of building and construction, 71 per cent of motor-vehicle production and repair work, 89 per cent of wholesaling and 80 per cent of mining and quarrying.

(*c*) The third group is a relatively small group, the **non-profit-making organizations**. The largest of these is the group of co-operative societies, which handle about £10000 million of trade every year. Others, like the Automobile Association, are quite large, but many clubs and societies are very small and serve to meet the needs of members for recreational purposes rather than as major businesses.

(*d*) The fourth major grouping in the mixed economy is the group of **nationalized industries and services**. In the United Kingdom these include British Rail and the Atomic Energy Authority. On the non-industrial side such services as the National Health Service and the social security services are less obviously productive, but their contribution in terms of human happiness and in the relief of distress of every sort is quite incalculable. Because these industries and services are so large and are often monopolies controlling the whole industry or service, they have the capital to set up the most advanced types of organization. Each nationalized organization is a study in its own right, employing thousands of workers at all sorts of levels and endeavouring to achieve the very best structure possible for the industry it controls, or the service it provides.

These four groups of organization make up the **'world of work'**. What do they need to use when they try to produce goods or services? The answer is three things: *land*, *labour* and *capital*. They are called the **factors of production**. A full explanation of these three factors of production is really the subject matter of economics and is given in another volume, *Economics Made Simple*. Very quickly we may list them as follows:

(*a*) **Land**. Agricultural land, business sites and premises, the minerals of the earth, the gases of the atmosphere, fossil fuels like oil and coal, forest products, animal products and the bounties of the sea. All these things are usually called **primary products**, because they were provided first by nature. Many of these products are also worked upon and improved into what we call **secondary products**. Crude oil is refined into petroleum, timber is made into furniture, iron ore is made into steel, etc. Clearly the word 'land' covers a great many things provided by nature originally.

(*b*) **Labour**. Before natural products can be turned into useful things, work has usually to be performed. Some processes are very simple, like freezing garden peas. Some are more complicated, like using atomic energy to generate electricity. There are many types of skilled and unskilled labour, but all of them are necessary. The lathe operator who works a difficult machine to make a motorcar component; the inspector who tests and packages it; the driver who drives it to the depot near your home; and the road-sweeper who makes sure the driver does not get a puncture are all doing useful work.

(*c*) **Capital**. Capital is often thought of as money, but this is only a special kind of capital, called **liquid capital**. Liquid capital is soon turned into **fixed capital**, which means buildings, machinery, tools and anything else which is used by organizations in the production process.

These three factors of production – land, labour, and capital – are illustrated in Figure 1.5. Study this diagram before we go on to consider how the mixed economy really works.

1.10 The world of work needs a money system

One of the results of working our system of production in the way that we do is that we have to invent a 'money' system. Money makes the world go round, but it is only an instrument of human activity, not a governing force. John Stuart Mill, a famous nineteenth-

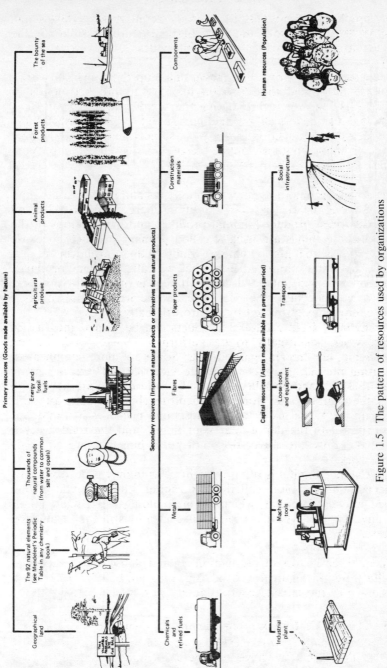

Figure 1.5 The pattern of resources used by organizations

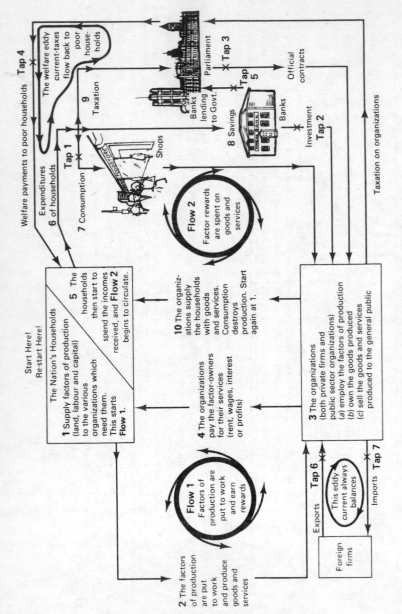

Figure 1.6 Flows of money round the mixed economy

Notes

(i) The first flow is of factor services into production and the payment of rewards to the factors, in the form of rent, wages, interest or profits. (Follow Flow 1 round the circle 1, 2, 3, 4; 1, 2, 3, 4, etc.)

(ii) Everything the firms receive in one period is paid out in the next period, either as rent, wages interest or profits – but there is also a very large flow of taxation to the Government which is used to finance the public sector services like defence, education, etc. In the first period these payments must come from the capital provided by those who start the firms up. In later periods the funds come from the sales of goods and services produced in the previous period.

(iii) The second flow is the expenditure of income on goods and services. The owners of the factors spend the incomes they receive. The income flows through a number of taps, which influence the level of activity in the economy. If a tap is closed off for some reason, activity in the economy declines (a slump). If taps are opened wide, activity in the economy increases (a boom). Let us look at each tap in turn.

(iv) Tap 1: Consumption. If the nation's households are spending a great deal on consumer goods and services business will be booming. If households are pessimistic about the future and only buying essentials, Tap 1 will be partially closed and the economy will slump.

(v) Tap 2: The Savings-investment tap. If savings are high consumption will be low (Tap 1 almost closed). This will not matter if the savings are borrowed by businessmen (or by the government through Tap 5 for the public-sector borrowing requirement – PSBR). An open Tap 2 means strong investment and the economy will keep booming along.

(vi) Tap 3 and Tap 4: These taps are controlled by the government. Tap 4 (welfare payments) allows tax money to flow back to poor families so that they can consume goods and services. This opens up Tap 1 and keeps the economy booming. Tap 3 allows more official contracts for all sorts of things (defence, education, health services, highways, etc.) to be placed. This gives employment to unemployed people and keeps the economy booming. If taxes are not sufficient to pay for these contracts the government borrows through Tap 5 the money that pessimistic householders are saving for 'a rainy day' when they might lose their jobs. The government contracts ensure that the 'rainy day' never comes.

(vii) Foreign trade always balances (the balance of payments) but sometimes it is a bit more difficult than others. The government does a good deal of manipulating to keep this balance right, and sometimes has to call in the *International Monetary Fund* to overcome a difficult period. Temporarily it is possible for Taps 6 and 7 to affect the working of the economy. A wide-open Tap 6 gives an export-led boom (funds flowing in to UK firms). A wide-open Tap 7 gives an import-led slump (funds flowing out to foreign firms, leaving UK firms starved of orders). However, as explained above, neither of these situations can continue indefinitely. A balance of payments has to be achieved. At present, we have ceased to be members of the Exchange Rate Mechanism (ERM) and consequently can influence the prices of our goods by allowing our currency to float downwards. Should we rejoin the ERM, we should have to induce a balance by influencing our own economy – closing off various taps – 1, 2, 3, and 4).

(viii) The reader should now return to page 21, Section 1.11.

century philosopher who lived in the early days of the capitalist system, was the first man to point this out. We have developed a powerful tool for creating wealth by specialization. We do not run a simple economy, like Robinson Crusoe on his island, doing a little fishing, and then a little hunting, and then gathering shellfish. We specialize. We take a full-time job in some organization somewhere and we keep at it. We grow skilled as a result. The tailor makes hundreds of suits a year, whereas Man Friday, and probably Robinson Crusoe too, were naked most of the time. The tailor wears one of his suits, but exchanges the rest for food, shelter, furniture, warmth, light, entertainment, personal transport. He eats out in restaurants, attends pop festivals, flies to the Mediterranean for holidays, has his teeth drilled and his appendix removed, courts his sweetheart, sets up home, educates his children, and it is all done by the money system. To ensure reasonable fair play those with secure jobs and steady incomes pay taxes to help those who have not.

As John Stuart Mill said, having created the wealth, it is a matter of human policy only how we share it out. The money system is the method by which our complex society shares out wealth. How this is done is illustrated in Figure 1.6. Before studying this diagram let us note the stages of activity which are organized by money flows.

(*a*) The factors of production − land, labour and capital − are needed to produce wealth. For the full story of this the reader should read *Economics Made Simple*.

(*b*) The owners of these factors all live in our country. Some have land, some have capital, but most of us, as Karl Marx said, have 'nothing but our labour power'.

(*c*) The owners of the factors supply them to the various organizations and receive in exchange a money reward for the use of the factor. The reward for the use of land is called 'rent'; the reward for the use of capital is called 'interest'; the reward for the use of labour is 'wages'. Any surplus over and above these rewards is called 'profit'. It goes to the owner of the business, which may mean the sole trader or the partners, or it may mean the shareholders of the company. For the public sector, and 49 per cent of British wealth-creating activity is in the public sector, the government is the owner of the industries and departments, and the profit goes, to the Exchequer. This is the first flow of money − from the organizations to the owners of the factors of production. Of course, the original flow of this money has to be found from somewhere. It is the capital collected by the organizations from the founders of the firms, and explains why every business needs some money capital.

(*d*) Now we all have money as a reward for using our factors, and as we have created some goods and services, we can begin to consume − but first we must pay our taxes. For most of us the system is called PAYE — Pay As You Earn. This ensures that all those who for some reason are without an income — the sick, the disabled, the unemployed — can be provided for.

(*e*) The rest of our income is now available to be spent on whatever we care to spend it on — consumption.

(*f*) If we have too much income, we save it in banks. The banks then lend it·

(i) to organizations that wish to expand their business activities, or

(ii) to government bodies that are authorized to expand services to the general public. They are also spending tax moneys of course.

(*g*) One other flow that takes place is the flow of foreign trade. Our money flows out to buy imports, and foreigners' money flows in to buy our exports. As these flows must always be made to balance (a balance of payments), they do not really affect the money system, but they do enrich the variety of goods we can buy and make our life much fuller and more enjoyable as a result.

(*h*) As the money flows back to the organizations, whether as payment for goods and services or as loans from the banks, they are ready to pay the next week's rewards to factors. The early Socialists used to have a slogan which said: 'We go to work, to get the cash, to buy the food, to get the strength, to go to work, to get ..., etc.' It was a protest against a tyrannical system of work, and in those days the money system was a tyranny. It is really a tyranny no longer. Instead it is an instrument of democratic policy, which alone enables the exchange of goods and services to take place in a modern advanced society. The reader should now study Figure 1.6 and the notes below it.

1.11 Business organizations in the private sector

A full description of the types of business organization in the private sector is not appropriate in a book about office procedures. The reader should refer to *Commerce Made Simple* for a full account. It is true though that most offices deal with every type of organization, and a preliminary comparison of the various types of business units described in Figure 1.6 above is helpful. This is most easily studied in chart form, and Table 1.1 compares and contrasts sole traders, partnerships, limited partnerships, private limited companies and public limited companies.

The reader should turn to pp. 22 and 23 to study this table. For the way in which a company is formed and financed, Figure 1.7 gives a simple explanation of the general pattern of arrangements. Starting as a small private company, the business grows to the point where it is able to meet the strict requirements of the Stock Exchange Council and then 'goes public' by issuing enough shares to make a

Table 1.1 Comparison of profit-making private-enterprise units

Aspect	Sole Trader	Partnership	Limited Partnership
1 Name of firm	Any name provided it is either the proprietor's true name or their names, or a notice giving their names and addresses is displayed at premises and on letterheads, etc.		
2 How formed	By commencing business without formality except (1) above	By agreement, which may be oral or written; limited partnerships must be registered.	
3 Control of the firm	Proprietor has full control	Every partner is entitled to manage	Only the general partner(s) can manage the business
4 Liability for debts	Liability to the limits of personal wealth	Jointly and severally liable for debts to limits of personal wealth	General partners fully liable; limited partners not liable beyond the capital contributed
5 Relationship between owner and business	The business is the owner, or owners, and has no separate legal existence		The business is the same as the general partners; the limited partner is not the business
6 Membership of firm	One	Two or more	Two or more
7 General powers	At will	At will, subject to agreement; if no agreement, *Partnership Act, 1890* applies	
8 Transfer of ownership	By sale of 'goodwill'	Only with unanimous consent	
9 Controlling Acts	None	*Partnership Act, 1890*	*Limited Partnership Act, 1907*
10 Disbanding of firm	At will or by bankruptcy	Firm may go bankrupt or be dissolved by notice, mutual consent or by death of a partner	
11 Advantages	Independence. Personal control of staff and granting of credit. Decisions acted upon at once	Increased capital. Days off and holidays possible. Wider experience of partners. Privacy of affairs	Limited liability for some partners. Larger capital
12 Disadvantages	Long hours. No holidays. Illness affects conduct of business. Unlimited liability. Small capital.	Unlimited liability. Death or retirement ends firm. Profits must be shared	Unlimited liability for the general partners. Also as for partnerships

	Limited Companies	
	Private	*Public*
1	The registered name, registered under the *Companies Acts, 1985–9* with the word 'Limited' for private companies, and the words 'Public Limited Company' for public companies	
2	By registration under the *Companies Acts*, with due legal formality	
3	Directors control the company. Members have no control at all, but may elect a new board at the Annual General Meeting, or at an Extraordinary General Meeting if they wish to do so	
4	Limited liability for all members – only liable to the limit of capital contributed	
5	The business is a separate legal personality from the members	
6	Minimum two, no maximum, under the Companies Acts, 1985–9	
7	As laid down in Memorandum of Association and Articles of Association	
8	Shares may only be transferred with consent of fellow shareholders	Shares are freely transferable
9	Companies Acts, 1985–9 control all types of company	
10	Company may go into voluntary or compulsory liquidation	
11	Limited liability. Death of shareholders does not affect the firm. Capital can be found from many members. Privacy to some extent on affairs	Limited liability. Death of shareholders does not affect the firm. Very large capital can be collected
12	Publication now required, but today turnover need not be revealed if it is below £8 million and profits need not be revealed if the turnover does not exceed £2 million. These figures may be revised from time to time	Full public knowledge of affairs

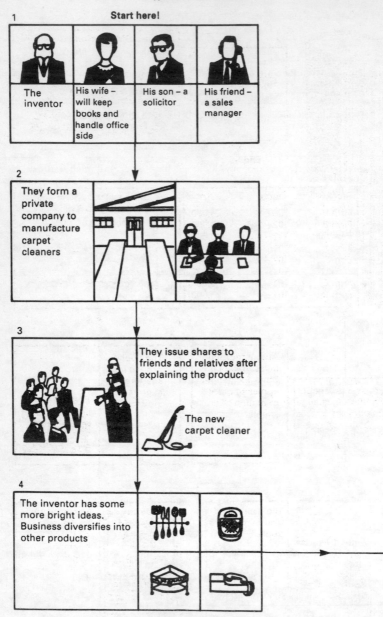

Figure 1.7   How a company is formed and financed

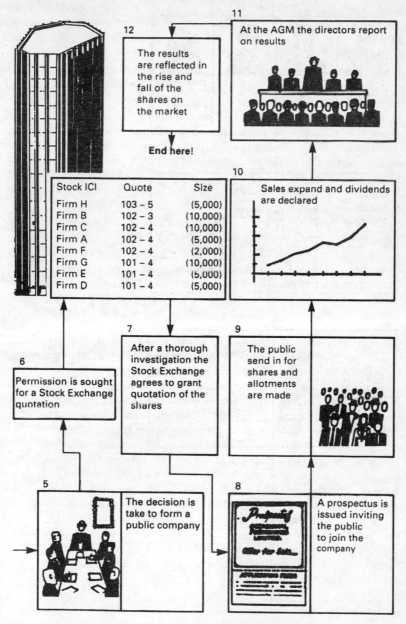

Figure 1.7 (*continued*)

worthwhile market. This enables extra capital to be collected from the general public and the business is then able to grow more rapidly.

1.12 Non-profit-making units (clubs and societies)

A certain number of business units are non-profit-making clubs and societies. They are formed to confer on their members certain benefits in the way of club facilities, discount trading, or value for money. Such clubs and societies often make profits on the year's trading, but these are not profits in the normal commercial meaning of the word. They really represent over-payments by the members for the services they have received, and are usually called 'surpluses'. Examples of such business units are the working men's clubs in the north of England and the co-operative societies.

Co-operative retail societies

The first successful 'co-op' store was founded in 1844 in Toad Lane, Rochdale, by twenty-eight weavers nowadays remembered as the 'Rochdale Pioneers'. The idea was to buy foodstuffs at wholesale prices and sell them (to members only) at market price. Profits were divided among members in proportion to the value of their purchases. The share-out (dividend) took place twice a year. By 1845 there were seventy-four members; the turnover was £710; the profit £22.

The co-operative movement spread rapidly. Societies were set up in towns all over the United Kingdom. In 1862 the members voted to set up a wholesale organization, the Co-operative Wholesale Society. This society not only supplied the retail societies like any ordinary wholesaler but also ran factories, farms, transport services, and even tea gardens to provide everything the retail societies needed. The chief aim in this activity was to ease the serious unemployment of those days. The retail societies joined the wholesale society in exactly the same way as the ordinary members joined the retail society. All the profits of the Co-operative Wholesale Society are shared among the member retail societies, and all the profits of the retail societies are shared among the members. Thus in the end all the profits return to the members of the retail societies, whose purchasing power actually keeps the co-operative movement going. These profits in recent years have been distributed by means of a trading stamp scheme.

Agricultural co-operatives

These are very common in many countries and enable the small-scale farmer to achieve some of the economies of large-scale organizations. They may be marketing co-operatives, which grade, pack and distribute farmers' produce; or purchasing co-operatives, which buy seed, fertilizer and equipment at discount prices, supplying or hiring these items to farmers.

1.13 Public enterprises

We have seen that the economy is divided into two main parts: the private sector and the public sector. The private sector comprises all those firms described earlier — sole traders, partnerships and limited companies. The public sector comprises all those other institutions set up or taken over by the authority of parliament for operation in the public interest and not for private profit. There is a wide variety of such institutions, and many of them were set up by Acts of Parliament which approved a unique framework appropriate to the particular industry under consideration. A full discussion of these institutions is a matter for students of the British constitution, and may be studied by those interested in a companion volume, *British Constitution Made Simple*.

Table 1.2 lists some of these major public institutions.

1.14 Local government institutions

In every economy an important part of the services required is local in character. Education, health services, drainage and sewerage works are required all over the country and are inappropriate to control by the central government. A lower order of government, which reaches out to every locality, is required. In the United Kingdom a comprehensive restructuring of local government took place following the Radcliffe-Maude Report. The number of local authorities was reduced from over 1200 to 421. Six of these, not counting London, were designated as metropolitan counties. There are 47 county councils in England and Wales, 35 metropolitan districts or boroughs and 296 non-metropolitan districts or boroughs. Parish councils in England and community councils in Wales operate at the very lowest levels.

Functions of the new authorities. The chief functions of the new authorities include major responsibilities in town and country planning, education, housing, police and fire services, traffic and highways, consumer protection, personal social services and many more. A full description of all these functions is given in *British Constitution Made Simple*.

Municipal undertakings. This type of organization used to be much more important than it is today, because many water companies, electricity supply companies and gas companies were municipally owned. The nationalization of such public utility services has reduced the scale of local enterprise, but it is still common to find such institutions as swimming pools, leisure centres, etc., run as municipal enterprises.

Table 1.2   Some public sector institutions

Name of organization	Reason for operation in public sector	Date of original act of nationalization
1 Atomic Energy Authority	Inappropriate to private sector	1954
2 Bank of England	To unify political and financial power	1946
3 British Broadcasting Corporation	Inappropriate to allow it to develop in private hands	1926
4 British Rail	To restore a declining industry	1947
5 Independent Television Authority (now Independent Broadcasting Authority)	To license and control programme companies	1954
6 National Coal Board	To nationalize a gift of nature in a depressed industry with a history of poor industrial relations	1946
7 National Health Service	To provide a health service to all irrespective of financial status	1946
8 County councils	To provide a wide range of local services, inappropriate to the private sector	1888
9 QUANGOS (e.g. the SITPRO Board)	To fulfil some useful public function (e.g. the Simpler Trade Procedures Board represents the UK in international negotiations about documents used in overseas trade)	Various dates (The SITPRO Board was set .up in 1970)

1.15   Central government departments

In recent years a certain amount of experimentation (with super-ministries, for example) has caused frequent changes in the running and responsibility of government departments, so that any list is subject to change at the whim of the Government in charge. In general there are about twenty ministries, with about two-thirds of them sufficiently important for the minister in charge to be of cabinet rank. The major ministries are the Treasury, the Foreign Office, the Home Office, and those of Defence, Social Services, Employment, Education and Science, the Environment, Wales, Scotland, Agriculture and Trade and Industry. All departments have considerable sums of money to spend in pursuing their activities, and are therefore influential in the economy. In 1990 the total expenditure of central Government departments was £200 000 million. This is equivalent to a pile of £10 notes seventy-two times as high as Mount Everest.

In all these different types of business organization there will be some sort of senior management staff charged with the major responsibilities of conducting their affairs. In small firms it will be the sole trader, or the partners. In large firms there will be some sort of departmental organization. The departments will vary with the organization itself. For example, a firm engaged in production of goods for sale will have a factory, under its factory manager. Such a department will not be needed for a service organization e.g. a bank or an accountancy practice. Nor will a government department usually have a factory – though there are some official factory organizations making items such as artificial limbs for disabled people.

A brief mention of some of the major departments in large-scale firms is given below.

1.16 The major departments in an office – an introductory description

(*a*) *The General Administration Office.* This department is a non-specialist department dealing with all those activities which promote the general organization of the enterprise. The **administrative officer** will be a person of wide experience, to whom all other departmental heads can turn for advice on general office procedures. In smaller enterprises he/she may be in charge of the appointment of staff, the ordering of equipment and stationery, the general supervision of the premises including security, caretaking and cleaning, canteen or refreshment arrangements and many other matters. Very often this office will have the inward and outward mail arrangements under its general control as well as reception and telephone services, safety and first aid arrangements and, very often, the typing pool.

(*b*) *The Personnel Department.* This department supervises all matters to do with staffing. It advertises for and appoints staff of suitable quality for the various activities of the business, runs induction and training courses and prepares updating lectures, demonstrations and seminars. These serve to bring existing staff to higher levels or to introduce new procedures.

The personnel department also preserves records of performance, considers candidates for promotion and circularizes regular reports for completion by supervisors and departmental heads. It hears complaints from staff and rearranges staffing to avoid conflict, where clashes of opinions or principle appear likely to prove troublesome. Finally, it deals with the dismissal of staff, prepares testimonials for personnel leaving employment and handles welfare problems when necessary.

(*c*) *The Accounts and Costing Departments*. These departments are concerned with the accounting records of the business. The accounts department deals with the book-keeping records of purchases, sales and expense items and with the purchase of capital assets. It carries out **internal audits** to ensure that money is being properly spent. The costing department deals with the estimating of production costs. Some costs, like raw materials, are **direct costs** and may be allocated at once to the product which has been manufactured from them. Others are **overheads**, which cannot be directly attributed to one particular product. They must be spread over all the units of output in some even way. The costing department also attempts to discover rising production costs while they are still changing, so the increases can be controlled or selling prices can be adjusted.

(*d*) *The Purchasing Department*. This department is responsible for buying the raw materials, machinery, office equipment, stationery and other items needed to produce the firm's products and market them effectively. Purchasing Department personnel will evaluate new equipment or new business systems to decide whether they should be adopted, and they will visit exhibitions, demonstrations or suppliers' premises for the purpose of discussing prices and delivery dates.

(*e*) *The Sales Department*. This department is concerned with the marketing of a firm's products at home and overseas. Home sales are usually secured by **commercial travellers** who are allocated a **territory** which they cover at regular intervals visiting established customers and attempting to secure new trade whenever possible. **Export trade** is handled in rather a different way, depending upon the size of the firm concerned. Two other departments are closely associated with the Sales Department. These are the **Advertising Department**, which handles day-to-day publicity and special promotions, and the **Servicing Department**, whose activities preserve **goodwill** by ensuring prompt repairs and the replacement of spare parts.

(*f*) *The Transport Department*. Today the typical method of delivering goods is by 'own account' vehicles. There are great advantages with many products in keeping delivery under personal supervision. Many products are small, technically complex and therefore expensive, and highly desirable as personal possessions. Such products are easily pilfered and difficult to trace once they have been stolen, and a transport department operating vehicles on its own account can supervise drivers much more effectively than can a public transport system. Even where goods are to be rail-freighted, shipped or airfreighted the **transport manager**, who has professional knowledge of **'freight forwarding'**, will secure the cheapest and most reliable operations for the company's needs. He/she will also evaluate vehicles, choosing the most useful and economical for the firm.

Today many firms work by JIT methods. JIT stands for 'just in time' and it means that the firms arrange for all the supplies they need to arrive 'just in time' before they are needed. Often the supplier has to deliver direct to the shop floor, where the production line is on the move already. Thus a motor vehicle manufacturer might order the seats for the vehicle to be delivered to the production line 200 at a time, at 8 am and 2 pm every day. A batch delivered to the unloading bay at 8 am will be fitted into place in the 100 vehicles made that morning and by the time the last one is being fitted the next batch will have arrived 'just in time'.

A transport manager who is bound to keep to this type of contract will need to ensure that the necessary vehicles to maintain the service are in good running order, and that drivers are available and know the importance of a JIT delivery.

(*g*) *The Production Manager's office*. This office is the centre of a firm's production activities. It is usual to call this the 'factory' rather than the production department. The manager will sometimes be a **production engineer** or **mechanical engineer**, and the office will be devoted to ensuring the most effective means possible of planning and executing production. Costings can be prepared as manufacture proceeds and temporary shortages are overcome by clerks called **progress chasers**, who 'chase' materials required or components being manufactured to ensure that they reach the production line in time.

(*h*) *The Research and Development Department*. Someone has to take a long-term view in any firm. Today's bestseller is tomorrow's 'has-been'. 'Fad today and fade tomorrow' is the rule of modern business. R & D, as it is called, tries to anticipate tomorrow's needs; tomorrow's new look; tomorrow's variation on the well-established product.

There are many small departments that have not been listed above, including the Post Department, the Central Filing Department, the Duplicating Department, the Addressing and Mailing Department. As most of these have specialized chapters in this book, a discussion of them is left until later.

1.17 Points to think about and discuss

(*a*) 'I hate you people who sit in offices, drinking cups of tea and giving yourselves airs and graces', said the factory worker. 'You're like the fountains in Trafalgar Square — you play from nine till four. We are the people who do the real work.'

How would you answer this sort of criticism to justify what is done in offices?

(*b*) 'In manufacturing 94 per cent of the firms only did 16 per cent of the work.' What does this tell us about the importance of large firms in the manufacturing trades? Is it a good thing that so many small firms have so little of the work?

(*c*) When a firm is set up in a district it immediately affects the environment, both natural and human. What are the dangers and what are the advantages which follow from industry moving into a district?

(*d*) 'We already have plenty of goods and services. Let us reduce consumption and preserve the natural world around us.' Do you support or disagree with this idea?

1.18 Rapid revision – business organizations

Cover the page with a sheet of paper and uncover one revision question at a time.

Answers	Questions
	1 Why are organizations formed?
1 There are eight main reasons: (i) To produce consumer goods. (ii) To produce producer goods (capital assets). (iii) To provide personal services. (iv) To provide commercial services. (v) To provide protective services (defence, police, fire prevention, etc.). (vi) To legislate (Parliament). (vii) To administer the country (Civil Service, etc.). (viii) To administer justice (the Courts).	2 What is the general aim of economic activity?
2 To obtain the greatest output of useful goods and services from the smallest input of our scarce resources.	3 Explain the stages in the cycle of production.
3 (*a*) 'wants'; (*b*) enterprise; (*c*) production; (*d*) distribution; (*e*) marketing; (*f*) consumption; (*g*) 'wants' again.	4 What are the two sectors of the economy?
4 The private sector and the public sector.	5 Name some private sector organizations.
5 Sole traders, partnerships, limited partnerships, private limited companies, public limited companies, clubs, Co-operative Societies.	6 Name some public sector organizations.
6 Autonomous corporations, QUANGOS, nationalized industries, local and central government departments.	7 How is wealth created?

7   Land, labour and capital are put to work by some type of organization. The result is a flow of goods or services which can be used to satisfy 'wants'.

8   What part does 'money' play in the 'world of work'?

8   It enables factors of production to be employed and their reward is paid in money. Then this money is exchanged by the workers, landowners, etc., for the goods and services needed. Each buys a balanced basket of goods for his own family's needs.

9   Go over the page again until you are sure of all the answers.

Exercises set 1

1   Copy out the lines below and fill in the missing words or phrases. Some answers are given at the end to help you.

(a) From the moment they are born people ...... things.
(b) To satisfy the demands of the public, businessmen engage in ....
(c) Many goods are produced, but we also need many ....
(d) Three industrial concerns would be: (i) a motorcar factory, (ii) a ...... and (iii) a ....
(e) Three commercial activities would be: (i) banking, (ii) ...... and (iii) ....
(f) The two sectors of economic life are the ...... sector and the ...... sector.
(g) A fully developed economy cannot work unless we have a ...... system to arrange the exchange of goods and services.

Answers: services, insurance, public, want, money, production, communications, private, printing works, cotton mill.

2   List the reasons why organizations are set up in society.

3   Distinguish 'personal services' and 'commercial services'. Refer in your answer to the eight services named below, and explain whether you consider them 'personal' or 'commercial'. Are any of them both personal and commercial? The eight services are: (i) dentistry, (ii) a news agency, (iii) surgery, (iv) insurance, (v) a bus service, (vi) road haulage, (vii) education, (viii) satellite communication.

4   Describe the public sector of the economy of your own country, naming major institutions which operate in the public sector, and explaining why they are not privately operated.

5   What is meant by 'the cycle of production'? Why has it continued constantly throughout man's history? Illustrate a typical cycle by reference to the life of one of the following: (a) a farmer, (b) a coalminer, (c) a merchant banker.

6   Make a detailed study of your own workplace, whatever it is, and pinpoint how it is organized. Use the names of official positions (i.e.

manager, supervisor, chief clerk, etc.) rather than the names of individuals. Indicate any chains of command which appear to exist. For those in full-time education, study the department in which you are following your main course. Assess the effectiveness of the organization you have studied and bring out clearly its strengths and its weaknesses. Keep the discussion of such matters impersonal, and consider them objectively (from the point of view of an outsider who is not personally involved).

7 (*a*) Money is the root of all evil!
   (*b*) Money makes the world go round!

Discuss these two views of money and explain which you consider to be the more sensible. In your answer explain how the money system affects a college leaver who is very good at mathematics, but not much else. He is proposing to marry a girl on the same course as himself, in the near future.

8 Why worry about an apprenticeship? – there are plenty of good jobs going in the public sector. Discuss this viewpoint expressed by a careers officer in an area where few apprenticeships were available.

2 Staffing the offices

2.1 Junior staff

It used to be the case that most junior staff were recruited at the school-leaving age and arrived in offices with little background knowledge of what would be required of them, except the elementary knowledge of English and commercial arithmetic acquired during their school years. Many left school at 14 years of age, but later this was raised to 15 years, and now the basic school-leaving age is 16 years. The traditional name for an office worker is 'clerk' and the work performed was called 'clerical work'. If we think of Victorian times, then Bob Cratchit, the clerk in Scrooge's office in Charles Dickens' *A Christmas Carol* is the archetypal 'clerk'. He is shown in Figure 2.1 working away at the ledger in Scrooge's counting house in the City of London.

Today things have changed a great deal. The vast majority of junior staff are now much better trained than the 'school-leaver' of earlier times. Many of them have pursued at least a 2-year course with some bias towards business studies. Many will have taken an actual course called Business Studies — those who have done so may have used a companion volume to this called *Business Studies Made Simple*. Many will have taken a secretarial course, and acquired keyboard skills of various types. Others will be knowledgeable about computers. All these background subjects will be very helpful to students of office procedures, for all these skills today are needed by those who carry out clerical activities. If you are one of those with such skills, you will find office procedures an easy subject to study. If you have not pursued any business-related studies before, do not despair. The present volume contains all you will need to know to make a successful start in an office career.

2.2 Building a successful office career

In Figure 1.2 (see p. 6) we studied a rather complex chart of a business organization run along functional lines. The word 'function' means 'a range of activities'. In many businesses it is convenient to organize along functional lines, because the business falls naturally into groups of related activities. For example, the production of goods is one range of activities (the production function) and the marketing of them is another (the marketing function). Getting paid

Figure 2.1 Bob Cratchit at work on the ledger in Scrooge's office (Charles Dickens – *A Christmas Carol*)

for the goods and services we produce is another range of activities – and there are many other 'functions' to be performed.

If we now look at the lowest level of staff on the Figure 1.2 chart we can see that there are many different types of staff listed, and it is at this sort of level that junior staff join the firm. There are a number of points to make about this first level of entry.

(*a*) All the different departments are engaged in office procedures to suit the particular needs of the department.

(*b*) Since it is helpful to know something about every department in your company or firm, and since it is almost always the case that the person who gets on best in the firm, and is the most use to the organization, is someone who does have contacts in other departments, there is everything to be said for learning as much as possible about the work of the department you are recruited into. You may later transfer elsewhere, but the skills you have learned and the contacts you have made will still be valuable.

(*c*) Learning the work of a department is done in two ways.

(i) People show you how to do a particular job; let you have a go at it; come back and check you on it from time to time, correcting your faults, and gradually relax control as they see you have mastered the job. This method is sometimes called the 'sitting next to Nellie' method of training, a term of disparagement which implies (and probably quite rightly) that it is a less satisfactory method of training than more formal training courses. The trouble with it is that the trainee may pick up Nellie's faults as well as her skills. On the other hand, we all know of people educated to a high level who find it very difficult to pick up simple practical jobs. We can all learn something from the Nellies of this world.

(ii) The second method of learning the work of a department is the more formal 'short course', where we are sent off for a week, or possibly longer, to learn a new skill that is used in the department. This may be linked with promotion of some sort or it may simply be a 'sideways move'. Having learnt one or two skills by 'sitting next to Nellie', we are seen by our supervisor as quite good material for development, and when an opportunity arises, he/she puts our name forward for a particular area of work, and a short course of instruction to start it.

Such courses may be 'in-house', run by our own firm in some special training school. Others will be run at manufacturer's training departments, or at technical colleges, commercial schools, etc. They are not cheap, and firms will not be pleased if the people they have selected fail the courses and waste their money. It is important to do well on such courses, not only for the firm's benefit but for your own. A skill can only be learned by the person under training, and once acquired you have it for all time. If you are forced to change jobs, or if you decide to do so, the skills leave with you. Naturally this makes your organization keen to keep you, but if they have to let you go because of redundancy or similar difficulties, at least you have a new skill, acquired at considerable expense (but not to you). As a general rule it is always worthwhile accepting offers to go on training courses. It is one more rung of the ladder you have to climb to reach the top of your chosen profession.

(*d*) Of course it is possible to accept a job in a field which you later find interests you very little, and for which you are totally unsuited. There are ways of dealing with this problem, but, first, a word of warning. Do not throw any job up at a moment's notice, or deliberately do it so badly that the firm decides to let you go as soon as any probationary period comes to an end. The trouble is that giving up a job like this looks like failure — even if you view it as a success because you wanted to leave anyway. Every job — even sweeping a factory floor — can have some interest. It can be done well or badly, and we can almost always learn something from it. If it seems of no interest at all — why is this? Oliver Cromwell told his army 'I beseech you — think it possible you may be mistaken?' Perhaps there are things in the job that you, as a newcomer, do not appreciate. Where does the job fit into the firm's or company's activities? Could it be done better, or more quickly (so it's not so boring)? Use your ingenuity to improve the job. Give it a fair chance, and, above all, master it so that you know absolutely how to do it, what it involves etc. In this way you will be able to discuss it intelligently and say why you want to be transferred to some other area of work. Then raise the whole matter, first with your immediate supervisor and later, if necessary, with some higher authority. However, that is a matter for a later chapter (see Chapter 17).

(*e*) If you are recruited into an area which you later find unsuitable, put in for a transfer to some other area you find of greater interest. You will find this easier if you have genuinely struggled to make a success of your present post and have drawn up a sound list of reasons why you feel the new area will be more appropriate to your skills and interests.

(*f*) The ultimate aim of anyone starting on an office procedures course should be full professional qualification in the field that eventually proves to be of interest to him/her. Full professional qualification means you become a member of the professional body that acts for the profession. It is usual to become a student member, or if you are already qualified, you enter at the lowest level — as an associate or perhaps they just use the term 'member'. Later you move up to higher levels as you qualify for higher grades (by examinations and experience). There are many such bodies, and a list of some of the more famous is given in an Appendix at the back of this book. Study the list for a short while now (see pages 487– 90).

2.3 Clerical posts

The term 'clerk' has a very wide meaning, and although we often think of a clerk as being a fairly low level post of the 'Bob Cratchit' type, in fact the name is used for many quite high-level positions. Thus the 'clerk of works' on a building site is the person in total charge of the activities on the site, and a 'town clerk' is the chief officer of a town council and acts as the secretary and agent of the council in all its activities. The 'clerk to the justices' is the person in a magistrates court who advises the justices on all legal matters and the correct sentences to impose, since magistrates are 'lay' persons not necessarily knowledgeable about law, but appointed for their common sense and upright behaviour. To be a clerk to the justices a person must be either a solicitor or barrister of at least 5 years' standing. We must therefore expect to find both young and more experienced people called by the term 'clerk' — though 'chief clerk' is a term used for many of the more experienced staff.

Today much clerical work of a routine nature calls for the use of equipment, particularly such devices as computer terminals, which feed data into a computer. Such a network of terminals is described and illustrated later in this book (see Chapter 14). At one time a great deal of clerical work called for the copying of letters. In the Gilbert and Sullivan opera *H.M.S. Pinafore* the First Sea Lord explains that although he is now the ruler of the Queen's Navy he actually began by 'Copying the letters in a big round hand':

I copied all the letters in a hand so free
That now I am the ruler of the Queen's Navee.

Today most copying is done with a plain-paper copier, and the best machines can make a copy of an A4 page in half a second.

It is impossible to describe or even to name the thousands of different posts coming under the heading of 'clerical' positions, but we could just list the following.

(*a*) *Junior clerks*. A wide variety of junior positions in all sorts of departments would come under this general heading. The work includes many activities, much of it concerned with simple documentation, the use of calculators, activities concerned with mail inwards and outwards, etc. The five main clerical activities are described in the next chapter.

(*b*) *Senior clerks*. As their name implies senior clerks are people who have served a reasonable time in a variety of junior clerical posts and have become sufficiently knowledgeable and experienced to take on a supervisory role as a head of some section of the work. They usually have a number of juniors to supervise and a general responsibility for the work in their section. If anything goes wrong, it will be the senior clerk who stays behind to solve the problem, and the senior clerk who will have to report the matter if it can't be solved.

(*c*) *Chief clerks*. A chief clerk is a person of real authority in a department, charged with the supervision of the department and reporting to senior management on any problems that arise. The chief clerk is at once the representative of the department to senior management, i.e. the board of a company or the partners in a partnership business, and also the representative of the management to his/her section. In this capacity the chief clerk conveys to the department the views and instructions of the management and implements the policies, reorganizations, etc., within the department.

2.4 Secretarial posts

The term 'secretary' is another word that has a wide meaning, and it is important to appreciate the various uses of the term. We usually think of a secretary as a person who takes dictation from a manager or other senior member of staff and turns the notes made into neatly typed correspondence. This is important work and is described later in this chapter.

First, note that the word 'secretary' really means a person entitled to initiate correspondence on behalf of some organization. As such, it is a key role — in many organizations it is the second most important position. Thus in any club, e.g. a golf club, a tennis club or a learned society, the secretary is the person who conducts all the correspondence with members and with 'outsiders' such as suppliers of equipment and services. The only other people of importance are the chairperson, who presides at meetings and is therefore the leading person in the club, and the treasurer, who collects the members' contributions and actually signs the cheques that the secretary sends off. The secretary organizes everything else: meetings, outings, the annual children's party, etc.

Another use of the word 'secretary' is in the organization of limited companies. Every company must have a company secretary, and his/her name must be registered with the Registrar of Companies at Company House, which is the central registry for all company affairs and has two main offices, one in London and one in Cardiff. A company secretary is the head of legal matters in a company, responsible for the issue of share certificates and the transfer of shares from one shareholder to another. He/she is also responsible for complying with the Companies Acts of 1985—9. The Acts contain detailed regulations for the honourable conduct of companies, and offences are punishable by fines (and imprisonment if necessary). Clearly the post of company secretary is a high-level post, often filled by a person who has qualified as a solicitor and elected to work in business instead of in a legal practice.

Leaving aside these special uses of the term and others (such as the term secretary of state which is used for top posts in the government), we may now list the types of secretarial post met with in most offices. It is a common error in textbooks to refer to such posts as being exclusively female occupations, though it is true to say that most top secretarial posts are filled by women. Fortunately this textbook attitude is changing, but it has always been true that men have held secretarial positions too. We may list the following.

(i) *Junior secretaries*. A junior secretary is a person who types correspondence from shorthand notes, from tape-recorded notes or from manually written letters supplied by executives. Junior secretaries often work for a group of middle management executives, e.g. in a school or college or in a large department. They may also act as general factotums for their departments, answering the telephone, taking messages, organizing inter-departmental meetings and helping with a variety of functions, seminars, conferences, etc.

(ii) *Personal secretaries*. Personal secretaries are usually secretaries to a named senior executive, whose work they organize and whose correspondence they type. They usually have excellent shorthand and typing skills, but may also type from tape-recorded memos prepared by the executive on a desk tape-recorder, or on cassettes from a portable recorder. Even top executives prepare manuscript letters and reports, because they are dealing with top-level difficult material which needs careful drafting and correction. Today almost all personal secretaries use word-processors, which not only produce impeccable correspondence but also store the material in electronic form so that first drafts of letters and reports can be revised later without major retyping.

Personal secretaries are responsible for all aspects of the executive's daily round, e.g. the opening of correspondence, the handling of routine correspondence to save the executive's time, the keeping of his/her diary, the reception of visitors and the minuting of departmental meetings of various sorts. Minutes are of course the notes made at a meeting of the matters discussed, the decisions taken and the responsibilities imposed on various committee members to investigate matters and report back.

(iii) *Personal Assistants (PAs)*. A personal assistant is the most senior secretarial position, usually to a top executive such as the managing director of a company or the company chairman. Frequently a PA will have a department of his/her own with assistants. A PA not only attends to secretarial matters at the highest level but exercises supervision over all personal secretaries and junior secretaries, and possibly such staff as reception staff, caretakers, chauffeurs, etc.

PA posts command excellent salaries, and the work PAs perform is highly confidential. It is concerned with the very top level work, such as acting as minuting secretary to company board meetings, supervising the organizing of top-level conferences, press conferences, briefings for television and radio interviews of top executives, presentation of matters at public inquiries of various sorts, etc.

2.5 Typing posts

Secretaries carry out many of the duties connected with correspondence but there are slightly lower posts that many juniors take to acquire skills and experience. In the typing field we may list the following divisions.

(i) *Copy-typing*. As its name implies, copy-typing requires the typist to copy manuscript letters written by junior executives, and other material, such as extracts from trade journals for library storage, digests of legislation (Acts of Parliament likely to affect a company or firm), advertising copy, press releases, etc. Copy typists often act as general factotums in the office, duplicating circulars, assisting with post, taking messages, etc. Often called Man/Girl Fridays (watch for this term in advertisements in the press), they are considered junior assistants (with skills up to Junior Secretarial level) who will help generally in an office – usually of a small business. The term comes from *Robinson Crusoe*, who, when on his island, befriended and was helped by a native whom he christened 'Friday'.

(ii) *Audio-typing*. Audio-typists work from tape-recorded letters dictated by executives. The messages may be from a dedicated tape-recorder (used by a single executive) or a mini-cassette from a portable recorder, but chiefly from a multi-bank system. This is a system where there are a number of tape-recorders in a central location to which all executives have access by telephone. The executive calls up the service, is connected to a recorder, dictates up to five letters and disconnects. This enables the audio-typist supervisor to start an audio-typist on that batch of letters. The executive calls in again if he/she has more correspondence and gets the next machine in the bank for another five letters.

An audio-typist controls the recorder with a foot-pedal, listening to a few words, typing them and then listening to a few more. It is essential for audio-typists to be good at spelling, for they have only the words they hear to type – nothing is written down – and a poor speller will produce poor correspondence.

(iii) *Medical secretarial work*. The work of the medical secretary is specialized because many medical terms are based on Latin and one needs at least some understanding of nursing and medicine to keep up with this rather difficult vocabulary. In addition, many medical words are similar to one another, and severe effects on the patient may be expected if the wrong tablets are prescribed or the wrong strength of a solution is given. It is usual to take a special course before qualifying as a medical secretary and one should hesitate to transfer into this field from an ordinary business field without taking a short course to learn the technical terms in use.

2.6 Accountancy and book-keeping

Accountancy is the art of keeping financial records, which are of basic importance to all offices. The chief accountant is almost always a member of the board of directors of a company, and the accounting function is one that influences the work of all departments. Young people who are good at figures will find that book-keeping and accounts offer interesting and worthwhile careers. Starting from the bottom and working upwards we may list the following positions.

(i) *Junior book-keepers*. There are thousands of jobs available for junior book-keepers. It is possible to learn the work as you go along, but those who have taken a 1-year course in book-keeping or principles of accounts will find no difficulty in securing a post and fitting easily into any accounts department. You might like to work through *Book-keeping Made Simple*, a companion volume to the present title, which will teach you all you need to know.

There are two levels of work — Book-keeping to the Trial Balance and Book-keeping to Final Accounts. Both levels are shown in diagrammatic form later in this book (see pp. 408–9). Book-keeping to the trial balance means you know how to make all the entries for purchases, sales, returns, receipts of cash, and payments of cash, and can keep a petty cash book. It is when all these entries have been made that a trial balance is taken out to check whether the working is correct. Book-keeping to Final Accounts means you know how to continue from the Trial Balance, and can prepare the final accounts of the business, to find the profit (or loss) for the financial year. This work leads on to **financial accountancy** work.

(ii) *Cost clerks*. A cost clerk is a book-keeper who specializes in costing production activities such as factory assembly work, process costing (for oil refineries, for example), distribution activities and all the various types of overhead expenses. This work leads on to an important branch of accountancy work called **Management Accounting**.

(iii) *Professional level work*. It is usual for those with book-keeping qualifications to pursue their studies into one of the main professional bodies in accountancy. There are the **financial accountants**, who look after the whole range of accounting activities of firms and companies. The **management accountants** look after the complex activities of industrial firms, costing projects and budgeting ahead to ensure that major projects costing millions of pounds are never starved of the capital they need — but also spending their money wisely. We often hear of films that cost $40 million. And who is in charge of this vast collection of funds? — the management accountant. Finally a special group of accountants work in national government and local government. They belong to a body called CIPFA — the **Chartered Institute of Public Finance and Accountancy**. Most councils have budgets that run into millions of pounds. Incidentally, a body that uses the term 'Chartered' has been granted a royal charter, which recognizes the important part it plays in the work of the nation. All the bodies referred to in this section have been granted royal charters; the work of accountants is crucial to the nation's prosperity.

2.7 Administrative and supervisory staff

Sections 2.3–2.6 above have described some of the main types of staff to be met in offices, although there are many more in the specialist departments such as the factory, the Transport Department, stores, etc. There are supervisory grades in all these areas, and they tend to be filled by the best qualified and most experienced members of staff. It is now time to look at one office, one that stands at the very centre of the activities of any firm, providing the framework for all departments and exercising general control. This is the general administration office, which is usually headed by an experienced administrator, whose post is designated as administration officer or possibly chief administration officer (CAO).

2.8 Functions of the General Administration Office

This office performs a wide range of activities providing office services for the more specialized departments such as production, buying, sales, advertising, despatch and transport. In particular, it often provides centralized services such as a computer network, typing and audio-typing pools or reprographic services. It may act as a **resource centre** providing handouts, publicity material, display facilities, etc., and it usually acts as a general reserve force to assist activities in other departments which come under pressure at times of peak activity.

The administration officer must be a person of wide experience and sound ability to whom colleagues at all levels can turn for help and advice in handling problems. He/she will usually have some control of the disbursement of funds between departments, and a general responsibility for the choice and supply of office equipment and business systems, both the hardware (machinery and equipment) and the forms and documentation. This will usually call for some decision-making about the provision of centralized office services.

2.9 Centralized office services

We live in a world where there are great economies to be achieved by the use of large-scale organization. A large firm can usually manufacture, distribute and sell more cheaply than a small firm, and a large office can similarly produce letters, circulars, invoices and other documents more economically than a small office. Top-class machines, highly skilled staff and subdivision of labour into specialized jobs and processes reduce the costs of each unit of office activity just as they do in a factory.

What is centralization?

Centralization is a system where control is exercised from the centre on the activities of all departments and branches. Detailed instructions on methods and procedure to be followed are issued from Head Office, and a system of 'reporting back' is instituted to keep Head Office informed of developments. In addition, those cost centres that can be more efficiently operated as large units — for example, accounting centres, typing pools and resource centres — are removed from the specialized departments and operated as central services. Very advanced equipment can therefore be employed at these service departments, including computerized accounting and data-processing installations and multi-user audio-typing systems.

The advantages and disadvantages of centralized services may be arranged appropriately in tabular form as follows:

Centralization of services

Advantages	*Disadvantages*
1 More economical operation. The specialist staff can perform the work more quickly and easily with proper facilities which are utilized more fully.	1 Impersonal nature of the employment. Some of the gains in economy of operation are lost in frustration of individuals resentful of the impersonal nature of the work.
2 Better administrative control. The supply and use of hardware, software, ancillary equipment and staff time are more easily controlled in specialist centralized offices.	2 Greater bureaucracy. Form-filling and similar time-wasting activities may mean an increase in 'red tape' and bureaucracy. Where departments are dependent on co-operation from other departments, a growth of inter-departmental committees and other time-wasting bodies is inevitable.
3 Better use of staff. Skilled staff can be more fully utilized, since interruptions by telephone calls or visiting staff can be circumvented.	3 Impersonal activity is subject to delay. Delays may occur in more important activities, e.g. senior staff must dictate letters in full instead of giving a secretary brief instructions like 'Write and say — no, we're sorry'. Boredom reduces work output if tasks become too repetitive, and bright staff go elsewhere.
4 Cheaper labour costs. Routine work can be performed by less skilled staff. Centralization gives a variety of graded employments at all levels of difficulty.	4 Impractical orders and procedures. The remoteness of managers from the actual scene of events leads to some procedures being unworkable or
5 Better layout and use of mechanical aids. Machines can be more fully utilized, and they can be isolated if they are noisy, away from the general office.	
6 Greater flexibility in the use of resources. Central pools enable flexible use to be made of available staff and equipment. A statistical department makes fuller	

use of computer software in the statistical field, and the capital tied up in this equipment is more intensively used.

7 Greater variety of service. A centralized service will usually be able to afford a variety of equipment which will increase the choice available to staff. For example, in reprographic activities a desktop publishing system can revolutionize the production of circulars, advertising materials, brochures, reports, house journals, etc., incorporating illustrations, colour, ring binding and other improvements. The resulting output will be appropriate to its final use — from boardroom reports of high quality to cheap handouts and documents for more routine activities.

inappropriate.

5 Segregation of staff. Many of the routine office practices which are most easily centralized employ less experienced staff. This separates staff into categories and reduces *esprit de corps*, the essential unity of the organization.

6 Job motivation is reduced. The routine work of centralized departments retards the training and development of personnel. The opportunities to experience all facets of business life are reduced, and work becomes a daily round of office chores. This must be overcome by planned progression from department to department to assist young staff to gain general experience.

2.10 Services commonly controlled by the General Administration Office

In the largest offices the general administration office would usually control:

(a) Mail inwards and outwards.
(b) The telephone and telex systems.
(c) Caretaking, cleaning and routine maintenance services.
(d) Reception and messenger services.
(e) Canteen, refreshment breaks and machine vending services.
(f) Stationery and office supplies.
(g) Holiday, sick relief and other staff rotas.
(h) First aid, fire and safety services.

It would be influential in deciding policy on central services, including the appointment of staff and exercising general supervision of the following:

(a) Typing and audio-typing services.
(b) Reprographic services.
(c) Filing and records services.
(d) Computer systems and networks.

The centralized services are dealt with more fully in the chapters that follow.

Every organization has to maintain relations with the general public, not only in order to maintain sales of goods or services but also to meet the many obligations which arise in the course of everyday life. The public today are very conscious of the need to preserve the environment, indeed there is a huge **Department of the Environment** to control the impact of industry on our national heritage. One nationalized industry which runs cross-channel ferries made a decision to change from paper cups to plastic cups. It was in the habit of dumping rubbish overboard in mid-channel. The new plastic cups, unlike the paper ones, did not become waterlogged and sink, but floated ashore, where they proved to be a source of almost permanent litter. Quite apart from this nuisance the matter brought to light the fact that to save emptying a few dustbins at each end of the journey the seas were being polluted with all sorts of waste products. Naturally the industry concerned had to revise its policy to meet the public indignation that arose.

The general administration officer often assumes responsibility for public relations in small firms. Larger organizations will appoint **public relations officers**, who are often members of the **Institute of Public Relations**.

2.11   Overcoming the disadvantages of centralized services

Some of the economies achieved by the introduction of centralized services are inevitably lost in the departure of formerly key workers who dislike the new arrangements. The departmental secretary who knows everyone and everything that is going on in his/her department resents being shifted into a more repetitive, less influential role in a typing or audio-typing pool. Anyone who has worked a plain-paper copier for an hour or two knows how boring and repetitive the activities become. One is reduced to reading bits of the material being copied to keep any interest going at all, and if it comes from several departments, it amounts to a miscellaneous collection of unrelated matters – whereas the secretary in a department can follow how the duplication work fits into the pattern of the other work done. Some of the ways of overcoming the disadvantages of centralized services are:

(*a*) *Varying the daily round.* It is undesirable for anyone to do the same job all day and everyday. The work needs to be rotated. After a certain amount of time on a particular activity, the member of staff moves to a different task, possibly in a different work area. If staff can be encouraged to plan their own day to a considerable extent, so long as the necessary work is eventually completed, the individual preferences of staff can be more easily accommodated.

One person may prefer a particular task, and will do it for longer than another.

(*b*) *Avoidance of excessive supervision.* Modern computerized methods give very close control of productivity, counting how many items are produced, forms are processed, calls are answered, etc. This gives a very tyrannical control over staff, which, if insensitively exercised, can cause great resentment, and even make staff ill. Such controls should be exercised as lightly as possible, and those subjected to them should not hesitate to complain if they are suffering stress. Top management should watch for high labour turnover; it is often the result of insensitive supervision, and a particular individual may be the cause.

(*c*) *Group working.* The loss of personal links between staff is one of the chief disadvantages of centralized services. One solution is to allow a certain degree of specialization. For example, two or three typists in a typing pool might always attend to the correspondence, invoices and other documents required by the sales department, and thus build up a strong link with that department as well as an expertise in its requirements.

(*d*) *Higher pay for boring work.* Sometimes the solution to boring, repetitive work may be to pay a little more for it. The person who particularly needs to earn a good salary may be happy to plod on with less inspiring tasks if the financial reward compensates for the repetitive nature of the work.

2.12 Points to think about and discuss

(*a*) Some people leave school at 16 and go straight into offices. Others stay on at school, college and university until much older. A student taking a full university course to qualify finally as a PhD (Doctor of Philosophy) cannot expect to leave university and take his/her first job until the age of 24 or 25. Discuss the advantages and disadvantages of leaving early, as opposed to leaving at 21 with a degree, 22 with a master's degree, or 24 with a doctorate. In your discussion consider both the point of view of the individual and that of society.

(*b*) A hospital has been storing its x-ray records departmentally; the various departments such as the orthopaedic department, ear, nose and throat clinic, casualty department, etc., keep their own records. The registrar is proposing to centralize all hospital records, and suggests a centralized x-ray records department. Discuss the advantages and disadvantages of such a system.

(*c*) The office has been supplied twice daily with tea, served to staff at their desks from a mobile trolley with urns. A vending machine system is suggested instead, located at convenient points on each floor and available at all times. Discuss the advantages and disadvantages of such a change.

(*d*) Argue a case for, or against, a change from a system where personal secretaries with shorthand and typing skills serve executives' correspondence needs, to a system where executives are connected by a hand microphone to a centralized dictation machine and letters are typed by a pool of audio-typists.

2.12 Rapid revision – staffing the office

Cover the page with a sheet of paper and uncover one question at a time.

Answers		Questions	
–		1	What is the traditional term for an office worker?
1	A clerk	2	Who was Bob Cratchit?
2	The clerk in Scrooge's office in Charles Dickens' *A Christmas Carol*.	3	Why is clerical labour more interesting than in Bob Cratchit's day?
3	(*a*) There are many sub-divisions of the work, each with its own skills and interests. (*b*) There are many mechanical and electronic aids, and many computerized procedures, which take the drudgery out of routine office work.	4	What should be the ultimate aim of every office employee?
4	Full professional qualification in the functional area in which he/she decides to specialize.	5	What are the grades of clerical work?
5	(*a*) Junior clerk, (*b*) senior clerk; (*c*) chief clerk.	6	What are the routine posts in typing?
6	(*a*) Copy typist, (*b*) audio-typist, (*c*) junior secretary.	7	What are the chief types of secretarial work?
7	(*a*) Junior secretary, (*b*) personal secretary, (*c*) personal assistant (PA).	8	What are the types of post in the accounts department?
8	(*a*) Junior book-keeper, (*b*) book-keeper, (*c*) accounting technician, (*d*) cost clerk, (*e*) financial accountant, (*f*) management accountant.	9	Why is the work of a medical secretary rather specialized?
9	Because it is a sensitive area, where, for example, a misspelling could lead to incorrect treatment, wrong prescriptions, etc.	10	Which official in any firm or company best represents the office?
10	The general administration officer.	11	What are the functions of the general administration office?
11	To control a wide range of activities within the firm, particularly the care and cleaning of buildings, the security	12	Which services are often centralized?

arrangements and the provision of centralized services used by other departments.

12 (*a*) The telephone service, (*b*) typing pools, (*c*) computerization and accounting services, (*d*) stationery and office resources.	13 What are the advantages of centralization of these services?
13 (*a*) More economical operation, (*b*) bulk purchase of supplies, (*c*) the best and most sophisticated equipment becomes economical, (*d*) better use of staff time, (*e*) cheaper labour can be employed because every activity becomes routine.	14 Are there any disadvantages?
14 (*a*) The work becomes impersonal, (*b*) a bureaucratic attitude may develop, (*c*) delay may occur because of the indirect nature of orders to staff, (*d*) segregation of staff causes resentment, (*e*) job motivation is reduced.	15 What type of person is required for the post of chief administrative officer?
15 A person of wide interests and abilities, who is equally at ease with all classes of visitors and staff.	16 Where is the general administration office usually situated?
16 Near the entrance to the building, on the ground floor, where it is at the centre of activities.	17 Go over the page again until you feel you are sure of the answers.

Exercises set 2

1 Write down the letters (*a*)–(*j*) in a list one below the other. Then write against these letters the word or phrase from the word list below which best fits sentence (*a*), (*b*), etc.

(*a*) The people who work in offices are called collectively the ......

(*b*) Today office work embraces many activities calling for a wide variety of office ......

(*c*) The majority of business ...... is produced in typewritten form.

(*d*) Today, although typewriters are still widely used, many of the best typists and secretaries use a ......

(*e*) An in-house course is a ...... course run within a firm – often at a special venue away from ordinary work areas.

(*f*) ...... is the art of keeping financial records of receipts, payments, costs, etc.

(*g*) The top secretarial posts in commerce and industry are those of ......

(*h*) Services that are provided to help all departments within a firm are called ......

(*i*) Work that seeks to promote the work of a company in the community and anticipate any adverse criticism is called ...... work.

(*j*) A ...... organization is one that seeks to represent employees in responsible positions and ensure a proper standard of qualification and conduct in their work.

Word list: skills, word-processor, centralized services, public relations, training, staff, correspondence, accountancy, personal assistants, professional.

2 Name four types of employee who might use typewriters.

3 List the characteristics that might be helpful to a person taking up work in the accountancy field.

4 Explain the use of the word 'secretary' in the following cases:

   (*a*) Personal secretary.
   (*b*) Company secretary.
   (*c*) Secretary of State for Social Security.
   (*d*) The secretary of the Happy Wanderers' Rambling Society.

5 What do you understand by the designation of 'chief administration officer'? What responsibilities would such a post carry in the large office block of an international company?

6 'Every one of these dictation machines will save you the wages of six short-hand-typists.' − Salesman to general administration officer.
   You are one of the shorthand-typists. Write a report objecting to the adoption of dictation machines, and justifying your opinion.

7 Your office has six members of staff who can do relief telephone operating. The telephonist has lunch from noon to 1 pm and coffee breaks from 10.30 to 10.45 am and 3 pm to 3.15 pm. Draw up a rota for relief telephone duties so that the work is fairly allocated between *A*, *B*, *C*, *D*, *E* and *F*. *C* cannot be available any morning and *F* cannot do any lunch-time work. *A* has Thursday off and *D* has Friday afternoon off.

8 What is meant by 'centralization'? What is meant by 'centralized services'? In your answer consider the application of these two principles in (*a*) the retail supermarket trade *or* (*b*) an oil company controlling a chain of garages *or* (*c*) a university with fifteen colleges.

9 You are asked to produce a holiday rota for the ten members of your staff covering the months of June, July and August (a period of 13 weeks). The staff consists of yourself and your assistant, one telephonist and a relief telephonist-typist, two general clerks, two shorthand-typists, one copy typist and a junior trainee clerk. Each member of the staff is allowed to take two weeks' holiday. Draw up the necessary rota, ensuring that the department's work is adequately covered.

10 In office practice there is an increasing tendency towards specialization and centralization of functions. State your views as to why this is happening and explain the advantages which can be obtained. Illustrate your answer by reference to one specific office procedure.

11 As administrative officer it is your duty to cover the absence of any clerk or specialist employee. Johnson, an export documentation clerk, is jealous of his specialist knowledge and secretive about the various functions he performs. Suggest arguments you would use to change his attitude. If he stubbornly refuses to train a replacement, how would you suggest this should be overcome?

12 Considerable trouble has developed among the caretaking staff in the Massive Office Company. The administration officer discovers the following chief complaints: (*a*) Bill Bloggs, the assistant chief caretaker, is universally disliked for his bad temper and foul language, (*b*) female cleaners consider that they receive an unfair allocation of the heavy work, (*c*) persistent grumbling by supervisors about the late arrival of cleaning staff is caused by the fact that the first bus does not reach the area until 10 minutes after the official starting time, and this grumbling is resented by the cleaners, (*d*) there is a shortage of cleaning materials of every sort although prices have not risen and the allocation of money has not changed, (*e*) increased bus fares have not been reflected in any increase in wages for the lowest paid staff but higher ranks have had a 10 per cent increase in pay, (*f*) Department 'D' is notoriously slovenly in its behaviour, and staff cleaning this department are thoroughly disgusted with the condition of desks and floors, which seems to be related to the installation of a coffee machine.

Suggest remedial action the administration officer should take on each of these points.

13 'Central services are more efficient than departmental services.' 'The impersonal relationships between staff and the central services who are supposed to be supplying them with correspondence, etc., lead to a reduction in efficiency.'

Discuss these two opposing views of central services. Which view is the more correct in your opinion?

14 Segregation of the sexes frequently results from a change to centralized services. Why is this? What solutions can be found to this problem?

3 The layout of the office: health and safety

3.1 The need for planning

If an office is merely a haphazard collection of desks, chairs, filing cabinets, telephones, etc., it will be inefficient and inconvenient. The office worker today will not continue in employment where work is badly arranged, facilities are outdated and the work is tiring and laborious. It follows that new offices should be thoroughly planned so that the work is easily performed and conveniently but unobtrusively supervised. Even older offices, which may fall below modern standards in many respects, can be greatly improved if the systems employed and the layout are regularly reappraised. The chief considerations are: (*a*) location of the office, (*b*) conditions, (*c*) the layout and (*d*) the provision of adequate business systems and aids.

We must consider some of the chief points under these headings, although even the best attempts at planning are subject to criticism in the light of actual experience. It follows that the young office worker actually performing the various tasks is often able to offer suggestions an enlightened management will gratefully accept. Some offices have a **suggestion box** in which staff may place written suggestions. They should in particular report anything they find tiring or irksome, such as uncomfortable seating, poor lighting, unnecessary lifting or walking about. A telephone wrongly placed may cause a junior employee to make endless journeys across a large office. Niggardly behaviour with the paper clips may fray tempers and waste time out of all proportion to the cost of a more generous supply.

3.2 The location of offices

Where a completely new office is being built, it is desirable to choose a location which represents the best possible site for the purpose of the business concerned. Important considerations are:

(*a*) The location of other parts of the business, factories, warehouses, depots, etc. It will be of great importance to locate the office as centrally as possible to ensure adequate control.

(*b*) The likely costs, particularly the cost of land, or the rent payable for the use of land. Other costs might include business rates for the area, parking costs, etc. The comparison of these costs at various sites may show one site to be more economic than another.

(c) Development authority incentives. Many local authorities, particularly development authorities, are keen to attract office development – for example, to areas of inner city decay. They may offer subsidies to assist with building costs, free rental for a period of years, etc.

Other points of interest about the office location are:

(a) Its closeness to the bank and the post office. If a local branch of one of the major banks is not available, great inconvenience may be experienced in obtaining money as and when required, or in disposing of cash takings. Similarly, country mail services are less reliable than town deliveries.

(b) Its convenience for customers and business contacts. A firm that regularly receives visitors from overseas will wish to set up not far from a major airport. Closeness to a railway station may also be an advantage. Pleasant country surroundings may be very expensive from the point of view of transport for visitors and staff.

(c) The availability of suitably qualified staff. If the area surrounding the office cannot offer a sufficient number of suitable employees, it will not be a convenient location. Future needs as well as present requirements should be borne in mind.

3.3 General working conditions – The *Health and Safety at Work Act, 1974*

In the United Kingdom general working conditions are controlled to some extent by the *Offices, Shops and Railways Premises Act, 1963*, a copy of which must be displayed prominently in all offices for the information of employees. A later Act, the *Health and Safety at Work Act, 1974*, is gradually introducing new regulations and approved codes of practice. The 1963 Act lays down many rules which employers must obey. Premises must be kept clean, adequate floor space must be provided for workers and their equipment, temperature must be kept above a minimum of 16°C, and ventilation must be adequate. Toilet facilities must be available, with running hot and cold water, soap and clean towels. Many employers not only meet these elementary conditions but recognize that good working conditions raise productivity. They therefore pay attention to many points not specifically required by the Act. The main points of interest are listed below.

(a) *Decoration*. Walls and ceilings should be tastefully decorated in carefully chosen colours. Furnishing and furniture should wherever possible be chosen to tone or contrast with the decorations.

(b) *Lighting*. The Act says that lighting must be adequate for the work required. Modern light fittings are generally inexpensive, and give out light of uniform intensity. Glare is avoided by suitable baffles which screen off the light from anyone who looks directly towards the source of light, yet at the same time the working surface is perfectly lit.

(*c*) *Safety*. The Act requires that personnel trained in first aid should be available at all times and that an adequate first-aid box should be provided in every office. The knowledge of first-aid staff should be retested every 3 years. The greatest care should be taken to ensure safety in the office. Electrical and other apparatus should be installed or repaired only by qualified electricians; office equipment should be shielded where necessary, e.g. guillotines and other cutting devices, and gangways should be kept clear, even marked out where necessary. Fire exits should be brought to the attention of staff and drills should be held to ensure that procedures are understood. Practical jokes should be severely discouraged – they often cause injuries.

(*d*) *Noise*. There is little excuse these days for noisy working conditions, since acoustic panels in ceilings and walls, double glazing and cork or rubber flooring can together deal effectively with most internal and external sources of noise. Doors can be fitted with devices that prevent slamming, and many modern machines are quiet in operation. The isolation of noisy equipment in alcoves or rooms where they are least disturbing to the general office is sometimes helpful.

(*e*) *Ventilation and heating*. Fresh air is essential to efficient clerical activity, but draughts can produce miserable working conditions, colds and rheumatic pains. Temperatures of about 65°–68°F (17°–18°C) are about the best for a busy office.

3.4 The employer's duty of care

The employer has a general duty under the common law to take reasonable care of all employees. This duty of care covers the provision of a safe place to work in, safe tools, machinery and other equipment, safe methods of work with safe materials and a properly supervised establishment at all times.

This general requirement under the common law has been extended by several Acts of Parliament, of which two have been mentioned – the Offices, Shops and Railway Premises Act, 1963 and the Health and Safety at Work Act, 1974. Two more are the Fire Precautions Act, 1971 and the Employers' Liability (Compulsory Insurance) Act, 1969. The latter Act makes it compulsory for all employers to insure against physical injury and disease sustained by employees. A notice must be displayed to show that the insurance has been taken out. The effect of insurance is to provide a huge pool of funds contributed by all employers from which any employee successfully suing for compensation for injury or ill health can be compensated.

The Fire Precautions Act, 1971 requires employers to provide adequate means of escape in case of fire, firefighting equipment, fire alarms, etc. A fire certificate will be issued to major firms after an adequate system has been installed, while a code of practice for lesser firms is given in a booklet from Her Majesty's Stationery Office.

The employer's 'safety policy'

If an employer has more than five employees, he/she must draw up a written statement of 'safety policy' and this must be drawn to the attention of every employee. The policy statement must refer specifically to any problem area on the premises and any special dangers to be avoided. It must lay down rules of conduct and procedures to be followed, e.g. about the use of electrical appliances, the avoidance of overloading circuits, the accumulation of waste materials, the blocking of passageways, the safe use of stairways, etc. Generally speaking, the occupier of premises is responsible under the Act for the general working conditions, but where the premises are controlled by an owner who leases off parts of the building to different firms, some of the duties and responsibilities are transferred to the owner.

All premises used as offices must be registered with the local authority, which must also be notified of any accident causing the death, or disablement for more than 3 days, of any employee. The 'safety policy' must lay down proper procedures for reporting accidents and 'near misses', preferably to a named person acting as 'safety officer', and that individual will report any serious accident by telephone or a tele-message to the local authority and follow this up by a formal report on a Form 2508 (Report of an accident and/or dangerous occurrence, and injuries sustained).

A recognized Trade Union has a right to appoint a safety representative to consult with the management on safety matters and make representations on behalf of its members.

3.5 Hazard spotting in offices

One element of the supervision of office safety is 'hazard spotting'. An exercise in hazard spotting can be carried out at any time and should be featured from time to time in all offices. Even more, departmental heads with areas under their control should be aware at all times of the need to watch out for possible hazards. This is particularly true at any time where an unusual set of circumstances has interrupted normal routines. Thus where redecorations have caused rooms or corridors to be cleared, the furniture removed and stored elsewhere may cause fire exits to be blocked or passageways to be obstructed. A head of department who notices such dangers should take steps to correct them.

Some of the common hazards to be met in offices are as follows:

(*a*) *Filing cabinets.* Filing cabinets are relatively lightly built, being made of fairly thin sheet metal. They do become very heavy when the drawers are filled with files of correspondence. The danger is that if the top drawers are filled with correspondence when lower drawers are empty, the whole cabinet will fall forward on to the secretary using the cabinet if one of the top drawers is pulled wide open. If the top drawer is pulled out and tips the cabinet, the second drawer may fly out too, causing serious injury. It is a common thing for a secretary to put personal belongings in the bottom drawer of a cabinet, but these are usually light items. A handbag or a luncheon snack box do not weigh much, and will help to make the cabinet unstable. It is better to put personal items in the top drawer and use the lowest drawers first for correspondence. Some cabinets have the top drawer as a lockable cupboard, and this is a safe place to put light personal belongings. Where a cabinet is slowly being filled with files as the months pass it is sometimes safest to fill the bottom drawer with heavy items (a few house bricks) as a safety measure.

(*b*) *Passageways.* An open-plan office generates a great deal of 'traffic' as staff visit one another for a variety of business purposes. With 'corridors of power', cubicle offices lead off on either side of a central corridor, which is usually completely free of obstruction except for the odd row of fire buckets or fire extinguishers. With open-plan offices there is no clear corridor, and visitors or people passing through from one area to another need some guide as to where to walk. It is a common practice to mark out the passageways with white lines. All such passageways should be kept clear. There is a tendency for the passageway to become a dumping ground, e.g. when stocks of copying paper are delivered, they may be kept in the passageway until the secretary concerned has time to put them away. The next person wheeling a trolley down the passageway has to negotiate the obstruction. Passageways should be kept clear at all times.

(*c*) *Waste material.* Accumulations of waste material are a major hazard. One thinks of a recent football disaster in which a huge stand filled with spectators became an inferno in which many people died because waste paper that had fallen under the stand over the course of months (and possibly years) had not been cleared away. Nobody had spotted the hazard, and taken steps to clear up the mess.

Some occupations generate a great deal of waste paper, e.g. in artwork departments, pattern designs in the clothing trades, etc. It is essential to have large, preferably metal, waste-paper baskets where such waste material can be collected; on no account should it be simply thrown on the floor.

Waste material such as cotton cloth, dusters, etc., which have been used to polish furniture, wipe down oily machinery or used to remove solvents, especially where a spillage has occurred, are a common cause of fires. They may slowly heat up and eventually catch fire. One chemical may react with another, or if left near a radiator, a cloth may burst into flames. Special care should be taken to dispose of such materials, e.g. it is unwise to put them in a waste-paper bin. Better to take them out to a dustbin in a back yard.

(*d*) *Swing doors*. Swing doors are a frequent cause of accidents. Not only do people get hit by the doors as they open suddenly but the person pushing the other side may come through the glass if the push is suddenly resisted. Never stand near such doors or engage someone in conversation on one side or other of them. In factories and warehouses fork-lift trucks often come through such doors without any real warning.

(*e*) *Electrical appliances*. A well-designed office will have a plentiful supply of plugs on what is known as a ring main, which simply means that electricity is made available at many points. Ideally each appliance should have its own plug, and the use of two-way plugs and three-way plugs should be avoided. The more appliances working off a single plug, the greater the 'load' on that plug and the greater the chance that (*a*) the fuse will blow or (*b*) over-heating of the cables will occur. Sometimes a device such as a computer configuration requires several appliances to be supplied with power but the actual current is not likely to be great and a single plug will be enough. In such cases it is usual to buy a special lead and junction box, with a single plug fitting into the supply point and leading to a four-way junction box into which the computer, the disc drive unit, the monitor and keyboard and the printer can all be plugged, each with its own separate socket.

Conclusions on hazard spotting. It is not possible in the space available to give detailed accounts of all the various hazards that might be encountered besides those mentioned above. Hazards can exist in many places, from the floor covering used to the paint on the ceiling, and with every piece of equipment in between. Students should try the exercise in their college classrooms, and those in employment should 'hazard spot' in the offices and other locations where they work.

3.6 Open plan and enclosed offices

Visitors to the House of Commons in London may occasionally be shown 'corridors of power' where all the doors leading off the central passage bear titles such as 'President of the Board of Trade', 'Foreign Secretary', 'Home Secretary' and so on. Small private offices of this type are very convenient for confidential private discussions of important matters, perhaps concerning state secrets. On the other hand, enclosed offices of this sort, which are not solely

Figure 3.1   An open-plan office (reproduced by courtesy of K + N International
(Office Systems) Ltd)

found in government departments, have disadvantages too. By contrast, many firms have adopted 'open-plan' offices, some of them
quite enormous, with 300 or 400 people working in the same room.
A list of the advantages and disadvantages of open-plan offices
would include the following:

Advantages
1   They are cheap to construct since lightweight partitions replace
    walls.
2   They are often single-storey buildings lit by natural daylight from
    overhead.
3   They are easy to supervise, since staff are in view at all times.
4   Communication is easy between staff in different departments,
    since it is not necessary to leave the office and perhaps walk long
    distances to visit colleagues.

5 Changes in the pattern of work and the size of departments are easily taken into account if expanding departments move over into the spaces left by contracting departments.
6 Open-plan offices are easy to decorate. The staff themselves provide part of the decor, making them pleasant places to work in.
7 They are democratic, since all grades of staff are on view. Senior staff must preserve their position by a display of character and efficiency rather than by imposing door-plates and illuminated 'Enter' signs.
8 Layout can be such that work flows on from desk to desk, with clerks contributing their special knowledge and skills to documents circulated into their in-trays.
9 A planned communications system can reduce movements about the office and put senior staff in instant touch with all departmental managers and clerks.

Disadvantages
1 There is a lack of privacy for confidential discussions.
2 They use land extensively rather than intensively, and are therefore less suitable for city offices where rents are high.
3 Idle chatter may disrupt the work of a greater number of people, reducing work output from the more responsible staff.
4 Senior staff may be more easily disturbed than in the cubicle type of office.
5 There are some machines that are inappropriate for open-plan offices, particularly some typewriters, computer printers and photocopiers. These pieces of equipment must be installed in cubicle type offices or alcoves on the edge of the open-plan office. Figure 3.1 is a photograph of the open-plan office at Barr and Stroud, part of the Pilkington Group.

3.7   Providing a suitable layout for an individual
Layout of the office depends very greatly upon the most careful choice of desks and equipment to ensure the convenience and comfort of the clerk. Clerical duties can be as effectively carried out as the work on production lines in factories if the functions the clerk is to perform are given the same thought beforehand. Since most clerks perform a variety of jobs at different times of the day, the layout should be such that each task is accessible and easily commenced when necessary while at other times it is tidily out of the way.

A firm which specializes in devising equipment appropriate to such a variety of activities is Flexiform Ltd, whose **Master Units**, while mass produced and therefore relatively cheap to purchase, are

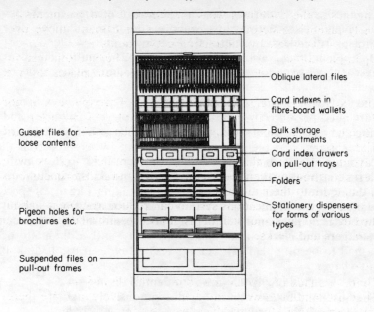

Oblique lateral files

Card indexes in fibre-board wallets

Bulk storage compartments

Card index drawers on pull-out trays

Folders

Stationery dispensers for forms of various types

Gusset files for loose contents

Pigeon holes for brochures etc.

Suspended files on pull-out frames

Figure 3.2 A Flexiform unit (reproduced by courtesy of Flexiform Ltd)

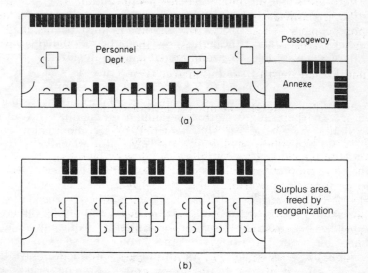

Personnel Dept.

Passageway

Annexe

(a)

Surplus area, freed by reorganization

(b)

Figure 3.3 Saving space by improving office layout (reproduced by courtesy of Flexiform Ltd)

flexible in nature. The same master unit may accommodate shelving units, pigeon-hole units, filing wallets and boxes, hanging filing pockets, card index drawers, a desk top and many other types of fittings. Such arrangements as those shown in Figure 3.2 are very convenient, very economical in the use of space and quite inexpensive, especially when their long life is considered.

A case study on office layout
Figure 3.3 shows the layout of office premises before and after serious thought had been given to the layout by experts from the Flexiform organization.

Before reorganization the firm concerned used the main room, and the annexe, to store personnel records, taking $14.5\,m^2$ of space. At times personnel records overflowed into the small passageway, shown clear in the diagram. Increased documentation of 20 per cent was anticipated as a result of expansion plans, and additional office area had to be provided. The equipment already in use included:

36 4-drawer filing cabinets
 1 3-drawer filing cabinet
10 2-drawer filing cabinets
33 9-tray visible index cabinets
 2 16-tray visible index cabinets
 1 work table
 3 pull-out working tops with cupboards
 1 20-drawer card index cabinet
 1 4-drawer card index cabinet

After reorganization the annexe was cleared completely and the main office was able to accommodate not only all the previous records but the anticipated 20 per cent increase as well. The area required had been reduced to $8.8\,m^2$, a saving of $5.7\,m^2$, despite the increased capacity. Clearly, with office accommodation costing on average £64 per square metre per annum, good office layout can contribute a great deal to the reduction of accommodation costs, and − by reducing distances travelled to secure information stored in the records − can reduce fatigue and increase efficiency.

3.8 Organization and methods (O and M)
Work study is a science in its own right today, and during the last 20 years it has begun to take more and more interest in office procedures. There are several reasons why this should be so. First, major economies of large-scale operation in factory production have been achieved in recent years, and many factory systems are now as efficient as they can possibly get. It follows that manufacturers, trying to keep ahead of their rivals in a competitive world, have had

to look elsewhere to achieve more economic operations. A great deal of their attention was turned towards the distribution system; transport and warehousing have been revolutionized as more and more attention has been given to the most economic and efficient distribution system. The only other field left where economies can be achieved is in the field of clerical duties and office practice. The O and M teams have therefore turned their attention to this new field, and have begun to analyse the work done in offices. A second reason for the new interest in office procedures is the switch to international companies and the international movement of goods. This has required a careful study of documentation to reduce as far as possible the legal disputes which so easily arise when businessmen deal with foreigners who, apart from language differences, have different laws and mercantile customs from ourselves. You cannot hope to secure good arrangements with overseas governments and overseas firms if your own organization and methods are slipshod and haphazard.

Generally speaking, the O and M team are specialists in work study, and do not normally work in the office that is being investigated. They bring an outsider's point of view to bear on the problems, asking employees what they do, what is the purpose of their activities, how long each process takes, etc. The stages of an O and M study include the following:

Stages of an O and M investigation

(a) Discover and record the present arrangements, including:

(i) What work is performed and by whom?

(ii) What is the purpose of this work in the firm's operations?

(iii) How does the work at present flow through the office? This may best be presented as a flow chart or model.

(iv) What are the links between this office and other departments — what part does this office play in the firm's whole scheme of activities?

(b) Draw up proposals for improving the system, including:

(i) Improvements in documentation; particularly the *alignment* of similar documents (see p. 200). The alignment of similar documents involves putting the same information in the same spot on each document. The required number of copies can then be run off in some sort of copier, or more probably today they will be printed out by a computer (see p. 276).

(ii) Improvements in work-flow: rearranging desks and working positions where necessary to improve the layout.

(iii) Improvements in technology: using labour-saving devices such as personal computers, computer networks, electronic calculators, visible index records, etc. Often convenient visual wall-displays, e.g. of telephone numbers, personnel in departmental listing, etc., improve the speed with which queries are handled.

(iv) Estimates of personnel changes required, including proposals for dealing with redundancy, etc.

(c) Implementation of the policy, including problem-solving where necessary, staff consultation, regular check-ups as the plans take effect and modification of the arrangements in the light of experience.

3.9 Simple office items of equipment

There are many minor office items of equipment which promote efficiency, and which every clerical worker should collect for his or her own use. Ideally the management should supply these for all staff. If it does not, and staff are continually having to walk about the office to borrow staplers, rulers and other items then they should point out politely that this shortage of equipment is wasting time and reducing their output of work. The following lists of essential and occasional requirements may help you to judge the adequacy of your own situation.

Essential requirements	*Occasional requirements*
1 Pencil.	1 Heavy duty stapler.
2 Rubber.	2 Heavy duty punch.
3 Red and black ballpoint pens.	3 Eyeletting tool.
4 Hand stapling machine.	4 Guillotine (paper trimmer).
5 Staple extractor.	5 Roller damper for envelopes, etc.
6 Light two-hole punch.	6 Electronic calculator, or prefer-
7 Scissors.	ably a printing calculator.
8 Ruler.	*Note:* Some offices issue blue ball-
9 Date stamp and pad.	point pens, but these can be a
10 Desk tidy – for pins, paper	nuisance if work is photocopied.
clips, etc.	Some photocopiers cannot 'see' blue,
11 Rubber stamps as required.	and consequently it is better to use
12 Rubber stamp rack.	black ballpoint pens.
13 Paste or gum.	
14 Desk diary.	
15 Magnetic pin dispenser.	
16 Telephone message pad.	
17 Post-it notes.	

3.10 Points to think about and discuss

(*a*) The professional body for office managers is the Institute of Office Management. What advantages might follow from securing membership of such bodies, which usually require both examination qualifications and proof of experience from applicants?

(*b*) A delivery man asks you to sign for 2 tonnes of coke which he has shot into the area at the back of your factory premises. It is lunch-time and no one is on duty in the yard. What is the best course of action? Would you reach a different decision if it was a small, hand-delivered parcel?

(*c*) Make a plan of any small office that you know, marking in as accurately as you can the following items:

  (i) The entrance door.
  (ii) The windows.
  (iii) The desk positions and seats.
  (iv) Using the letters OL mark in the positions of overhead lighting.
  (v) Use the letters DL for marking in any desk lights.
  (vi) Use the letters ET and IT to mark the position of external and internal telephones. If the same telephone is used for two purposes mark it E & IT.
  (vii) Mark the position of the filing cabinets, cupboards, work surfaces and other items of furniture.
  (viii) Mark the position of any notice boards or display surfaces with the letters NB.

In a suitable place alongside or below your diagram list any suggestions you have for improving the layout of the office in view of your knowledge of the work done there. Head these suggestions with the title 'Recommendations for improving the office layout'.

(*d*) Consider whether the room you are now sitting in would be acceptable as an office under the *Health and Safety at Work Act, 1974*. In particular consider: (i) cleanliness; (ii) adequate floor space for each employee (how many clerks could it accommodate); (iii) temperature; (iv) availability of toilet accommodation; (v) adequacy of the lighting; (vi) safety aspects, particularly the possibilities of fire.

3.11 Rapid revision – office location and layout
Cover the page with a sheet of notepaper and uncover one question at a time.

Answers	Questions
–	1 List the points to be borne in mind when choosing the location of an office.

1 (*a*) Closeness to other parts of the business, factories, depots, etc.
(*b*) General cost considerations, based on costs per square metre per annum.
(*c*) Local authority incentives.

2 What other considerations enter into the choice of locality?

---

2 (*a*) Availability of bank and post office services nearby.
(*b*) Convenience of customers and business contacts, particularly overseas contacts.
(*c*) Availability of qualified staff.

3 What Acts of Parliament control office conditions?

---

3 The *Health and Safety at Work Act, 1974*, and the *Offices, Shops and Railway Premises Act, 1963*.

4 List the important points in the Acts.

---

4 (*a*) Premises must be clean.
(*b*) Adequate floor space for each employee.
(*c*) Temperature at about 17°−18°C.
(*d*) Toilet facilities and hot and cold water, soap, etc., to be provided.
(*e*) Adequate lighting.
(*f*) Trained first-aid staff and retesting for these staff every 3 years.

5 (*a*) With whom are office premises registered?
(*b*) What particular events must be reported to them?

---

5 (*a*) With local authorities.
(*b*) Accidents causing death, or incapacity for more than three days.

6 What is 'hazard spotting'?

---

6 It is the study of a working area such as an office to pinpoint dangerous situations, with a view to correcting them before a hazardous situation develops.

7 Whose duty is it to spot hazards?

---

7 Everyone should play his/her part, but the chief responsibility lies on Heads of Departments and the General Administration Officer.

8 What does the common law say about hazards?

---

8 It says the employer has a general duty of care towards those employed in the enterprise.

9 Employers of more than 5 people must . . .
(continue)

---

9 . . . draw up a written 'safety policy' which must be drawn to the attention of every employee.

10 What are the chief types of office?

---

10 (*a*) Enclosed offices, or 'cubicle' offices.
(*b*) Open-plan offices.

11 What are the advantages of enclosed offices?

---

11 (*a*) More private for confidential discussions.
(*b*) Quiet to work in.
(*c*) They isolate noisy equipment.
(*d*) They confer status on top-level staff.

12 What are the advantages of open-plan offices?

12 (*a*) They are cheap to build.
(*b*) They are easy to supervise.
(*c*) They are democratic and sociable places to work in.
(*d*) They are adaptable as work patterns change.

13 What is an O and M department?

---

13 A department that appraises organization and methods and recommends changes in layout and procedure.

14 What aspects might it consider?

---

14 (*a*) The present arrangements and system of work.
(*b*) The possible improvements in:
(i) general layout,
(ii) the documentation procedures,
(iii) the 'flow' of work around the office,
(iv) the individual work positions, and their layout.

15 Go over the page until you feel you are sure of the answers.

Exercises set 3

1 Write down on your answer paper the letters (*a*)–(*j*), to correspond with the sentences below. Against each letter write the word or phrase, chosen from the word list, which is needed to complete the sentence.

(*a*) Many ...... help firms to find offices in suitable locations.
(*b*) An idea for improving the working of your office should be contributed to the ......
(*c*) The Act of Parliament controlling working conditions in offices is the *Health and ...... Act, 1974.*
(*d*) Modern office lighting is fitted with baffle screens to prevent ......
(*e*) Noise can be reduced by using ...... ceiling panels in offices.
(*f*) Fresh air can be assured by adequate ...... systems.
(*g*) Greater privacy for senior staff is possible with small ...... offices.
(*h*) Open-plan offices are easier to ...... than enclosed offices.
(*i*) Good internal telephone networks reduce the need to ...... colleagues to clarify difficult points.
(*j*) The department responsible for improving office layout is the ...... and ...... team.

Word list: suggestions box, glare, ventilation, development authorities, O M, enclosed, supervise, Safety at Work, sound absorbent, visit.

2 In each of the following questions select the best answer from the four alternatives given; (*a*), (*b*), (*c*) or (*d*).

(i) Closeness to a large housing estate may be an advantageous location for an office because: (*a*) an adequate bus service is sure to be available, (*b*) there will be a post office nearby, (*c*) industrial sites are often unpleasant and pollute the atmosphere, (*d*) a large labour force will be available for employment.

(ii) The *Health and Safety at Work Act, 1974*: (*a*) lays down clear limitations on the height of office buildings, (*b*) controls the general working conditions in offices, (*c*) was repealed in 1976, (*d*) nationalized all offices employing more than 100 staff.

(iii) In all offices there should be, according to the 1974 Act: (*a*) lifts to serve all floors, (*b*) lighting to a standard of 120 lumens per square foot, (*c*) trained first-aid personnel whose knowledge should be retested every 3 years, (*d*) welfare and recreation club facilities.

3 Write short paragraphs (5–6 lines each) about any five of the following, to mention possible hazards that might be met with in offices:

(*a*) floor covering   (*b*) passage ways
(*c*) swing doors   (*d*) desk lamps
(*e*) electric points   (*f*) waste paper
(*g*) filing cabinets   (*h*) ceilings

4 Which of the following are *not true* of open-plan offices? (*a*) They are often well-lit and well-ventilated, (*b*) they are easy to supervise, (*c*) they are very suitable for confidential interviews, (*d*) they help the easy flow of documents, (*e*) they reduce the disturbance caused by idle, chattering, staff, (*f*) they are generally speaking cheerful places to work in, (*g*) they are democratic, giving all staff the same working conditions.

5 Compare the advantages and disadvantages of the large open office with those of a group of small enclosed offices.

6 What do you understand by 'office methods'? How might they be improved in a firm operating in a traditional way?

7 Tom Smith advertises himself as an 'office consultant'. What services do you think he might offer to businessmen?

8 Write short notes about: (*a*) open-plan offices, (*b*) office fire drill, (*c*) guillotines and similar dangerous equipment, (*d*) document flow.

9 Write a memo for the manager of your office about the provision of minor office equipment items. Advance reasons for increasing the available equipment, and justifying the initial expense. Suggest control procedures to prevent waste of such items.

10 (i) Suggest a layout for a work position, including a diagram if you wish to draw one, for an employee who (*a*) regularly types for about half her working day, (*b*) spends half of the remainder of her time assembling and stapling speeches of senior executives for distribution as handouts at staff conferences (they are usually at least 12 pages thick), (*c*) is a telephone link-girl for her department answering both internal and external calls.

(ii) Would you change your layout if she were left-handed?

11 What part can office equipment play in improving the layout of work positions? In your answer refer particularly to (*a*) filing cabinets, (*b*) wall notice boards, (*c*) desks.

4 Communication on routine matters

4.1 Communication

Communication is the art of passing on news and information from one person to another. There are two main sub-divisions of communication: we can pass information in written form or in spoken form (orally, by word of mouth). For convenience we can further sub-divide each of these into two groups, into personal messages and mass-media messages. Thus the prime minister may discuss an international incident with the defence secretary in one of the rooms at No 10 Downing St, or he may go on television to tell the nation what the United Kingdom government thinks of the matter. The marketing manager may send a memo to a representative in East Anglia about a new product or he/she may issue 500 copies of a press release about it. Figure 4.1 shows a chart of the methods of communication used in offices and by people in offices. The notes to the figure explain some of the important features of the chart, but most of the individual methods of communication are described later in the body of the text.

Today so much of the work of communication is done electronically that it is important to be aware right from the start about computerization and the way that information can be passed over telephone lines in data form. Every office is a communication centre. It receives instructions, information and reports from other offices, by telephone, in data form or in correspondence of various sorts and after processing and reacting to it within the firm it sends out instructions, explanations and responses to those awaiting them.

Some attempt has been made in Chapter 14 to give an account of computerization, so that those who are unfamiliar with the subject can follow what happens. Even the law has had to be amended to take account of electronic developments, e.g. one Act of Parliament says that as far as the law is concerned a document shall be deemed to be in existence even if it is only stored electronically in someone's computer, so long as it is possible for both parties to access the computer and call the document out of the computer's memory on to a monitor (television) screen. Such screens are called visual display units, and if a suitable printer is attached, it is possible to print off a copy of everything on the screen. This means that a document can be made to appear at the touch of a single key. Such

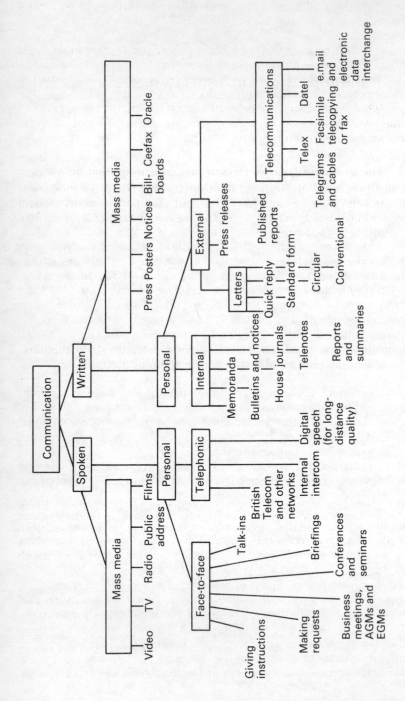

Figure 4.1 The pattern of business communication today

a copy is called a 'hard' copy, presumably to distinguish it from a document that is held by the 'software' — the programs in the computer.

In establishing links between offices there are a number of basic clerical and communication activities which form the vast majority of communications sent. The various departments have their separate functions to perform, but the results have to be passed to the end-user, whoever that may be, while head office and other supervisory bodies will need to be kept informed. We must first look at these basic clerical and communication activities.

4.2   The five main types of clerical and communication activities

In the processes of starting, developing and controlling business activities the manager and his office staff take part in many clerical and communication activities. There are five main fields of activity in all offices. They are:

(*a*) Routine procedures.
(*b*) Calculations.
(*c*) Records.
(*d*) Reports.
(*e*) Communications.

While many of these activities are described in detail in later chapters, a brief look at each of them seems appropriate here.

Notes

(i) The chart divides business communication into two parts, oral communication and written communication.

(ii) Each of these parts is then divided into two parts, mass media methods of communication and communication with individuals.

(iii) When communicating orally, we may do so in a face to face situation or over the telephone. We may deal with individuals or with groups at briefings, conferences, etc.

(iv) When communicating with business associates in writing we may be dealing with individuals or groups within the business, or with outsiders (suppliers, customers, officials of various sorts, professional advisers, etc). Much of this written communication will be in the form of correspondence, but some of it may be electronic in form, e.g. telex, or facsimile copying or telemessages. E-mail is electronic mail sent by computer over the telephone network. Documents and information can also be sent in this way by a system known as 'electronic data interchange' (EDI).

(v) In all these types of communication a good command of the English language is helpful, and practice in each method of communication is essential. Students interested in improving their ability to communicate might like to read a companion volume *Business English Made Simple*.

(vi) Mass-media methods of communication generally call for professional expertise, because the impact is on a very wide audience and a poor presentation can have an adverse effect on the whole business. Such work falls to the senior staff in a special **public relations department**, or in a small firm it is usually handled by the proprietor, senior partner or managing director.

(a) Routine procedures

Many routine activities must be carried out regularly if the office is to function properly. At the lowest levels these may include the replacement of clock cards ready for a new week or the collection and posting of letters from various departments. At higher levels routine check-ups on the progress of junior staff, following up of overdue credit accounts, checks on vehicle safety and maintenance procedures on plant and machinery are typical routine duties. **The essence of business organization is the establishment of routine procedures**. No one can claim to be organized until he/she has established a routine procedure to deal with the work in hand. Many people who find themselves attending a hospital, a mortuary, or a police station for the first time are surprised to find that these places have their own routine procedures. What is a memorable event for the member of the public involved in an accident, a burglary or a murder is mere routine to the nurse, the pathologist, the policeman or the judge.

Whenever any new activity is to be started, the manager, or the management team, will consider how the new activity is to be dealt with. They may decide that *A* will be in charge of the activity, that mail connected with it will be delivered to *B*, who will refer any difficult points for decision to *A*, and who will have *C* and *D* to help with routine activities.

Once this sort of procedure has been devised, the whole operation should proceed smoothly, at a minimum cost and under good control right up to top management level. Forms can be designed to assist the activity, e.g. a form to list names and record payments or a form to instruct the despatch department daily of the destination of goods to be sent out. The whole activity is systematically performed.

The rules for drawing up an office procedure are as follows:

(*a*) The system must be simple (so that highly skilled labour is not required).

(*b*) It must trigger into action everyone who needs to play some part in it. Thus the passing of a daily 'list of orders' to a typist may trigger her into preparing invoices and labels for the despatch of goods.

(*c*) The procedure should make use, wherever possible, of mechanical aids and labour-saving devices.

(*d*) The principle of 'exceptions' should be followed – i.e. only unusual items should be referred to higher authority. The mass of routine matters will be handled by junior staff.

(*e*) Too intricate a system costs money. One famous firm found its system was so complicated that paper work was costing millions of pounds. The rules were changed and 6 million forms were saved every year.

Figure 4.2 shows a possible plan of procedure for the despatch of a mailing to schools and colleges in connection with a series of books.

Computer routines

Computers are described more fully in Chapter 14, but these increasingly important activities for younger members of staff must be mentioned at this point. They concern activities necessary to input data into computers and to solve problems arising from the computerization of records. For example, in banks all cheques now have a line of magnetic material at the foot of the cheque, which tells us the number of the cheque, the branch to which the customer belongs and the account number of the customer. What it cannot tell us, because until the customer writes out the cheque no one knows, is the amount that the cheque will be made out for. When a cheque is paid in over the counter of a bank, the amount of the cheque has to be encoded with the figure which the bank is ordered to pay. This is done in a machine called a document handler, which

Spring mailing procedure – educational textbook series

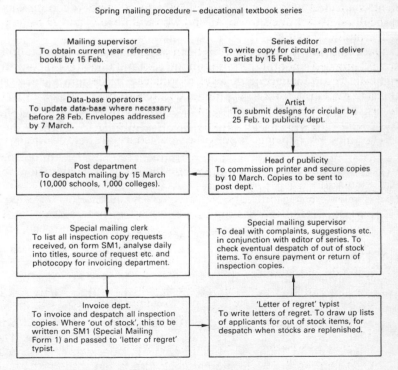

Figure 4.2   Laying down office procedures

lines the cheque up correctly and enables the key operator to key in the correct figures. At the same time as the figures are encoded the document handler sorts the cheques out into their separate banks so that they can be sent to the clearing house. Eventually the electronic reading of the cheque will enable each bank to extract the funds from the account of the person who wrote the cheque and give them instead to the account of the person who paid the cheque in. This MICR (magnetic ink character recognition) ability of the computer depends for its success on the young person who is keying in the figures.

Another example might be where a telephone complaint is received from a debtor who claims the amount charged on a particular statement is incorrect. The book-keeper concerned will call up the account on the visual display unit (VDU) and can discuss it with the debtor. If the debtor is correct and an error has occurred, the matter can be put right. If the debtor realizes that a particular item has been overlooked, he/she will apologize and will pay the account.

Manual of office procedures

Some firms draw up manuals of procedure to assist new staff in fitting themselves quickly into the organization. A clear statement of the activities performed in each department is given in the manual, and staff asked to undertake a particular activity are able to read up the procedure for themselves. This is clearly very desirable in some situations, e.g. where absolute security of documents is required, or where dangerous materials are concerned. Documentation in such cases needs to be very carefully checked.

There is the possibility that such handbooks or rules of procedure may become a drawback, rather than an advantage, e.g. where they may be used as an excuse to 'work to rule'. Here a group of clerks who perhaps wish to express their resentment of management policies might use the manual of office procedures as a justification for working less hard than normally.

(b) Calculations

Very few of the activities of business can be carried on without calculations or figure work of some sort. Factory output, construction work of all sorts, the consumption of gas, electricity and water, wages payments and countless other items have to be measured, priced and computed. The range of aids to help these activities is now very great, from the simple hand-held calculator to the computer. Some computer packages are particularly sophisticated and will calculate every statistic you require in the twinkling of an eye. The popular term for them is 'number-crunching packages'. Although such calculations are performed at huge speeds and without the help of the clerk or other employee, the results do have to be interpreted and call for a knowledgeable, skilful and conscientious approach. A fuller description of calculators and other devices is given in Chapter 14.

(c) Records

Records are important if business is to be conducted efficiently. It is often necessary to prove that contracts were made, or that obligations have been fulfilled. It is vital, too, to be able to answer queries from employees, customers and others efficiently and quickly. Accurate records enable such queries to be dealt with easily, and in many cases they may enable us to compare present performance with past achievements and to detect problems that are arising long before they would otherwise be noticed. Such systematic records have saved many firms from bankruptcy.

Probably the most vital records of all are the book-keeping records, which enable us to tell how much we owe our **creditors**, and how much we are owed by our **debtors**. They also enable us to prepare the financial accounts of the business each year so that profits can be ascertained and **dividends** paid to our shareholders.

In Figure 4.3 a simple ledger account shows a record of our dealings with Henry Wills, a supplier. The notes to the illustration explain what this record tells us. Study them now.

Computerized accounting records

If we now look at this same account as if it had been kept by a computer, it would be in running-balance style. This is shown in Figure 4.4 and explained in the notes below it (see p. 78).

(d) Reports

The basis of control activities is the report. If a member of staff notices something wrong he/she should report it. The astute office junior who notices that a bill has remained unpaid may save his/her firm money in future bad debts. Many reports are required as routine procedures from departments to head offices. There the reports are considered and analysed to discover whether the affairs of the firm are being properly conducted. Managers look for exceptions. The vehicle using more fuel than the others may have a dishonest driver. The department with the heaviest telephone bill may be poorly controlled. This is known as **management by exceptions**.

Computers are particularly helpful at picking out things that are possibly going wrong, and can be programmed to print out a report at once. For example, it is possible to ask the computer to print out a list of overdue accounts, so that the **credit controller** can phone the firm concerned requesting immediate payment. In many schools and colleges the heads of departments have a budget for a year's expenditure and, except in special circumstances, would be expected to spend one twelfth of the budget each month. If the computer detects that a head of department is going over budget, it will print out a report for the head teacher or principal, who will then ask the head of department to explain why. If there is no good reason, the person concerned will be told to reduce expenditure in the month ahead.

Consider the examples shown in Table 4.1 of sales figures reported for representatives in six areas of a firm's activities (see p. 78).

Which set is exceptional, and needs to be investigated? An examination of the figures reveals that while most sales staff are selling considerably more, in fact between 14 per cent and 80 per cent more, in May than in January, Mr C is selling a mere 1 per cent more. Clearly he is either experiencing special difficulties or is not doing his job properly. Either way his case should be investigated.

This shows the usefulness of reports.

(e) Communications

Every office is to some extent a communication centre. It receives instructions, information and reports from other offices, and after

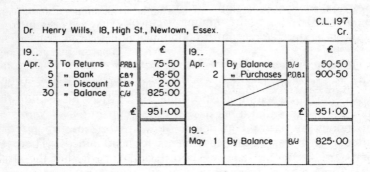

Figure 4.3   A simple book-keeping record − a creditor's account

Notes

(i) The ledger is the chief book of account.

(ii) Each page in it is called 'an account'

(iii) The page is divided down the middle (although there is a kind of ledger called a 'running balance' ledger that is not in this form).

(iv) The left-hand side of the account is called the debit side of the account or the debtor side of the account. A debtor is a person who owes us money, because he/she has received goods or services or money. The rule is: **Debit the receiver of goods or services or money**.

preparing or processing forms and documents it passes instructions or explanations to those awaiting them. These may be internal memos, or letters to outside bodies.

Information is the chief interest of those who control offices. They need to know as much as possible about the influences at work in the world of business if they are to make the right decisions and run their businesses properly. A lack of information causes costly errors to be made. The chief types of information collected are production reports from factories and mines, sales reports from home and overseas wholesale and retail outlets, and official statistics from Government or international bodies which show the trends and developments in world population, prices of commodities and growth of national incomes. On the basis of this information, which is arranged and classified into a more digestible form by specialist office employees of various sorts, top management makes **decisions** that are issued out to lower levels of staff as **memos** and **communications** of various sorts.

Nothing is so useful in maintaining good communications as the provision of suitable forms for internal and external use. The **memo**

Notes to Figure 4.3 (continued)

(v) The right-hand side of the page is called the credit side of the account. A creditor is a person to whom we owe money, because he has given us goods, or services or money. The rule is: **Credit the giver of goods, or services or money**.

(vi) On 1 April there was a credit balance of £50.50 on the account, so we owed the person named at the top, Henry Wills, £50.50.

(vii) On 2 April he gave us goods (purchases to be re-sold at a later date) worth £900.50. We credited him as he is the giver of the goods.

(viii) On 3 April we returned goods worth £75.50 so we debited him (he received the goods back).

(ix) On 5 April we paid him by cheque from our bank the sum of £48.50 and we were allowed discount of £2.00. Both these items were debited on his account, because he received the cheque and forgave us the other £2. This cleared the debt of £50.50 owing on 1 April.

(x) On 30 April there was a balance of £825.00 owing to Wills. This was brought down to show the final balance owing on 1 May, £825.00

(xi) Note that when we say a balance is brought down we mean it is entered on one side (as if Wills had received the money). This enables the account to be balanced off (£951.00 on each side). Then the £825.00 is brought down to the start of the next month to show that Henry Wills is a creditor – he has given us £825.00 of goods that we have not yet paid for. Now return to the main text on page 75.

Henry Wills, 18, High St, Newtown, Essex					CL197
Date	Details	F	Debits	Credits	Balance
Apr. 1	Balance				50.50 Cr
2	Purchases			900.50	951.00 Cr
3	Returns		75.50		875.50 Cr
5	Bank		48.50		827.00 Cr
5	Discount		2.00		825.00 Cr
May 1	Balance				825.00 Cr

Figure 4.4   An account in running-balance style

Notes

(i) Since the computer works so fast it has no difficulty adding or subtracting money. Therefore it works out a new balance every time an entry is made.

(ii) This means we have a running balance which we can refer to should any query arise on the account. Of course to see such a balance we have to call it up on the visual display unit (VDU) of our computerized system.

form (Figure 4.5) will be useful in ensuring that messages state clearly from whom they come and to whom they are sent, that the date is clearly stated and that any difficulties may be clarified by a simple procedure. Sometimes the use of different coloured memo pads for senior staff ensures prompt attention to their urgent requirements.

A very effective type of memo set is illustrated in Figure 4.6. It is a three-part NCR memo set. NCR means 'no carbon required' and refers to the fact that the memo set is coated with globules of invisible ink. When someone writes on a memo set (a ballpoint pen is best), the globules of ink break and the message becomes visible

Table 4.1   Sales of Product 'X'

Representative		Jan. £	Feb. £	Mar. £	Apr. £	May £
Mr A	Area 1	14 000	15 400	17 000	17 000	20 000
Miss B	" 2	27 000	29 200	33 000	33 900	37 500
Mr C	" 3	140 000	130 500	141 000	116 000	142 000
Mrs D	" 4	130 000	140 000	147 000	148 500	155 000
Miss E	" 5	180 000	195 000	199 000	198 500	206 000
Mr F	" 6	7 250	9 100	10 700	11 000	12 800

Memo from...

To................................. Date...............

Message :

Should there be any difficulty over this matter
you can contact me as follows:

Place.............. Phone No........... Time.........

Figure 4.5 An internal memo form

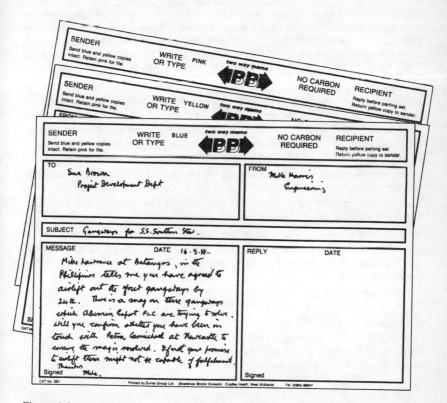

Figure 4.6 A ping-pong memo set (courtesy of Evrite Ltd, Cradley Heath, West Midlands)

on all three copies. The sender writes on the top copy whatever query he/she wishes to raise, and then tears the top copy off, leaving the other two linked together. The sender retains the top copy and puts it in a tray marked 'pending'. The other two copies are sent to the addressee, who writes a reply on the bottom half of the memo slip. He/she then retains one copy and returns it to the enquirer. Both parties now have a copy of the original memo and the response. If the enquirer does not receive a reply, the original copy in his/her pending tray is a reminder that as yet no answer has been received.

The illustration is from Evrite Ltd, of Cradley Heath, Warley, West Midlands. They call their sets 'ping-pong' sets, a happy choice of name, which conveys the idea that these memos should pass to and fro, like a ping-pong ball (and the enquirer hopes just as rapidly).

Electronic memos

As mentioned earlier, the computer today can offer us solutions to almost every problem, and the electronic memo (called e-mail) is one of the most useful. Where a large firm has a network of computer terminals all feeding in to a host computer, and all able to send messages to one another, it seems only sensible to send our memos at electronic speeds. By keying in a message and its destination terminal you can send the memo in a second or two, and the response can be just as immediate. Microsoft, the largest software company in the world, claims its employees receive 100 memos per day, on average. It does not say where they find the time to answer them. The point about such e-mail is that it can be individually addressed to a particular colleague, or it can sent to a group (say all departmental managers) or even to all members of staff. Staff who receive computerized memos cannot claim 'They don't tell me anything' if they have failed to read their e-mail.

A further point about electronic memos is this. You receive a memo, and it shows the sender's name and computer terminal and your name and terminal as the receiver. By a simple keying code you can tell the computer to reverse the roles. You become the sender and your correspondent is now the recipient. You key in your reply, and a touch on the transmission key sends the reply at electronic speeds.

A good network of communication trays is desirable, and ensures that everyone has a tray in which messages may be left. Trays of the type illustrated in Figure 4.7 are very economical in the use of space, can be labelled with the names of staff and are often anti-static treated. (Sheets of paper easily become charged with static electricity, and the lowest sheet can often remain in the tray when a pile of papers is removed hurriedly.) Such trays can also be used by

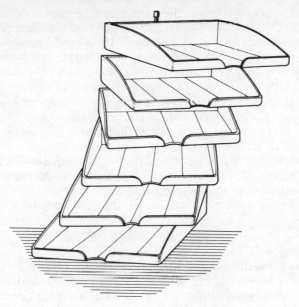

Figure 4.7   A set of trays for ensuring good communications (courtesy of Wilson & Whitworth Ltd)

a single individual for a variety of work, and labels such as ACTION, FILING, PENDING can be attached to indicate the tray's purpose.

The **telephone system** is an essential link in the chain of communications and is fully described in Chapter 6. Direct links over telephone circuits are also possible for the transmission from branches to head office of computerized information about sales, daily takings from debtors, cheques banked and so on. This type of information is called 'data' and its despatch or reception and processing by calculators and computers is called **data-processing**. As mentioned earlier this is more fully discussed in Chapter 6.

4.3   Subsidiary clerical activities

All these types of clerical activity necessitate what may be called **subsidiary activities**, i.e. activities that give additional help to the main activities. The subsidiary activities are:

(*a*) Writing (including typewriting, shorthand and other devices for speeding up the writing process).
(*b*) Copying (both manually, mechanically and photographically).
(*c*) Filing (including sorting, numbering and indexing).
(*d*) Checking.

Staff at all levels perform these activities, but much of the routine work is performed by office juniors. Many of their activities form the subject matter of this book. Here we will briefly refer to some of the more general points about these subsidiary activities.

Writing

This implies the creation of new original records by hand or by typewriting. Decisions that are made have to be recorded, orders must be sent out, enquiries put in hand and explanations given. They must then be communicated to the parties interested by post, or messenger, or by being circulated to the personnel concerned either in the form of e-mail (electronic mail) or in document form to their in-trays in the various departments.

Copying

This is the reproducing of information so that all those interested in a particular matter receive a copy. There are many ways of copying, e.g. many firms still use carbon paper to take copies of a letter being typed by a secretary, but those who use word-processors simply print off at the end the number of copies required. Each copy then is as good as the original, whereas carbon copies deteriorate if we try to take too many of them. Copying is dealt with more fully in Chapter 15. It is one of the best ways to communicate instructions to several people, or the entire staff. It is of great importance that memos of this sort are read at once by staff who receive a copy. Your employer will be entitled to complain if you fail to act on instructions given in this way. During the Second World War an enthusiastic commanding officer wrote in his daily routine orders that all lower ranks should not only salute their officers, but should shout 'Hi-de-hi' as they did so. To this the officers were to reply 'Ho-de-ho'. Many personnel of both types who had failed to read their memos were charged with an offence against good order and discipline. The commanding officer was, of course, right, but it was several months before derisory cries of 'Hi-de-hi' and 'Ho-de-ho' ceased to ring round the bars and canteens whenever an officer was sighted. It is important to read all memos and routine orders.

Filing (sorting, numbering and indexing)

Filing is perhaps the most necessary and important clerical activity. No office can run its affairs properly without filing items away in some sensible order where they can be quickly rediscovered. Consider a firm making and installing lifts. As the years go by, it becomes responsible for the maintenance and care of lifts in every part of the country. They will vary slightly in many ways. One will invariably be overloaded – another will often break down in a particular way. An accurate file in the maintenance department will warn a fitter called out in an emergency which faults are likely, which spares are necessary, etc. He will arrive equipped to correct the fault with the necessary spare parts. The filing systems described later in this book give some idea of the different types of equipment in use, and the different procedures adopted by firms. Do not throw pieces of documentary information away – file them where they can be found when required.

An essential first step in any system of filing is the sorting out of papers into some sensible and convenient order. The 'work-organizer' shown in Figure 4.8 may be used as a first step in this process. Documents may be roughly sorted into alphabetical or departmental order first. Then each section is taken to the appropriate filing cabinet and filed. Alternatively the work-organizer may be used to contain folders and papers which could otherwise clutter up the desk. An executive may have tabs prepared for the folders covering the various departmental managers or foremen. Papers referring to departments or activities are sorted into the folders as the mail is opened ready for the day's work. The various managers are then called in, the appropriate folder – containing all the current items for that department – is discussed, and it is then handed over for action by the manager or foreman concerned.

Checking

Checking is necessary at all levels of activity, and enormous expense can be saved if careful checks are instituted. In the United Kingdom today it costs about 24 pence to send the cheapest type of letter.

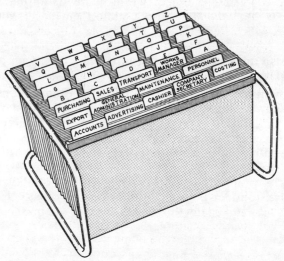

Figure 4.8   A work-organizer (courtesy of Twinlock Ltd)

Imagine a firm circulating 5 000 customers to announce an exhibition in London. Because of weak checking the date of the exhibition is omitted from the circular. To send out again will cost £1 200 for postage, besides the cost of envelopes, the second letter and the labour of sending them out. Before this can be done the switchboard will be jammed solid with calls asking for the date of the exhibition. **Junior staff should check their work at every stage, to ensure accuracy**.

4.4 Job specifications

While most clerical workers expect to do a variety of jobs as the situation requires, some degree of specialization is desirable, and a strong trade union may even insist on a clear designation of duties. This helps in the grading of jobs and also separates the work from the individual doing the work at present. Dr Jekyll may do his present job in a very helpful and co-operative way, doing twice as much as Mr Hyde who succeeds him. Clearly this is not really good for Dr Jekyll or Mr Hyde. The former overworks and is underpaid, the latter slacks and does not really earn his salary. A good 'job specification' will require Mr Hyde to reach a reasonable standard of work, while it may also remind Dr Jekyll that he is overworking and deserves to relax a little.

Good job specifications have the following advantages:

(*a*) They define the jobs carefully, listing the work to be performed.
(*b*) They make it easier to decide what class of staff is required, and to appoint properly qualified applicants.
(*c*) They enable the jobs to be graded for salary purposes.
(*d*) They enable training schemes to be devised at appropriate levels.

4.5 Points to think about and discuss

(*a*) Many young people now stay on at school or proceed to a college or university in order to qualify by examinations and by intensive study for a future career. They then expect to start work at least some part of the way up the promotion ladder. Is this desirable? How can management ensure that the late entrant really does understand the routine office procedures which he or she will one day have to control?

(*b*) Four jobs are available, for which the six candidates shown below apply. Consider the specification carefully for each post and appoint the 'best' candidate, thus deciding which two must be rejected. Explain why they are unsuitable.

Job (1) (*a*) Some copy-typing.

(*b*) Needs to be able to use audio-typing machine − or be prepared to learn.

(*c*) Relief telephonist.

(*d*) Relief messenger.

(*e*) Filing and general duties under supervision (of R. Brown).

Job (2) (*a*) 140 wpm shorthand.

(*b*) 50 wpm typewriting.

(*c*) Fluent French essential.

(*d*) Occasional Spanish and German.

(*e*) Public relations responsibility.

Job (3) (*a*) 40 wpm typewriting.

(*b*) Relief telephonist.

(*c*) Occasional use of datacard address equipment.

(*d*) Electronic calculator use required daily.

(*e*) Prepared to work to 9 pm when required.

Job (4) (*a*) Book-keeping to Trial Balance and Final Accounts level.

(*b*) Preparation and typing of confidential audit reports.

(*c*) Assistance at times to chief accountant in extraction of quarterly figures. Computer experience desirable.

(*d*) Presentation of statistical data.

(*e*) Occasionally required to visit outlying branches suspected of unreliability over cash payments.

Candidate No. 1. Bachelor of Arts Degree. Member of the Institute of Freight Forwarders. No accountancy knowledge. Not interested in salaries below £15 000 per annum. Male with a public school background.

Candidate No. 2. Female. 23 years of age. Reasonable typing. Can operate switchboard and datacard address equipment.

Candidate No. 3. Typing very good (50 words per minute). Aged 16 years. No shorthand or book-keeping knowledge. Pleasant speaking voice. Likes to meet people. Prefers routine work without too much responsibility.

Candidate No. 4. Fluent shorthand typist. Speaks French excellently and some Spanish. Very sophisticated girl with a charming personality.

Candidate No. 5. At present chief book-keeper in a small firm. Studying accountancy at local technical college. Desires more responsibility. Cannot type but has keyboard skills and experience in operating computers. Male.

Candidate No. 6. Age 16. Types at 40 words per minute. Prepared to learn adding-listing machine and address equipment. Very immature and nervous, but willing.

4.6   Rapid revision — basic clerical activities

Cover the page with a sheet of notepaper and uncover one question at a time.

Answers	Questions
—	1 What is communication?
1 It is the art of passing on news and information from one person to another.	2 What are the chief sub-divisions in communication?
2 Spoken communication and written communication. Each of these may be sub-divided into personal communication and mass-media communication.	3 What is the result of good communication activities in a firm or company?
3 A host of low-level clerical activities.	4 Why are so many people engaged in clerical activities.
4 Because mass production creates a flood of goods which have to be distributed quickly and easily to consumers. This requires documentation, instructions, orders and reports.	5 What are the five main types of clerical activity?
5 (*a*) Routine procedures. (*b*) Calculations. (*c*) Records. (*d*) Reports. (*e*) Communications.	6 What are the subsidiary clerical activities?
6 (*a*) Writing, typing, shorthand, etc. (*b*) Copying (manually, mechanically or photographically) (*c*) Filing, sorting, numbering and indexing (*d*) Checking.	7 What is the purpose of a job specification?
7 (*a*) To define the job, so that its difficulty can be assessed (*b*) To grade the job for salary purposes (*c*) To assist the appointment of suitable staff (*d*) To enable staff training schemes to be devised.	8 What is a manual of procedures?
8 It is a book of rules laying down procedures to be followed when an activity is undertaken. It establishes routines for each activity.	9 Go over the page again until you feel you are sure of the answers.

Exercises set 4

1 Complete the following sentences by inserting a word or phrase from the word list below.

(*a*) The people who perform clerical duties are called ......
(*b*) Clerical duties are performed in a building called an ......
(*c*) The branch of mathematical science dealing with numerical facts is called ......
(*d*) Writing letters has been largely mechanized since the invention of the ......
(*e*) The establishment of an internal memo system improves ...... within the organization.
(*f*) In order to answer queries from management and customers it is necessary to have a good system of ......
(*g*) To ...... things is to store them in such a way that they can be easily rediscovered.
(*h*) To investigate items that appear to be different from the usual run of things is called ....
(*i*) The reproduction of letters photographically is called ......
(*j*) A ...... lays down all the activities that should be performed by a particular employee.
(*k*) In the computer age it is essential for all junior staff to acquire ...... skills.
(*l*) Today a firm which has a network of computers may send its memos by ...... The abbreviation e-stands for ......
(*m*) A ledger account that shows us exactly what the balance on the account is after every entry is said to be in ...... style.
(*n*) Computers that can read account numbers off the bottom line of a cheque are using ...... techniques.
(*o*) MICR stands for ......

Word list: office, records, clerks, job specification, communication, file, keyboarding, MICR, management by exceptions, e-mail, running balance, statistics, magnetic ink character recognition, photocopying, typewriter, electronic.

2 The following memo is distributed to all staff in their in-trays: 'Kindly remember to complete the forms already distributed and return them before 5 pm.' Prepare a list of criticisms of this memo, explaining why it is an inadequate communication to staff.

3 Select the correct answer or answers to the questions below from the sets of answers supplied.

(i) What is the purpose of regular reports: (*a*) to record systematically the facts affecting a particular aspect of office work; (*b*) to welcome visiting personalities; (*c*) to enable management to assess changing situations, and pursue 'management by exceptions'; (*d*) to give regular opportunities for supervisors to complain about staff whose activities are below standard?
(ii) Which of the following may be described as clerical duties: (*a*) the

typing of letters from a tape-recorded audio system, (b) the copying of a circular letter to 500 doctors notifying them of changes in Health Service charges, (c) the decision to spend a large sum of money on an extension to the factory, (d) the inspection of burned-out premises for signs of arson?

(iii) What is a manual of office procedures: (a) a list of promotions to be displayed on the office notice board, (b) a handbook made available to new staff describing the system used for certain routine office activities, (c) a hand-operated device used in the training of staff during the induction period, (d) a guidebook reference work as to the status of individuals in a company?

(iv) What is a job specification: (a) a detailed explanation of the materials to be used and the method of construction of a particular object, (b) a remedy for an illness, (c) a clearly given order, (d) a precise account of the activities to be performed by a particular class of employees?

4 List the chief types of duty described as 'clerical duties' and give an example of each as it might be performed in: (a) the factory office of a large manufacturing firm; (b) the accounts department of a busy Government department.

5 What is a job specification? Make out such a specification for a part-time employee who assists (afternoons only) in the general office. She can type and knows how to keep books, but cannot do shorthand. Invent appropriate activities for her to perform.

6 Explain the functions of a school office in a busy school catering for pupils aged 11–18.

7 List at least five clerical activities. Then choose *one* of the activities you have named and explain its importance to (a) the large office of a public company, (b) the small office of a suburban solicitor.

8 Communication is a major function of offices. How may communication be improved within the office? Refer in your answer to both (a) organization and (b) electronic devices.

9 Susan Smith has joined the staff this morning. Suggest how she may be introduced to the various duties she will be required to perform so that she quickly reaches a good level of performance and later may deserve promotion.

10 Suggest suitable clerical assistance for the following senior members of staff: (a) the chief accountant in a busy accounts department, (b) the works manager – a small factory unit only, (c) the head of research and development department, (d) the sales manager, (e) the chief buyer.

You are now told that only nine staff can be employed for clerical duties. What allocation would you make to the senior staff concerned? The sales of the firm are spread over five counties, employing eleven commercial travellers.

11 What is the procedure when complaints are received? Draw up a suitable procedure for dealing with complaints: (a) about the repeated

failure of a component you manufacture, (*b*) about an insufficiently stamped letter which has suffered delay as a result.

12 All business organizations and institutions, e.g. hospitals, colleges, etc., have offices. Describe the clerical functions that these are likely to have in common.

(RSA Stage II)

5 The reception office

5.1 The importance of the receptionist

Many young people are attracted to clerical positions by the idea of reception work. Receptionists are important because they are often the public's first contact with a firm, and first impressions are often the most enduring. A surly or aggressive reception, or a 'couldn't care less' attitude, can do a firm irreparable damage, by rebuffing clients, customers and potential new staff.

A good receptionist must have many important qualities: a smart appearance, a pleasant speaking voice, a willingness to assist the visitor, and a sound knowledge of the organization. This enables the receptionist to attend to visitors' enquiries quickly.

The last requirement, a wide knowledge of the organization, means that it is usually impossible to perform the duties of a receptionist adequately until one knows something about the firm's activities, its layout and its personnel. Perhaps, therefore, 18 years is the minimum age for a receptionist, since by then most young people will have mastered several routine activities and have acquired poise, maturity, knowledge and experience.

5.2 The work of the receptionist

Not every firm has such an endless stream of callers that it needs the services of a full-time receptionist, although it is important for the reception desk to be manned at all times. It follows that a variety of work may fall upon the receptionist. The type of work performed will vary with the office, but may include the following:

(a) Control of the switchboard and telephone system.
(b) Supervision of messengers and porters.
(c) Book-keeping records, particularly in hotels.
(d) Typing, filing and envelope-addressing.
(e) Petty cashier duties.
(f) Small sales, e.g. of brochures and handbooks published by the organization.
(g) The receipt of packages and messages for onward transmission to departments.
(h) Use of a computer terminal, e.g. in hotels to check the avail-

ability and allocation of rooms, or in hospital services to check the appointments of patients with consultants.

Where the duties of a receptionist are combined with other tasks, posts are advertised for clerk-receptionist, typist-receptionist, telephonist-receptionist or book-keeper-receptionist. Such posts give valuable training to young staff wishing to acquire experience for a later position as a full-time receptionist.

5.3 The location of the reception office

The reception office must be in the entrance hall of the building or at the entrance to the suite of offices. Often a hall porter will be in charge of the main hall, and will assist visitors to find the suite they require with the help of messenger boys or lift attendants. Where the receptionist is in the main hall, he or she will usually have a full working position, including the switchboard, a typewriter, perhaps book-keeping records, and possibly a computer terminal and other facilities.

Where the receptionist is in a small suite of offices, clear instructions to visitors are necessary. Adequate notices reading 'Enquiries' or 'Receptionist' help the visitors to gain immediate access to the suite at the most appropriate point for receiving attention. A bell, or buzzer, should enable them to summon attention at an unmanned reception point. A name-plate, made up of white plastic lettering on a triangular black plastic block, is a great help to visitors, who often prefer to know with whom they are dealing. One should be provided for each person who mans the reception position. A typical reception point is shown in Figure 5.1.

5.4 The reception of visitors

The following rules are helpful in receiving visitors at a reception point:

(*a*) Do not continue with an obviously trivial task while a visitor waits for attention.
(*b*) If you are engaged on the switchboard, you should at least glance up and smile to show that you have noticed the visitor's appearance and will attend to his/her needs at the earliest possible moment.
(*c*) The best form of greeting is 'Good morning/afternoon. May I help you?'
(*d*) It is useful to make a list of callers, as a routine record of reception activities. This list will often prove helpful, as when the member of staff visited forgot to ask the caller's initial(s) or his/her telephone number. This register should be prepared

Figure 5.1   The visitor's reception should be friendly and efficient

Date	Name of caller	Business or other address	Person or Dept. visited	Time of arrival	Time of departure
19... May 5	J. Goldfarb (Mr.)	San Francisco (staying at Ocean Hotel)	Mr. Lyonnesse	10.30	12.30
5	J. Fellowes (Miss)	20 Golding's Crescent Newtown	Personnel Dept	10.50	11.15
5	R. Bacon (Mr.)	Imperial Typewriter Co.	Miss Hachett	10.55	3.30
5	T. Brownjohn (Mr.)	Elite Display Co.	Advertising Dept.	12.15	12.25
6	R. Lucas (Mr.)	Engineering Consultants Ltd.	Works Manager's Office	3.30	4.45

Figure 5.2   A reception register

quite openly and the caller should be asked for any details that are not volunteered. A typical ruling for such a register is given in Figure 5.2.

(*e*) If possible, you should invite the visitor to take a seat while you speak on the telephone to the person he/she wishes to see.

(*f*) It is desirable to escort the visitor personally to the office of the person he/she wishes to see, or ask a messenger to act as an escort. If the interview is to be conducted in an interview room near the reception area, seat the visitor in the interview room before making arrangements to summon the person who is to conduct the interview.

(*g*) It is wise to check up to ensure that the visitor does in fact receive attention; if the contact fails to arrive, remind the contact over the telephone that the visitor is still waiting for attention.

5.5 Problem-solving by receptionists

In many respects the receptionist is like a buffer between the firm and the world outside. When the private world of the office wishes to make contact with the outside world, or vice versa, the parties concerned will usually make appointments. Visitors who have an appointment present little difficulty to the receptionist, who deals with them in the ways suggested above.

Other visitors may present difficulties; for example, their visit may be unexpected and therefore inconvenient. Generally speaking, uninvited visitors are prepared to wait until someone can see them, or will philosophically accept the fact that their calls are so inconvenient that it is quite impossible for them to receive attention. Such a call may result in the receptionist's arranging an appointment, usually in consultation with the personal secretary of the person concerned, for a later date.

A third type of visitor may represent what can only be regarded as an emergency. Such visitors should always be given immediate and courteous attention, according to the urgency of their request. For example, at education offices an irate parent, breathing fire and sulphur against a local head-teacher and demanding to see the district education officer, would probably be accorded an interview without a previous appointment. Similarly a police officer or a journalist from a local or national newspaper would certainly be accorded immediate attention. Quite apart from possible bad publicity resulting from any discourtesy to such people, most firms feel a sense of social responsibility towards the law, the press and local authorities.

Sometimes it is necessary to cover up for a member of staff who for some reason does not wish to see a particular visitor. If there is any likelihood of this, it is best to speak impersonally on the internal telephone. Do not say, 'Mr Payne, there is a representative here to see you from Colour Display Co.' Instead, say, 'There is a gentleman here from Colour Display Co. who would like to speak to Mr Payne if he is available, please'. This gives Mr Payne the opportunity to excuse himself. The telling of *white lies* is almost inseparable from reception work. In most cases the motive is to avoid embarrassment to both parties. A direct statement that Mr Payne thinks the Colour Display's Co.'s products are poor value for money and he does not wish to discuss them might upset the representative concerned.

5.6 Confidential matters

An employee is in a special position with regard to his or her employer. A receptionist is to some extent the employer's agent, acting on the employer's behalf in many matters that arise during the day's work. One of the rules about such agents is that they have a duty of care not to disclose confidential matters regarding the employer's business affairs. An indiscreet receptionist may easily disclose matters which are of use to callers, even by such apparently innocent remarks as disclosing the names of other visitors. Consider the following conversation:

'I have an appointment with Mr Rogerson, I am from Universal Take-overs.'
'I'm so sorry, Mr Rogerson is busy at present. He is having a discussion with the Chairman of Amalgamators Incorporated.'

Clearly the receptionist has 'let the cat out of the bag'. The visitor now knows that the employer is negotiating with two possible purchasers of the business at the same time. This is a breach of the duty not to disclose confidential information.

Similarly, the response to the question 'How's business?' is ideally a noncommittal remark like, 'Oh, pretty hectic, you know'. To reply, 'Dull as ditchwater!' will perhaps cause the visitor to revise his/her ideas of whatever bargain it is proposed to make with the firm. Prices may be hardened or shorter delivery dates than are normally conceded by a supplier be demanded.

In particular, receptionists should be careful that visitors do not 'pump' them for information. 'I'm afraid I don't know anything about that', is the discreet answer to loaded questions.

5.7 Receiving parcels

It often happens that parcels, packets and other communications are delivered to the receptionist, and a signature is demanded on a delivery note. Such notes should not be signed without inspection of the goods, since a 'clean' signature, i.e. one that makes no comment upon the number and condition of the packages, will usually absolve the carrier from any blame should the consignment be incomplete or damaged.

If the parcel or packet, or number of packets, appears to agree with the description in the consignment note it is best to sign 'Received in apparent good order and condition'. This still leaves the firm free to claim if in fact the contents are damaged and if the damage could not be seen from the outside. If they do not appear to be in good order then it is best to describe on the note the actual condition, i.e. 'Arrived open' or 'Parcel damp and stained — contents may be broken'. This is better than saying 'Signed unexamined', which appears to imply that there was nothing apparently wrong with the parcel.

5.8 A panel-strip index

A device called a 'panel-strip index', marketed by Kalamazoo Ltd, is very useful to telephone operators, receptionists and others who need quick references to a range of information. The illustration in Figure 5.3 shows how it is used. Strips of a specially designed shape are typed or handwritten to give the information required. They may then be inserted in a few seconds in panels which form part of a visi-index alphabetical desk display. Some displays are wall-mounted, to keep the desk top clear.

Imagine that a salesman has called and given the receptionist his business card to take to a departmental manager with whom he has an appointment. The receptionist asks permission to return it on his way out. The register of callers and a visi-index strip are then prepared before he leaves. We now have a convenient visual record of the name, phone number, address and other details and the person he is most likely to wish to speak to. Should someone from his office call him, we will be able to locate him in the building in a few seconds, and similarly if the person he visited later phones us with some query, we shall be able to answer such questions as 'What are his initials?', 'Does he have letters after his name?' etc.

5.9 Points to think about and discuss

(*a*) How should a receptionist deal with the following two situations:

(i) A commercial traveller who usually comes on the first Monday of the month for a regular appointment with the chief buyer arrives on the first Wednesday of the month regretting that he has been indisposed.
(ii) An elderly gentleman demands to see the manager in order to lodge a complaint about a product. The manager is on vacation.

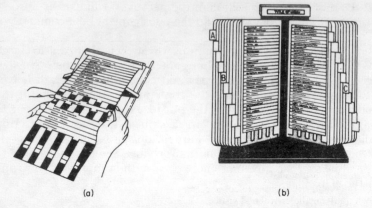

(a)   (b)

Figure 5.3   A visi-index desk unit holding 3 400 strips of information (courtesy of
Kalamazoo Ltd)

(*b*) Three applications are received for a receptionist's post,
which comprises switchboard operation, keeping a register of visitors, and controlling a staff of three messengers. The ability to give
first aid is also desirable. The three are (i) a disabled telephonist,
male, aged 44, using his own wheelchair, trained Post Office telephonist, (ii) an ex-Post Office telephonist, female, aged 50, a
competent typist but untrained in first aid, (iii) a smart young lady
of good appearance, who learned relief telephonist work at her
former post, and wishes to 'meet people' in her employment, although
she already has a well-paid post as a copy typist.
Discuss the merits of these three applicants.

5.10   Rapid revision—reception activities
Cover the page with a sheet of paper and uncover one question at a
time

Answers	Questions
—	1 Where should the reception office be located?
1 (*a*) In the main foyer of the building. (*b*) In the entrance to the suite of offices.	2 Where a reception point is not manned all the time what arrangements should be made?
2 (*a*) Clear notices to indicate the reception area. (*b*) A bell, buzzer or telephone system to attract attention.	3 What attributes should a receptionist have?
3 (*a*) Good appearance. (*b*) Pleasant speaking voice. (*c*) Courteous approach.	4 What duties are often associated with the receptionist, besides the reception of visitors?

(*d*) A good knowledge of the business, its layout and chains of responsibility.

---

4 (*a*) Control of the switchboard.
   (*b*) Supervision of porters and messengers.
   (*c*) Bookings (in hotels) and other book-keeping records such as petty cash.
   (*d*) Small sales of brochures, etc.

5 What points must a receptionist watch to prevent the disclosure of confidential matters?

---

5 (*a*) Keep conversation with visitors at an impersonal level.
   (*b*) Watch out for the visitor who asks leading questions.
   (*c*) Talk indirectly over the telephone when notifying the arrival of a visitor.

6 How should parcels, etc., be signed for?

---

6 So that a 'clean' signature is not readily available, e.g. 'in apparent good order' is the best signature to be given. In doubtful circumstances state them, i.e. 'parcel open on arrival'.

7 What is a register of callers?

---

7 A register recording the names initials and other details about callers, and the purpose of visits made to the premises.

8 Go over the page again until you feel you are sure of the answers.

Exercises set 5

1 Write the letters (*a*)–(*j*) on your answer paper to correspond with the sentences below. Against each letter write the word or phrase from the word list required to complete the sentence.

(*a*) The receptionist needs a sound knowledge of the firm's ......
(*b*) The receptionist is the first person in the firm that the visitor meets, and should always try to create a good ......
(*c*) A receptionist should keep his/her work position tidy and in appearance should be smart and ......
(*d*) The reception office must be near the ...... to the building or suite of offices.
(*e*) The best greeting is 'Good morning/afternoon. May ......?'
(*f*) Wherever possible callers should have previously arranged an ......
(*g*) It is good practice wherever possible to ask to see a visitor's ......
(*h*) A ...... should be kept to assist in recalling later who came, at what time, etc.
(*i*) It is important not to disclose ...... information of use to callers.
(*j*) When using the internal telephone it is best to speak ...... if there is any chance that a visitor may not be welcome.

Word list: impression, impersonally, entrance, organization, appointment, business card, register of callers, I help you, well groomed, confidential.

2 In the following questions select the best answer out of the four alternatives given:

(i) A receptionist should be knowledgeable about the firm and its affairs because: (*a*) the receptionist can deal with visitors personally instead of bothering other staff, (*b*) the receptionist will feel more confident, (*c*) the receptionist will be able to bring the visitor into contact with the right member of staff with the minimum delay, (*d*) it will save listening-in on the telephone.

(ii) A receptionist should preferably have a name-plate at the reception point because (*a*) visitors prefer to address the receptionist by name if possible; (*b*) it makes it easier for visitors to 'date' the receptionist, (*c*) complaints about the receptionist's behaviour and attitude may be more easily made, (*d*) it creates an impersonal atmosphere.

(iii) Emergency visitors who arrive without an appointment on very urgent affairs should (*a*) be given an opportunity to calm down before meeting a member of staff; (*b*) be told that they can receive attention only if they make an appointment in a proper way, (*c*) be invited to wait in a convenient waiting room while the receptionist contacts the most likely person to deal with the matter, (*d*) be taken in at once to the manager, however busy he is.

(iv) The best response to a visitor who expresses his appreciation of your services is (*a*) 'That's quite all right sir (or madam)', (*b*) 'Bring a box of chocolates next time,' (*c*) 'You are very welcome', (*d*) 'Good morning, sir (or madam)'.

3 Which of the following are *not* true of a receptionist's work? (*a*) It is easy, routine work, (*b*) it calls for tact in dealing with callers, (*c*) it is of little importance to the firm, (*d*) it makes an instant impression on visitors, (*e*) it needs maturity and a wide knowledge of the firm's personnel and organization, (*f*) the hours are short and untroubled by emergencies or sudden pressures.

4 What is a register of callers? Draft the likely headings on such a register and enter the name and other details of four visitors.

5 Draw up a message pad which might be of use to a receptionist showing the following points: (*a*) date, (*b*) time, (*c*) to whom addressed, (*d*) message, (*e*) by whom was the message received.

6 You are a relief receptionist in the lunch hour and no one else is available. The canteen is accessible by telephone and has a loudspeaker call system for emergency use. How would you deal with the following situations? (*a*) A traffic warden informs you that the firm's car is causing an obstruction and must be moved immediately; (*b*) a carrier arrives with two parcels, the smaller of which is clearly damaged and some of the contents may even be missing, and demands an immediate signature; (*c*) a member of a visiting party of foreign buyers arrives to say that he has been separated from his party and is not sure where they are lunching (you know that foreign buyers are always entertained at Rule's Restaurant).

7 One of your duties is the reception of visitors to your chief. List four simple rules to be observed.

8 Suggest five pleasant remarks you might make to a caller while you were waiting for his contact to come down and collect him from the reception area.

9 What do you consider would be (*a*) the pleasant parts of a receptionist's work, (*b*) the most difficult matters to deal with?

10 Your work as a receptionist has grown more and more hectic recently as the firm's activities have expanded. Draft a letter to your employer pointing out the difficulties you are experiencing and suggesting how the work load could be reduced.

11 List the chief qualities you would expect from a receptionist. Select two of these qualities and explain why you consider them to be important.

12 A receptionist is often required to perform routine work during intervals between the arrival of visitors. What sort of activities might be carried out in this way? Explain why each is an appropriate activity for a receptionist.

13 A receptionist is faced by the following situations during a busy morning. Explain what action should be taken in each case.

(*a*) An important client from overseas is cut off by the receptionist. He was not ringing from his usual office, and the sales manager is furious.
(*b*) The office boy is hit by a swing door and his nose bleeds furiously.
(*c*) The local police call in to check security arrangements in connection with their campaign 'Look out — there's a thief about'.
(*d*) The Post Department asks the receptionist to obtain postage stamps to the value of £100.00.
(*e*) A parcel delivered by special messenger appears damp from internal damage. It also smells strongly, of something rather like petrol or lighter fuel.

14 Miss Brown, the new receptionist, has been promised that before taking up employment on the first of next month her working accommodation will be improved. What points would you consider when providing her with a satisfactory work-position? The reception office is close to the entrance of your suite of offices in a large multi-occupied building.

15 The receptionist is at lunch from 1 to 2 pm. There are seven other employees who share the duty of relief receptionist at this time, and also when necessary during the day. They are *A*, *B*, *C*, *D*, *E*, *F* and *G*. *A* is always absent on Monday, and *E* on Thursday. *G* is not to be left in sole charge at lunch-time as she is inexperienced, but it is desired to give her some opportunity of reception work at other times of the day. *C*, by special arrangement, always lunches from 1 to 2 pm so that he may care for his invalid mother. Draw up a rota of duties to ensure that the reception desk is always manned.

6 The telephone and switchboard

6.1 The importance of the telephone network

When Alexander Graham Bell, a teacher of the deaf, patented the telephone in 1876, he surely could not have dreamed of the revolution he was making in communications, and the effect it would have on the business world in particular. The whole quality of our lives has been transformed by this facility to speak personally and instantaneously to almost anyone else in the world. It is now possible to dial business associates almost everywhere in the world directly, without any assistance from the operator. Half the world's population watches pictures of a royal wedding, a presidential assassination, or an Olympic Games. There seems to be no limit to the technical skill of the telecommunications engineer. Already proposals are being made that the telephone system should read our gas and electricity meters for us without any human assistance. Television-linked telephone circuits, which enable us to see our caller, are already in use, and may be said to have perfected Alexander Graham Bell's invention, for they enable the deaf person to lip-read what his/her caller is saying.

The telephone is the most vital communications link in business. It is direct, personal and immediate. The most modern switchboards are miracles of ingenuity, linking department to department, branch to head office, international company with foreign subsidiary, ship to shore, aircraft to base; with every refinement to ensure speed, economy and, if necessary, secrecy. The telephone operator holds one of the key positions in any organization. Consequently the young office worker should always be prepared to learn how to operate the telephone console, which has replaced the switchboard in most offices. It brings immediate recognition of his or her ability, and a knowledge of the affairs of the firm which cannot be acquired so quickly in any other way.

6.2 The principle of the telephone

Figure 6.1 illustrates the principle of the telephone. Study the diagram now and the notes below it.

This traditional telephone system is called an analogue system. It works from the waveform created by human speech at one end, which is turned into an electric current with a similar wave pattern.

This is transmitted along a wire to the receiver's telephone, where the wave pattern is turned back again into a sound wave that can be picked up by the receiver's ear. The word 'analogue' means 'a parallel system', with the final wave pattern very similar to the original wave pattern. This is the system illustrated in Figure 6.1 and explained in the notes below it.

The trouble with the traditional system is that the wave pattern of speech produced at the caller's end becomes weaker and weaker the farther it travels, and distortions in the cables make it difficult to pick out the signal easily, because of background noise. The more modern system is to send the message in digital form, that is to say as a series of numbers. The two parts of Figure 6.2 show what happens.

6.3   Advantages and disadvantages of the telephone system
These may be listed as follows:

Advantages

(*a*) It is a very fast communications system, taking only fractions of a second to bridge gaps of thousands of miles.

(*b*) It is a direct link person to person, giving an extremely individual and personal character to the contacts made in this way.

(*c*) It is relatively cheap, especially if good control can be exercised.

(*d*) Calls can be received on automatically operated telephone answering services, at any time of the day or night. This enables agents and commercial travellers to phone in cheap calls at off-peak periods for attention the next day.

(*e*) Now that the telephone lines can be used for facsimile copying (fax) and computer networks, written records are available of the messages sent by these means.

(*f*) The changeover to fibre optic cables is revolutionizing telecommunications. The messages travel as beams of light at the speed of light, and consequently huge volumes of data can be handled as a bitstream. There is no background noise and reception is perfect. This high capacity enables pictures to be relayed over the new videophones. Only one country, Iceland, has a completely fibre optic system, but then it is a tiny place. Eventually the whole world will be linked by fibre optic cables. These developments have now made possible the transmission of complex streams of data so that the videophone can be introduced (see Figure 6.3).

Disadvantages

(*a*) There are no written records of the actual conversations, though they may be recorded fairly easily. Contracts made by telephone could thus be proved in a court of law if tape-recordings were admissible as evidence, but generally speaking such contracts are

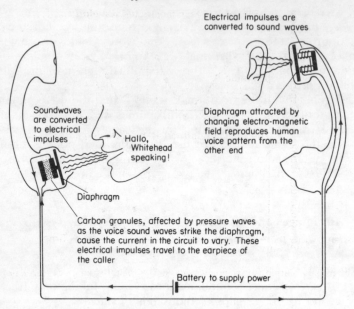

Electrical impulses are
converted to sound waves

Soundwaves
are converted
to electrical
impulses

Hallo,
Whitehead
speaking!

Diaphragm attracted by
changing electro-magnetic
field reproduces human
voice pattern from the
other end

Diaphragm

Carbon granules, affected by pressure waves
as the voice sound waves strike the diaphragm,
cause the current in the circuit to vary. These
electrical impulses travel to the earpiece of
the caller

Battery to supply power

Figure 6.1 The principle of the telephone

Notes
(i) The human voice makes sound waves which strike the diaphragm of the microphone in the telephone handset.

(ii) The pressure waves cause the diaphragm alternately to compress and release the carbon granules behind it. This alternately increases and decreases the flow of current in the circuit passing through the telephone network to the earpiece of the caller's handset.

(iii) In the earpiece the current is led around an electro-magnet which becomes more or less magnetized as the current varies. The strong current attracts the earpiece diaphragm strongly − the weaker current releases the diaphragm.

(iv) This movement of the diaphragm imitates the movement of the human voice box miles away that is causing the current to vary, and we hear the same sounds the speaker is making.

made between members of honourable bodies, e.g. Stock Exchange contracts, Lloyd's insurance contracts and other contracts are made by those who live by the motto 'My word is my bond'.

(*b*) Although relatively cheap, telephone services may be abused, e.g. for private purposes of staff. Good control is necessary, or devices like 'trunk barring' may reduce the abuse.

(*c*) Although the videophone is now in use, and will come into wide use no doubt during the last decade of the twentieth century, for most telephone users the caller cannot be seen, and the personal contact established depends upon the voice; one cannot see facial expressions or gestures which may convey much in a completely personal confrontation.

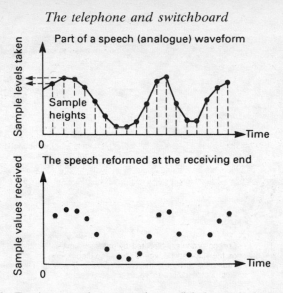

Part of a speech (analogue) waveform

Figure 6.2 Turning an analogue wave into a digital stream of information

Notes

(i) The original voice pattern can be seen as a wave in the top half of the diagram.

(ii) The size of the wave can be measured at any given moment by measuring how far it is from the two axes which meet at 0. Thus the position of any part of the wave can be stated by measuring its height above the horizontal axis and its distance from the vertical axis.

(iii) This is actually done every 125 millionths of a second, in other words 8 000 times every second.

(iv) If these millions of measurements are then sent over a first-class quality line as a 'bitstream', i.e. a stream of data in computerized form, they can be used to reassemble the wave at its destination so accurately that the speech produced in the earpiece is clear and free of background noise. It is possible to have 'dedicated' lines always available for your exclusive use and free from any interference. This is particularly useful for television companies, press agencies, etc.

(v) The actual device for turning the analogue speech into a pulsed code of measurements is called a **modem**. This stands for modulator-demodulator. To modulate is to vary the frequency or pitch of the human voice. The modem measures the pitch of the voice, converts it into a machine language that can be transmitted, transmits it and then turns the resulting set of measurements into a wave again at the other end of the telephone link.

(vi) The use of the modem not only enables one conversation to be sent, but up to 2 000 conversations can be sent on a single cable, or in radio form to a satellite in space, without getting them mixed up. This requires 140 million bits of information to be sent every second. It is difficult to imagine such huge movements of data.

6.4 Making a telephone call from an office

Simple installations

British Telecom no longer has a complete monopoly of the telephone network but a very high proportion of offices make their initial application to BT for telephone services to be connected to the

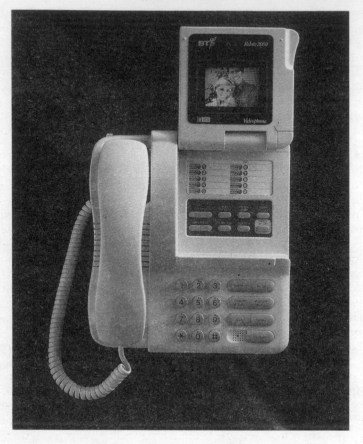

Figure 6.3 The videophone (courtesy of British Telecom)

premises. A hire charge is made for the use of facilities installed, and also for the calls made, which are metered automatically. Quarterly accounts are then rendered to the subscriber. It follows that telephone calls from an office do not depend on the insertion of money in coin boxes. The local telephone directories now include all the dialling codes for particular areas, and calls can be dialled almost worldwide without the aid of an operator. There are one or two countries, however, where repressive governments do not allow direct access to their citizens over the worldwide telecom networks.

The simplest installation merely consists of a hand-set, which is connected directly to the telephone system. Other systems have a simple hand-set with a switch and connection to another hand-set. The switch has four positions. By repositioning at points (*a*), (*b*), (*c*) or (*d*) it is possible to connect (*a*) to the exchange to make or receive outside calls; (*b*) to the other extension (in this case the outside caller cannot hear what is being said); (*c*) the outside caller to the extension; (*d*) the two hand-sets as an intercom unit.

In these cases immediately the hand-set is lifted a dialling tone is heard, and the subscriber may then dial or key in any number required in the enormous range of numbers given in the booklet. There are about 3000 exchanges within call, with thousands of subscribers on each exchange, so that virtually anyone in the country is within reach. For these simple installations the best course of procedure is as follows:

(*a*) Find out the telephone number of the person or firm you wish to ring. This may be given on their letterhead if you have been in correspondence with them, or on their documents such as invoices or statements. Well-designed letterheads or documents will give both the code number and the telephone number. Poorly designed letterheads may not give the code — they might for example say Cambridge 123456. This is a great nuisance, because the caller has to find the code for Cambridge. The designer of the letterhead could so easily have given the code, in the form (0223) 123456.

(*b*) Have a pencil and paper ready before you start the call in case you need to make any notes during your conversation.

(*c*) Lift the receiver and listen for the dialling tone (a continuous purring sound).

(*d*) Dial the exchange code first, and then the personal number of the business associate. When dialling, it is best to dial carefully but quickly — do not leave too long an interval between each digit. The dial should be allowed to return freely to its starting point between each digit. If the telephone has a key pad, do not linger on the keys or they are liable to send the number keyed more than once. Keying has to be firm but staccato, moving on to the next key at a steady pace.

(*e*) Wait for an interval of anything up to 15 seconds.

(*f*) Listen for either:

   (i) A ringing tone (burr-burr) which tells you the number is being called.

  (ii) An 'engaged tone', a repeated single note, which tells you to try again later.

 (iii) A number unobtainable note (a steady note). You should replace the receiver, check your information about codings, etc., and then redial.

(*g*) At the end of the call replace the receiver carefully. This action disconnects the charging equipment. A badly replaced receiver may cost a great deal of money if the charging meter is not disconnected.

Today even the simplest telephones have a variety of services that can be of great assistance to the small trader or householder. Names of these appliances change from year to year as a range of new services is offered. The only sensible thing is to consult the current BT *Business Catalogue* and buy the telephone that meets your requirements. The catalogue may be ordered by dialling 100 and asking for Freephone Telecom Sales. Some of the features of ordinary handsets are:

- A number memory – for the most common numbers you use. This saves dialling the numbers when you require them.
- Last number redial. It remembers the last number you dialled and will try it again without redialling. This is helpful if the line was engaged.
- A secrecy button. This cuts off the caller while you speak to someone in the room.
- A number-called panel – to show you the actual number dialled. This will help you detect a 'repeat key' error, for example.
- Lamp signalling. Besides ringing, a lamp flashes to draw the attention of the hard of hearing.
- Notepad memory. A memory in the phone unit in which you can key another number for your next call while you are making the first call, e.g. if your call is answered by a machine that says 'I'm not here today, but you can reach me on 071 000 0000'.
- On-hook dialling. You can dial without picking up the phone – you only pick it up if your call is answered.
- Loudspeaker function. The phone contains a loudspeaker, leaving your hands free to write while you are making a call.

There are several more features, and they are added to every year.

PBX and PABX

These terms are still in use but are becoming dated and will eventually disappear. They stand for Private Branch Exchange and Private Automatic Branch Exchange, and imply that the business has an exchange for its own personal use just like the public telephone exchanges. Progress in telecommunications began when the operator became much less necessary with the introduction of STD (subscriber trunk dialling and GRACE (Group routeing and charging equipment). In fact the progress in telecommunications is so fast that it is now possible to have an advanced system in any office, offering a huge range of services. Again it is necessary to use the current BT *Business Catalogue* or the Mercury *Business Catalogue*, and of course a visit by the sales staff to evaluate the exact needs of the firm or company concerned is desirable. There are Telecom solutions to almost every communication problem. The switchboard has now become an electronic console.

The system offers a large range of services to the subscriber, which may be selected or rejected when the original installation is made and adapted easily from time to time as business patterns change. The SL-1 system illustrated in Figure 6.4, for example, is very flexible. The flexibility of the SL-1 system stems from the fact that the central control is a computer. The system's features and services are defined by a software program rather than circuit wiring. Features can be added, deleted or modified by changing the software program rather than the hardware.

In the description of the features and services of the SL-1 system below the author is grateful for permission to use material supplied by Reliance Systems Ltd.

Access to paging. Extension users and attendants have access to loudspeakers or radio-paging equipment.

Access to dictation. Extension users have access to and control of dictation equipment, so that they may dictate letters to a typing pool.

Digital transmission multifrequency calling (DTMF) allows the use of telephones equipped with pushbutton dials to transmit digits via audible tones to the switching equipment.

Access to services and trunks. Extension users can either dial or press a key to gain trunk lines or services from the telephone exchange.

Call forward − First number busy. This service automatically routes incoming calls to a pre-selected extension when the called directory number is busy. A busy executive can thus pass calls to a secretary or assistant.

Call forward   First number does not answer. Automatically routes incoming calls to a pre-selected extension when the called directory number does not answer within a prescribed time.

Figure 6.4   The SL-1 attendant's console (courtesy of Reliance Systems Ltd)

Call forward — Follow-me. Automatically routes incoming calls to an extension defined by the absent extension. An executive who has to see a colleague elsewhere in the building can route all his/her calls to the extension concerned.

DTMF to dial pulse conversion. Automatically converts DTMF signals from a key telephone for transmission over rotary-dial-only trunk lines.

Direct inward dialling (DID). Allows an incoming call from the exchange network to reach a specific extension without assistance from the attendant.

Direct outward dialling (DOD). Allows an extension user to gain access to the exchange network, without assistance from the attendant, by dialling an access code.

Class-of-service restrictions. This enables managements to control calls originating from extensions, e.g. to prevent junior staff using outside lines at peak periods in the day.

Code restrictions. Denies or allows selected extensions access to international, national and local public exchange codes. The degree of restriction provided can be automatically varied at pre-selected times of day and on switching to night service.

Hunting. This service routes a call to an idle extension number in a prearranged group, when the called extension number is busy.

Extension-to-extension calling. An extension user can dial other extensions within the same system directly without the assistance of the attendant.

Night service. Allows incoming calls to be directed to selected extensions or directory numbers after normal business hours or at times when the console (switchboard) is unattended.

Call pickup. Allows an extension user to answer an incoming call to another extension belonging to the same call pick-up group.

Handsfree operation. Permits the extension user to speak without using the handset.

Hold. Allows an extension user, without assistance from the attendant, to hold any active call and use the telephone to call another number for consultation purposes. The user may then return to the held call and continue the interrupted conversation.

Call transfer. Allows an extension user, on any established two-party call, to hold the existing call, and originate another call to a third party for a private consultation. The user may either release from the consultation and return to the original call or transfer the original call to the third party.

Call waiting. Informs an extension user by tone buzzing and lamp flash signals, that another call is waiting to be connected during an established call.

On-hook dialling. Allows a user to dial without lifting the handset.

Override. Enables an extension user, after reaching a busy number, to override the busy condition and enter the existing conversation on a bridged basis, preceded by a warning tone.

Conference (three-party). Allows an extension user, while on any two-party connection, to hold the existing call, and originate another call to a third party for a private consultation. The user may then add the held party to the call for a three-party conference.

Conference (six-party). A similar feature to conference (three-party) except that six conferences are allowed.

Pushbutton dialling. A dial pad consisting of twelve non-locking pushbuttons (4 × 3) is provided on all SL-1 telephones and consoles.

Release key. A dedicated key can be provided on the SL-1 telephone to allow an extension user to release from an active call without having to go on-hook.

Telephone expansion. The complement of key/lamp facilities on the SL-1 telephone may be expanded by simply installing add-on key/lamp modules on the right-hand side of the basic telephone.

Tone buzzing. Provides an audible tone through the speaker to alert the extension when on-hook.

Voice calling. Allows the originating extension user to page over the speaker in the called party's SL-1 telephone.

Volume control. Provides independent volume control of tone buzzing, tone ringing and voice calling.

Ring again. Alerts a calling extension when a busy number becomes idle.

Speed calling. Permits an extension user to dial frequently-called numbers using only one or two digits.

Figure 6.5 shows the basic SL-1 telephone which an ordinary extension user would be provided with and the variety of keys available to him/her.

6.5 Answering the telephone

Just as the receptionist is the caller's first link with the firm, and it is important to receive callers courteously and attend to their needs promptly, the telephonist is the telephone caller's first introduction to the firm. Always answer calls promptly, deal with callers courteously, and ensure that you convey, by your interest in the callers and their requirements, the impression that your firm is efficient and businesslike. Under the STD system all calls are metered and charged. Formerly many local calls were not metered and were very cheap. A caller who is kept waiting for an extension today may elect to ring again later since he/she will be charged for the call while holding on. Time can be saved to callers if the following procedure is adopted, not only by telephonists but by all who answer extension telephones:

(*a*) Announce your identity, and state the name of the firm, or the department. 'Whitehead speaking. Accounts Department. May I help you?'

(*b*) Listen to the caller and assess the quality of the enquiry. The following alternatives may occur:

(i) It is a routine enquiry which can be answered directly. Do so courteously and fully, without being repetitive. The caller will be satisfied and ring off.

(ii) It is a specialized enquiry but one which the telephonist is competent to deal with. In this case it is useful to make a note of the call and a pad of scrap paper should be handy to record any necessary details. It is sometimes difficult to remember exactly what was said without a note of this sort. A phrase like 'Told him we'd deliver by the 30th' may prove invaluable next day when trying to recall the conversation.

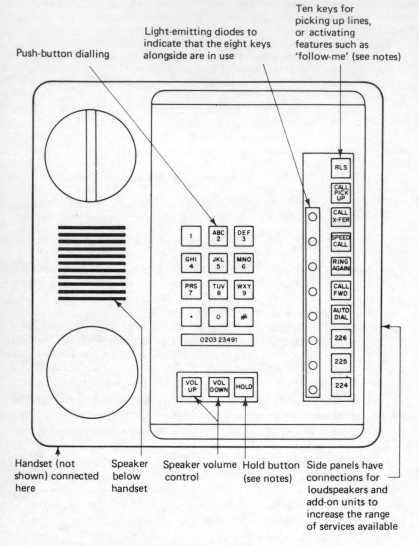

Push-button dialling

Light-emitting diodes to
indicate that the eight keys
alongside are in use

Ten keys for
picking up lines,
or activating
features such as
'follow-me' (see notes)

Handset (not
shown) connected
here

Speaker
below
handset

Speaker volume
control

Hold button
(see notes)

Side panels have
connections for
loudspeakers and
add-on units to
increase the range
of services available

Figure 6.5   The basic SL-1 telephone (courtesy of Reliance Systems Ltd)

(iii) The person the caller wishes to speak to may not be available. The telephonist has a choice between taking a message for the absentee, or asking the caller to wait while he/she is located. It is often cheaper for the caller to leave a message and the responsibility then rests upon the telephonist to ensure that it reaches the absent colleague.

```
┌─────────────────────────────────────────┐
│         Telephone  Message  Form          │
│                          Date............ │
│                          Time............ │
│                                           │
│    Caller's name........................ │
│    Address.............................. │
│    Telephone No.............  Ext. No..... │
│    ─────────────────────────────────────  │
│    Message for.......................... │
│    Message:............................. │
│    ------------------------------------- │
│    ------------------------------------- │
│    ------------------------------------- │
│    ------------------------------------- │
│    ------------------------------------- │
│    ------------------------------------- │
│                                           │
│         Message taken by.................. │
└─────────────────────────────────────────┘
```

Figure 6.6   A telephone message form

The best way to take a message is upon a printed message pad which conveniently reminds the operator of most of the essential details. Figure 6.6 shows such a pad, with spaces for the date, time, name and address of the caller, his/her telephone number and the detailed message. It is best to read the message back to the caller.

6.6 Special telephone services

A wide range of services is available to the general public and all subscribers through the telephone system. The most important of these are as follows:

(*a*) *The emergency services*. Dialling 999 gives everyone a priority answer from an operator, who will ask which service is required. The services available are Fire, Police, Ambulance, Coastguard (sea and cliff rescue), Cave Rescue and Mountain Rescue. The operator connects the caller to the service, who will then ask for the address where help is needed. In public call boxes a press-button connection, instead of a 999 call, enables direct contact with the operator to be made without the payment of money in the slot machine.

(*b*) *A. D. and C. calls*. Sometimes subscribers wish to know the charge for a particular call − possibly to charge a member of staff for it. The phrase 'Advise duration and charge' is used to book such a call through an operator. When booking the call the subscriber says 'and may I have A.D.C. please'. The operator meters the call and a few minutes after the end of the call will ring back to say, 'Your call to New York was timed at 5 minutes 48 seconds and cost £6.40'.

(*c*) *Alarm calls*. Subscribers who have urgent early morning business appointments can ask for an early call. 'Alarm' calls can also be booked for any time of the day or night. The charge is low. Precautions are usually taken by the telephone company to avoid hoax calls. The person booking the call is asked to hold on. The operator then dials the number and on hearing the engaged signal knows that the request is coming from that number.

(*d*) *Information services*. These can be very valuable, particularly the weather reports and the motoring reports. The 'speaking clock' service is one of the most widely used services in the country. 'A teletourist service supplies information on shows, sporting events, etc., in five languages, for tourists visiting the United Kingdom. Test match scores, cookery recipes, share prices and other information are also available.

(*e*) *Transferred charges, telephone credit cards and Freefone services*. These services help the subscriber who wishes to pay for incoming calls. It is, for example, convenient when travellers wish to call head office, or executives who are away from home wish to call their families to transfer the charge and have it added to the ordinary telephone bill. The only additional cost is a small charge to pay for the recording of the transfer. A **credit card** system operates differently. Selected staff, usually commercial travellers, are given a credit card, which they use from any ordinary telephone box in the country. By dialling the operator and giving details of the credit card account the caller will be connected free, and the charge will be passed on to the credit account. The Freefone service enables business subscribers to pay for incoming calls. This may be an attraction to customers. The caller simply asks the operator for the special 0800 numbers. The charge is recorded against the subscriber, with no charge to the caller.

(*f*) *Person to person calls*. These are available, at a small extra charge, to enable long-distance callers to save time on their calls. By paying the 'personal' charge. whether or not the person required is available, they ensure that they are not charged for the time spent locating their business contacts. Only one personal charge is made in any 24-hour period even if two or three attempts are necessary before the call is finally connected.

(*g*) *Data transmission services*. Head offices very often wish to receive data from branches, factories, etc., with the utmost possible speed. A series of data services is available to send computer data quickly and safely across country − or across the world. BT's Global Network Services offer businesses the means to transmit data nationwide and worldwide, at electronic speeds.

If a business uses computers or word-processors, and people at different desks or different locations want to be able to share the information stored in them, all you need is a **modem**. This is a simple, inexpensive device that translates computer-generated data into signals suitable for transmission on local, national and international telephone networks and then turns them back into computer code at the other end. This makes it as easy to send an urgent report from one personal computer (PC) to another as it is to pick up the phone and call someone.

Another useful device is the **multiplexer**. Quite simply the multiplixer is the data-communications equivalent of a traffic controller. It enables many users to connect their desktop terminals to a single line without causing traffic jams. It does this by collecting the data voice traffic from each terminal, packing it into concentrated bundles and then simultaneously shooting it accurately to its different destinations.

Any office requiring data services should approach the British Telecom or Mercury sales offices.

(*h*) *Disabled services.* A wide variety of appliances and services for different kinds of disablement is available. Some of these may be provided free, e.g. under the 'Special Aids to Employment' scheme. A free guide is available on 0800 800 878.

(*i*) *0800 and 0345 lines.* While the telephone is the easiest (and, when properly costed, the cheapest) way of contacting anyone, customers often hesitate to call long-distance. It is possible to ensure that they can always afford to call you if you register an 0800 or 0345 line. The 0800 number gives them a free call, wherever they are – there is even an international 0800 number. The caller simply lifts the phone and dials the 0800 number you have mentioned in your advertisements or on your letterhead. The 0800 number is charged to the person called, not to the caller. The customer gets the call free, but you get the order you wanted. The cost of the call is usually tiny relative to the profit on an order.

The 0345 line is slightly different. Here the charge is split – the customer pays the cost of a local call, and you pay the 'long-distance' element of the charge. Most customers are prepared to pay a local charge, but hesitate to phone if the call will incur a long-distance charge.

There is another system called Freefone name. You register a Freefone name, such as Freefone British Telecom. The caller dials the operator and asks for the Freefone name. The call is connected free of charge, but the person who registered the Freefone name is charged the cost of the call.

(*j*) *Conference calls and video-conferencing.* To bring people together – say a sales team – is expensive and time-consuming. There are travelling expenses, hotel bills, rooms to hire, etc. A telephone conference facility can link up to sixty people around the country and around the world, at any time of the day or night.

Video-conferencing depends on the use of special centres, which can be linked by satellite (or land line within the UK). Each centre is equipped for television and what takes place can be seen at each centre.

(*k*) *Security services.* The telephone system can now provide customers with security sensors that detect intruders, fire, failure of deep-freezer devices, cutting of telephone lines and other malfunctions. Calls may be made direct to the police or to the fire station, or to a central control office, which is manned 24 hours a day.

(*l*) *Special number services.* There are a number of widely used services that give up-to-date information. For example, the 'talking clock', the weather service, AA road advice, the BBC Newsline and many others. To find the numbers consult your local telephone directory.

6.7   Intercom links

At one time intercom links (the word is short for intercommunication) were widely used in business to link up all the important executives in a factory, office or warehouse. By pressing a single button the executives could call one another directly. The system is much less used today because modern console systems enable anyone to dial anyone else on an ordinary telephone, which thus serves both as an intercom service and a telephone service.

6.8   Paging devices

Originally a paging device was used in places such as hospitals to alert a busy doctor or key executive that he/she was wanted elsewhere. A 'bleep' device about the size of a fountain pen worn in the doctor's pocket uttered a 'bleep' when he/she was required elsewhere. Today they are called 'celebrity' bleepers.

Other systems use loudspeaker links which can be heard throughout the premises of a large organization, and in the car park, restaurant and similar areas. They are often referred to as Tannoy systems from the name of one of the earliest systems of this sort. The message usually given is only brief, e.g. 'Michael Smith to the General Manager's office, please − Michael Smith!' One leading firm in this field is Planned Equipment Ltd, Belvue House, Belvue Rd, Northolt, Middx (Tel 081 841 6251).

More recently, paging has been extended across the whole country by the setting up of paging zones covered by radio frequencies. A variety of paging devices enables the subscriber to be called in any zone for which he/she has registered. Some pagers just 'bleep', inviting the subscriber to call his/her home number for a message.

The message master receives messages that appear on a screen. A numeric pager can receive numbers, such as telephone numbers the subscriber out in the country is invited to call. Many small businesses and one-person firms find the use of a pager keeps them in touch with customers, suppliers and their home bases.

6.9 Directories

Directories are very important to any telephone service. They are printed for each area of the country, and most of them today group all the business numbers together in a special section. In London there are so many of them that they have a special directory all to themselves. Besides the telephone directory in each area there is a *Yellow Pages* directory, which lists all the various trades in alphabetical order and all the firms in that particular trade. A firm may have only a single line entry, but many firms pay for a 'display' advertisement, which gives them a chance to tell everyone the services they offer. It is very informative to study the *Yellow Pages* directory, particularly the index pages showing all the trades. If your business needs a particular service, such as a 'graphic designer' or a 'company formation agent', a few seconds spent with the *Yellow Pages* directory will find you one near your office, and only a telephone call away.

6.10 Telex and fax machines

The telex system is a system of printed communication between firms, a copy of all messages sent being produced on teleprinters at both the receiving and transmitting installations. Teleprinters are hired to firms by British Telecom at nominal charges of a few pounds per week. The subscriber is given a telex number similar to a telephone number, and business associates around the world can obtain access to this teleprinter 24 hours per day. The time gap between countries in different time zones therefore makes no difference to the effectiveness of the telex system. A London firm calling the number of an Australian subscriber whose offices are closed because it is night time, will automatically switch on the Australian teleprinter and the message will be passed. On arrival next morning the Australian telex operator will pass the messages to the department concerned. A reply can be prepared and sent, although the London offices are now closed in their turn.

Charges for actual calls are low, e.g. at the time of writing about 16p per minute to Belgium and £0.98 per minute to Australia from the United Kingdom.

Telex revolutionized communication between firms when it was first introduced. It is now computerized, and since telex lines are dedicated lines, it always gives accurate messages unspoiled by any loss of transmission quality. All telex machines send an answerback code at the conclusion of a message to prove that the full message has arrived. In many countries these are recognized in law (as proof of the conclusion of a contract, for example). Telex messages are used rather less than in former times because of the development of the Fax machine.

Facsimile copiers (Fax) are machines that transmit whatever appears on a sheet of A4 paper, whether it is text, diagrams, maps, drawings, designs, photographs etc. The whole page is scanned and every mark is transmitted over the telephone lines as an electronic message. It takes about 20 seconds to scan the page and transmit it anywhere in the world. The charge is the same as the cost of a telephone call to the same destination. There are 12 million fax users in the world, and the number is growing fast. You can also call in to many shops that act as Bureaufax centres. They will send a fax for you at a fairly nominal charge to any fax subscriber. Even those who do not have a Fax machine can therefore make use of the Fax communication network. It is also possible to link a fax machine with an 0800 or 0345 number, so that customers can send fax messages to you at your expense. This is an inducement to customers to get in touch with you.

6.11 Telephone management: call control

It is a sad fact that the use of the telephone is often abused. For example, employees make calls at the expense of their employers; even people who would never dream of making an international call at their own expense do not hesitate to do so if the employer is paying. One Italian 'au pair' was actually sent to prison for phoning her boyfriend in Italy, because the judge held that making telephone calls without permission was 'stealing from the employer'. Mind you, the bill was not small − she spent over £4 000 before the bill came in.

If we think about the problem of telephone abuse more deeply, we find it has much wider implications than just the cost of the call. For example, while the line is blocked by an unauthorized call, outside callers trying to phone in are getting the 'engaged' signal. They may have orders for the firm and be unable to pass them. Goodwill is easily lost if people say 'Oh they're always engaged − it's no good phoning them'. An irate caller who does finally get through may say to the managing director 'For heavens sake − you need more lines! We can't get through to you when we want you!' Every extra line not only means a high installation charge but extra rental every quarter for the use of the line. Similarly, while a line is occupied by an outgoing private call, other extension users who want to make a business call cannot get a line to use.

A call management system detects every call made, which extension made it, and how long the call took, and it prints out a detailed report. The very fact of probable detection reduces the number of private calls, and enables those who do make them to be charged the correct charge. It can also tell management how long it took staff to respond to an incoming call − thus pinpointing staff who are absent from their desks or deliberately fail to answer the telephone. Efficiency increases, and overworked areas that do need extra lines can be given them, while spare lines can be taken away from areas not under pressure.

To cut the cost of telephone services we could do the following:

(*a*) Train staff in the use of the telephone − how to answer, how to be brief, how to close off a call when the caller is only chattering.

(*b*) Ask for fully itemized bills. They give details of every call, and private calls and lengthy conversations can be investigated.

(*c*) Install 'trunk call barring' to extensions that don't need to make long-distance calls. Trunk call barring prevents unauthorized calls except local, inexpensive ones.

(*d*) Install a system such as the Ringmaster Call Management System, which gives full control. It is available from Cristie Electronics.

6.12 Answering machines

There is now a wide variety of answering machines available, at prices to suit all pockets. You can buy them outright or have them supplied and fitted by British Telecom for rental on a quarterly basis. The machines are electronic devices that will receive incoming calls, play a message to the caller regretting the subscriber's inability to answer the telephone at the moment and inviting him/her to leave a recorded message after the tone. Some machines count the messages so that on your return you find a small dial reading 3 or 5, or however many calls have been received. Touching a single key, saying 'play', for example, rewinds the tape and plays the messages. On most machines they can be replayed as often as required.

When about to rewind a tape, be ready with a notepad and pencil to record any names, telephone numbers or other details that will be provided by the caller. Replay the tape if necessary to ensure nothing has been missed. Then take appropriate action on the messages to ensure that the caller's requirements are satisfied.

Some machines are provided with remote interrogators. These are devices that can be used from a telephone anywhere in the world. The business person who is away from the office or home can call from any telephone and use the remote interrogator to operate the answering machine and listen to any calls. Action can then be taken to deal with the calls, e.g. calling back the person who has left a message, or passing the message on to the sales department or some other part of the business.

Some machines have a paging device that will page you when a message comes in. The paging device warns you that someone has left a message, and so long as you have not been paged, there is no need to contact the machine.

Some people use their answering machines to screen calls. This means they leave the answering machine on and, instead of answering the call, listen to each messages as it is recorded. If the call is an urgent one, they can break in on the recording and say 'hello, I've just come in. How may I help you?' If the call is not urgent, they let the caller complete the message and then deal with it at a convenient moment.

Many people misunderstand the telephone answering machine. 'I won't have one', they say, 'because I don't often get important messages.' This overlooks the fact that what you need to know, usually, is that no one has been trying to get you. If the machine has no message on it, that too is information. You can get down to work straight away, knowing that no one is pressuring you for anything.

An amusing sideline to answering machines is that some people go to great pains to make up appropriate outgoing messages. One golfer who enjoyed a reputation for being fond of female companionship left his message:

I've gone to play golf in the Open at Troon,
I'm on the first tee at a quarter past noon;
So please leave your number right after the tone,
If your voice sounds attractive I'll *certainly* phone.

You might like to try making up an outgoing announcement for some celebrity, and ask your fellow students to guess for whom it is intended. If you do have an answering machine in your own home, you could certainly make an announcement to suit your own personality.

6.13 Points to think about and discuss

(*a*) British Telecom is much concerned about the needs of handicapped people. It has a free help-line on 0800 800 150 to tell handicapped people about its services, and sends out brochures about appliances. (i) Why is it desirable that the telephone system should pay particular attention to the needs of handicapped people? (ii) How can the telephone be made more readily available to (*a*) the bedridden at home; (*b*) the chronically sick in hospitals; (*c*) the disabled?

(*b*) The *Yellow Pages* directory is issued in addition to ordinary directories giving a classified list of business addresses. What are the advantages of this arrangement to (i) the subscribers and (ii) the businesses.

(*c*) Your business delivers cream, yoghurts and similar fresh food to restaurants, dairies and other catering establishments. You have an A4 page laid out in pad form with all the various items you offer. The proprietors of shops phone in daily for their 'next day' orders and these are noted down on the pad. You are at present considering installing a fax machine which would enable firms to send in their orders by fax instead. Discuss the points in favour of such an idea, and the points against.

6.14 Rapid revision − the telephone system

Cover the page with a sheet of notepaper and uncover one question at a time.

	Answers		*Questions*
	−	1	Who invented the telephone?
1	Alexander Graham Bell.	2	How does it work?
2	Voice sound waves are converted by the microphone mouthpiece into electrical waves that travel to the earpiece of the person called. Here they are reconverted to sound waves.	3	What is a wave that is similar to the human voice called?
3	An analogue wave.	4	How else can we send a wave pattern?
4	By computer, as a stream of numbered measurements, called a digital bitstream.	5	How fast is the wave measured?
5	8 000 times a second	6	What are fibre optic cables?
6	Cables made of glass fibres, which carry messages at the speed of light	7	What do the letters PBX and PABX mean?
7	PBX = private branch exchange PABX = private automatic branch exchange	8	What are the meanings of STD and GRACE?
8	STD = subscriber trunk dialling. GRACE = group routing and charging equipment.	9	What do these systems do?
9	They enable the subscriber to dial directly to all parts of the country without any need to call the operator at the exchange.	10	How should the telephone be answered?

10 (*a*) Announce your identity, and the name of the firm or department.
(*b*) Answer directly if it is a routine matter which you are competent to deal with.
(*c*) Answer a specialist matter that you are competent to deal with and record any vital details on a telephone memo pad.
(*d*) Other callers should be connected to someone competent, or a detailed message should be taken.

11 The answers are too complex to describe here. The reader should refer to the text.

12 It is a device to call members of staff who are busy about the region.

13 A machine that not only types out a telex message as the teleprinter operator keys it in, but also transmits it to a remote destination, where it is printed out again.

14 You type in the code for your correspondent's telex.

15 It sends an answerback code. I am then free to send the message.

16 The machine sends its answerback code at the conclusion of the message.

17 A facsimile copier, which can scan a page and send every mark on the page as an electronic message to another fax machine at the destination address.

18 British Telecom and Mercury, but more competition is planned.

11 Explain the following:
(*a*) How to use the emergency services.
(*b*) What is an ADC call?
(*c*) What are transferred charges, credit card services and Freefone services?
(*d*) What are person-to-person calls?
(*e*) What are data transmission services?

12 What is a paging device?

13 What is a telex machine?

14 How do you access a distant telex machine?

15 How do you know the machine is ready to receive your message?

16 How do you know the message has been received?

17 What is a fax machine?

18 What organizations run the telephone system in the United Kingdom?

19 Go over the page again until you feel you are sure of the answers.

Exercises set 6

1 Write down the letters (*a*)−(*j*) and against them write the phrases from the word list necessary to complete the following sentences:

(*a*) The telephone was invented by ......
(*b*) The sound waves of the caller are turned into ...... in the telephone circuit and are then reconverted to sound waves at the receiver's telephone earpiece.
(*c*) PBX stands for ......
(*d*) PABX stands for ......
(*e*) The more modern switchboards, where many of the connections are made automatically, are called ......

(*f*) GRACE stands for ......
(*g*) STD stands for ......
(*h*) *Yellow Page* directories are ...... directories, listing firms under the type of trade or service performed.
(*i*) The letters A D C stand for ......
(*j*) Devices which locate busy staff wherever they are working in a building are called ...... devices.

Word list: Alexander Graham Bell, private automatic branch exchange, classified, group routing and charging equipment, advise duration and charge, electrical waves, private branch exchange, subscriber trunk dialling, paging, consoles.

2 On a half sheet of A4 paper type or write out a telephone message form as shown in Figure 6.6. Then record on it the following message. 17 May 19... Mr A. A. Kenningham of Moulded Plastics Ltd wishes to speak urgently with Mr R. Roberts of Sales Dept. He particularly wishes to know the prices of 'ordinary' and 'extra quality' shelving units, and to know whether both qualities of shelving can be mounted on the same brackets. If not, what are the gauges and prices of the 'extra quality' brackets. Will Mr Roberts phone him at Burdon 13475, Ext. 12, before 5.15 p.m. If Mr Kenningham proves to be not available, will he leave a detailed message with Miss Chalmers. Message taken by R. Ford, telephonist.

3 In the following questions choose the best answer to the question from the answers given, (*a*), (*b*), (*c*) or (*d*).

(i) The principle of the operation of the telephone is: (*a*) that the voice travels along a wire to the receiver's earpiece; (*b*) that the pressure waves of the voice striking the diaphragm of the mouthpiece cause a pressure wave to flow along the copper conductor; (*c*) that the sound waves of the voice patterns are converted into electrical waves along a conductor to the earpiece of the receiver, where an electro-magnet reconverts them to sound waves which can be heard by the person called; (*d*) the movement of molecules of copper along a conducting wire.
(ii) The good telephonist will always answer calls (*a*) by saying 'Hallo'; (*b*) by announcing his/her identity, or the firm's identity; (*c*) in strict rotation as they arrive at the switchboard; (*d*) by saying 'Hold on. I'm busy'.
(iii) Trunk call barring is a system used on PABX consoles (*a*) to stop junior staff making long-distance calls, (*b*) to stop unauthorized staff making long-distance calls, (*c*) to prevent anyone having private calls, (*d*) to stop long-distance calls coming in without going through the operator.
(iv) A telephone credit card (*a*) enables a credit-worthy businessman to buy telephone equipment on credit, (*b*) enables senior staff to draw money from any branch of the 'Big Four' banks, (*c*) enables a caller to credit his charges to his own home telephone account, (*d*) enables the bearer, by quoting the number of the credit account, to telephone any number and have the call charged to the head office of his organization.

4　Which of the following could be said to be true of the work of the telephone operator: (*a*) it requires tact and diplomacy at all times; (*b*) it is not essential to most offices; (*c*) it has been made easier by the use of automatic devices; (*d*) it sometimes requires the telephonist to deal with emergency situations coolly; (*e*) it never has spells of intense activity; (*f*) it sometimes requires the telephonist to act in other capacities, for example as a receptionist; (*g*) it is best carried out by someone who knows the organization of the firm very well; (*h*) it does not require special training.

5　Suggest four ways in which a manager, wishing to cut the cost of telephone services, could economize in its use without reducing the effectiveness of the service.

6　The telephone gives direct communication between businessmen and their clients or customers. What are the advantages of such links? Are there any disadvantages?

7　A new junior has been appointed in your office, one of her main duties being to answer the telephone. List four *practical* hints to help.

8　Name three of the special telephone services provided by British Telecom which give, by dialling particular codes, immediate information on certain matters or events.

9　What do you understand by the following terms: (*a*) STD, (*b*) fixed-time calls; (*c*) data transmission services, (*d*) the speaking clock?

10　Write about eight lines about each of the following: (*a*) personal calls (*b*) early morning alarm calls, (*c*) transferred charge calls, (*d*) cheap rate calls.

11　What is subscriber trunk dialling? How has it changed the work of the telephonist as far as outgoing calls are concerned? What difference has it made to local calls?

12　What do you understand by the terms PBX and PABX? Explain the use of these systems to a business house conducting a major part of its business by telephone.

13　(*a*) What is a fax machine? (*b*) What are the advantages of a fax machine to (i) an editor wishing to see an artist's ideas for the cover of a book, (ii) an exporter wishing to get documents to a foreign seaport.

14　(*a*) What is a modem? (*b*) How does it improve the quality of a telephone conversation to a foreign country?

15　You are employed in the office of Super Stationery Limited and at 10.30 am on 3 June you receive the following telephone call: 'John Brewster here, Bennington Limited; is Mr James there?' You are the only person in the office, so you ask if you can take a message; Mr Brewster replies:

'Yes, please. We're shipping agents and Mr James has an African consignment. Will you tell him that there's some cargo space available on SS *Orono* to Mombasa. It's loading at Tilbury Dock, London. They're starting on the 7th June and won't take anything after the 11th.

I'd like confirmation before 4.30 this afternoon, so ask Mr James to ring back, please, before then. Would you like to take the number? It's (9154) 37184. If I'm out ask for Mr Smith — he'll be able to deal with the job. Thank you, goodbye.'

Draw up a suitable telephone message form for general use, and record the essential points of the conversation ready for Mr James' return.   (RSA)

16   (*a*) What should a junior do to ensure that an incoming call is dealt with intelligently? (*b*) Some firms forbid personal calls for their employees. Why do you think this is done? (*c*) Why do people sometimes make 'Personal calls?' What is the procedure?   (RSA)

17   (*a*) You are looking after the telephone switchboard and also the paging system. A visitor, Mr Blake, has called to see Mr Martin, the chief engineer, by appointment. The visitor is on time but Mr Martin is at the other end of the factory. Write out the exact message you would speak into the microphone of the paging system. (*b*) What is the main advantage to a business of an internal telephone system? (*c*) What particular advantage is it for a business to install a PABX switchboard? (*d*) A company has branches in the six largest cities in the United Kingdom. The managing director has some urgent news to pass on to the branch managers. Ideally he would like to tell them all at once and at the same time have some opportunity for a brief discussion in which they could all participate. Discuss how this could be done.   (RSA)

18   (*a*) In what circumstances might you wish to make use of (i) a telephone answering machine, (ii) the transferred charge call service, (iii) a telephone credit card, (iv) the personal call service? (*b*) Explain fully *one* of the above telephone services.   (RSA)

19   What is a multiplexer? Why are telephone services essential to people who use computer networks to link factories and warehouses with head offices?

20   Your employer is concerned because a number of incoming messages received by telephone have not been dealt with efficiently. (*a*) Draft a telephone message form which could be used on all occasions when the person required is not available. (*b*) What would you do if a telephone caller would not leave a message?

21   What is a fibre optic cable? How is it of use to the electronics engineer working on the development of the videophone and video-conferences?

22   What is a telex machine? Why is it able to work 24 hours a day even though offices are closed at night times?

23   What part can the telephone play in giving added security to buildings?

7 Mail inwards

7.1 Introduction

Mail inwards and mail outwards are clearly both connected with the postal services, but they are not handled in the same way. While mail outwards calls for the weighing, stamping and actual despatch of letters and parcels, and is usually the main function of the post department, mail inwards does not involve quite the same sort of routine activity.

In many firms much of the correspondence is addressed to the firm as a whole, not to particular persons or departments. Some firms even print on their letter headings 'All correspondence to be addressed to the general manager' or some other official. It follows that a preliminary sort-out is necessary to ensure that letters reach the proper department. This preliminary sort-out is best carried out by experienced staff, often the personal secretaries of the various departments or even the office manager personally. In many small firms the proprietor always opens the mail personally, it is the only way to detect underhand practices by staff, who may, for example, misappropriate notes and cheques sent by post, or order items at the firm's expense. In larger firms it is a common practice for members of lower management staff to open the mail together, sorting it into departmental trays. In other offices a supervisor controls the incoming mail, with more junior staff doing the routine activities of opening letters and rough sorting.

7.2 Collecting the mail

Mail is usually delivered to the addressee by the postman, and it arrives at times convenient to the Post Office organization. Firms wishing to collect at times convenient to them may do so through the 'private box' or 'private bag' service. The former enables the firm to hire a box in the Post Office sorting department into which their mail will be placed, and from which it can be collected. The 'private bag' service enables a firm to send a driver to collect the firm's mail, which will be handed over in a suitable locked bag provided by the firm. The bag must conform to the corporation's specifications. The charge, at the time of writing, is £20 per box or per bag per annum. A separate box or bag is required for parcels, and if one or the other is used for both, a double fee is payable.

The service enables firms to ensure that mail is collected, opened and distributed to departments early in the day, so that correspondence can be read and action taken at the earliest possible moment. It is usual for mail inwards staff to start work earlier than other employees, sometimes on a rota basis.

7.3 Rules for opening incoming mail

Mail should be opened systematically, with particular attention to the security of incoming cheques or money. It is also important to ensure that all the contents of envelopes are removed and secured together before the envelope is thrown away. Some departments prefer to keep envelopes with the contents: for example, personnel departments can often learn a lot about an applicant from the way an envelope is written. The following rules might apply, but every office will have its own special procedures, which the reader should discover on taking up emloyment.

(*a*) *Carry out a preliminary sorting.* Separate the **first-class** from the **second-class letters**. Arrange both types in tidy packs with the addresses all facing the same way.

(*b*) *Extract the personal letters.* Extract any envelopes marked 'Private', 'Confidental', 'Personal', or 'To be opened by addressee only'. Stamp these letters on the envelope with a **date stamp** to show the date of arrival, and perhaps the time of arrival, using a stamp such as those in Figures 7.1 and 7.2. Then place them unopened in the trays of the individuals to whom they are addressed.

(*c*) *Open the non-confidential sealed letters.* Sealed letters should be opened either with a **paper knife** or with a **letter opening machine**. This is a machine that shaves off a very tiny sliver of paper from the edge of an envelope, so that the contents may be removed. The small slice is only about two thousandths of an inch thick, so that it is impossible to damage the contents of the envelope. Figure 7.3 shows such a mail opener

(*d*) *Remove and sort the contents.* After removing the contents, the clerk should ensure that the envelope is empty by holding it up to a desk light. Then the correspondence removed should be opened out, and date stamped with the date, or time and date, of its reception.

If it has any 'enclosures' mentioned at the foot of the letter, ensure that they were in fact enclosed. If any are missing, make a note of the fact against the 'enclosure' and sign it, for example, 'Not enclosed − R. Smith'. The supervisor should be informed so that action may be taken. Finally, sort the correspondence into the most appropriate tray.

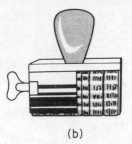

(b)

This date stamp can be altered to read
Answered, Supplied by, Ordered,
Cancelled, Invoiced, Checked,
Delivered, Received, Entered,
Telephone, Acknowl'd, and Paid

(a)

A self-inking date stamp

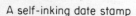

Figure 7.1   Devices for date-stamping letters

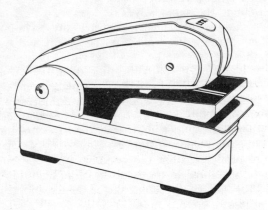

Figure 7.2   A device for time-stamping mail inwards

(*e*) *Record important documents in the mail inwards register.* It
sometimes happens that important documents arrive in the ordinary
post; at other times they arrive in special post such as registered or
recorded delivery post. Many offices require the supervisor to record
all such mail in an **inwards mail register**. Solicitors, for example,
might record the receipt of deeds, conveyances and depositions.
Publishers might record manuscripts of books, or artwork, and most
offices would record registered and recorded delivery letters. The
arrival of money, cheques, bills of exchange and so on should be
recorded in a **remittances inwards book**. Payments, whether by cash

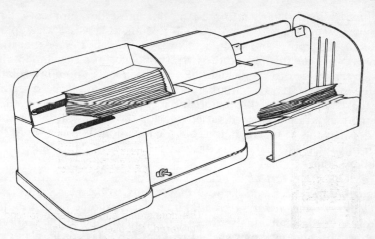

Figure 7.3 A mail-opening machine (courtesy of Messrs Pitney-Bowes Ltd)

Notes

(i) Mail of varying sizes and thicknesses is placed in a stack on the feed plate.

(ii) An electric drive feeds the letters into the machine, where two rotary knives cut off a thin strip, without damaging the contents.

(iii) The opened letters are stacked in a hopper ready for the removal of their contents. The 'chips' cut from the letters are ejected into a separate hopper.

or cheque, should be compared with the **remittance advice note** that accompanies them. Registered letters should preferably be opened only by the supervisor. Any disparity between either cheques or money and the advice note should be reported at once. When all the mail has been opened, the cashier should be requested to sign the remittances inwards book for those items involving payments, to confirm that he/she has received them. Where **loose postage stamps** are received, e.g. in requests for samples, patterns and recipes or to cover return postage, the cashier will eventually pass them on to the post department for use, charging them out as part of the **petty cash imprest**. Alternatively, the Post Office will repurchase them, subject to a 10 per cent discount.

Special note on recorded delivery. A lot of important mail is sent **recorded delivery**, which is a way of proving that the posted item reaches its destination, and a less expensive method than registering it. For example, colleges often use recorded delivery to send certificates to students who have passed examinations. Such deliveries must be signed for on an individual basis, otherwise no reponsibility is accepted by the Post Office. Thus where five recorded delivery letters arrive at the same time, each one should be signed for; it is incorrect to bracket them together and sign once only.

(*f*) *Prepare circulation slips if necessary.* In many offices it is the practice for certain types of mail to be circulated to several departments, so that all are informed of the latest developments. The duplication or photocopying of such documents gives each department a file copy, and a full record of events. Less expensive, however, is the affixation to the correspondence of a **circulation slip**, which shows the order in which the correspondence should circulate. Thus, in Figure 7.4, the circulation slip is routed to all the directors of the company, and the company secretary and the accountant. Sometimes a rubber stamp is used bearing the names of the persons or departments to be circulated, but a circulation slip overcomes the difficulty met when there is insufficient space on the item for a rubber stamp.

(*g*) *Open the unsealed letters.* Then place the contents, often circulars, into the trays of those most likely to be interested.

(*h*) *Distribute the trays of mail.* Finally, trays should be distributed carefully to the individuals concerned, so that none of the contents are lost. Empty envelopes should be kept for 3 days at least in case they are needed for reference, and before finally being disposed of, they should be checked again to make sure they are empty.

In Figure 4.7 (see p. 81) we saw a group of trays typical of the sort of anti-static tray used for circulating mail and memos around the offices. The trays in Figure 4.7 were linked together for use at a single work-position. Loose trays, one for each department or each senior member of staff, are used in the mail inwards department at the start of the day. Upon distribution after the mail has been sorted, they would be placed at a convenient point in each department

Circulation Slip Please read the attached correspondence, and pass at once to the next person on the list	
Name	Please initial when read
Director No. 1	
" No. 2	
" No. 3	
" No. 4	
" No. 5	
Company Secretary	
Chief Accountant	
Received by Mail Inwards department and circulated on :-	
Date Stamp here	

Figure 7.4   A 'mail inwards' circulation slip

to receive all mail outwards and memos for other departments from various members of staff throughout the day. A junior member of staff would make regular collections from these trays, say every 2 hours. Any memos or files for other departments would be circulated as the collection round continued, while the mail for dispatch would be taken to the post department for franking and dispatch. This is explained in Chapter 8

In these days of eletronic communication by computer networks some of the mail, especially between departments, will be e-mail (electronic mail) sent from one computer terminal to another. However, totally paperless communication is still some way off in the future, and for the present a good system of trays with a reliable messenger service is essential in most offices. The last collection of the day usually requires the actual trays to be collected for return to the mail inwards department ready for the arrival of the post next morning.

7.4 Sorting the mail − a desk sorter

If mail is sorted into departments, without being opened, a *desk sorter* is a convenient piece of equipment. It consists of a flat base-plate, to which is connected a series of hinged metal flaps. Each flap projects a short distance beyond the previous one, and bears a visible index panel which can show the various names of the departments. Letters and documents placed between the flaps are held in position by the weight of the flap. Other sorters consist of filing pockets conveniently arranged in concertina style, pigeon-holes and work-organizers such as the one illustrated in Figure 4.8 (see p. 83). Figure 7.5 shows an Ambidex desk sorter of the type mentioned above.

7.5 Electronic mail (e-mail)

Today there is a new type of mail inwards − electronic mail or e-mail. It is mail of every sort, sent in electronic form over the data links of a computer network. Data links may be ordinary telephone cables, fibre optic cables which transmit electronic messages as pulses of information carried in glass fibres at the speed of light, and satellite links. Networks can be small in-house networks within a single building or organization − wide networks linking head offices with factories, depots and branches, or world-wide links such as GEIS. This name rhymes with nice − GEIS is nice. It is the American company General Electronic Information Services, which offers everyone a global link-up.

Today anything can be sent electronically. It may be a simple memo, a short report, a legal deed, a document or a drawing. So long as the necessary preparation has been done, every piece of

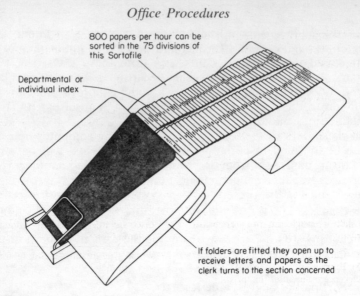

800 papers per hour can be sorted in the 75 divisions of this Sortofile

Departmental or individual index

If folders are fitted they open up to receive letters and papers as the clerk turns to the section concerned

Figure 7.5　An Ambidex desk sorter (courtesy of Ambidex Equipment Sortofiles Ltd)

information can travel by e-mail, be viewed on a screen (visual display unit or VDU), be printed off as a hard copy or stored in a memory bank. The layout of a 'network' is illustrated more fully in Chapter 14.

7.6　Points to think about and discuss

(*a*) As an office manager it is your duty to draw up a roster of staff to come in half an hour early each week and open the incoming mail. Miss Smith, a personal secretary, objects to taking her turn on this duty. (i) What arguments could be used to justify the requirement to come in early? (ii) Miss Smith refuses point blank to come in. How should the problem be dealt with?

(*b*) A registered letter addressed to 'The Administration Office' was opened by a junior member of staff who reported that money was short. Upon telephone enquiry the chief cashier of the firm concerned reports that on making up the registered envelope for post he called two witnesses to see the notes inserted in the envelope and sealed it in their presence. What should be done about the £20 that is missing?

(*c*) In a small office there are five people. They are (i) Mr Jones, the manager, who never arrives until 10.15 am; (ii) Mrs Pike, his secretary, a very experienced and trustworthy member of staff; (iii) Mr White, chief clerk and cashier; (iv) Miss Trimble, a junior secretary who joined the firm last week; (v) Miss Brown, the postal clerk. What arrangements should be made in such an office with regard to the opening of mail, much of which is remittances inwards for mail-order goods advertised in the national press?

7.7 Rapid revision — mail inwards

Cover the page with a sheet of paper and uncover one question at a time.

Answers	Questions
—	1 How is mail collected for a large office?
1 Usually through the private box or private bag system.	2 List suitable rules for opening incoming mail.
2 (*a*) Carry out a preliminary sorting. (*b*) Extract the personal letters, marked 'confidential' or 'private'. (*c*) Open the non-confidential sealed letters, and sort them. (*d*) Record remittances inwards. (*e*) Prepare circulation slips if necessary. (*f*) Sort the unsealed letters into appropriate trays. (*g*) Distribute the trays of mail.	3 Which type of staff should open and sort the mail?
3 (*a*) Responsible staff of middle management level or personal secretary level. (*b*) A specialist mail inwards supervisor.	4 Why do some firms ask correspondents to address all mail to 'The General Manager', or some similar addressee?
4 It gives better control of correspondence and reduces undesirable, or corrupt, practices.	5 What is a mail opening device?
5 It is a device that cuts a thin sliver off sealed envelopes without damaging either the contents or the envelope.	6 What action should be taken when money reputed to be enclosed in a letter is reported short?
6 Rigorously investigate the affair to determine the cause of the shortage.	7 What should be done with envelopes after opening mail?
7 Keep them for 2–3 days until it is quite certain they will not be required. Check them against a desk light before final disposal.	8 What is e-mail?
8 Electronic mail coming into a computer terminal.	9 Where does it come from?
9 It can come from any other computer terminal in the network, whether it is somewhere else 'in-house' or scattered across the globe world-wide.	10 Go over the page again until you feel you are sure of all the answers.

Exercises set 7

1 Choose the best word or phrase from the word list below to complete these sentences.

(a) Mail should be distributed ...... after it is received from the Post Office.

(b) Mail marked ...... or ...... should not be opened.

(c) Important letters such as registered letters or recorded delivery letters should be recorded in a ......

(d) A paper knife is a device for ...... letters.

(e) A ...... will remove a tiny sliver of paper from the edge of an envelope.

(f) Always test envelopes to see if they are ...... before discarding them in the waste-paper basket.

(g) All mail should be ...... on arrival to indicate when it was received in the mail inwards office.

(h) If a letter has ...... sent with it the fact will usually be noted at the foot of the letter.

(i) It is best if the ...... opens letters likely to contain money or cheques.

(j) A ...... may be made out if a letter has to be read by several members of staff.

Word list: personal, confidential, opening, as soon as possible, letter opening machine, date stamped, circulation slip, mail inwards register, supervisor, enclosures, empty.

2 Suggest why mail inwards should be opened only by experienced staff.

3 In what ways may mail inwards reach the office? How should it be dealt with on arrival?

4 Describe the procedure that would be adopted by a large organization for the speedy opening, sorting and distribution of the morning post. What special security precautions might be introduced?

5 A firm frequently receives (a) registered letters, (b) cheques, (c) loose postage stamps in payment for items requested by customers. How should these be dealt with on arrival, and what will eventually happen to each?

6 What action would you take about (a) an envelope that arrived empty; (b) a registered envelope, signed for by the telephonist, which proves to have been carefully cut at the bottom? The valuable contents are missing.

7 You are in charge of the mail inwards room. Write out a list of instructions to guide your relief in dealing with the incoming mail each day, while you are on holiday.

8 Today's incoming mail includes the items listed below. You have instructions to sort mail into four departments:
(a) Accounts, (b) company secretary and administration office, (c) purchasing department, (d) sales department. List the items suitable for each department.

(i) The telephone account.

(ii) A brochure on electronic calculators.

(iii) Four orders from customers.

(iv) A credit note from a supplier.

(v) A bank statement.

(vi) An insurance policy for a commercial traveller's car.

(vii) Twelve invoices from suppliers.

(viii) The deeds to a new factory.

(ix) The monthly correction list for the Post Office's *Mailguide*.

(x) A testimonial regarding an applicant for employment.

(xi) A brochure about office equipment.

(xii) A Home Office enquiry about a work permit for an overseas trainee from a foreign branch.

9   An important document, received in the post at 8.30 am and recorded in the mail inwards register, did not reach the company secretary in his tray. Suggest a procedure for tracing the missing document.

10 Write against the items of mail listed below the most likely department to be interested in them: (*a*) new booklet of tax instructions, (*b*) price list of office equipment, (*c*) notification about trainee schemes for transport staff, (*d*) the Lloyd's shipping list, (*e*) an invoice for goods ordered from a supplier, (*f*) a cheque from a debtor, (*g*) a request for information from the Chamber of Trade, (*h*) a Department of Health leaflet about earnings-related contributions, (*i*) a copy of a government white paper on the auditing of company accounts, (*j*) an employee's P45 from a previous employer.

11 In what circumstances should incoming mail be: (*a*) photocopied, (*b*) recorded in an inwards mail register, (*c*) handled by the supervisor only, (*d*) left unopened?

12 There have been complaints from the other departments in your organization that the postal and telephones department, in which you work, is often left unattended at lunchtimes. The lunch hour may be taken from 12 to 1 or from 1 to 2. There are six staff in the department:

A   a switchboard operator

B   a receptionist who can also deal with the switchboard

C   a postal clerk responsible for all outgoing mail

D   a postal clerk who can also operate the photocopiers

E   a secretary in charge of photocopying of incoming and outgoing mail

F   a junior responsible for preparing parcels, franking envelopes and preparing letters for the post.

Make out a lunch rota which will ensure that there is always someone in the office who can deal with post and telephones. D and F are on day-release courses on Tuesday and Wednesday respectively.   (RSA)

13 Explain fully a procedure for the handling of incoming office mail so that it is dealt with systematically and efficiently.   (RSA)

14 The senior executives of your firm have complained that the morning's mail is late in being delivered from the mail room to their offices, with a consequent delay in starting the day's business. The office manager

has asked you to investigate the present method of handling the incoming mail and to devise a more satisfactory system which will not only ensure that the correspondence is available for distribution before the senior executives arrive in the morning, but will also take into account the need for security in the handling of remittances. Write a memorandum to the office manager setting out the procedure you would recommend. (RSA)

15 You work for a manufacturing company and you are responsible for the incoming mail. In this morning's post you found (i) a letter from a skilled operator asking for a job in the factory, (ii) a credit note for returnable containers, (iii) a letter making a special offer of an exceptionally large discount on some raw materials used in your company's manufacturing processes, (iv) a cheque, accompanied by a remittance advice, in partial settlement of one of your customer's accounts.

(*a*) To which departments of your office will you direct these documents?
(*b*) What action will then be taken within those departments? (RSA)

16 Give *four* practical hints for junior clerks to help them in their duties of opening and sorting incoming mail in a large organization. You should bear in mind the importance of getting everything to the proper recipients as quickly as possible. (RSA)

17 What is e-mail? How is it used in offices?

8 The Post Department − mail outwards

8.1 Introduction

The post room is one of the most important departments in any firm, and one where many office juniors start their employment. It is an excellent point to begin work, for by spending some time in the post department the young clerical worker quickly learns the layout of the firm, its organization and staff, and the chains of responsibility in various departments.

In former times the postal services have been the chief means of communication between firms, and an enormous staff was at one time employed in the General Post Office to provide an efficient service. In Queen Victoria's time seven deliveries a day was not uncommon. Today the postal services are supplemented by the telephone, telex and fax systems, so that less emphasis is placed upon speed in the postal services. Two deliveries a day are usual; only one in some areas. Firms with urgent business to transact do it by telephone; the written documents which eventually travel by post merely confirm the oral agreements made on the telephone. Some years ago the Post Office in the United Kingdom ceased to be a government department, and began to operate as an independent corporation, **The Post Office Corporation**. Shortly after this the telephone service was separated off as a separate corporation, **British Telecom**, while other organizations were licensed to operate competitive telephone networks. The chief of these companies are **Mercury Communications** and **Vodophone**. Today the Post Office Corporation consists of three separate businesses, *Royal Mail*, *Parcelforce* and *Post Office Counters Ltd*.

8.2 Organization of the Post Department

The size of a firm dictates the organization of this department. In many firms a single individual called the **postal clerk** will handle all outwards postal transactions. Often it is convenient in such firms to make this person a **petty cashier** as well (see below).

In larger firms a more complex organization may be required, and some firms, such as **mail order houses**, even have complete post offices controlled and operated by the Post Office built into their premises to handle the enormous volume of mail outwards.

The following rules should apply to most 'mail outwards' departments:

(*a*) Good links should be established with all departmental managers to ensure that they lay down firm procedures about outgoing mail. The late despatch of 'emergency' correspondence at the very end of the day will thus be reduced to a minimum.

(*b*) Collection points and collection times should be clearly designated, and adhered to rigorously.

(*c*) Staff should be trained to mark in pencil in the top right-hand corner all special mail, i.e. airmail, foreign mail, recorded delivery and registered mail.

(*d*) First-class mail should be rubber-stamped 'First-class' in the **top left-hand corner**.

(*e*) Practices should be established for the recording of important letters as they are despatched, and for the checking of 'enclosures' by the clerk responsible for folding and sealing mail after signature.

(*f*) Franking machines should be used wherever possible, and procedures for recording the use of adhesive stamps established.

(*g*) Rules should be laid down to prevent the despatch of private correspondence at the expense of the firm.

(*h*) Establish procedures for recording and preserving receipts from the Post Office for registered letters, recorded delivery letters, COD packets and other parcels.

8.3 Mailguide

This is a loose-leaf reference book which is issued annually, and is supported by periodic up-dates of revised pages. The first year's revision pages are included in the purchase price. It contains full details of thirty-five services available to businesses, and explains how to obtain these services and how to use them. The chief points are:

- What special collection & delivery services are available for businesses? How, where and when do they operate?
- What are 1st and 2nd class services? How do they work? How much do they cost?
- What's the difference between recorded delivery, special delivery and registered post? How to choose and use the most cost-effective service for a particular business.
- How to prepare international mail, and how to choose the right service.
- What discounts are available for larger mailings? When does a business qualify for discounts?

- How direct mail — a powerful and cost-effective method of advertising — can work for a business. How it can target customers and bring in more business.
- What other specialist publications are available? Where to get help and further information.
- What to do if something goes wrong. Who to talk to, and how the Post Office can help sort out any problems.
- How to prepare post. Which envelopes and wrappings are recommended. What is a correct address? How to find an unknown postcode.
- Where to buy Royal Mail services. How to pay. What alternatives to stamps are available and which is best for a particular business.

A description of some of these services is given in Section 8.8 (p. 143)

8.4 Collecting mail outwards
Every firm must have an adequate system for posting outgoing mail and for avoiding sudden rushes of post that would overwhelm the staff. Points to be considered include the following:

(*a*) *Collection points.* A tray for outgoing mail should be placed in every department from which mail can be conveniently collected by a messenger and brought down to the Post Department for despatch. Regular times should be arranged for the collection — say at every even hour, 10 am, 12 noon, 2 pm, 4 pm, etc. This will not only spread the work of the post department over the working day, but will ensure more rapid handling by the postal authorities. Letters posted early in the day are cleared easily and quickly by the Post Office, but the great mass of post despatched in the early evening is inevitably subject to some delay. In particular, a final collection time should be laid down by which mail must be ready if it is to be handled by the Post Department that night.

(*b*) *Unusual mailings.* Many firms circularize their customers at regular intervals. Such mailings put the Post Department under pressure, but this can be avoided if the mailing can be arranged to fall at a time when routine postal activities are likely to be slight. Also much of the work can be avoided by using the **bulk mailing service** of the Corporation. Letters may be delivered in bulk to the Post Office, together with a cash payment for the total postage. At its convenience the Corporation will then frank the postage paid onto each envelope and despatch the letters.

(*c*) *Letters for signature.* When letters have been typed and are ready for signature they should be checked, signed and put into the departmental post tray at once. If staff delay doing this until late in the day, they will cause a pressure of work in the Post Department, which is unnecessary. The postal clerk is entitled to protest if a particular department offends regularly in this way.

8.5 The petty cash (imprest) system

In many small offices the postage clerk acts as a petty cashier. The word 'petty' means 'small' or 'minor'. A petty cashier is responsible for all sorts of cash payments e.g. the refund of bus fares to messengers. Since postal clerks must have sums of money available for stamps and other items, and must account for these expenditures, it is a simple matter for them to account as well for other small items. It saves the time of the chief cashier, who prefers not to be interrupted for trifling payments of this kind. A special type of system, the **imprest system**, is used to control the sums of money spent. Under this system the postal clerk is given a sum of money called the **imprest** or **float** for use in purchasing stamps, etc. Suppose an imprest of £100 was agreed as being sufficient for a week's activities. As money is spent, the petty cashier records it in a petty cash book. At the end of the week the book is totalled and presented for checking. After this the cashier '**restores the imprest**' — the money spent is replaced. The postage clerk thus starts the new week with a £100 imprest.

Figure 8.1 illustrates the imprest system. The notes explaining the keeping of the petty cash book have been set across the page for easier reading. Study this illustration now.

Petty cash vouchers A voucher is a document authorizing some expenditure. All petty-cash disbursements should be authorized by a petty cash voucher. The best voucher is one from outside the business, such as a bill for items purchased at the local stationers or a bus ticket showing an amount paid for a journey by a messenger. If the voucher is small, it is usual to clip it to a larger piece of paper for easy filing.

Where a voucher cannot be obtained from an outside body, it is usual to make out an internal petty cash voucher. This is made out by the person claiming the money, and authorized by his/her supervisor.

Petty cash vouchers are numbered PCV1, PCV2 etc and filed in a weekly or monthly package of vouchers. Figures 8.2 and 8.3 show external and internal petty cash vouchers.

8.6 The franking machine or postage meter

Postage stamps are easily stolen, difficult to identify, unhygienic to lick and difficult to handle in large quantities. Much better control and more efficient methods are made possible by the use of a **postage meter** or **franking machine**.

The rules for using these machines are as follows:

(*a*) The machine must be presented at a specified office for meter setting with the amount required, say £200, which is paid in advance. However, the latest machines can be reset electronically without any need to take the machine to the Post Office.

(*b*) Machines may be purchased, leased or rented from any one of a number of approved suppliers, who will arrange a demonstration and a training session for staff if required.

(*c*) Some machines can be linked to electronic scales for weighing and pricing postage automatically. A touch on a button will give a display showing alternative prices at first and second class levels. Machines can also be linked to automatic sealing and stamping machines.

(*d*) The date has to be set at the start of each day unless the machine does this automatically. Incorrectly dated mail may be subject to delay. The mail franked by the machine must be posted with all the letters facing the same way and secured in bundles with elastic bands. It should then be placed in appropriately coloured pouches as follows:

Red	1st class mail
Green	2nd class
White	International mail
Yellow	Local mail

It should then be posted at an agreed local post office, or a collection may be specially arranged for large mailings.

(*e*) Franked mail should be kept separate from stamped letters, as it does not need to be postmarked, and goes through the sorting office more quickly.

(*f*) The licensee must have the machine tested at least once a year by the manufacturer to ensure clear impressions on envelopes and packet labels, and accurate records of the postage paid.

Figure 8.4 shows an electronic postage meter mailing system (E 501). The caption notes bring out the advantages of the machine. Figure. 8.5 shows a high-speed version, the mail processor, capable of handling 12 000 items of postage per hour. Letters of all sizes and thicknesses can be moistened, sealed, imprinted with postage and postmarks, counted, recorded, printed with a personalized advertisement chosen by the user and stacked ready for despatch.

8.7 The postage book

In earlier days it was usual for a note to be made of every letter despatched, so that some proof was available that letters had actually been sent and accurate checks on postage could be maintained. Today this is not the usual practice: clerical labour is too expensive

Dr.	Date	Details	PCV	Total	Postage	Fares	Cleaning	Sundry expenses	Stationery	Folio	Ledger a/cs
	19..										
20.00	Mar. 25	To Imprest	CB9								
	25	By Stamps	1	1.50	1.50						
	26	" Postage	2	0.65	0.65						
	26	" Cleaning	3	0.45			0.45				
	27	" Sundries	4	0.32				0.32			
	27	" Fares	5	1.45		1.45					
0.30	28	To Telephone call	L3								
	28	By R. Jones	7	1.34						L19	1.34
	29	" Cleaning	8	0.65			0.65				
	29	" Sundries	9	0.40				0.40			
	29	" Travelling	10	1.65		1.65					
	30	" Envelopes	11	0.45					0.45		
	30	" Office equipment	12	1.65						L15	1.65
	30	" Sundries	13	0.15				0.15			
	31	" Totals	—	10.66	2.15	3.10	1.10	0.87	0.45		2.99
20.30	31	" Balance	c/d	9.64	L5	L11	L27	L36	L49		
				20.30							
9.64	Apr. 1	To Balance	b/d								
10.36	1	" Restored imprest	CB11								

Figure 8.1 The petty cash book

Notes

The following points will explain the operation of the Petty Cash imprest system, shown in Figure 8.1 above.

(*a*) The page is divided into two parts, debit and credit, but the 'centre' of the book is offset towards the extreme left of the page. This gives only a very small amount of debit side, while the credit side is expanded to make room for a series of analysis columns.

(*b*) The details are written on the credit side, since there is no 'details' column on the debit side.

(*c*) The chief source of cash received is the cashier, who provides the original imprest, but other small sums may be received from staff, for private telephone calls, etc. All receipts are debited (the rule in book-keeping is 'debit the receiver').

(*d*) On the credit side, money spent is first entered into the total column, but is then extended out into one of the analysis columns. This enables the total postage, fares, etc., to be collected together. A special column at the end is used to extend out any items which cannot be mixed with other items, e.g. the payment to R. Jones can be posted eventually only to R. Jones' account.

(*e*) At the end of the week, or when the imprest is nearly all used, the petty cashier rules off the page in such a way as to total the 'Total' column, and the analysis columns. These are then cross-totalled to ensure accuracy. The balance is found, the book is closed off and the balance is brought down.

(*f*) The cashier then checks the petty cashier's work and restores the imprest by providing enough cash to raise the balance to the original imprest figure.

(*g*) The book is now posted to the ledger accounts, using the totals of the analysis columns and the individual special items in the end column. Folio numbers are entered as shown. A folio number is a page number which cross-references to the books of account. Note that this is page 5 of the petty cash book (PCB5).

(*h*) Note that the money for private telephone calls is posted to the telephone a/c (L3 in the ledger), where it reduces the losses due to telephone expenses in the year.

(*i*) The petty cash vouchers, which authorize the payments made, are arranged in order, numbered and the PCV numbers are entered in the column provided. The vouchers are then filed away. The petty cashier is now ready for a further week's business.

White — Customer's copy
Buff — Store copy

Customer's
receipt for
cash purchase

(U.K.) V.A.T. Registration No. 232 5555 75
(R.I.) V.A.T. Registration No. 8/K/56287

Ref. No. 728149

Store address stamp

F. W. WOOLWORTH P.L.C.

19-24 Sidney Street
Cambridge OB2 3HI

Sales receipt   Date 14 July 19..

Qty.	Item Group like rated items together	Unit S.P.	V.A.T. %	Incl. V.A.T. £	p
6	100 Watt Light bulbs	75p		4	50
1	Candle Lamp	7·95		7	95
1	13 Amp plug	1·15		1	15

Received
with thanks   R.T.   Total £ 13 60

Complete this section only if requested by customer	Totals excl. V.A.T. £	p	V.A.T. %	Amount of V.A.T. £	p	Totals incl. V.A.T. £	p
			Zero				
Totals							

Customer's name   G. M. Whitehead

Address   2174 Camside
                     Cambridge

S.75 (V.A.T.) — 11/80

Figure 8.2   An external petty cash voucher

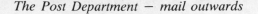

Petty Cash Voucher

Folio *PCV 27*

Date *15 May* 19..

For what required	AMOUNT £	p
Fares to Harlow	3	85
Jane to publisher	2	35
£	6	20

Signature *G. M. Jones*

Passed by *A. A. Kenningham*

Manager.

Figure 8.3   An internal petty cash voucher

and the volume of post is too great. There are, however, certain offices where it is essential to keep a record of at least some of the mail despatched — solicitors, for example, might keep a record of conveyances or other important documents despatched by post, and government offices dealing with passports would keep a record of such mail outwards. Very often this type of mail would be sent by **registered post** or **recorded delivery** and receipts would be obtained anyway. Figure 8.6 shows a typical ruling for a Postage Book.

8.8   Some Post Office services

The following special services, among others, are offered to the general public by the three businesses that make up the Post Office Corporation.

(*a*) *Registered post.* This is a first-class letter service offering the transmission of valuable items in return for a registration charge. It covers compensation up to various levels, reaching a maximum of £2 200 at the time of writing. Registered letters must be handed to an official of the Post Office, who will issue a certificate of posting that also acknowledges payment of the registration charge. Packages may also be registered, if posted at 'first-class' letter rate. Parcels are no longer accepted as registered mail, but on payment of an extra 'compensation fee' the Corporation will pay compensation up to a maximum limit of £250, at the time of writing. (See Figure 8.7).

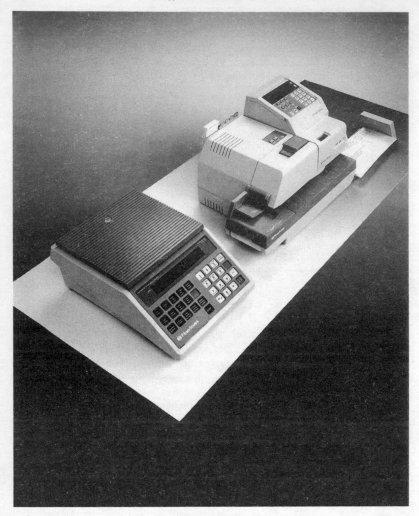

Figure 8.4 An E501 mailing system (courtesy of Pitney-Bowes Ltd)

Notes

(i) The machine operates automatically as soon as an envelope is placed on the scale and the keys for the service required are touched. This sets the postage meter.

(ii) The postage set on to the meter is automatically franked on the letter, and the charge is deducted to show the amount of postage still stored in the machine.

(iii) The letters franked by the machine do not have to be 'cancelled' like stamped letters, but go straight into the sorting office for despatch.

(iv) The machine prints gummed labels with the correct postage for use on parcels, packets and envelopes too large to be fitted into the machine.

(v) Advertisements and sender's address (for return if undelivered) can be printed on every franking, giving a very professional appearance to the mail.

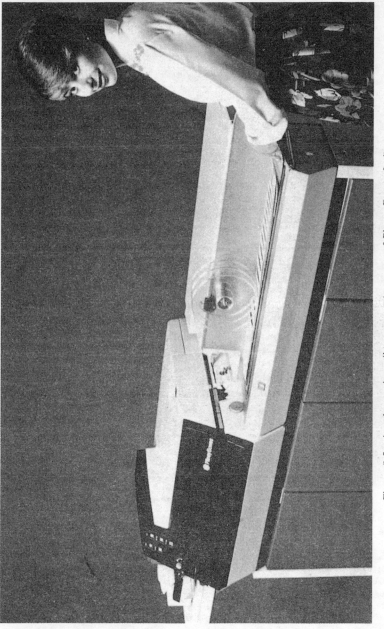

Figure 8.5 An electronic mail processor (courtesy of Pitney-Bowes Ltd)

Postage Book				Page 1
Date	Addressee	Address	Type of Enclosure	Postage value
19. April 4	T. Hill	7, Coombe Lane, Exeter	Conveyance for signature	64p
4	R. Jones	15, Hill Rise, Newtown	" " "	74p
5	M. Peters	21, Lodge Lane, Grays	" " "	64p
6	L. Long	17, Mill Rd, Buxton	Deposition	£2·05
6	R. Smart	34a, Lorings, Newtown	Conveyance for signature	£1·08
7	M. Smith	15, High St, Leamford	Will (duplicate copy)	£1·08

Figure 8.6   A postage book for important mail outwards

(*b*) *Recorded delivery*. This is a service designed to ensure safe delivery. Compensation is available only to a nominal amount (£24 at the time of writing). The Post Office issues a certificate of posting to the sender, and obtains a written acknowledgement of delivery from the addressee. This is useful in many circumstances, e.g. when legal documents, certificates of educational qualifications and other important papers are sent through the post. (See Figure 8.8.)

(*c*) *Special delivery*. This is a fast, reliable, guaranteed next-day delivery for first-class letters. Parcels may be sent if they pay first-class letter postage. It is the equivalent of a courier service at a very cheap rate (£1.95). Double the fee is refundable should the letter or package not be delivered next day. However the service is not available to some remote areas, where next day delivery cannot be achieved.

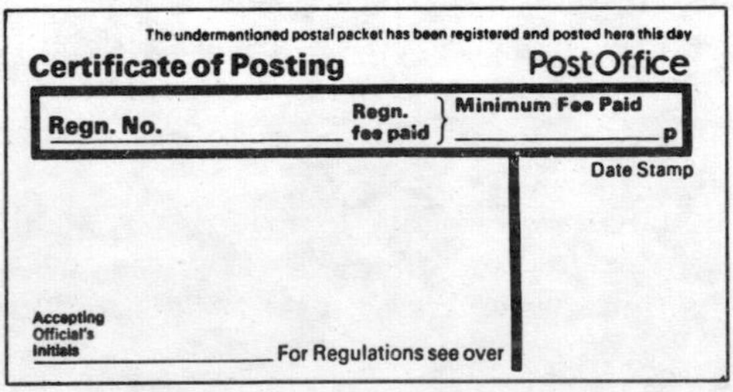

The undermentioned postal packet has been registered and posted here this day
Certificate of Posting   **Post Office**

Regn. No.	Regn. fee paid	Minimum Fee Paid p

Date Stamp

Accepting Official's Initials _____ For Regulations see over

Figure 8.7   A 'registered letter' receipt (reproduced by permission of the Post Office)

Certificate of Posting for Recorded Delivery

How to post

1 Enter below in ink the name and full address as written on the letter or packet.

2 Affix the numbered adhesive label in the top left-hand corner of the letter (or close to the address on a packet).

3 Affix postage stamps to the letter for the correct postage and Recorded Delivery fee.

4 Hand this certificate, together with the letter, to an officer of The Post Office.

5 This certificate will be date-stamped and initialled as a receipt. Please keep it safely, and produce it in the event of a claim.

Name

Address

Postcode

Recorded Delivery should not be used for sending money or valuable items.

For Post Office use

Accepting Officer's Initials

Date stamp

Recorded Delivery no

J 9598820

P2297 Nov 90

Figure 8.8   A 'recorded delivery' receipt (reproduced by permission of the Post Office)

(*d*) *International registration*. This service offers similar cover to inland recorded delivery. Letters are signed for at every stage of their journey and on final delivery to the addressee. However, this is not an insurance service. An *international insured service* is available to many countries, but not to all. The limit of cover, for a fee of £3.90 at present, is £1 500.

An international service called **Swiftair** is available for airmail letters to and from foreign countries. Swiftair packages receive accelerated attention during transit and accelerated delivery in the country of destination. Post Office services to exporters are described in the publication *Mailguide*.

(*e*) *Poste restante services*. The phrase 'poste restante' means 'remaining at the post office'. It is a useful service for travellers, and is limited in time. It may not be used for more than 3 months in any one town. Letters are addressed as follows:

> J. Green Esq.,
> Poste Restante,
> Post Office,
> Richmond,
> Surrey.

Instead of 'poste restante' the words 'To be called for' may be substituted. A person wishing to collect a 'poste restante' letter must be able to produce proof of identity. If the item is to be collected by someone else, he/she must produce a letter from the addressee and proof of both his/her and the addressee's identity.

(*f*) *Business reply service*. Under this service businesses which wish to obtain an answer from clients without putting the client to the expense of postage, may obtain a licence from the local head postmaster to enclose reply paid cards or leaflets in their correspondence with customers. A deposit is required of an estimated month's postage likely to be incurred under the scheme. The design of the card or leaflet proposed must be included with the application, and must conform to the specifications laid down in Mailguide. The licensee pays the postage, and a further charge of $\frac{1}{2}$p per card, as well as a licence fee of £55. This service is very popular with business houses seeking custom through postal and magazine advertisements.

(*g*) *Cash on delivery services*. This is a service of cash collection linked to registered mail. A trader who receives an order for goods valued up to £500 can send them as registered post COD (cash on delivery). The charge is small, less than £2 at the time of writing. The postman when delivering the package will not deliver it until the amount of the COD payment has been handed over to the addressee. If the amount of the 'trade charge' is £50 or less, the postman will take the money and deliver the package. If it is more than £50, the postman will not accept the money, but will merely advise the addressee that the package is available and will be released on payment of the sum due at the local Post Office or delivery office. In both cases the sum of money collected is banked in the Royal Mail account and a girocheque is sent to the trader in due course. If the packet is not claimed, it will be returned to the sender. If the addressee pays by cheque in a proper manner but the cheque is subsequently dishonoured, the Royal Mail reserves the right to turn to the trader for a refund of any money paid over to him/her.

(*h*) *Faxmail*. A fax (facsimile copier) will send messages on A4 pages over the ordinary telephone lines to a destination machine. It takes about 20 seconds. If an addressee does not have a fax machine, the faxmail system allows the message to be sent to a local faxmail office, from which it will be delivered in special envelopes (like a telegram). Delivery may be same day, or next day, as required. The service also operates around the world to some fifty countries. There is also a broadcast fax service, which lets the same message be sent to multiple destinations, e.g. for advertising purposes.

(*i*) *Electronic post.* This is a computerized system for sending personalized mail to selected contacts in a format that has been pre-registered with the Royal Mail's Electronic Mail Centre. Imagine that a company regularly offers holidays at its prestige hotels to groups of past customers. Each letter has to be addressed with the name and address of the customer and other personal details, e.g. the salutation might read 'Dear John' on one letter, 'Dear George' on another, and so on. These personal details are sent to the Electronic Mail Centre, where the Centre's computer merges the personal details with the standard text and sends off the mailing by first class post.

Conclusion on Royal Mail services. Clearly it is impossible to describe all the services of Royal Mail, Parcelforce and Post Office Counters Ltd. The publication *Mailguide* describes the Royal Mail services in great detail. Enquiries about it should be made to:

Royal Mail Mailguide,
FREEPOST KE 8421
76 Turnmill St,
London
EC1B 1ES

8.9 Bulk mailings — computerization of mailing activities

When a large mailing is being undertaken, e.g. an annual mailing of catalogues or a quarterly mailing of price lists, there are a number of ways the mailing can be handled:

(*a*) By an outside, specialist, mailing organization, which simply takes over the whole mailing, prepares suitable mailing material in consultation with the sales manager and does the whole thing. Naturally such a firm employs all the latest equipment; it is able to afford the best machines since it is doing such mailings all the time.

(*b*) By a specialist department within the firm, which handles such mailings with a small specialist team, helped out by other staff seconded to it for the purpose of the actual mailing period.

(*c*) As a spare-time activity carried out by the post department in odd moments. This is of course a cheaper way to do such mailing, but the work will take longer and the mailing is therefore not so well organized, some parts of the mail shot going out before the rest, as the work can be fitted in.

Today nearly all such mailings are computerized to some extent, though there are firms with old mechanical installations still in use. Names that were famous in their day, such as Addressograph, have now been superseded by such companies as Data Card UK Ltd, which specialize in computer-driven addressing systems.

Machines for large mailings

(*a*) *Direct impression printers.* These machines print addresses directly onto the envelopes or reply-paid cards from a computer memory bank of addresses, at speeds up to 10 000 addresses per hour. The blank mailing media is simply fed into the machine in stacks. Each item is then fed through the printer, automatically impressed with the address of an addressee, and carried away by a conveyer—stacker to form a stack of mailing material now ready for posting. Such a system avoids the need for costly pressure-sensitive labels, which then have to be applied to the envelope or other item to be mailed.

Take the very largest organization with, say, 8 million customers, sending a monthly mailing (say 20 working days in a month). It needs to send out 400 000 letters every day. Even at 10 000 items an hour that is 40 hours continuous production every day. Such machines need continuous attention as new stacks of envelopes are fed into them and the addressed envelopes are stacked at the exit point. A leading name in this field is Addressograph & Farrington Ltd of Feltham, Middlesex, now part of Data Card UK Ltd. Drawing up data banks of addresses is an important part of such mailings. The entries should be proof-read to ensure correct initials, house numbers, postal codes, etc. There will then be no possibility of transcribing mistakes, mis-spelled names to offend customers or transposed street addresses to misdirect cheques, invoices, etc. Once the plate is perfectly prepared every mailing from it will be perfect.

(*b*) *The folding machine.* The impact made on the customer by a leaflet or other document may depend upon the folding of the document. Figure 8.9 shows eight possible folds which can be made by a typical folding machine. The folding of leaflets, etc., is a time-consuming activity, disliked by staff who are sometimes loaned to the post department from their ordinary duties to help with a mailing. The folding machine, with a single operator, can fold between 5 000 and 12 000 sheets per hour, giving clean, accurate folds, never taking more than one sheet or skipping a sheet, and eliminating the need for overtime payments in busy periods.

(*c*) *The collating-inserting-sealing-mailing machine.* This machine, with a single operator, can do the work of many people. It will collate (arrange several sheets in order, neatly, for insertion into the envelopes), insert, seal, stamp, count and stack ready for posting as many as 7 500 envelopes per hour.

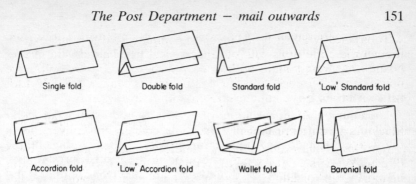

Figure 8.9 Folds made by a folding machine (courtesy of Pitney Bowes Ltd)

(*d*) *The mail tying machine*. These machines will tie packages of any size or shape in a few seconds. They are particularly useful for mail order houses and for individuals such as nurserymen who send trees and plants by post at certain times of the year.

(*e*) *Automatic labellers*. An automatic labeller is a machine that transfers labels that have been printed with the addressee's address on to the mailing medium, whatever it may be. Widely used in the mailing of magazines, it can achieve speeds of up to 10 000 labels per hour; it is computer-controlled and counts electronically the number of items prepared for mailing.

(*f*) *Card embossing and encoding*. Although not strictly a mailing device the ability to emboss and encode label sized cards is an important development from ordinary labelling. Widely used in the security, banking, medical and hotel fields, the 'credit card' is ideal for many situations not related to credit. For example, these cards are widely used as proofs of membership by social clubs, sports centres and motoring organizations. They are used as identity cards for access to places of employment, industrial sites and other secure areas, e.g. airports subject to 'terrorist' restrictions. They can have magnetic strips like bank credit cards, and when wiped through a 'magnetic swipe reader', can tell security gate staff who the bearer is, who he/she works for, etc. They can have photos implanted into them, and some 'smart cards' have a wafer-thin microcomputer inserted into them with basic data about the bearer. Some wafer-thin cards have electronic calculator chips inserted into them also and, with solar panels to provide free electricity, give a card-sized calculator for everyday use.

One machine, made by Data Card (UK) Ltd, is capable of creating cards instantly and on site, without reference to any central bureau, and the data stored on the microcomputer chip embodied in it can be up-dated as and when required, as people change jobs or sites.

The electronic screen display gives clear prompts to the user, and consequently staff can be trained to issue cards in about 2 hours only.

8.10 Address lists

A large number of organizations offer 'lists' of addresses in particular fields, e.g. one offers lists of all the schools, colleges and Universities in the United Kingdom. Another might offer lists covering all the industrial firms, or all the publishers, or all the dentists. Today such lists are usually computerized, and they are sold (for use once only) at reasonable prices, say between £20 and £100 per 1 000 addresses. Some houses, known as 'fulfilment houses' do huge mailings of between 250 000 to 1 000 000 addresses for anyone requiring this type of mailing.

8.11 Points to think about and discuss

(*a*) Office juniors working in the mail inwards and outwards section are complaining that they have to arrive earlier than other staff and invariably leave later. They also complain that the last hour of their working day is so exhausting that they are quite unable to enjoy the evening even when they do finally get away. What improvements could be made to meet these objections?

(*b*) A firm with an address-list of 15 000 customers is introducing two new models of its most important machines. At the same time it is diversifying into a related field, producing a range of equipment likely to appeal to about two-thirds of the firms only. Leaflets cost 1p each to produce and postage will be 24p per letter. Would you recommend:

  (i) Sending all three leaflets to all the firms?
 (ii) Sending separate mailings, the leaflets about the new models going to all firms and the leaflets about the new range of equipment going under separate cover to the 10 000 firms likely to be interested?
(iii) Some other scheme?

Give your reasons.

(*c*) A burglary during the night has meant that the cash in the petty cash till and the postage stamps have been stolen. It is proposed to claim from the insurance company for these losses, and also for the cost of repairs by a carpenter, a locksmith and a glazier. How would you set about discovering the correct sum to be claimed?

8.12   Rapid revision — mail outwards

Cover the page with a sheet of paper and uncover one question at a time.

Answers		Questions	
	–	1	What organization conducts the postal services in the United Kingdom?
1	The Royal Mail, which is part of the Post Office Corporation.	2	Which reference book describes the services offered.
2	*Mailguide*	3	Outline a suitable system for dealing with mail outwards in a large organization.
3	(*a*) Arrange suitable collection points in the departments, (*b*) fix the last time for collection from these post trays, (*c*) lay down rules to arrange an even despatch of mail throughout the day, (*d*) lay down rules for marking letters with the service required (first-class; recorded delivery, etc.), (*e*) collect and despatch mail at regular intervals.	4	What is a postage meter?
4	A meter that automatically franks letters with the required postage, so that stamps are unnecessary.	5	How does the Post Office control the use of postage meters?
5	It requires them to be presented at post offices for resetting (or they may be reset electronically). They must be serviced annually.	6	What system is used for petty cash?
6	The imprest system.	7	What is an imprest?
7	A sum of money set aside for a particular purpose.	8	What are the advantages of the imprest system?
8	(*a*) It saves bothering the main cashier, (*b*) little risk, and little temptation, (*c*) it trains young staff, (*d*) it saves time on posting to the ledger because of the analysis columns, (*e*) it is easily checked.	9	Where is the 'middle' of a page in a petty cash book?
9	Set towards the left-hand side of the page.	10	Why is this done?
10	Because the petty cashier does not often receive money.	11	When is money received?
11	(*a*) When the imprest is drawn from the cashier, (*b*) when members of staff pay for telephone calls, etc.	12	Why does the credit side need more room than in an ordinary cash book?

12 Because there are extra analysis columns.	13 What is the point of these analysis columns?
13 To collect together similar minor expenses and to make it possible to post the total· each week to the ledger with only one posting per column.	14 Go over the page again until you feel you are sure of the answers.

Exercises set 8

1 Copy out the sentences given below, and complete them by using an appropriate word or phrase from the word list.

(*a*) The postal services are provided by an organization called ......

(*b*) Postal deliveries are less frequent today than in earlier times because other means of ...... are available.

(*c*) The postal clerk in many firms also acts as the ...... disbursing small sums of money as required.

(*d*) The most important reference book for a postal clerk is ......

(*e*) A ...... is a machine which prints the postage paid on to letters, so that they need not be stamped.

(*f*) To prevent excessive work in the post department late ·in the day, departmental managers should read and ...... letters for despatch as they are typed throughout the day.

(*g*) A ...... is used to record important outgoing letters.

(*h*) Letters which are sent by the ...... service travel through the mail system in the usual way but are delivered by special messenger if they arrive at the destination office after the usual mail delivery has taken place.

(*i*) The business reply service is one where the ...... is prepared to pay whatever postage is due when he receives the letter.

(*j*) A ...... is a machine which arranges papers or leaflets in order for despatch by post, or in readiness for a meeting.

Word list: communication, sign, postage book, *Mailguide*, special delivery, addressee, The Post Office Corporation, petty cashier, collator, franking machine.

2 In each of the following select the best answer (*a*), (*b*), (*c*), or (*d*) to the question.

(i) A poste restante letter (*a*) is one addressed to the local head postmaster, (*b*) is one addressed to a post office for collection by a genuine traveller, (*c*) is one delivered to a letterbox mounted on a post at the end of a long drive, (*d*) is·a type of express delivery?

(ii) A service by which a letter is sent out to the addressee by Post Office messenger if it has missed the daily delivery is called (*a*) 'express all the way', (*b*) express at the request of the addressee, (*c*) special delivery, (*d*) Swiftair.

(iii) An addresser−printer is (*a*) a Post Office employee who rewrites badly written envelopes to save unnecessary delay, (*b*) a printer who specializes in mailing systems for other firms, (c) a machine for printing envelopes from a computerized address data bank, (d) a machine for filing, stamping and despatching bulk mailing?

(iv) A posting list is (a) a list of registered envelopes to be sent off at the same time, presented to the Post Office counter clerk for signature. (b) a list of staff transfers to other departments, (c) an extract from *Mailguide* listing postal charges to foreign countries, (d) a disability suffered by postmen as a result of carrying heavy sacks of mail?

3 What are the advantages gained by the use of 'postal franking' over the use of postage stamps?

4 Outline procedures for the efficient handling of outgoing mail in a large organization. What equipment would be useful and what records should be kept?

5 Write about five to eight lines on any *three* of the following. Refer to *Mailguide* if necessary.
(a) postal franking, (b) special delivery, (c) how to address an envelope, (d) postage books, (e) recorded delivery, (f) registered parcels.

6 Draw up a list of instructions for a junior member of staff with respect to (a) collection of mail outwards from departments, (b) duties as a messenger with respect to registered letters, recorded delivery letters and parcel post. *Use such imaginary names of individuals and departments as will make the instructions sensible.*

7 What points would you pay particular attention to in preparing addresses to be stored in a computerized data bank.

8 What mechanical aids are available to make the stamping and despatch of mail outwards more efficient?

9 In what circumstances would you despatch a letter by 'recorded delivery' rather than ordinary post? Describe the 'recorded delivery' service.

10 Your firm proposes to mail 24 000 customers with a special leaflet about a new product. Describe stage by stage the procedure you would use in such a mailing, referring to any machines that would be helpful. You may assume that such mailings are made regularly by your firm.

11 Describe briefly the Post Office services you would use in each of the following instances: (a) to enable customers in this country to reply to you without having to pay postage, (b) to enable customers abroad to reply to you without having to pay postage, (c) to collect money from customers in mail order transactions, (d) to send a legal document in which proof of delivery may be required in a court of law, (e) to ensure that a faxed letter to Nigeria reaches an addressee who has no fax machine, (f) to obtain correspondence in advance of the normal time of delivery. Refer to the publication *Mailguide* if available. Give reasons for your answers.

12 You are employed in the mailing department of a large organization. Name three machines which would simplify and speed up the handling

of incoming and outgoing mail. Describe these machines and their functions.

13 Rule up a petty cash book with analysis columns, and enter the following items:

19..

		£
March 2	Balance in hand	2.56
	Received from cashier	77.44
	Bought stamps	23.60
3	Postage on parcel	4.25
	Bus fares	1.36
	String and gum	2.45
4	Bought pencils	2.36
	Surcharge on letters	1.18
	Tea and milk for office teas	4.55

Balance the book on 5 March.

14 From the information in the following petty cash book (which is kept on the imprest system) answer the questions given below.

Dr   Cr

Cash Received £	Date 19..	Details	Totals £	Postages and faxes £	Carriage £	Stationery £
4.61	Jan. 1	Balance				
95.39	2	Imprest				
	3	Postage	4.10	4.10		
	5	Stationery	23.41			23.41
		Carriage	12.45		12.45	
	6	Postage	14.25	14.25		
	7	Fax	6.45	6.45		
		Carriage	11.55		11.55	
	8	Stationery	15.18			15.18

(*a*) What is the amount of the petty cash float? (*b*) What was the balance of petty cash on the first day of the year? (*c*) How much was spent in postage and telegrams during the period? (*d*) How much was spent in stationery during the period? (*e*) What was the total amount spent during the period? (*f*) How much must the petty cashier receive at the end of the period to make up the float?

15 (*a*) Whose signature(s) will appear on an internal petty cash voucher? (*b*) What is an 'external' petty cash voucher? (*c*) What is a 'float'? (*d*) What is the imprest system of petty cash?

16 You are responsible for writing up the petty cash book in your office. The three analysis columns are headed 'Office expenses', 'Postage and stationery', and 'Cleaning'.

(*a*) State under which heading you would enter the following payments: refills for ballpoint pens; laundering of towels; erasers; tea, milk and sugar; stamps; tip for a van driver; a roll of Sellotape; magazines for the waiting room; dishcloths; airmail letter forms. (*b*) What do you understand by analysis columns? (*c*) Explain fully the uses of the petty cash book.

9 Stationery and stock

9.1 Stationery

The term 'stationery' implies office supplies of every sort. Without an adequate supply of letterhead, plain paper, envelopes, documents such as invoices and credit notes, and many other forms for special purposes it is impossible to run an efficient office. We also need such items as paper clips, pins, rubber stamps, sellotape, wrapping paper, labels, string and sealing wax. While such items seem very obvious requirements in any office, every one of them poses special problems. For instance, the firm's letterhead requires careful planning. It must state the name of the firm, its address, telephone number, fax number, and many other details. It must comply with the requirements of the Company Acts if the firm is a limited company, or with the Business Names Act, 1985 if the firm is a small organization run by a sole trader or partners. We must hold adequate stocks of these stationery items so that we do not run out of any particular item. We must have a system of *requisitions* so that staff needing supplies can put in a request for them. We must have secure control of stocks, so that they are not misused.

Control of stationery is exercised at different levels. At the top level we must have an official, often the general administration officer, who supervises the availability of such items as letterhead, invoices, credit notes, debit notes, order forms and any other specialist forms carrying the firm's name, address and other details. All such documents can be used to establish contractual relations with other firms. They may need to comply with international arrangements made at the United Nations or within the European Community. They may need to comply with Inland Revenue or HM Customs requirements. Clearly this is quite high-level work − not at all the sort of thing that an office junior could arrange. Printers must be consulted and quite heavy costs are incurred.

At a lower level there may be stationery items that are used internally. Many of these will be designed by heads of departments, but again they may need to call in expert help. For example, some factories use computerized job cards and progress cards to travel round the factory with various components as they move from workshop to workshop. A computer consultant may advise about their design.

Finally, at a more routine level, where the correctly designed letterheads and forms have been printed and supplied in bulk, someone must take charge of them and supply them to staff who need them. This sort of responsibility can be undertaken by a junior employee who has proved his/her reliability, and who has a reasonable understanding of the firm or company. A routine is established, e.g. stock may be requisitioned on Mondays and will be made available on Tuesdays. There will always be times when it is necessary to bother the stationery clerk for emergency supplies, but the idea is to set up a system that covers 99 per cent of the office's needs, and only requires emergency distributions of supplies at rare intervals.

9.2 Letterhead

A firm's letterhead is a very important piece of stationery, and it is worthwhile at this point drawing the reader's attention to some important features of any letterhead. First, a letter is an important item because it almost always plays some part in a contractual relationship between firms. It therefore has legal force, and may be produced in court as evidence of statements made in the course of discussions leading up to the contractual arrangements made. Even if there is no contract to be concerned about, a letter may come into court for other reasons, e.g. if it shows a failure to show due care. We owe everyone around us a duty of care in many ways. This legal use of letters means that we must know who is writing the letter, and the name and address of the firm concerned must be printed on the letterhead, with other useful details. We may list the most important points of a good letterhead as follows:

(*a*) The name of the individual, the partners, or the company, and if it is a company the name must end in the word 'Limited' or Public Limited Company (PLC) or the Welsh equivalents. If the name of the firm is a made-up name (such as 'Beautiful Gardens'), the names of the proprietor (or proprietors) must be stated in the following form:

Beautiful Gardens
   Props: Donald and Ann Greenfingers

(*b*) The address, postcode, telephone number (including the code) and if it applies any fax number or telex number. The telephone number may also show an extension number.

(*c*) An indication of where the date might go, e.g. Date: ......

(*d*) An indication of the references for filing purposes, both in the firm itself and in the addressee's firm, is useful. For example, it may read:

Our Ref: JT/AK
Your Ref: BG/MN 5 Oct 19. .

The author of the letter is JT, the secretary is AK and the letter is a reply to one sent on the 5 October by BG and typed by secretary MN.

(*e*) If it is a company, the European Communities Act requires the letterhead to show the registered number of the company and its place of registration. It must also show the address of the registered office (not always the same as the address on the letterhead) and the amount of the paid-up capital.

(*f*) The Companies Act requires the names of the directors of a company to be shown, and this must include their first names. The titles of peers of the realm must be shown.

A collection of letterheads

One of the best ways to learn about letterheads is to make a collection of letters from various firms. A classful of students each contributing one or two letters from parental and other sources can quickly provide a variety of letterheads for appraisal. Consider them from the point of view of the list of features given above, and also from the aesthetic viewpoint. Are they attractively laid out? Is the print style clear?

Security of letterheads

It is very important to keep close control over letterheads. Since letterhead has legal implications, we do not want copies of our letterhead falling into the hands of people who might misuse them. In large organizations quite a few people may have the right to use letterhead, and if two or three of them are careless about the availability of it, unauthorized users may easily obtain it. Never be slack about letterhead – keep it secure at all times.

9.3   Stock records

In this chapter we are concerned with stationery and stock, but stocks can be of many kinds, and the principles discussed here with reference to stationery can also apply to all other kinds of stock. We obtain stocks either by purchasing them or by making them out of raw materials purchased earlier. Thus we may purchase letterhead from a printer, but we may purchase plain paper and print up in-house the various forms we require for factory, warehouse and office use. Some stocks are of **finished goods**, which have been manufactured for resale. Others are **stock-in-trade**, which means goods purchased for resale. Then there are **raw material stocks** and **components**, waiting to be manufactured; **spare parts** purchased in anticipation of the breakdown of plant, machinery and motor vehicles; and **consumable stocks** of such items as stationery, to be used in the course of business. All these items require supervision, for if stocks are exhausted the activities which depend upon them will come to a halt. Thus the factory must not be deprived of raw materials or components needed for manufacture or assembly, shop counters must be refilled with stock as soon as the customers empty them, lorries must not be kept idle for lack of spare parts and packs of invoices and other documents must be ready for office staff to complete their day-to-day activities.

The following considerations enter into the keeping of stock records for a simple part of the stocks, such as the stationery stocks.

(*a*) What is it that we need?
(*b*) How much of a particular item is required, week by week, to keep us operating efficiently?
(*c*) What is the minimum stock?
(*d*) What is the best re-order quantity?

We must consider each of these in turn.

(*a*) *What is it that we need?* The stationery clerk must keep an open mind about the stocks that are needed. If a new member of staff wants a particular type of book or form or piece of equipment, it should be considered and ordered if necessary. Nothing is more frustrating to a reasonable member of staff than to be refused the use of a vital item because 'Well, we've never used them before'. Sometimes a new machine, say a fax machine, calls for a special type of paper, and clearly it must be added to our list of requirements and ordered. The usual procedure is that staff are allowed to put in requisitions for the stock they need on a particular day each week. Routine items will be supplied from stock next day. Unusual items will be ordered, and in due course will arrive and be supplied to the person who requested them.

(*b*) *How much is required?* We need to have some idea of what the normal requirement for a particular item is. Thus a plain-paper copying machine may use 6 reams of paper in an average week. There are 500 pages in a ream (strictly speaking 480 pages, but reams are always made up in packs of 500). This machine will therefore be recording about 3 000 copies run off each week. If we ordered 6 reams every week, this would mean placing a small order each week, and the consequent ordering costs and delivery costs would probably make the order uneconomic. We have to strike a balance between having too large a stock (which ties-up capital in unused stocks) and placing too many small orders (which do not attract the discounts that larger orders can command).

(*c*) *What is the minimum stock?* There are two ideas here. How long does it take for an order from our suppliers to arrive? Suppose it is 3 weeks. If we know what our average requirement is for a week, then the minimum stock is three times that figure. For the plain-paper copiers, mentioned above, needing 6 reams a week, the minimum stock is 18 reams. Our stationery clerk must not let the stock of paper fall below 18 reams. Sometimes a special notice is made out to mark the minimum stock level — or a little bit higher. It might read 're-order now', and when the quantity left reaches the re-order point, the stationery clerk asks the purchasing department to place an order for a further supply.

(*d*) *What is the optimum re-order quantity?* The optimum means 'the best possible'. When we re-order an item, we want to avoid buying too much (because excessive stocks tie-up our capital, which might be better employed elsewhere). At the same time we can often get 'quantity discounts' by placing a larger order. Although it is the work of the purchasing department to negotiate the terms of supply with all suppliers, the stationery clerk will usually be told what is the best re-order quantity, and when stocks fall to the re-order point, will requisition that quantity to replenish the stock cupboard.

9.4　Stock requisitions

The simplest type of stock requisition is an in-house form, drawn up by the general administration officer, or more likely by the store-keeper concerned under instructions from the general administration officer. The whole idea is to establish a routine procedure, which should be made clear on the form, and have copies available at some convenient spot where those needing supplies can obtain a blank form for submission to the storekeeper. Alternatively the person concerned, say the stationery clerk, may distribute copies of the form on the day requisitions may be submitted.

Where a firm has some sort of in-house printing, the form will be passed to the printing department once its design has been finalized, and a batch will be run off. Where there is no such department, a number of forms will be run off on a plain-paper copier. It would be economical to type up the form several times on an A4 sheet, and thus obtain, say, four copies off each A4 sheet of paper. Figure 9.1 shows a typical layout for a stationery requisition.

9.5　Stock control cards

We have said that the possession of any stocks means that capital has been expended on buying them, and consequently every effort should be made to keep stocks as low as is possible, without running the risk of being 'out of stock' and thus delaying the operations of the company. Stocks are also pilferable. It is a great temptation to staff to take small quantities of stock home — paper is always useful, for example, in any family, as are envelopes, pencils and almost every other type of office stationery. It follows that reasonable

Stationery requisition: Please submit
your requests on Mondays to Helen Boalck.
Supplies will be distributed on Tuesday afternoon.

Item	Qty	Item	Qty
Letterhead A4		Ballpoints (black)	
Letterhead A5		Ballpoints (blue)	
Bond A4		Pencils	
Bank A4		Erasers	
Bank A5		Paper clips	
Envelopes white A4		Tippex	
Envelopes manilla A4		**Other items**	
Envelopes brown 9 × 5			
Envelopes small white			
Adding machine rolls			
Fax rolls			
White copier paper		Name...........................	
Shorthand books		Dept	

Figure 9.1   A stationery requisition

control has to be exercised over stocks of every type, and managers
and supervisors must be quick to detect minor thefts before they
prove habit-forming. Theft of any sort is punishable by dismissal,
and although dismissal for a first offence might be held to be unfair,
it would certainly be applied for a second offence.

Leaving such considerations aside, there are two reasons why
some sort of stock control procedure is essential. First we need to
know what stocks we have available, when they are likely to reach
re-order level, and how much to order when they do reach danger
point. Secondly, at the end of every year we need to know the value
of the stock in hand so that we can work out the profits for the year.
This is referred to more fully in the notes to Figure 9.2. Today
many stock records are kept by electronic methods, which are
referred to below, but the traditional methods are still widely used.
They depend largely on the use of some kind of stock control card.

Stock control cards may be kept in a card index system. Sometimes it
is more convenient to have the stock card actually kept in the
container used to store the parts of which it is a record. For

STOCK CONTROL CARD : FIFO

Location ..Miss. Peacock's. Store..........
Code number ..S.124/CIMD..........
Description ...A4: Letterhead..........

Unit ..Reams..........
Delivery time ...2. weeks..........
Re-order level ...30. reams..........

Re-order quantity .50. reams.
Maximum stock ..80. reams..
Minimum stock ..20. reams....

Receipts					Issues					Balance		
Date	Supplier	Quantity	Price £	Value £	Date	Req. No.	Quantity	Price £	Value £	Quantity	Price £	Value £
19 --					19 --					32	2-20	70-40
8 Jan	Quick-Print Ltd	50	2-20	110						82	"	180-40
					9 Jan	74	8	2-20	17-60	74	"	162-80
					16 "	89	9	2-20	19-80	65	"	143-00
					23 "	112	12	2-20	26-40	53	"	116-60
					30 "	115	30	2-20	66-00	23	"	50-60
3 Feb	Quick-Print Ltd	50	2-40	120						73	Mixed	170-60
					4 Feb	123	3	2-20	6-60	70	"	164-00

Figure 9.2 A 'running-balance' stock control card

example, small components are often kept in bins, and the 'bin card' is either kept with the parts or used as a label for the bin, in a small mounting on the outside. When a part is required for use, its removal from the bin is recorded on the bin card. A typical stock card is shown in Figure 9.2. The reader will note that a running balance total at the edge of the card keeps an up-to-date record of the stock in hand. 'Spot' checks held by the internal audit department will reveal whether any stock is missing from the bin or compartment where it is usually stored.

The running balance in Figure 9.2 is seventy items (in this case reams of A4 letterhead). The value is also shown: £164.00. Study Figure 9.2 now, noting how fresh stocks were received from the supplier, consequently increasing the stocks in hand, while the issue of stocks to those requiring them reduces the stocks available. Note that on 30 Jan thirty reams were issued (15 000 sheets of letterhead). Clearly some major mailing was done in the early part of February.

9.6 Computerized stock controls

We have all been into shops where the goods we buy are priced by a computer, which reads a bar code to tell us what the item is and how much it costs. It also finds the stock record for that particular item and reduces the balance in hand by one unit. Of course the

---

Notes

(*a*) The card is largely self-explanatory, but the word 'mixed' in the price column of the running balance needs to be explained.

(*b*) The seventy items in stock on 4 February were purchased at different prices: 50 reams have just been purchased at £2.40 per ream, but 20 reams of old stock were purchased at £2.20.

(*c*) There are three ways of valuing stock, FIFO, AVCO and LIFO. We don't need to go into this too deeply, but FIFO means First-In, First-Out. Our card is a FIFO card. So the next time we issue stock we shall use up the old stock (priced at £2.20) first and eventually we shall use it all up and only the £2.40 stock will be left.

(*d*) AVCO means 'average cost' and this means we find the average value of the 70 reams. This works out to £2.3429 per ream − a rather awkward figure.

(*e*) LIFO means Last in, First Out, which is a system where we issue stock (whenever we bought it) at the latest price we had to pay.

(*f*) Whichever system is adopted produces slight differences in the costing of jobs, processes, etc., and also a slight difference in the profit calculations at the end of the financial year. When working out the profits, we need to find the cost of stock sold and take it away from the selling price (the total sales for the year). To work out the cost of stocks sold, we need to do a 'stocktaking', in which we count the stocks in hand, i.e. the unsold stock, and value it at a fair price. This is called the **annual inventory**. The rule is to value it at cost price, or lower if it has depreciated while in stock and is now worth less than cost. Stocktaking can be a tedious process, but by using our stock control cards, or even better, a computerized system (see below), we can reduce the work to some extent.

stock record is not kept on a stock control card but in the computer's memory. In the fraction of a second after the sensing device has read the bar code the computer searches its memory for the stock record and records the sale of the unit of stock. If this reduces the stock level to the re-order point, the computer will print out an order for a new batch of stock, i.e. the re-order quantity, which is also stored in its memory. Clearly this gives a very efficient control over stocks.

The stocktaking can be simplified with a well-programmed stock control system, and the value of closing stock can be found at any time. Such a system is often called a **perpetual inventory system**.

The same procedure can be followed in an ordinary office if the computer system is a network. A network is a system where every department has a terminal linked to a central, host, computer. The stationery clerk has only to go to the terminal and key in the stock issued today to various members of staff. The host computer will reduce the stocks on the various control records, and if any of them have reached re-order point, it will print out an order for the re-order quantity.

9.7 Points to think about and discuss

(*a*) Peter's car is stopped at a barrier as he leaves the staff car park. It is found to contain 200 sheets of A4 white paper and a printing calculator from his office. It also contains two files of Peter's current work. Peter claims he is taking work home because he is unable to get everything done in office time. What action should the chief administration officer take on the gateman's report next day?

(*b*) The examination of stock records reveals that plain paper for the photocopier is being used at twice the rate of last year, and the actual copies printed as counted by the machine are about $1\frac{1}{2}$ times as great. You are asked as stationery clerk to investigate the matter and make a report about it. What points would you investigate to get at the facts?

9.8 Rapid revision − stationery and stock

Cover the page with a sheet of paper and uncover one question at a time.

Answers		Questions
−	1	What is stock?
1 Reserves of goods of various sorts.	2	How is stock obtained?

2 By purchasing or manufacturing the items.

3 What problems arise whenever stocks are held?

3 (*a*) Security problems – most stocks are pilferable, and attractive to thieves;
(*b*) storage problems – stocks may be perishable, or liable to deteriorate under the influence of temperature, humidity, insect pests, microbes, etc.;
(*c*) financial problems – stocks represent capital tied up unproductively.

4 What is a maximum stock?

4 The largest stock that may be held of a particular item. It sets the upper limit for any orders.

5 What is a minimum stock?

5 It is the lowest level to which stock must be allowed to fall before re-ordering.

6 What determines the minimum stock level?

6 (*a*) The time for delivery, between ordering and receiving the goods, (*b*) the average consumption of that item in the delivery period.

7 What is the 'optimum order size'?

7 It is the best size of order to place, so that the best quantity discount possible is obtained, without tying up excessive capital.

8 How is stock usually made available to staff?

8 Against a stock requisition form, completed by the member of staff, and according to a set procedure.

9 What is a stock control card?

9 A card dealing with a particular type of stock, recording the amounts received from suppliers and the amounts issued to staff.

10 What is electronic stock control?

10 It is a computerized system of stock control in which stock records are adjusted electronically as goods are sold, or issued, and as further stocks arrive from suppliers.

11 How are stock movements notified to the computer under this system?

11 A bar code reader reads the bar code and enters it into the computer in machine-readable form.

12 Go over the page again until you are sure of all the answers

Exercises set 9

1 Copy out the following sentences filling in the gaps with a word or phrase from the list below:

(*a*) A form for requesting a supply of office stationery is a ......
(*b*) Most stationery clerks ...... stationery on a set day in each week.

(*c*) It is a waste of ...... to keep larger stocks than are necessary.

(*d*) When stocks are in danger of running-out we re-order the ......

(*e*) What decides when we should place a further order for an item is the ...... specified on the stock control card.

(*f*) At the end of the financial year we must ...... the stock before we can work out the profits of the business.

(*g*) A ...... detects the code of each item sold at a check-out in a supermarket.

(*h*) A stock ...... keeps a record of arrivals and issues of stock.

(*i*) At any moment the stock control card should show a ...... of stock in hand.

(*j*) The stock of any item should never be allowed to fall below the ...... shown on the stock control card.

Word list: distribute, optimum re-order quantity, value, control card, requisition, running balance, capital, bar code reader, re-order point, minimum stock level.

2 You are responsible for the ordering and issuing of stationery in your department. What precautions would you take to ensure (*a*) that you do not keep too large a stock, (*b*) that the stock does not run out? Give a sample of a ruling for a stationery stock card.

3 What is meant by (*a*) minimum stock level, (*b*) maximum stock level, (*c*) re-order point, (*d*) optimum order size?

4 (*a*) Rule up a stationery stock record card for A4 typewriting paper and make the following entries:

Maximum stock   Minimum stock   Optimum re-order quantity
60 reams   20 reams   40 reams

1.3.19.. Balance in stock: 45 reams at £2 per ream.
8.3.19.. Issued 10 reams to sales department.
10.3.19.. Issued 18 reams to typing pool.
22.3.19.. Bought 40 reams from L.P. Stevens & Co. Ltd at £2.10.
1.4.19.. Issued 8 reams to buying department.
12.4.19.. Issued 10 reams to typing pool.
23.4.19.. Issued 10 reams to works department.

(*b*) Explain the importance of the maximum and minimum figures in connection with stocktaking. (*c*) What do you understand by (i) a ream, (ii) A4?

5 (*a*) What is letterhead? (*b*) Explain the advantages of letterhead over plain paper. (*c*) Why is it necessary to keep letterhead secure?

6 On 1 April 19.. the central stores of G. Smith & Co. Ltd, High Street, Welbridge, had 48 reams of A4 lined paper in stock. During April the following issues were made. The re-order point is 30 reams and the optimum re-order quantity is 60 reams.

5 April Sales Department   10 reams
7 April Planning department   6 reams

  9 April Publicity department   8 reams
15 April Accounts department 10 reams
26 April General office   8 reams

The maximum stock level is 100 reams and the minimum stock level is 25 reams. On an appropriate date an order for a further supply was placed with G. Roberts Ltd, 15 Low Road, Welbridge, and this supply was received 5 days later.

(*a*) Enter all the above details in a stationery stock record card ruled up for the purpose, invent your own document numbers, inserting them in the appropriate columns, and complete the balance in stock column.

(*b*) Using a form of your own design, make out the order for the further supply of stationery mentioned above.

10 The Purchasing Office (or Buying Department)

10.1 Purchases

Three main kinds of purchases are made by firms. They are:

(i) *Purchases of assets*, such as plant, machinery, motor vehicles, office equipment or fixtures and fittings. These items are purchased for long-term use in the business and are sold only when they have depreciated over many years in the service of the firm.

(ii) *Purchases of consumable items*, such as solvents and lubricants used in manufacture, petrol and oil for motor vehicles, stationery for office use and postage stamps. These items are consumed more rapidly than assets, and become losses of the business during the year in which they were purchased.

(iii) *Purchase of goods for resale, or of raw materials for manufacture into goods for sale*. These items are passed on to the eventual customer at a profit, and are the source of the profits of all trading firms. Firms that offer services only do not handle this class of purchases, since they do not deal in *goods*.

10.2 Centralized buying

In small enterprises the proprietor may be solely responsible for buying the goods required. In larger firms a central buying department will usually handle all purchases. The head of this department may be a member of the Chartered Institute of Purchasing and Supply.

There are certain advantages in centralized buying. These may be listed as follows:

(*a*) The Buying Department has the time and the organization to evaluate various products on the market and to pick the most appropriate for the firm's purposes. Cheapest is not necessarily best, and delivery dates may be more important than uniform quality.

A purchasing officer will discover the names of suitable suppliers (i) from past records maintained in the purchasing department; (ii) from trade journals, published weekly or monthly; (iii) from a trade organization which is prepared to supply lists of members that offer particular products or services.

Difficulty is sometimes experienced if suppliers do not fulfil orders on time, or demand payment at once because their own financial organization is weak and they are short of working capital. The purchasing department may consult the records at Companies House to attempt an evaluation of such firms, or may require clauses about **liquidated damages** to be inserted into the contract. Such a clause attempts to estimate the loss late delivery will cause, and requires the supplier to pay compensation if goods are not delivered according to contract. Many firms today are operating on a 'just-in-time' basis (JIT). JIT systems require suppliers to send supplies 'just-in-time' for use by the customer. The Purchasing Department will ring every day to notify the supplier how many items it requires for manufacture next day. The supplier undertakes to deliver to the factory floor at the agreed time. This requires the seller to show great discipline in producing goods of the right quality and in time to meet the JIT requirements.

(*b*) A system of records built up in the purchasing office enables supplies to be ordered as they are required. Calculations are made to discover the minimum stock levels necessary to keep production going until further supplies arrive, and as these minimum stock levels are reached, orders will be passed to suppliers to replenish stocks. Catalogues and price lists will be collected and filed for future reference. A catalogue gives a detailed description of goods, reference numbers, etc. It is usually expensive to produce and cannot be reprinted too frequently. For this reason firms publish price lists separately, and they can be reprinted at regular intervals to take account of price changes.

(*c*) Centralized buying results in the placing of larger orders, which therefore qualify for **quantity discounts**. For example, if stationery supplies are ordered by departmental heads, they will each place small orders. A centralized Buying Department buying for the whole firm achieves very great economies by demanding 'quantity' discounts. In times of shortage they may also receive more favourable treatment than competitors because the supplier is anxious to preserve the goodwill of larger customers.

(*d*) Budgetary control is easily achieved where a single purchasing officer supervises the activities of a number of buyers. Calculations can reveal the limits to which each buyer may go in purchasing items for a department, and an '**open to buy**' figure will tell a buyer how much he/she is entitled to spend in the week or month ahead.

10.3 The index of suppliers

The work of the purchasing department will result in a list of suppliers whose products are of the type sanctioned by the purchasing officer, and whose terms and conditions of sale are acceptable. A succession of orders will then be placed over the years with these firms, and should result in the establishment of sound links with these suppliers. Naturally such firms would hesitate to offend a valued customer, and will abide by the agreements made over the years.

An index of suppliers should be created, and it should list all the details of the firms dealt with. Such an index would include the names, addresses and telephone numbers of suppliers, the personal contact within the firm, the type, quantities and quality of goods usually ordered, the terms agreed for delivery and payment, etc. Such an index saves time, and also disappointment, which may be caused if there is no clear policy on such matters and buyers approach untried firms of doubtful integrity.

10.4 Purchasing routines

The procedure adopted for any order may be something like the following:

(*a*) A requisition form is raised by the department concerned. Usually this will be handwritten, and most probably it will not be in the correct terminology. For example, translucent paper might be incorrectly described as 'transparent'. The Purchasing Department will amend the requisition, and produce an 'order master' for a plain-paper copier so that copies can be run off.

(*b*) This matter will be used to prepare several copies of a tender-quotation form. This form will invite **quotations** from suppliers. A quotation is an offer to supply at a firm price, and if accepted it will become a binding contract on the supplier. These are sent out to suitable suppliers.

(*c*) On the closing date for receipt of quotations the tenders received will be considered and the best quotation will be accepted. The master will be used to prepare an official 'order form' − which will be sent to the supplier − and several copies, including two for the goods inwards department. They will thus know that an order is expected.

(*d*) Upon receipt of the goods the goods inwards department will observe the rules laid down by the purchasing officer. Typical rules might be the following:

(i) No delivery note is to be signed unless the goods it refers to have been personally checked by the clerk signing.

(ii) A 'clean' delivery, i.e. a signature without comment of any sort, must not be given if there is any sign of damage to cartons, or cases. Damage, discoloration or dampness is to be recorded on the sheet where the signature is given.

(iii) Deliveries made at lunch-time are to be signed for by the duty clerk. No delivery is to be refused because the duty clerk is not available.

(iv) Once the goods have been accepted, complete one copy of the order form, which becomes a goods received note. This will be passed to the Purchasing Department. This proof of receipt will be kept in the Purchasing Department until the statement requesting payment is received by the accountant. He will seek the Purchasing Department's acknowledgement that the goods have arrived, and they will confirm that this is indeed the case. Approval will be given to the accountant to pay the statement and it will be included in the next batch of remittances. Figure 10.1 shows a typical order form.

10.5   The order form

As will be seen in Figure 10.1, the order form should have certain information on it. The chief matters given are:

(*a*) The name and address of both parties to the contract. Orders are offers to buy, or they may be acceptances of quotations. Whichever they are, they are vital elements in a contract. A contract consists of an offer, validly accepted. Usually the supplier will be asked to acknowledge the order, and a tear-off portion may be provided for this purpose.

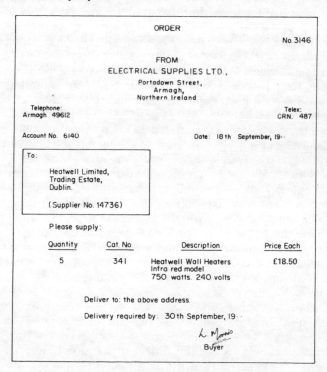

Figure 10.1   An order to a supplier

(*b*) A clear description of the goods or services required, giving price, colour, discount and carriage terms as quoted.

(*c*) The date, and a reference number.

(*d*) Clear instructions with regard to time and place of delivery.

(*e*) A warning that no goods are accepted unless supplied against a signed order.

The top copy of the order, sent to the supplier, will bear the signature of the Purchasing Officer.

10.6 Electronic ordering

Many wholesalers today offer facilities for electronic ordering of various sorts.

(a) Telephone ordering

Once a customer link has been established, which is achieved on the first occasion an order is placed, the customer is given an identifying code, which is the starting point for each order placed. One firm of office suppliers uses the customer's telephone code and number as the identifying code. This is convenient because the customer cannot easily forget his/her code. Immediately the code is keyed in to the computer the customer's details are retrieved from the data bank and show his/her current status. For example, what has been ordered recently? Has the last order been paid for? If not, what is the balance outstanding? What is the customer's credit limit? The customer then proceeds to state what items are required. If the customer has a catalogue and can give the order references for the item, so much the better; if not, the telephone operator will call up the details of the item from the data bank and key the required details into the order. The payment arrangements are then discussed.

Preferably a customer will pay by credit card, giving the necessary details. Often payment by credit card earns a cash discount on the price, because there is no problem about payment and the supplier's cash-flow position is eased by immediate payment. While the customer holds, the supplier gets through to the credit card company, and in seconds the payment is confirmed and the customer's order is processed. The computer prints off the invoice (to go to the customer), the advice note (to be wrapped with the goods before they are dispatched) and a stores copy (to be retained in the stores and showing where the goods went). At the same time the stock records have been adjusted; if they show that the re-order point has been reached, the computer will print out an order for the 'optimum order quantity'. This ensures that the supplier never runs out of stock. Such systems reduce the delays in the ordering process considerably. Within seconds of the customer's telephone call ending, the warehouse (which may be miles away from the head office and quite close to the customer's place of business) is receiving the print-outs of the 'advice note' and the 'stores copy' and the warehouseman will 'pick' the various items from their place on the shelves. They will be packed in the Dispatch Department and be delivered next day.

(b) Fax ordering

Since many firms have fax machines today, catalogues sent to customers frequently have fax order forms. These enable customers to photocopy the order form, enter the items required and fax it through to the supplier, a procedure that costs very little and takes 20 seconds. The receiving machine sends its confirmation that the order has been received and a key operator starts to key in the order to the supplier's computer. The procedure is then the same as for telephone orders, described above. The Freepost priority order form shown in Figure 10.2 is for customers who do not have a fax machine and instead send their order by post at the supplier's expense, i.e. FREEPOST. However, the same order may be faxed through by those who do have a fax machine, and it will receive

NEAT IDEAS

FREEPOST PRIORITY ORDER FORM

Complete using BLOCK CAPITALS –
If posting – no Stamp Required

Send to: Neat Ideas, FREEPOST
Kirk Sandall, Doncaster DN3 1BR

Customer Code

INVOICE INSTRUCTIONS

Company ____________

Address ____________

Postcode ____________

Telephone No. (STD) ____________

Contact ____________

DELIVERY TO (if different)

Company ____________

Address ____________

Postcode ____________

Telephone No. (STD) ____________

Contact ____________

Catalogue Order Ref.	Description (including Size and Colour)	No. of Cartons or Items	Price Per Carton/Each	Total Goods Price £

IMPORTANT: When ordering furniture or heavy items please indicate floor level. (Ground, 1st, 2nd etc.) IS LIFT AVAILABLE? YES/NO

ML17

PAYING BY CREDIT CARD

VISA

Card No.

Expiry date of Credit Card ____________

Cardholders Name ____________

Cardholders Address ____________

Signature ____________

GOODS TOTAL	
LESS 5% PRE-PAYMENT DISCOUNT	
SUB TOTAL	
CARRIAGE ON GOODS VALUE (under £200)	
NEXT DAY DELIVERY	
ADD £1 INSURANCE	
SUB TOTAL	
VAT	
FINAL TOTAL	

FAX ORDERING, ANYTIME – 0302 886605/885303

Photocopy these Priority Order Forms to fax your order without delay!

Figure 10.2 A FREEPOST Order form, which may also be faxed to the supplier

immediate attention. The supplier will confirm the credit card payment with the appropriate credit card company and the order will be picked and dispatched.

10.7 Some purchasing terms

(*a*) *Ex works*. This means that the price quoted is the price at the time the goods leave the supplier. Carriage charges will be additional to the price quoted.

(*b*) *Carriage paid*. This means that the price quoted includes delivery to the customer's door.

(*c*) *Carriage forward*. This means that the carriage will be payable by the purchaser to the carrier. The latter will usually insist on payment before delivery.

(*d*) *Terms net*. This means that no cash discount or settlement discount is allowed.

(*e*) *Trade discount* is a reduction in the catalogue price of an article to enable the retailer to make a profit. Thus, a suite of furniture advertised to the public at £300.00 might be sold to a retailer at 40 per cent trade discount, i.e. at £180.00.

(*f*) *Shortage*. A shortage arises when an order is only partially filled by a delivery. The discrepancy between the quantity ordered and the quantity supplied may be due to theft, accidental loss or deliberate short delivery by the supplier. He may acknowledge this by some phrase like 'Balance to follow' on the advice note.

10.8 Rapid revision − purchasing

Cover the page with a sheet of paper and uncover one question at a time.

Answers	Questions
−	1 What are the three classes of items purchased by firms?
1 (*a*) Assets like plant, machinery, etc., (*b*) consumable items used up in the manufacturing or office procedure, (*c*) goods for resale.	2 What are the advantages of centralized buying?
2 (*a*) The specialist buyers have time to evaluate products and equipment, (*b*) they establish links with accredited suppliers so that many purchases become routine, (*c*) better terms are negotiated in return for bulk orders, (*d*) a system of budgetary control supervises the expenditure of departments.	3 What is an index of suppliers?

3 A list of approved suppliers whose goods conform to agreed standards and who can be relied upon to meet the terms and conditions usually required by the firm.

4 List the forms or documents used in a modern purchasing department, in ordering and authorizing payment for goods.

4 (*a*) A requisition, (*b*) a quotation, (*c*) an order, (*d*) a 'goods received' note, (*e*) a statement, (*f*) a remittance advice note.

5 What is the meaning of 'ex works', when being quoted prices by suppliers?

5 It is the price of the article when it leaves the supplier's premises, without any carriage or other charges.

6 What is a shortage?

6 It is the amount by which an order received from a supplier falls short of the actual quantity ordered. The discrepancy must be reported so that an investigation can take place.

7 What is electronic ordering?

7 It is ordering in such a way that the order can be immediately keyed into a supplier's computer and the documentation, order picking and dispatch can begin at once.

8 Go over the page again until you feel you are sure of all the answers.

Exercises set 10

1 (*a*) Describe the office routine necessary for purchasing goods from the time that the buyer learns that goods are needed until the goods are received from the supplier and the invoice checked and passed for payment.
   (*b*) Explain the relationship of the purchasing department to the other departments of a medium-sized manufacturing concern.
   (*c*) Prepare an order form, setting out all the essential information.

2 A buyer is offered goods by one supplier at *45 per cent trade discount, ready delivery, cash one month net, carriage paid*. Another supplier offers goods at the same price with *25 per cent trade discount, 2 months delivery, carriage forward and 5 per cent cash discount within 10 days from date of invoice*.
   What factors will the buyer have to take into account in deciding which of the quotations to accept? In your answer show that you understand the terms in italics used above.

3 (*a*) State how the purchasing officer of a manufacturing business might obtain the names of suppliers of the commodities he needs.
   (*b*) Presuming that for a particular commodity you have found six possible suppliers, draft a letter of enquiry, which can be sent to all six, setting out your requirements, and requesting quotations.

4 You are about to place an order for £200 worth of goods with Unreliable Ltd. You have not done business with this company before and know nothing of its financial circumstances. What action do you recommend before sending the order?

5   A purchasing officer wishes to lay down a set of rules to be followed when goods inwards are received. Draw up a set of rules mentioning in particular what to do about damaged cases.

6   What considerations should be borne in mind before an order is placed with a new supplier?

7   The purchasing department of a firm wishes to order a large quantity of a new item which it has not obtained previously. Describe the office procedure to be followed and the documents necessary up to the stage when the firm pays for the items obtained.

8   A buyer receives quotations from three suppliers, as follows:

	Trade discount	*Delivery*	*Terms of payment*
A:	$22\frac{1}{2}$%	Ready	One month net
B:	30%	3 months	$2\frac{1}{2}$% cash discount
C:	45%	14 days	CWO

By referring to the above quotations, state the factors the buyer should take into account before he decides which supplier's offer to accept.

9   Prepare and complete an order form, setting out all the essential information for 250 loose-leaf folders (Catalogue No. A412) as quoted by Superb Stationery Ltd, 146 Paramound Road, Silvertown, at 25p each, less 30 per cent trade discount.

10 What is the difference between a catalogue and a price list? Some manufacturers issue price lists separately from their catalogues, and at more frequent intervals. Why do they do this? Do the purchasers derive any advantage from this practice?

11 You are employed as a typist in the order department of a large manufacturing concern. Much of your work consists in typing orders. Explain what you have to do and give a brief account of the working of the department.

12 Write brief notes on three of the following in connection with the buying of goods or services: (*a*) quotation, (*b*) tender, (*c*) trade discount, (*d*) goods received note, (*e*) 'to follow'.

13 Obtain for class use a mail-order catalogue such as is issued by many mail-order houses. Draw up a list of goods required, with their reference numbers, etc., and use this as a basis for a mail-order exercise in which you order by telephone. Don't forget you need a personal code − invent one − the exact details of the things you want to order and an 'imaginary' credit-card number, its date of expiry, etc. Using a dummy telephone (if available) and a class-mate to play the part of the electronic booking clerk, place your order. The class might then appraise your call, and also the way that the booking clerk responds to it. Remember that as the computer data base will be calling up its records, there is no need to give your name and address. Instead the booking clerk will say 'Are you Mary Jones of 20 Hill Road, Congleton, Cheshire', etc.

11 The Sales Department

11.1 Wholesale selling

In a free-enterprise economy goods flow to the consumer through a variety of channels. Each channel has developed over the course of the years as a particular solution to the problems facing producers and consumers, and with every product there are least two or three ways in which the product is transferred from the producer to the eventual user. The two routes for the sale of fish outlined below will illustrate the differences.

Route one

1   Caught by local fishermen. 2   Auctioned on the quay to local housewives or hoteliers.

Route two

1   Caught by a trawler. 2   Frozen in the ship's factory. 3   Stored in the refrigerated warehouse of a frozen food company. 4   Transported in a refrigerated container to a warehouse operated by a supermarket chain. 5   Delivered to branches of the company in a refrigerated van. 6   Sold to housewives from refrigerated counters.

In route one a single selling activity was sufficient. In route two the goods changed hands three times. At each point where they change hands goods are said to be 'sold' by one party to another for a consideration called the 'price'. The goods then become the property of the purchaser who has given value for them, and it is immaterial whether he pays at once (a cash sale) or pays later (a credit sale).

The two major divisions of selling are **wholesale selling** and **retail selling**. Retail selling is the final link in the distribution network, where goods are sold in small quantities to the final consumer. Wholesale selling is bulk selling, in which a large quantity of goods is sold to a middleman, or wholesaler. The wholesaler then sells them to several retailers, who eventually market them to the final consumer.

The practices followed in these two branches of selling are rather different and require different documentation. First we shall consider wholesale selling, by a typical sales department of a manufacturing company.

11.2 The functions of the Sales Department

The sales department has the following functions:

(*a*) To prepare or commission attractive brochures and publicity material for the company's products.

(*b*) To obtain and train a sales force of **representatives**, or **commercial travellers**, who are knowledgeable about the company's products and will find customers for them.

(*c*) To devise, in consultation with organization and methods staff where necessary, a system of documentation and controls which will keep selling expenses as low as possible and inform top management about developments.

(*d*) To stage demonstrations of the company's products at appropriate times and places, and to participate in exhibitions organized by trade associations and similar bodies.

(*e*) To explain the complaints of customers to the production department with a view to improving the product.

(*f*) To rebut the complaints of customers on behalf of the firm if the complaints are unjustified and result from the customer's failure to follow the recommendations given in the company's literature.

(*g*) To take responsibility for all those obligations that exist between the organization and its customers and clients. These may include liaison with the Production Department to maintain product quality, so that customers are pleased with their purchases; the observance of contractual terms so that, for example, if a warranty is offered that guarantees free servicing or maintenance it is carried out; delivery at the time required, at the place required, in the way agreed, etc.

These activities may be only regional or national in character but in recent years it has become more and more necessary to market a product on a world-wide basis and set up overseas agencies, or branches, to sell products internationally. Sales forces of this size require careful control if they are to fulfil their functions properly and yet still contribute to the profits of the company.

Advertising and the Sales Department

Advertising is a necessary adjunct to selling. The old proverb 'Good wine needs no bush' (a vine hung up at the door was the sign for a wine shop in days before people could read) is not true today. A product cannot achieve any reputation unless it is widely advertised in the competitive world of modern commerce. One advertising consultant uses the slogan 'If you don't advertise, you certainly know what you're doing – but you're the only one who does'. The enormous costs of laying down a production line, which may have cost millions of pounds, can be recovered only if the product sells, and the best way to achieve sales is to advertise. The Advertising Department may be a part of the Sales Department. If not, the two departments will work closely with one another, and the return from particular promotions will be rigorously investigated to determine which method of advertising gives the best results.

11.3 The sales force

The marketing manager or sales manager of a large company will control the operations of a sales force of representatives and agents throughout the country, and possibly the world. He/she is usually a strong personality, and will usually be a director of the company. The director represents the selling organization at the board meetings, helping to formulate company policy and objectives in the selling field. He/she then has the task of implementing this policy, conveying it to the area managers and agents, briefing representatives about the targets set by top management in the months ahead and adapting procedures and organization to achieve them.

Such a director will examine reports of sales achieved and problems that have arisen, pinpoint weaknesses and investigate staff activities where it seems that the potential sales are not being realized.

Sales representatives will be assigned to a particular territory, where they establish a personal link with the company's customers. They demonstrate and explain products, arrange for the service of equipment, up-date customers on the latest development and methods, and listen to the customer's particular needs. Some system of reporting back on all calls made will ensure that the marketing manager is informed about the needs of the customers, the success or otherwise of the calls made and the time spent on the enquiry. Sometimes a traveller may make considerable efforts on the customer's behalf and then not be rewarded with an order. At other times a very large order may follow from a simple phone call or the provision of an illustrated brochure. Frequently a representative is given a card record system which is small enough to put into a traveller's pocket, and which when that particular set of enquiries has been dealt with, can be posted back to Head Office to inform it of the results achieved, and the necessary action required in each case.

The representative's itinerary is important, since correspondence and messages must be able to reach the representative daily. This programme will be drawn up in consultation with the area manager, who will operate from a central point in each group of territories. Procedures will be laid down to enable the area manager to be kept fully informed, with reports being written up in the car before driving away from a call, and arrangements prescribed for ringing in at agreed times to acquaint the area manager with his/her position. To enable these calls to be controlled, travellers will usually have a credit card that connects them by telephone at the expense of Head Office. Alternatively, a mobile phone or car phone is supplied to the traveller, giving two-way communication between Head Office and the sales representative. This enables Head Office to control the representative more closely. Sometimes a paging device may be provided, and then the representative knows he/she is required to telephone in. A message-pager can actually record a written instruction to the representative, e.g. to pay a visit to a potential new client in the area.

11.4 Attracting customers

In order to attract customers it is necessary to keep one's products constantly before the public, by a succession of presentations, demonstrations and advertising campaigns. It greatly assists such campaigns if continual revision of the appearance and design of the product takes place, so that there is some refinement to discuss or some new model to introduce. It could be argued that some of this innovation is wasteful or socially unnecessary, but as far as the particular firm is concerned, it is justified by the increased sales which result.

The following ways of attracting customers are regularly used:

(*a*) *Exhibitions and trade fairs*. Here the firm, in conjunction with other firms in the industry, participates in a national or international demonstration of its products. Such shows as the Motor Show, the Farnborough Air Display and the International Business Show attract buyers from all over the world.

(*b*) *Wholesalers' displays*. Many wholesalers at regular intervals put on demonstrations and displays of the products they handle. Retailers who live in their particular areas visit the showrooms to hear accounts from representatives of the variety and purpose of the equipment their firms supply. These events are usually held on the 'early closing' day of shops in the area. Often sales managers will appear personally to demonstrate the products and discuss their features, assisted by the representative who travels in the area.

(*c*) *Illustrated brochures, leaflets and price lists*. A good supply of brochures should always be available for despatch to customers who enquire by post or telephone. This is at once convenient to the sales department, since special letters are not required, and satisfactory to the potential customer. The immediate despatch of the material required gives an impression of efficiency, and keeps interest in the product alive. The provision of **business reply cards**, asking for a demonstration or a visit by a representative, will again assist the sales department to follow up the enquiry.

(*d*) *Magazine and press advertising*. This type of advertising is not cheap but it is selective to some extent and therefore effective in directing the advertisement towards a particular section of the population. There are several hundred specialist magazines catering for the interests of groups, from archaeologists to zoologists. Some of these groups are enormous — teenagers, for example. Others are less numerous, such as brass-rubbing enthusiasts. Particular products that interest these groups will sell well if featured in this type of magazine. Even the national press, while less varied than the magazine industry, has a variety of appeal which leads sales managers and advertising departments to choose one paper rather than another to feature a particular product. There is also a special section of the magazine market catering for the business field, in many cases providing 'freebie' magazines dealing with particular industries. (A 'freebie' magazine is sent free of charge to interested people in a particular profession.) Magazines such as *Business Equipment Digest* and *Accountancy Age* cater for their specialist markets and welcome new readers. They are financed by the industry-orientated advertisements they contain. Each year the advertising in this field is worth about £350 million, more than one third of the total business to business advertising budget.

(*e*) *Television advertising*. The greatest impact on the general public can undoubtedly be made on the television screen. By entering the homes of practically everyone in the land a television advertisement can create an enormous demand for a firm's products. It does not follow that all such campaigns are successful, but where a product meets a popular need and is competitively priced, the television advertisement more than repays its extra cost.

(*f*) *Special campaigns*. These may take the form of a special mailing to interested parties, using address lists purchased for the purpose. Thus local authorities sell the electoral register, which may be used to prepare a mailing to a particular town or rural locality. Many professional bodies issue membership lists, and the yellow pages of telephone directories give classified lists of retailers in a particular field. Representatives may also be enlisted in special campaigns to enlarge trade in their areas, often with special prizes for the best sales person.

Free samples and coupons are popular ways to encourage the sale of goods in such special campaigns. The retailer who supplies goods in exchange for the free coupon is compensated by the firm for the value of the coupon.

Such campaigns need considerable planning and often require that stage or screen personalities who are to assist with the campaign are booked up in advance. Special publicity material must be prepared, supplies be made available in the shops and the general organization in the proposed sales area be improved to ensure full coverage during the actual campaign.

(*g*) *Fax campaigns*. The fax machine has several advantages for advertising purposes. You can design an attractive layout, with illustrations and descriptive material about your product, and then 'broadcast' it to many different locations at cheap rates in off-peak times. A fax always gets through to the official to whom it is addressed. It is not likely to be intercepted by other staff and treated as junk mail. It is more personal than a mail shot, and if you make your fax number an 0800 number, those wishing to place an order can fax you one free of charge. Alternatively, they can place an order by phone on an 0800 phone number free of charge, or on an 0345 number at the local call rate.

(*h*) *Promotional videos*. Many products are expensive, and those requiring them need a good opportunity to see the product in action. This is easily accomplished by a promotional video, which explains the product, shows it in use, relates it to the needs of the customer, etc. Such videos are quite expensive to produce, especially as they frequently feature famous personalities, require skilled camera work and possibly background music, etc. They can be shown in shopping arcades, large stores or in the homes of customers who have a video machine.

11.5 Documentation of sales

The sale of goods is the chief activity of a trading concern, and every aspect of a sale must be adequately documented. The sequence of operations is as follows:

(*a*) *The enquiry*. An enquiry may arrive by post, telephone or fax. It should be forwarded at once to the sales manager, who will take appropriate action to follow it up. Brochures and price lists may be sent, with a personal letter. It may be desirable to phone the enquirer immediately to give information about the product, or to arrange for the local representative to call on the enquirer.

(*b*) *The quotation*. Where necessary, the enquirer will be given a quotation. This is an offer to supply, at a stated price, goods in the quantity and of the quality described, on the terms and conditions described in the quotation. If accepted within the time limit stated, or within a reasonable time if no time limit is given, it becomes a legally binding contract between the parties.

(*c*) *The estimate*. A rather similar response to an enquiry is an 'estimate'. This is slightly less contractual in nature, in that it does not amount to an offer which the customer can accept to make a binding contract. It gives the same information, but leaves the matter open. It is up to the customer to make an offer based on the estimate, which the supplier will then accept if circumstances have not changed. Thus an estimate could be revised if costs of material or labour, say, had risen in the interval between sending the estimate and the customer offering to buy.

(*d*) *The order.* It must be carefully scrutinized to ensure that it is correct in every detail and if defective in any way, a phone call should be made to clarify the detail. If it is a telephone order, it should be confirmed in writing. It may be necessary to acquaint the Accounts Department with the details if the order is from a new customer who is asking for credit. They will then institute the necessary enquiries for references before sanctioning credit.

(*e*) *The invoice.* An invoice is a business document that is made out whenever one person sells goods to another. It is made out by the person selling the goods, and in large businesses it may have as many as eight copies, of different colours.

Figure 11.1 shows the usual form of invoice in use in large firms. It includes the VAT details required on tax invoices (see Chapter 18). It will usually have the following information: (i) names and addresses of both the interested parties to the sale; (ii) the date of the sale; (iii) an exact description of the goods, with quantity and unit price, and details of the trade discount (if any) given; (iv) VAT details; (v) the terms on which the goods are sold, i.e. the discount that may be taken and the credit period allowed. 'Terms Net' means no discount is allowed. The words 'prompt settlement' mean no credit period is allowed. In that case the customer must pay the invoice at once.

Lastly, many firms write 'E & OE' on the bottom of the invoice. These letters mean 'Errors and Omissions Excepted'. If an error or omission has been made, the firm selling the goods may put it right.

Trade discount is a reduction in the catalogue price of an article, given by the wholesaler or manufacturer to the retailer, to enable the retailer to make a profit.

Take the example of a manufacturer of bicycles. Leaflets will be produced about a particular brand of bicycle, explaining the merits of the machine. The price will either be printed on this literature or on a separate price list supplied on request, but the important point is that the manufacturer, and everyone else, will think of this particular machine as the £178.50 model. When invoicing a supply of machines, the simple way to invoice them is to list them at the catalogue price. The invoice might therefore read:

6 'Mercury' bicycles, 26-inch frame at £178.50 = £1 071.00

Clearly the retailer cannot sell these at the catalogue price if they have been purchased at the catalogue price. The manufacturer therefore deducts trade discount at an agreed rate, usually somewhere between 10 per cent and 45 per cent of the catalogue price. If these figures seem high, the student must remember that durable goods of this sort may remain in stock for some considerable time before being sold, and the profit margin must be fairly large on such slow-moving items.

6 'Mercury' bicycles 26-inch frame at £178.50 = £1 071.00
Less trade discount 45% = £ 481.95

£ 589.05

Value added tax is a tax that is added whenever goods or services are supplied by one person to another. At present (1993) there is only one rate of tax, a standard rate of $17\frac{1}{2}$ per cent, the higher rate having been abandoned. Since it is added at every stage of production, everyone who buys goods for resale, or for use in a business, pays tax on the goods purchased.

This is called **input tax**. Later, when selling the goods, or charging people for services, the appropriate rate of tax is charged to the customer. The business thus collects tax from customers every time it supplies an output of goods or services, and this is called **output tax**. Of course this output tax has to be paid over to the collecting authority, which is HM Customs and Excise Department (VAT), but before doing so the business is allowed to deduct the amount of input tax which it paid when the goods, raw materials, etc. were purchased. It therefore only pays over the *extra tax* it has collected from its customers, since the output tax will usually be bigger than the input tax because we sell at a higher price than we buy. The formula is:

Output tax − input tax = Tax payable to HM Customs

The four copies of the invoice shown in Figure 11.1 are processed as follows:

Top copy. This is sent by post or by hand to the person buying the goods, who uses it to record the purchase in the purchases day book.
Second copy. This is usually the sales day book copy, which is kept by the seller, entered in the sales day book, and then filed to be kept as a copy of the contract of sale.
Third and fourth copies. These are sent together to the stores department of the seller, where the storekeeper takes the goods out of the store. The third copy, often called the **delivery note**, is given to the driver of the goods vehicle in cases where goods are being delivered to the buyer's warehouse. The driver presents it with the parcel of goods and gets a signature on it to prove that the goods arrived safely. This copy is then taken back by the driver to the storekeeper and is filed in the stores department after being entered in the stores record book. The fourth copy is wrapped up in the parcel before it is given to the driver. It is often called the **advice note** and it enables the buyer's storekeeper to check the contents of

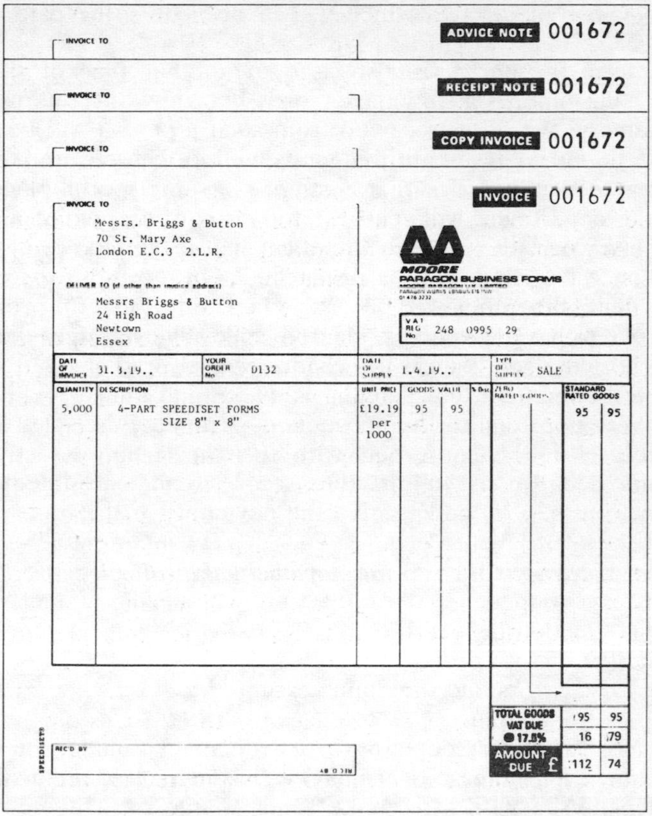

ADVICE NOTE 001672

INVOICE TO

RECEIPT NOTE 001672

INVOICE TO

COPY INVOICE 001672

INVOICE TO

INVOICE 001672

INVOICE TO
Messrs. Briggs & Button
70 St. Mary Axe
London E.C.3 2.L.R.

MOORE
PARAGON BUSINESS FORMS

DELIVER TO (if other than invoice address)
Messrs Briggs & Button
24 High Road
Newtown
Essex

VAT REG No 248 0995 29

DATE OF INVOICE	YOUR ORDER No	DATE OF SUPPLY	TYPE OF SUPPLY
31.3.19..	D132	1.4.19..	SALE

QUANTITY	DESCRIPTION	UNIT PRICE	GOODS VALUE		% Disc	ZERO RATED GOODS	STANDARD RATED GOODS	
5,000	4-PART SPEEDISET FORMS SIZE 8" x 8"	£19.19 per 1000	95	95			95	95

TOTAL GOODS	95	95
VAT DUE @ 17.5%	16	79
AMOUNT DUE £	112	74

REC'D BY

Figure 11.1 A four-copy invoice set

the parcel and record in the stores record book the stores that have just arrived.

Other copies. Where a set of invoices has more than four copies, they will usually include (*a*) a representative's copy, which is sent to the traveller handling the order; (*b*) a traffic planning copy for the transport department; (*c*) a consignee's copy for the actual consignee, as distinct from the head office of the buyer's firm.

Pro-forma invoices

Sometimes goods are sent 'on approval'. As they have not been sold, an invoice cannot be made out, but an exactly similar document called a **pro-forma invoice** is sent instead. If the customer approves the goods he/she will notify the seller and the pro-forma invoice will then become an invoice, which will in due course be paid by the customer.

The term *pro forma* is also used in another type of situation where a customer is a slow payer, or is not known to the owner of the business. An order received from such a person will be put in hand in the normal way but the goods will not be delivered, though they may be set aside for that customer in some special place. The invoicing department will send the top copy of an invoice as a pro forma invoice, with a note to the effect that if the invoice is paid in full at once the goods will be dispatched. On receipt of the cheque in payment, the goods will be dispatched, but a careful proprietor might pay to have the cheque cleared 'specially', or might delay the dispatch of the goods until the cheque was cleared.

From the moment that delivery is made, and the second copy of the invoice is passed to the accounts department, the sales department ceases to be concerned with the transaction directly. The accounts department will in due course render a statement of account (see p. 191) and receive the payment for the order.

Some abbreviations used in the documentation of sales

COD: Cash on delivery.
CWO: Cash with order.
E & OE: Errors and omissions excepted.

(*f*) *Debit notes.* A debit note is a document made out by the seller whenever the purchaser has been undercharged on an invoice, or when he/she wishes to make some charge on a debtor which increases the debtor's debt. It may also be made out whenever a purchaser returns goods. It then advises the creditor what goods are being returned, and invites the creditor to send a credit note.

Suppose that an invoice has been sent to a purchaser of a typewriter valued at £300.00, but by mistake the typist had typed £30.00 as the purchase price. Clearly the seller will want to correct this undercharge, but another invoice would not be appropriate since no 'goods' are being delivered. A debit note for £270.00 treated exactly like an invoice and put through the accounts in exactly the same way as an invoice will put this matter right. In the same way charges for carriage, or insurance, which were not known at the time the invoice was made out, could be charged to the debtor by means of a debit note.

(*g*) *The credit note.* We must expect in the course of business that some of our customers will return goods for valid reasons. Purchasers are not entitled to return something just because they have changed their minds about having it; but occasionally we may oblige a client by accepting this type of return. The usual reasons for returning goods are:

(i) The purchaser holds that the goods are unsatisfactory for some reason, e.g. wrong colour, wrong size, not up to sample, not up to specification, imperfectly finished, damaged in transit, etc.

(ii) The purchaser is entitled by contract to return goods, for instance goods sent on approval.

In these circumstances the document used is the credit note.

A credit note may be defined as a business document made out whenever one person returns goods to another. It is usually printed in red, to distinguish it from an invoice, and, like an invoice, is made out by the seller of the goods, who is now receiving them back again. Usually there are only two copies.

The credit note should show:

(i) The names and addresses of both parties to the transaction.

(ii) An exact description of the goods being returned.

(iii) The unit price, the number and the total value of the goods returned.

Other reasons for sending a credit note include:

(*a*) Sometimes goods that are unsatisfactory for some reason are not returned because of the inconvenience and cost. A piece of furniture that has been damaged by rain in transport may only need repolishing. The purchaser may be perfectly prepared to have this repolishing carried out by one of his/her own employees, provided the seller will make a contribution to cover the cost. This will be done by sending a credit note for the agreed amount. This is called an **allowance**.

(*b*) We saw above that when an undercharge is made on an invoice, a document called a debit note is sent to increase the original invoice to the proper figure. Invoice typists can make errors resulting in overcharges instead of undercharges. Supposing the typewriter valued at £300.00 was invoiced at £3 000.00. Clearly a credit note for £2 700.00 will be required to correct the overcharge.

Credit notes may therefore be sent for three reasons:

(*a*) To credit a debtor with returns.

(*b*) To credit a debtor with an allowance.

(*c*) To credit a debtor to correct an overcharge.

(*h*) *The statement.* We have seen that the sale of goods calls for an invoice to be sent to the customer, and the return of goods considered unsatisfactory for some reason calls for a credit note. Although these documents record the sale and return, they do not

CREDIT NOTE

Messrs Brewis and Jeffrey,	No. 7864
Cherrydown,	RIDER & Co. Ltd.
Newtown,	High Street
Essex.	London, W.C.2.

DATE   20th May   19..   REP.   M. TYLER.

No.	Description	Cat. Price (£)	Value (£)	VAT (£)	Total value £
3	Dining Chairs (damaged in transit)	£21.50	64.50	11.29	75.79

Figure 11.2   A credit note (the original document for returns), usually printed in red

necessarily secure payment for the goods or a refund for the returns. It is true that a new customer will often be dealt with on a *pro forma* basis, as explained above, and the invoice must be paid before the goods will be dispatched. In addition, some firms print on their invoices 'Please pay on this invoice within ... days; no statement will be sent'. However, for the vast majority of business-to-business arrangements, trading on monthly terms is usual. Under this arrangement a monthly statement is sent out, and this is the document that signals payment is due for the goods supplied in the previous month. We shall see that there are two types of statement, but first note this. If we send out all our statements on the last day of the month, it makes a rush of work at the end of the month, and absolute chaos at the Post Offices, as millions and millions of statements (often called bills) are sent from firm to firm. The better way is to adopt the system called **cyclical billing**. Cyclical billing means we send out 1/20 of all bills every day (in a 4-week month there are 5 working days in each week, so 1/20 is about the best fraction to send out every day). This spreads the work of sending out the statements evenly over the month, and also brings in some cash every day. It is very helpful to have a steady 'cash flow' into the business, as a result of cyclical billing.

Simple statements. Figure 11.3 shows a simple statement used by firms that do not have a computerized system of accounts. The

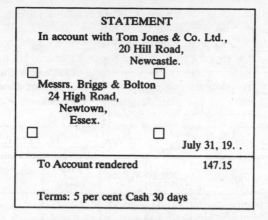

Figure 11.3   A simple statement

statement carries the names of both parties and reminds the debtor, Briggs & Bolton, that the total value of invoices sent to them in the previous month (after making adjustments for any credit notes sent) is £147.15. The term 'To account rendered' is the equivalent of saying 'You have had various documents sent to you this month. Now please pay us the outstanding balance of £147.15'. The statement also says that if the account is settled within 30 days a 'settlement discount' of 5 per cent may be taken. The cashier who decides to pay this account will write on it the discount taken and will pay the net amount. Thus:

To account rendered	147.15
Less 5% discount	7.36
Cheque herewith	£ 139.79

Cash discounts and settlement discounts are very similar. Cash discount *is given to customers who pay 'prompt cash'*. Settlement discount *is given to debtors who pay promptly for their goods when the time for payment arrives*. It is a great inconvenience to businesses to have debtors who are slow in settling their accounts, because it means that their capital is being used by somebody else. To encourage prompt payment, a cash discount is offered. Naturally this means a smaller total profit than would otherwise be earned, but it may be cheaper to give this discount than to allow debts to accumulate and perhaps suffer bad debts.

Computerized statements. Many firms today are using computerized forms of book-keeping. There are many such systems. The statement shown in Figure 11.4 is printed by kind permission of British Olivetti Limited. You will notice that it does not just contain the words 'To account rendered' but instead contains details of all payments by the debtor and of goods sent to him and items returned by him. This is because under computerized book-keeping the statement is printed automatically from the entire data file for the month concerned. At electronic speeds it is no trouble for the computer to give all the details.

(*i*) *The remittance advice note.* Some computerized systems send out the statements in duplicate form, and label the copy **remittance advice note**. This enables the customer to keep the statement, and use the remittance advice note to act as a covering document for the cheque. Remittance advice notes are also frequently attached to invoices as a perforated, tear-off section of the invoice. The customer is asked to pay the invoice by tearing off the remittance advice note and returning it with a cheque for the amount (less any settlement discount taken).

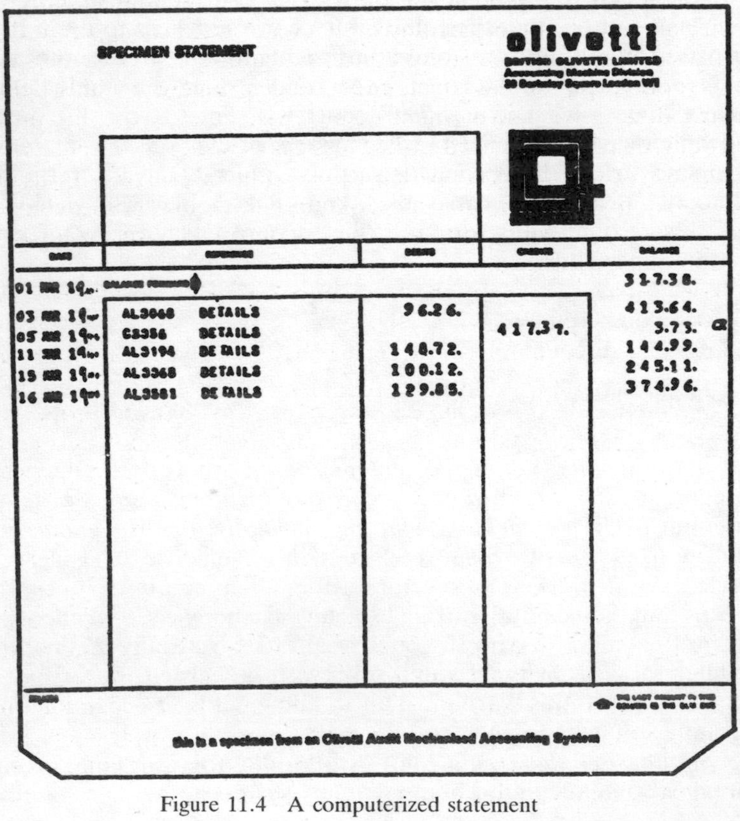

Figure 11.4   A computerized statement

11.6   Retail selling

Retail sales are usually cash sales, though a variety of other methods of payment have been devised. A full description of the types of retail outlet is not appropriate to this volume, but is given in a companion volume, *Commerce Made Simple*.

The chief office activities required in cash-selling are those described in Chapter 18: the recording and banking of cash takings. Where retail sales are not cash sales, but credit sales, there is a need to record and control the credit granted to customers.

The chief types of non-cash-selling carried on in retail trade are hire purchase selling, selling against credit-card payments and selling on 'budget accounts' or 'monthly credit terms'.

(a) 'Hire purchase' selling

At one time hire purchase was the most important of all the methods of selling expensive items to people whose incomes were relatively low. As its name implies, the hire purchase contract is a mixture of activities. The customer 'hires' the product required, paying regular instalments of money, and at the time when the full amount has been paid, the contract is completed by the last instalment and the customer 'purchases' the item. Sometimes a nominal amount (say 10 p) is added to the last instalment and payment of this 10p is regarded as the actual moment of purchase.

Today the system is used rather less than formerly, because many items are now purchased with the use of credit cards. These are explained below. First we must explain hire purchase selling in greater detail, because it is still very widespread, especially in the purchase of motor cars.

Hire purchase is the purchase of goods under an agreement called a **hire purchase agreement**. This permits the buyer to pay only a small part of the purchase price, called the deposit, at once. The rest is payable over a period of time by regular instalments.

The essence of a hire purchase agreement is that the property in the goods does not pass until the final instalment is paid. This means that the vendor owns the goods right up until the last moment of payment.

In the past this led to widespread abuse by finance companies, e.g. a person who had paid all but one instalment on a car but then was made unemployed and could not pay by the agreed date had the car re-possessed. Today the whole field of 'consumer credit' is controlled by the Consumer Credit Act, 1974 and the Office of Fair Trading lays down strict procedures. These procedures include a requirement to draw up an agreement, signed by both parties in a special form laid down in the regulations. This consumer credit agreement replaces the invoice as the sales document. It must contain the following information.

(i) A statement of the cash price, the total HP price, the number, due dates and amount of each instalment.

(ii) A list of the goods sufficient to identify them.

(iii) The provisions for layout, legibility, and wording prescribed by the Board of Trade. This includes in particular a clearly marked box like that shown below.

(iv) A statutory notice of the hirer's rights under the Act.

(v) A clear statement of the true rate of interest. This is called the **APR (Annual Percentage Rate)**. It enables the customer to know the true rate of interest, and consequently he/she is able to compare the various ways of purchasing an item from the interest point of view.

(vi) A box called the signature box, which records the agreement of the customer to the terms of the agreement. This box must read as shown below.

This is a Hire-Purchase Agreement regulated by the Consumer Credit Act 1974. Sign it only if you want to be legally bound by its terms.

Signature(s)
of Debtor(s)

Date(s) of signature(s)

The goods will not become your property until you have made all the payments. You must not sell them before then.

The memorandum must be signed by the hirer or buyer in person, and by the owner or his agent. A wife cannot sign for her husband, even if she has her husband's authority.

Frequently the retailer is not rich enough to finance hire purchase schemes, and merely completes the memorandum as agent for a finance company, which pays the retailer the balance of the purchase price and arranges to collect the instalments from the customer. As a result of the new regulations the hire purchase field has become a very reputable area of trading, and finance companies are now a very professional part of the financial sector of the economy.

(b) Payment by credit cards and debit cards

The most striking development in retail trade in recent years is the switch to payment by credit cards or debit cards. These are methods by which the financial sector has assumed the risks on countless transactions in retail trade, especially that section of the trade where customers are absolutely creditworthy (or believed to be so). The risks assumed are therefore not as great as one might think. The procedures are as follows:

(i) *The credit card.* Customers wish to buy goods, but do not always have the money. Retailers wish to sell goods, but cannot afford to give credit because of the risks of bad debts. If a specialist in lending money – a bank – steps in between the two and agrees to take the risks, trade can expand.

The bank issues a 'credit card' to any customer whose reliability is fairly certain because of an established record, a sound job, etc. In practice nearly everyone gets a credit card, but the amount of the credit varies – from a few hundred pounds to £100000. This may be spent in any retail outlet that is an accredited 'merchant member', with certain safeguards. For example, a floor limit is set for each firm, and anyone trying to buy more than the permitted floor is the subject of a telephone call to the credit-card centre. This confirms whether the card-holder has enough of his/her credit limit left to afford the item. If so, an authorization number is given and the sale proceeds. If not, permission is refused.

The sale having gone ahead, the trader is happy and simply pays in the credit card vouchers to the bank concerned. It is for the bank to make sure the customer pays, which is arranged on a monthly basis. The customer may pay as he/she likes, but must pay at least 5 per cent of the outstanding balance each month. The bank charges interest (at fairly exorbitant rates actually) stating the APR (annual percentage rate) each time it sends out a statement. Typical rates vary from about 19 per cent per annum to 34 per cent per annum, which is a very high rate of interest.

(ii) *The debit card.* A debit card is a more straightforward arrangement. It is called a debit card because it enables the bank to debit a customer's account directly by computer (or it would do if the account was 'on-line', i.e. available to the computer at all times). In practice many accounts are not 'on-line' until the daily records are passed through the computer overnight. Since a debit card is only supposed to be used by someone who has a favourable balance on his/her bank account, its use when such funds were not available would mean an unauthorized overdraft had been taken out, and this calls for quite a heavy penalty – say £25. It varies from bank to bank. The advantage of the debit card to the customer is that there is no need to write out a cheque – the mere wiping of the card through the card-reader deducts the amount from the customer's balance at the bank. Some retail outlets are also allowed to give customers money off their debit cards, usually up to £50. A customer who cannot get to a bank can draw money from the local grocery store and they will collect it from the bank through the EFTPOS system. EFTPOS is the correct name for these systems – it means 'electronic funds transfer at the point of sale'.

Budget accounts

Many retailers allow customers to run a budget account. This entitles the customer to buy goods up to eight times the value of a monthly budget figure, or up to thirty times the value of a weekly budget figure, which the customer is prepared to pay regularly. Thus a customer who can afford to pay £5 per month would be permitted to buy up to £40 worth of goods. At any time the customer who has partly extinguished his/her debts may purchase a further supply of goods provided the total does not exceed the total of £40.

Credit accounts and credit control

Here the retailer permits the customer to buy on credit, but renders a monthly account in the usual way. For many firms, especially those in very competitive trades, the granting of credit is inevitable in modern conditions. Cash payments are very inconvenient; but credit enables a host of transactions to be settled with a single payment. A sound credit control system is essential.

The following points may be listed as important features of a credit control system:

(*a*) Always take up references on new customers before granting credit. A banker's reference, or a reference from a trade association or professional body, is easily obtained by creditworthy customers.

(*b*) Exercise strict control of credit levels until a customer is well-known and well-regarded. A customer who wishes to exceed his credit level for some reason is free to ask that the level be raised, but goods ordered in disregard of the agreed level will not be supplied, except on COD (cash on delivery) terms, or on a *pro forma* basis (see p. 187).

(*c*) An overdue account should be placed on a 'stop' list. Coloured flashes are sometimes used, particularly on visi-index systems, to indicate a 'stop' on an account. There is one danger when 'stopping' supplies to late payers: if a customer could claim that it amounted to breach of contract, damages could be claimed, e.g. if his/her factory stopped work because you withheld supplies. To be sure of your right to 'stop' an overdue account, put such a clause in your conditions of trading, e.g. 'If an account is not paid on time the supplier reserves the right to "stop" supplies until the account is paid'.

(*d*) Similar 'flashes' may be used to indicate habitually slow payers. Here supplies will be stopped whenever shortages arise, preference being given to customers who pay promptly.

(*e*) Persistent follow-up of overdue accounts is essential. Do not wait too long. An overdue account calls for an immediate letter of remonstrance, accompanied the same day by a warning telephone call. If the account is still not paid within 7 days, it is best to put the matter in the hands of a solicitor. The charges are relatively small, and most solicitors today have a computerized system that follows a sequence of procedures. Failure to pay on the first letter is followed by a writ — a summons into court to show why the plaintiff should not have the justice he/she is asking for. It costs very little to issue a writ, and when we issue one, we do not expect to go through every court in the land. What we do expect is for the customer to pay up right away. Bad payers always pay the person who is worrying them most. If the debtor cannot pay, the failure to do so may result in the bankruptcy of the debtor. Bankruptcy is a legal process that sets the debtor free from debt, but only after his/her effects have been sold to pay as much as possible of the sums owed. The debtor is also prevented from obtaining any further goods on credit. Some firms, known as **debt factors**, buy up the bad debts of other firms, usually for about half their value. By making appropriate arrangements to collect the money owed, often by instalments, they eventually make a profit on their purchase. A business person who is too busy to collect such debts personally, and who feels that legal action will injure his/her goodwill in the locality, may think this assignment of debts to a debt factor the best way to 'cut his/her losses'.

(*f*) In the case of limited companies particular care is necessary in granting credit. The only really safe way to deal with a limited company is to make a preliminary examination of its affairs by consulting the records at Companies' House, in London and Cardiff. These will indicate the size, profitability and rate of growth of the company. If the records are not kept up to date, this fact alone is enough to create suspicion in the mind of a shrewd accountant, and credit should not be granted. The reason why companies have to be treated with care is that those who run the company have limited liability. The directors and other officials cannot be held personally liable for the debts of the business, so if they do not pay, we can only look to the company's assets for compensation. A company's assets, when sold off, rarely raise enough to pay the debts of the company.

11.7 Exporting activities

Every country has to import some goods and services from other countries. To pay for these goods and services she must export her own products and skills. In this way a country earns sufficient foreign exchange to be able to pay for the imported raw materials, finished goods and services. This type of international trade enriches the countries who take part in it, because it increases the variety of foods and manufactured products which their peoples can enjoy.

11.8 Problems faced by the exporter

(*a*) *Language*. When we enter an export market we must expect to translate the packaging, informative literature, and technical handouts into the language of the country concerned. We must have salesmen who are able to speak the language fluèntly and qualified to sell the product in that language.

(*b*) *Standardized units*. There are a great many technological problems arising from the use in different countries of different units of length, weight, capacity, voltage, screw threads, etc.

In North America and many Middle Eastern countries the domestic electricity supply is 110−120 volts only, and the frequency is 60 Hz; in Britain it is 240 volts and 50 Hz. This means that special motors, transformers and other equipment are needed if a British firm is to succeed in these export fields. One of the reasons that Britain is changing over to metric units is to enable us to adopt the same threads and the same units of length, weight and capacity as our competitors abroad.

(*c*) *Currency*. Clearly, prices of goods sold abroad have to be converted into the currency units of the country where they are to be sold. Since rates of exchange fluctuate, particularly in some politically unstable countries, the prices decided upon may prove to be insufficient to yield a profit if the rate of exchange alters. An exporter who contracts to supply goods at a fixed price may find that this contract price is no longer satisfactory.

(*d*) *Licences and other documentation*. There are a host of regulations to fulfil in most branches of the export trade. Not only may a licence be required before goods can enter a foreign country, one may even be needed from this country before they proceed overseas.

(*e*) *Risks of the export trade*. These are numerous. We have the sheer physical hazards of crossing oceans by sea or air, the corrosion that comes to iron and steel products from the salt air spray, the chance that goods will be damaged in rough weather or even jettisoned to save the vessel. There are the risks of theft at the docks, or in transit; the risks of non-payment by the buyer or refusal by his government to release foreign exchange. Even where these risks can be assumed by insurers or *del credere* agents, the premiums paid or the commission given eat into profit margins and make export trade less attractive than home trade.

Against this formidable list of problems can be set the very great rewards to be won by successful overseas trade where sound arrangements can be made with foreign buyers.

11.9 Functions of the Export Department

The export department has to overcome the problems outlined in Section 11.8 above. Some of the staff must be fluent in the foreign languages required. The firm must appoint agents overseas who will sell the firm's products. If foreign branches are opened they will usually be supervised by the export manager. Foreign staff may be brought in to attend training sessions or 'familiarization seminars' to enable them to know more about the products they are selling. They may assist in the preparation of sales literature, brochures, posters and other advertising material in their own languages while they are in this country. Listed briefly, the functions of the export department are:

(*a*) *To ensure that the product conforms with the technical requirements of the country of destination*. This may mean modifying the product in consultation with the production department to fit electric motors and other equipment appropriate to the country concerned.

(*b*) *To arrange adequate documentation*. Documentation must comply with the requirements of (i) the country of destination, which may require special documents for its import department, customs, central bank, etc.; (ii) the international conventions on road, rail, sea and air transport. In particular the TIR regulations, which allow loaded road haulage vehicles to go through customs without being inspected, are very strictly controlled. The **TIR carnets**, or books of documents, are purchased from the controlling offices in Switzerland. For EC countries similar T forms used to be required, but they were phased out on 1 January 1993, when goods were allowed to cross frontiers within the Community without inspection.

(*c*) *To communicate with overseas agents and branches*. This may be by air mail, or sea mail, but more often communication is achieved today by electronic data interchange (EDI). This is explained below. Fax and telex are also widely used.

(*d*) *To arrange packaging and despatch*. This may involve special considerations with regard to packing; times of departure of vessels and aircraft; compliance with insurance requirements and possibly with legal controls if goods are dangerous.

(*e*) *To ensure that financial safeguards over payment are arranged*. There are several different methods of arranging payment, of which the commonest are:

(i) Irrevocable credits confirmed by a London bank. When made available by the foreign customer these enable the London bank to pay the exporter, or accept a bill of exchange for him, which he can then discount on the London Discount Market.

(ii) Irrevocable credits with a foreign bank. These are similar to confirmed credits, but the London bank operates only as a correspondent and forwards the documents abroad for payment or acceptance by the foreign banker.

A full description of these and other methods of payment is given in Chapter 18.

11.10   Documents used in the export office

Overseas trade has to be particularly well documented, since government controls on both goods and finance are usually strict. Traditionally, merchants have devised their own documents to suit their own needs. In the last few years it has become increasingly obvious that much routine clerical time was being wasted in completing forms that carried the same information, but differently placed on each form. Some years ago the Board of Trade set up a joint liaison committee to investigate the whole problem of export documentation, with a view to preparing an **aligned series**, i.e. a complete set of documents of standard size with the same information in the same position. Modern duplicator techniques permit all the documents to be run off from a 'master document', and where certain details are not required on a particular form, a mask is fitted over the 'master', which obliterates the details not required. This work is now carried out by the **SITPRO Board** (the Simpler Trade Procedures Board). This body has now aligned some fifty forms, all of which can be run off either completely or partially from a SITPRO master document. The latest version of this document is reproduced in Figure 11.5. From this it is possible to reproduce all the main export documents. These are (*a*) the export invoice; (*b*) the bill of lading, or the short-form bill of lading or the sea waybill: (*c*) the single administrative document (SAD); (*d*) the national standard shipping note; (*e*) the insurance certificate; (*f*) the export consignment note; (*g*) the export cargo shipping instructions; (*h*) the certificate of origin; and (*i*) the air waybill.

With so many documents to prepare the advantages of SITPRO aligned documents are obvious. However, to some extent, technology has overtaken paper technology, for it is now possible to scan documents and turn them into a stream of electronic data that can be transmitted around the world. The documents required in the overseas country are sent in seconds and reconstituted at destination. (See EDI below, p. 204.)

A word about the various documents is now helpful:

(*a*) *The export invoice*. This is similar to an ordinary invoice but contains details of the vessel carrying the goods, the shipping marks used on the packages and the charges made.

(*b*) *The bill of lading*. This is the most important document in the export trade, because it represents the goods while they are in transit, and can be sold to transfer their ownership. Since the buyer of a bill of lading might run some risk if the goods were lost at sea, it always has attached to it the insurance policy which covers the consignment. If the goods are lost the buyer claims from the insurers.

In addition to the ordinary bill of lading described above, two new varieties are available in recent years. The **short-form bill of**

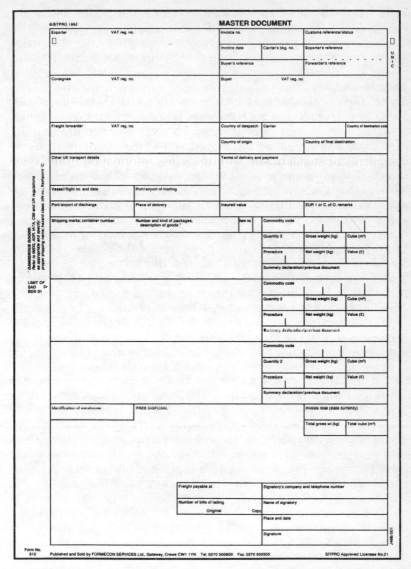

Figure 11.5 A master document (courtesy of the SITPRO Board)

lading is a very simple version of the original bill of lading, because it does not carry on the back of the form the very long and detailed contract of carriage between the shipowner and the consignor. Instead it refers in a box on the front to the standard terms and conditions offered by the shipowner to all those whose goods he carries. The other version is called the **sea waybill**. This is non-negotiable, which means the cargo cannot be transferred from one owner to another while it is on the high seas. This type of waybill is perfectly satisfactory when, for example, a multinational company sends goods to one of its subsidiaries overseas, and does not intend to sell the cargo to anyone else.

(*c*) *The single administrative document (SAD)*. This form used to be more important than it is today, because it was the single document used to control movements of goods between members of the European Community. This has now ceased but the form is still used to 'enter' goods at Customs for the wider world. To 'enter' goods at Customs is to notify Customs of the movement of goods through ports and airports. This is mainly a statistical procedure (to collect data about the volume and value of exports and imports), but it also gives control of drugs, armaments, etc.

(*d*) *The standard shipping note*. This has replaced all the shipping notes formerly issued by various ports around the country. Designed by SITPRO and now reproduced from their master document, it may be submitted to any port authority that is taking over goods for shipment. It tells them what goods are being handed over to their care, which ship they are to be loaded on, etc.

(*e*) *The insurance certificate*. A certificate proving that a policy has been taken out either with Lloyd's or with an insurance company to cover the goods while in transit.

(*f*) *The export consignment note*. This is a delivery note given to the road haulier who is taking goods to the docks to instruct him when and where to deliver the goods, and to secure a signature for them from the port authority or other warehouseman.

(*g*) *The export cargo shipping instructions*. When goods are sent to a freight forwarder to be packed for export and shipped by him, he has to be instructed on the nature of the goods, destination, etc. This form gives him all the details that he needs to know.

(*h*) *The air waybill*. Under the *Carriage by Air and Road Act, 1979*, which revised the rules of the Warsaw Convention in 1929, every consignment of goods by air must be covered by an air waybill in three parts. Part one is marked 'for the Carrier' and signed by the consignor. Part two is marked 'for the Consignee' and travels with the goods. It is signed by both the carrier and the consignor. Part three is signed by the carrier and returned to the consignor. We thus have each of the parties receiving a copy of the waybill signed by the other parties to the transaction.

(*i*) *The certificate of origin*. Certificates of origin are needed only where a free-trade area is afraid that its tariffs to non-members will be avoided by circuitous routings. For instance, if India allows British goods in duty-free, but charges German goods a tariff, a German firm might seek to evade the tariff by sending the goods to

Britain first and having them re-exported to India. A certificate of origin is usually issued by the Chamber of Commerce to certify that goods have been either entirely, or largely, manufactured in the country stated.

11.11 Standard terms and conditions

Goods are sold on certain standard terms, the meanings of which are understood by businessmen all over the world. They are published in a booklet produced by the International Chamber of Commerce, called *Incoterms 1990*. At present there are thirteen Incoterms with three-letter symbols to identify them. They are:

EXW (Ex works). The seller's duty is to make the goods available at his premises. The buyer must move the goods from the works and pay all charges for transport, insurance, etc.

FCA (Free carrier). The seller's duty is to deliver the goods to the carrier at a named point. The buyer must pay all charges and assume all responsibilities from that named point.

FAS (Free alongside ship). The seller's obligations are fulfilled when the goods arrive alongside the ship. The foreign importer must then pay for loading, freight and insurance charges.

FOB (Free on board). This means that the price quoted covers all charges up to the time the goods cross the ship's rail; after that the foreign importer becomes liable. The export office must notify the foreign buyer so that he can arrange insurance.

CFR (Cost and freight). Here the seller pays all charges up to the arrival of goods on board ship and the freight to the port of destination. The risk passes to the buyer as the goods cross the ship's rail, and insurance cover must be arranged by the buyer from that point.

CIF (Cost, insurance and freight). Here the final price on the invoice includes the cost of the goods, the insurance charges and the freight charges as far as the foreign port.

CPT (Carriage paid to). This is similar to CFR in that the seller pays the charges for carriage to the named destination, but the risk passes to the buyer as soon as goods are handed over to the first carrier, and not as they cross the ship's rail.

CIP (Carriage and insurance paid to). This is the same as CPT except that the seller must also arrange and pay for insurance of the goods to the named destination.

DAF (Delivered at frontier). The seller delivers the goods at the frontier, but before they go through the customs point of the country of arrival. The buyer must pay any customs duties on entry.

DES (Delivered ex ship). The seller must make the goods available to the buyer on board the ship at destination. The buyer must then unload and clear the goods from the port area.

DEQ (Delivered ex quay). There are two types of contract: 'ex quay duty paid' and 'ex quay — duties on buyer's account'. The seller must deliver the goods on the quayside at destination, either duty paid or duty unpaid. The buyer bears all charges from that point, including customs duties if the second alternative applies.

DDU (Delivered duty unpaid). The seller delivers to the destination address but any duty on entering the country is for the buyer's account.

DDP (Delivered duty paid). This is the term with the maximum burden for the seller. Goods must be delivered to the buyer's premises, duty paid, but terms like 'DDP exclusive of VAT and/or taxes' may be agreed.

11.12 Electronic data interchange (EDI)

Some of the problems of export trade have always been concerned with the difference between documents and goods. Whatever the goods are, we tend to move them separately from the documents. The goods are delivered to the port or airport, and are taken on board (shipped on board is the traditional term) and move to destination. While they are *en route*, the document represents ownership in the case of the bill of lading, and in the case of the air waybill it represents the right to claim the goods from the carrier, which usually takes place at destination of course. The documents have to move to the person who is finally going to claim the goods at destination, or claim on the insurance policy if the goods are lost. As the documents move they may themselves be lost, or stolen, and the wrong person may claim the goods at destination.

Clearly, if we can move the documents electronically (at the speed of light), we can save a lot of uncertainty, and the documents arrive at destination not only before the goods reach their destination, but possibly before the goods have even set off. Electronic data interchange is the interchange of information, formerly provided on documents, by electronic means. To do this we need a world-wide network, with all exporters, importers, carriers, customs authorities, banks, etc., interlinked and able to gain access to the information stored within the various computers in the network. We also have to exclude all those who do not have any interest in the cargoes on the move around the world. All this is not easy, and requires internationally agreed procedures, e.g. we must know how a document is to be turned into a collection of electronic impulses that can be sent along a wire, or a glass fibre, or on a radio wave from one part of the world to another; and how when it reaches its destination it can be turned back into a screen display or a hard copy (a document).

The basic principle of EDI

The basic principle of EDI is the transfer of 'structured business information' from computer to computer, to eliminate the need for paper documents. 'Structured business information' means any typical body of information, such as an invoice, a credit note, a bill of lading, a certificate of origin, etc. If we can turn such forms into a *standard message format*, they can be sent as a stream of data, to be reassembled at destination. The message can be stored in a computer's memory somewhere along the line − for safety's sake some organizations store everything in two places − usually on different continents. Thus a message sent from London to Honolulu might be stored in Holland and New York, giving four places that would get the message. It is unlikely a message could be lost if four places as far apart as that have it stored. They won't all suffer a power failure at the same time. Having a standard message format means that all the computers know which bit of message is coming first and which bit is coming next, and so the whole thing arrives in the expected sequence. The United Nations is active in this field, getting nations to accept an agreed format.

We cannot go any deeper into this system here, but those who work in export and import offices need to get to know all about EDI, and to join the growing number of firms who use this method of 'paperless trading.' The forms sent can be followed by personal messages to meet individual needs and situations, and to give any explanations or special details.

11.13 Points to think about and discuss

(*a*) You are about to set up in business with your best friend as couriers, delivering urgent packages, letters, etc., around a city area, and to two airports within easy range. How would you advertise such a service? Your premises are small, but convenient to the city centre, and you will use motorcycles and mopeds for most deliveries, but a light van is also available.

(*b*) A large firm for which you do regular work is a slow payer. How would you deal with the problem? Although they signed your conditions of trading, in which you required them to pay 30 days after invoice date, they now laugh at you and say 'We never pay anyone in less than 90 days!'

(*c*) Your manager asks you to give him sound reasons for moving over to electronic data interchange in export trade. What reasons could you give?

11.14 Rapid revision − sales

Cover the page with a sheet of paper and uncover one question at a time.

Answers	Questions
–	1 What are the two chief aspects of selling?
1 Wholesale and retail.	2 Which of these do we usually associate with a sales department?
2 Wholesale selling	3 What are the functions of a sales department?
3 (*a*) To prepare and commission brochures, posters and other advertising material about the firm's products, (*b*) to train a staff of representatives or commercial travellers, (*c*) to stage demonstrations of the firm's products at appropriate places and times, (*d*) to deal with all orders, including documentation, and passing them to the dispatch department. (*e*) to keep the management informed of progress, problem areas, etc.	4 What are the functions of advertising?
4 (*a*) To inform the public about the firm's products, and explain their uses and attributes, (*b*) to persuade the public to buy the product, especially where it is in competition with other brands, (*c*) to keep the firm's name constantly before the public.	5 What problems arise in dealing with a sales force?
5 (*a*) The sales representatives must be knowledgeable about the product. This requires training courses, and seminars to update their information, (*b*) the sales territory must be defined and arrangements made to contact the representative, (*c*) an adequate scheme of remuneration must be devised.	6 What means may be used to bring the firm's products to the notice of the public?
6 (*a*) National press and television, (*b*) magazine advertising, (*c*) local press, and local campaigns aimed at doorstep sales, (*d*) special mailings and free sample offers, (*e*) wholesalers' demonstrations, (*f*) exhibitions and fairs, (*g*) fax campaigns.	7 What is the sequence of documents that might be used in the course of a sales transaction?
7 (*a*) The enquiry letter, (*b*) estimates or quotations; (*c*) an order, (*d*) acknowledgment of the order, (*e*) invoice, (*f*) debit note, (*g*) credit note, (*h*) statement, (*i*) cheque, (*j*) receipt.	8 What is trade discount?

8 It is a reduction in the catalogue price of an item. It is given to the retailer so that he/she can make a profit when selling at the catalogue price.	9 What are cash discounts and settlement discounts?
9 Cash discounts are discounts given to customers who pay cash at once. Settlement discounts are discounts given to account customers who pay promptly when a statement is rendered.	10 What is VAT?
10 A tax levied by the government whenever goods or services are supplied to a customer. The amount added to the bill belongs to HM Customs and Excise Dept.	11 How does a firm account for VAT?
11 It pays over the VAT it has collected from customers (the output tax) less the VAT it has paid to its suppliers (the input tax). As a result the tax it pays is tax on the value added – hence the name Value Added Tax.	12 What is an invoice?
12 A business document made out whenever one person supplies goods, or provides services, to another person.	13 What is a credit note?
13 A business document made out whenever one person returns goods to another, or is made an allowance that reduces his/her debt.	14 When does a hire purchase agreement come to an end?
14 When the purchase takes effect because the last instalment is paid. From that moment on the arrangement ceases to be a hire and becomes a purchase.	15 Go over the page again until you are sure of all the answers.

11.15 Rapid revision – exports

Cover the page with a sheet of paper and uncover one question at a time.

Answers	Questions
–	1 Why are exports important?
1 Because the only way to pay for the goods we need to import from abroad is to earn foreign exchange by selling to other countries.	2 What particular problems face the exporter?

2 (*a*) Language problems, (*b*) currency problems, (*c*) licensing regulations, (*d*) problems of documentation, (*e*) controls over quality, safety, packaging, etc., vary from country to country, (*f*) marine and aviation risks, (*g*) risks that debtors will prove to be bad.

3 What documents are met with in the export trade?

---

3 (*a*) Export invoices, (*b*) bills of lading, (*c*) sea waybills, (*d*) customs entries, (*e*) shipping notes, (*f*) insurance certificates, (*g*) export consignment notes, (*h*) export cargo shipping instructions, (*i*) air waybills; (*j*) certificates of origin.

4 What is the meaning of FAS?

---

4 Free alongside ship.

5 And of FOB?

---

5 Free on board.

6 And of CIF?

---

6 Cost, insurance, freight.

7 What is the significance of these different abbreviations?

---

7 There are thirteen of them altogether. They are called Incoterms 90. Each one tells the parties engaged in international trade the point to which the exporter will be responsible for the goods. With FAS the exporter sees them to the ship's side. With FOB he/she pays all charges until the ship's rail is crossed. With CIF he/she covers the property until it reaches the foreign port.

8 What is EDI?

---

8 Electronic data interchange. The movement of structured business information (forms) as a stream of electronic messages that transfer the document around the world and reconstitute it when desired as a screen display or hard copy at destination.

9 What is the essential basis for such transfers?

---

9 An agreed 'standard message format,' so that all computers know which part of the form is arriving first, and which next, until the whole form has moved.

10 Go over the page until you are sure of all the answers.

Exercises set 11

1 Write down the letters (*a*)–(*j*) on a sheet of paper and against each letter write the word or phrase from the word list at the end of the exercise which best fits into the gap in the sentences below.

(*a*) In a large company the official in charge of the whole area of sales management would probably be designated ......

(*b*) A ...... is a person who visits wholesalers and large retailers around the country seeking orders for his company by showing products and giving demonstrations.

(c) ...... are shows at which a wide variety of firms can display their products and solicit orders from wholesalers and retailers.

(d) A quotation is an offer to supply that is susceptible of immediate ...... by the enquirer.

(e) The document made out whenever one person supplies goods or services to another is the ......

(f) When a customer orders more goods when he/she has not paid for the previous order, we can protect ourselves by sending only a ...... invoice.

(g) My Barclaycard statement arrives each month on about the 12th day of the month; they must use ......

(h) A person who sends us an invoice for goods they have supplied becomes one of our ......

(i) If one of our customers returns goods because we have sent the wrong product, we send them a ......

(j) The letters APR stand for ......, and are required by law on all hire purchase agreements.

Word list: Exhibitions, invoice, marketing director, cyclical billing, acceptance, credit note, annual percentage rate, commercial traveller, creditors, pro-forma.

2   You are setting up a small business to be called 'Beautiful Gardens'. It will offer all sorts of garden products. Although most customers will pay cash, some local firms will want to be invoiced for goods and to pay on monthly terms. Devise an appropriate invoice. To conform with the Business Names Act, 1985 you must show the names of the proprietors – yourself and a partner.

3   Draw up an estimate to be sent to Green and Robertson Ltd, 22 Mayview Road, Charlestown, CH4 1PQ, notifying them that you estimate the cost of their proposed extension to premises at Materials £4725; Labour £7924, design and other costs £12425. VAT is to be levied at 10 per cent. Give your own name and address as Master Builders Co., 135 High St, Charleston, CH3 1BA.

4   Your company wishes to sell goods in the following ways: (a) on credit, (b) by COD, (c) against cash with order. Outline three suitable office routines, one for each of the above methods, from the time when an order is received until the times when goods are despatched and payment is made.

5   (a) What is the difference between trade discount and cash discount?
    (b) A business sells goods to R. Martin for £600 on 1 January, subject to trade discount of 40 per cent and $2\frac{1}{2}$ per cent cash discount within 1 month of receiving the monthly statement. This is sent out on the 25th of each month. What would be the amount that Martin would pay if he settled his account on 17 February? What must he pay if he settles the account on 28 February?
    (c) Give the meaning of three of the following terms and abbreviations: E & OE, CWO, net, APR, deposit, instalment, HP.

6 Explain the hire purchase method of selling. What are its advantages and disadvantages?

7 (*a*) List four ways in which a supplier may draw his products to the attention of customers. (*b*) Explain one of the methods in reasonable detail.

8 Which types of products would respond to the following methods of advertising.

(*a*) Leaflet distribution from house to house.
(*b*) Local newspaper advertising.
(*c*) Advertising in trade journals.
(*d*) Television advertising.
(*e*) Promotional videos.

In each case justify your answer by a short explanation.

9 (*a*) A firm receives an order from a customer who has no credit account with that firm and does not enclose any payment with its order. What action should be taken by the firm?
(*b*) What records about customers would you expect a firm's credit control department to keep? What would the firm do if one of its customers had not yet settled an account which was several months overdue?

10 (*a*) You are employed as a sales clerk with responsibility for credit control and you receive an order to the value of £500 from a firm with whom you have had no previous dealings. The representative who was successful in securing the order asks you to consider giving the purchaser one month's credit. What action would you take before executing the order?
(*b*) What information about customers would you require on your sales record cards?

11 What problems face the exporter of goods? Describe the special features of an export department designed to overcome these problems.

12 What documents met in the export trade are not necessary in the home trade? How may such documents be prepared economically?

13 Explain briefly the difference between the export of goods on FAS terms and export on CIF terms.

14 Two identical consignments of goods are being exported to Japan. One consignment is on FOB terms, the other on CIF terms. Which will have the larger invoice price, and why?

15 An insurance agent is drawing up a 'statement of risk' slip for an exporter, with a view to obtaining insurance cover for him. The cargo consists of twenty crates of furs to be shipped from Leningrad to London. List the risks that should be considered in such a consignment, so that the exporter will be adequately covered.

16 What is a bill of lading? What is its importance in the export trade?

17   An export house is arranging the purchase of textile machinery for a Hong Kong mill. What chain of events will lead to the eventual arrival of the machinery in Hong Kong?

18   'Export documentation is more expensive than home documentation.' List the documents likely to be necessary in (*a*) a home sale of five pieces of machinery, delivered by road and paid for COD; (*b*) an export sale of five pieces of machinery, air freighted to Australia and paid for by irrevocable letter of credit.

19   What is electronic data interchange. Explain the advantages of EDI to the various parties in an export transaction.

20   What is a 'standard message format' in EDI? Why is it important to agree to such a standard?

12 Filing, indexing and record-keeping

12.1 Introduction

Every firm receives and despatches a great deal of correspondence daily. All letters, circulars, information bulletins and reports received will eventually be put away where they can be found when required for reference purposes. Of course there will be a certain amount of 'junk mail', which is of no interest to us at all, and this will be discarded. One famous office tycoon recently declared that the most important piece of filing equipment in any office is the waste-paper basket. Against that we may say that much of the mail of a promotional nature that is not of immediate interest to us may at some future time become of interest. It is a good idea to appoint a special person to receive all this material and file it away under various headings, so that when some need arises for that particular class of material, it can be considered.

Most correspondence going out will have copies taken for our own purposes, and such copy letters must be stored away where they can be easily located when needed. This type of work is called **filing**.

Filing may be defined as the storing of letters and documents in a systematic way so that they may be retrieved at a later date for reference purposes. The work of filing is the responsibility of filing clerks and the supervisors of centralized filing systems. The organization may vary from a simple filing cabinet to a huge, but compact, electronically controlled storage system such as Conserve-a-trieve, a system controlled by a single operator. A piece of correspondence may be retrieved when required by calling electronically for its storage container. Figure 12.1 illustrates the system.

12.2 Essentials of a good filing system

A good filing system should have the following characteristics:

(a) *Simplicity*. The system should be easy to follow and simple to operate, even by a non-specialist member of staff.

(b) *Security*. The system should be as secure as is required by the matter concerned. Personnel records, wages records, company policy records, etc., should be very secure. Catalogues and similar items should be more generally available and accessible to all staff.

Figure 12.1 Automated electronic filing

(*c*) *Compactness with comprehensiveness*. Clearly it is not easy to reconcile these two opposite requirements. Generally speaking, we need files to be comprehensive about the matter they are concerned with but we need a compact system to enable files to be stored conveniently and with easy access. A clear policy of **document retention** will enable compactness to be more easily secured. If documents have to be retained forever, then adequate reserve storage should be provided, and a clear policy about transfer into the reserve stores should be laid down. If documents may be destroyed after a given time, then this should be clearly laid down and **document shredders** might well be provided. (A document shredder reduces a document in seconds to a mass of paper waste, which may be used as packing materials in the despatch department.)

(*d*) *A clear cross-reference system* to enable staff who look for documents in a wrong section to find the correct section where the file required has been stored (see p. 220).

(*e*) *A systematic 'tracer' and 'follow-up' system.* Senior staff may call for a file at any time to deal with an emergency situation. If the file required is out, they may be in difficulty unless it can be traced. An 'out' card tracer system (see p. 221) will overcome this difficulty. Similarly, a 'follow-up' system (see p. 222) will chase up files kept for longer than necessary and reduce the numbers of files missing from the filing system. Should they be required, these files will then be available for special action.

(*f*) *An appropriate classification system.* There are a number of alternative methods of storing records. The most satisfactory system should be selected, bearing in mind the requirements of the business. This sometimes leads to conflicting systems in some businesses, one department preferring records to be arranged geographically, for example, while another prefers a subject classification. Conflict is most likely where the adoption of a centralized system is forcing departments that have formerly pleased themselves to align their arrangements.

12.3 Centralized filing systems

Whether or not it is advisable to centralize filing systems depends upon the size of an organization and the extent to which different departments need to consult the same records. Centralized filing is never desirable for confidential records, such as personnel, wages and salary records. Briefly the relative advantages and disadvantages may be set down as follows:

Advantages of a centralized filing system

(*a*) Clear responsibility will be laid down for filing. Adequate equipment will be provided and qualified staff will be appointed or trained.

(*b*) Related matter from all departments will be filed together, so that staff consulting a file will be fully informed.

(*c*) Records will be better maintained, better supervised and properly controlled by management. Staff who are inefficient in their attitude to record-keeping will be pinpointed, and may be educated and trained to improve their attitude.

Disadvantages of a centralized filing system

(*a*) It is time-consuming to have to order files and wait for them to appear.

(*b*) Filing staff cannot have the departmental knowledge that is so helpful when filing departmentally. They must therefore rely upon the filing indications given by the departmental staff submitting material for filing.

(*c*) Filing in departments is often used as a routine time-filler, which enables staff to employ themselves busily at times when other work is not available. If these activities are performed centrally by specialists, then total staff employed must rise.

12.4 Filing systems

In ordinary filing, correspondence is placed in a **file folder**, and is given a title before being filed under one or other of the major filing systems. It is worth starting a file folder for correspondence only if there is some probability that a lengthy course of correspondence will develop with that firm. Other letters are filed in a **miscellaneous file**, in alphabetical order with the letter A on the top, B below it and so on. When several letters for the same firm have accumulated, it is worth opening a file for that particular correspondence.

The major filing systems may be listed as follows:

(*a*) The alphabetical system.
(*b*) The numerical system.
(*c*) The alpha-numerical system, which combines the above systems.
(*d*) The subject system.
(*e*) The geographical system.

The alphabetical system

The alphabetical system of filing is the commonest in business. It is most easily understood, and is direct. This means that the filing clerk goes directly to the filing tray with the correct initial letter and searches it to find the file, which will be in alphabetical order in the tray. To assist the clerk to find the file quickly, the following guides are available:

(*a*) The trays have a name-plate in the front to indicate the contents, e.g. A–E.

(*b*) Primary guide cards are inserted with the visible portion sticking up on the left-hand side of the tray.

(*c*) Secondary guide cards are inserted with the visible portion sticking up in the centre of the tray.

(*d*) The labels on the individual files are placed at the right-hand end of the file.

A good filing clerk will therefore cast his/her eye first to the left to locate the primary section required, then to the centre, to locate the sub-section required, and then to the right to pinpoint the actual file. Figure 12.2 illustrates these points.

To assist the reader with the many rules of alphabetical filing a special section at the end of this chapter (see p. 225) explains them fully.

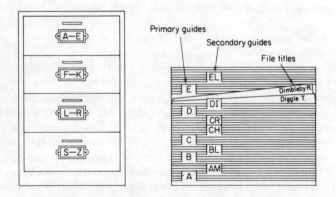

Figure 12.2 Alphabetical filing

The numerical system

The numerical system of filing has an advantage in that there is a vast range of numbers that can be used, whereas there are only twenty-six letters in the alphabet. It is not direct, like the alphabetical system, for it is impossible to go directly to the file in the cabinets. Instead the filing clerk must refer to a reference index, to find the number allocated to that file. This reference index is itself in alphabetical order, and is known as the alphabetical index file. The index gives the numbers of the files which may then be found in the filing cabinets. Figure 12.3 shows the two different arrangements. The numerical system shown is the simpler of the two possible numerical systems. It is called the **consecutive digit system**, since a new file is simply given the next consecutive number.

A variation upon the numerical system, which has the advantage of spreading the new files over the range of filing cabinets, is called the **terminal digit filing system**. The idea is to put new files into successive filing cabinets rather than into the same filing cabinet, as with the consecutive digit system. Since new files tend to be more active than old-established files, a large number of new files in the same drawer may cause delays. Several staff may wish to consult a file in the same drawer.

If the files occupy the cabinet displaying the terminal digit, only every tenth new file will be in any given cabinet. Thus if we take the first ten files numbered 1–10, file No 1 will be in No 1 cabinet, file No 2 will be in the second cabinet, and so on down to file No 10 which will be in cabinet No 0. As new customers are dealt with and are added to the filing system, they are given the next number available. Suppose in a busy office the next three numbers available are 3285, 3286 and 3287. The files opened for these customers will not all be in the same cabinet. The first will be in the fifth cabinet, the next will be in cabinet No 6 and the third will be in cabinet No 7. This reduces the chances of a clash between staff trying to use the same cabinet to extract the details they require from the files stored away.

More advanced terminal digit systems can be used, where each indexed item will be given three numbers: a document number, a file number and a cabinet number. These might read 32 : 14 : 03. The letter concerned will be the 32nd item in the 14th file in the 3rd cabinet.

The alpha-numerical system

This system is a combination of the other two systems. Files are entered in the major sections of the system in alphabetical order, but each letter section is then filed in numerical order, with a **guide card** at the start of each section listing the numbers of the files in that section of the filing system. A typical guide card would be as

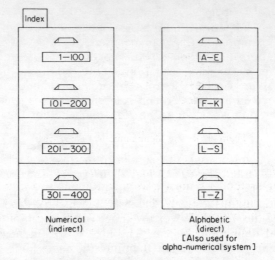

Figure 12.3   Alternative filing systems

shown in Figure 12.4. The index letter would indicate clearly the start of files beginning with L. The guide card would then pinpoint the particular file required. Periodically the filing clerk would update the guide card, putting the files listed into alphabetical order. As the reader will notice, the early files are listed alphabetically, but filed numerically. Recent additions are listed numerically, but at a later date will be incorporated into the alphabetical list.

Classifying files by subject

Some firms find it convenient to file under subjects, at least for part of their work. Thus, the general administration office may file items under the main subject headings of its activities, premises, staffing, insurance, equipment, contracts, telephones, sublettings, etc. As the firm grows, some sub-division within these major headings may become necessary. Premises may require files on leases, repairs, cleaning, lighting and heating, plant layout, drainage, electricity and telephone systems, etc. Once again primary and secondary guides will lead the filing clerk through the intricacies of the system, and an alert clerk will be ready to recommend to a superior any sub-divisions that become necessary. For example, the clerk might receive repeated requests for a file for the Alpha Omega Repair Co. Ltd. The clerk knows that this material is filed under 'General repairs', but it might be more convenient to allocate this correspondence to a separate file since the company's services are being used repetitively for a wide variety of repair jobs. Figure 12.5 shows a typical subject classification, with primary, secondary and tertiary guides.

L				
	No.			No.
Lanham, E.	7	Lucey, R.		1
Lawrence, T.H.	2	Luckford, H.		6
Lee, J.	5	Larkin, T.		10
Lott, R.	4	Lee, V.		11
Love, P.	9	Leary, P.S.		12
Lovegrove, S.	3			
Lovett, T.D.	8			

Figure 12.4   An alpha-numerical guide card

Card indexes for 'subject' filing systems. Whenever we have a subject filing system, we must have a card index showing the names of all correspondents and the files where their information is filed. For example, a request from a departmental head to 'Bring me the file for Porlock and Sons' might be difficult to fulfil if the filing clerk was not sure which subject it was filed under. A reference to a card index would quickly reveal that Porlock and Sons were lift repairers, and their correspondence was filed under lift repairs.

Card indexes may be purchased very cheaply from any stationer's shop. They consist of a neat box, either with a drawer to pull out or a lid to be opened up. Inside is a pack of white or coloured cards and a set of index cards A, B, C, etc., which may be used as guide cards. Each card has a top edge which is used for the name of the firm concerned, and details are given about the place where the firms' records are filed. Figure 12.6 shows a typical card for such an index system.

Classifying files by geographical area
It is sometimes convenient to file information geographically. Thus a large sales force may be divided into counties, with the representatives

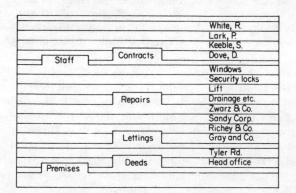

Figure 12.5   Filing by subjects

Porlock & Sons
Lift repairers
See 'lift-repairs'
Also 'Emergency arrangements'
227 Kiln Road
Muswell Hill
London
N10 2DT   081 000 0000

Figure 12.6   A card for a card index

or agents in each county filed alphabetically. An export house may
file under the countries to which exports are sent. Within these main
filing divisions the material may be filed under firms or under subjects. Once again a card index would be necessary if a 'subject'
classification is adopted.

12.5   Cross-referencing

It often happens that a name consists of several words, and staff will
request files in different ways. Thus British Air Ferries Ltd might be
wrongly rquested as Air Ferries Ltd, or even as 'the air ferry firm'.
To save trouble in future the filing clerk should make out a cross-
reference card (for a card index system) or a cross-reference sheet
for an alphabetical system. The next time she receives a request for
Air Ferries Ltd the index card or reference sheet will tell her 'Air
Ferries Ltd – see British Air Ferries Ltd'.

**A cross-reference card, or cross-reference sheet, should be made
out whenever a file may be requested under a title other than its true
title.**

Cross-references may also be recorded on the **file title** itself, on a
special guide card, or on the cover of a file folder. The latter
method is most useful where one firm is a subsidiary of another, so
that two files of correspondence might well be existence. Thus if
Supergrowers Ltd has a subsidiary Chemical Fertiliser Co., the
file for Supergrowers Ltd might bear the cross-reference (see also
Chemical Fertiliser Co.) while the file for Chemical Fertiliser Co.
would bear the cross-reference (see also Supergrowers Ltd).

Many foreign names are confusing to filing clerks. The Chinese
always begin with the surname, while Mohammedans have all their

names as surnames, taking the father's name, the gradfather's name and the great-grandfather's name. Often they will use these names in any order.

As an alternative to cross-references it is sometimes better to make a photocopy of an important letter. This is then filed in the less important file, the original letter being filed in the more frequently requested file cover.

Some typical cross-reference guides, or guide cards, are illustrated in Figure 12.7.

12.6 'Out' markers

When a file is removed, or when a letter is removed from a file, it should be replaced with an 'out' marker. These may be of several types. One of them is shown in the Expandex Filing System illustrated in Fig. 12.12 on p. 233. It shows the 'out' tab sticking up to indicate which file has been removed. On the card itself spaces are ruled so that information can be written in as to the destination of the file and the likely date of return. This information will enable the file to be traced and retrieved after it is no longer required. A system of follow-up procedures can be instituted to ensure that files are returned.

Sometimes, instead of recording this information, the 'out' card has a simple pocket into which the original **request slip** for the file can be inserted. This saves times, since the person requesting the file has already written all the information on the request slip.

A further method of recording files which are out is to keep a book record of the files sent to staff. This is like a 'day book' in accounting, recording every file going out and its destination.

We thus have three methods of recording 'out' files. These are:

(*a*) 'Out' cards, the same size as a file, with a projecting tab saying 'out', and room to record where the file has gone. On return the file is replaced, the 'out' card is removed, and the line recording

Figure 12.7 Typical cross-reference cards

who had this particular file is closed by inserting the date of return in the space provided. The 'out' card may then be re-used elsewhere.

(b) 'Out' cards with a pocket for 'request slips'. On return the file is replaced, the 'out' card removed and the request slip destroyed.

(c) A 'files requested' day book which lists all files sent out, and records their return.

Each of these methods may then be used in some sort of follow-up system.

12.7 Follow-up systems

One of the chief problems with any filing system is the tendency of executives and other staff to hold on to files and documents longer than necessary. This makes serious difficulties for the filing clerk, since correspondence is arriving all the time and the file will be out of date, and letters awaiting its return must be stored in a temporary file. The filing department therefore operates a follow-up system.

The follow-up systems most commonly in use are as follows:

(a) The daily scanning system

Here a small filing system is scanned every morning by the chief filing clerk, who lists any overdue files. The member of staff who has borrowed the file is then requested to return it, or to book it out for a further period. This daily scanning system is very easy if the 'files requested' day book is in use since it is only necessary to look through the book to see which files are still out, and overdue.

(b) The 'tickler' system

This is a more useful system in many ways, since it provides a method of securing not only the return of files, but also other regular check-up procedures. For example, the production manager might wish to review the progress made on a particular project at regular intervals, and might therefore request that the file on this project be sent to him as a matter of routine on the fifteenth day of every month. This request would be recorded in the 'tickler' system and would 'tickle' the filing clerk's memory on the correct day. Similarly, a bad payer's file might be requested by the accountant, who would stop further supplies to the customer if the account had not been settled by a certain date each month.

The 'tickler' system consists of two sets of cards, a set headed with the names of the months, and a second set headed with days, 1−31. The system enables records to be placed in the system at a point where action is to be taken, and a daily and monthly review can thus be made. The system is illustrated in Figure 12.8.

Its use may be described as follows:

Figure 12.8   A 'tickler' system

Daily system. When files are sent out, the file requisition slip is placed in the section of the daily list at the point where the file should be retrieved. Thus, a file requested on the 10th for three days should be returned on the 13th. The request slip would be inserted into the 'tickler' system on the 14th, by which time it will definitely be overdue. If it is returned before that date, the request slip will be extracted and destroyed. If it is not returned, the member of staff will be contacted and the file retrieved.

Monthly system. Some routine procedures are carried out at regular intervals, e.g. the removal of 'dead' files to storage. The monthly card system enables such routine work to be spread around the year adequately. For example, it might be best to review these matters in months which were known to be 'slack' months, when little other work was available. This would be recorded on the monthly card system and the necessary action taken. Similarly, certain actions, such as the renewal of fire insurance premiums, occur only in a particular month of the year. A record on the monthly card system that Mr Jones was to receive the fire insurance file on the Lea Bridge Road premises on the 15 October every year would remind Mr Jones that he must review the policy and contact the insurers if any updating of the 'cover' is necessary.

Every day, and every month, the card for that day or month is moved to the back of the file and the next day, or month, with its duties, is commenced.

12.8 How to file a letter

The following procedure is recommended:

(*a*) Discover whether there is a file folder for that particular letter. This may mean looking straight into the files if the system is alphabetical, or there may be card index to help the search.

(*b*) If there is a file folder, find it and place the new letter on top, since letters are filed in date order with the most recent letter highest in the pile. This order of filing is called *chronological order* (from the Greek word *khronos* = time). Letters filed in chronological order assist staff who know roughly when a letter was written, or a contract made, and can turn, in the correspondence, to that date and search through until they discover the letter concerned.

(*c*) If there is no file folder, file the letter in the miscellaneous file. Here the letters are filed in alphabetical order, i.e. Allen before Allsop, and Barker before Brown, and in each firm's correspondence the new letter is placed on top of the batch. If half a dozen letters have accumulated, consider whether a file folder for that set of correspondence should be opened.

(*d*) Consider whether any cross-referencing is necessary. If the letter relates to more than one aspect of the business and should be filed in two or three places we can either copy it and file the copies in each place, or put the letter in the chief place and a cross-reference to it in the other places.

12.9 How to find a letter

To find a letter the following procedure is recommended:

(*a*) Discover whether there is a file folder for that particular letter. This may mean looking straight into the files in an alphabetical system, or there may be a card index to help the search.

(*b*) If there is a file folder, find it and remove the file.

(*c*) If the whole file is to be sent to a particular person, record its destination by the use of an 'out' marker.

(*d*) If the file is the 'miscellaneous' file, remove only the desired correspondence from it, marking its position with an 'out' marker placed in the pile of correspondence at the appropriate point. Send the correspondence required in a temporary file folder to the person who wants it.

(*e*) If the request slip calls for only a particular letter from a file, remove that letter, mark its position with an 'out' marker and send it in a temporary file folder to the person requiring it.

(*f*) If the office uses a 'tickler' system, record in the system that the file is out and its destination so that it does not get lost and its return can be requested at a later date if the applicant fails to return it.

12.10   Rules for filing alphabetically

To assist the reader with the many rules of alphabetical filing the next few pages have been divided into a series of **alphabetical filing rules**. Each group has been given a number, and short practice exercises are included to help the reader to master the rules. The answers are given at the end of this section (see Section 12.17, p. 244).

Alphabetical filing rules 1 − indexing units

The ordinary alphabetical index is used in alphabetical filing to decide in which order the files shall be stored. The sequence is decided by considering the name of the person, or firm, and regarding every element in it as an **indexing unit**. Thus, Margaret Potter has two indexing units, while J. V. H. Knott and Overseas Groupage Forwarders Ltd each have four indexing units.

These indexing units are then inspected to decide which is the first indexing unit. With personal names the surname is usually chosen as the first indexing unit, and the 'given' names or initials then follow, as second, third, etc., indexing units. With impersonal names, such as the Borough Council of Newtown and the Diocese of Oxford, the first indexing unit is the first word that distinguishes that body from all other bodies. Thus:

Borough (there are many boroughs)
Council (there are many councils)
Newtown (this is − if not unique − at least very distinctive)

We would therefore index the title as: Newtown, Borough Council of.

Two important rules are 'nothing comes before something' and 'short before long'. Thus Potter comes before Potter, H., which comes before Potter, Harry.

Practical exercise 1   Select the correct first indexing unit in the following names (for the answers see p. 244).

(*a*) Alfred J. Marshall
(*b*) Peter R. Cummings
(*c*) Daniel Daniels
(*d*) M. V. T. Potterton and Co. Ltd
(*e*) Liverpool Wheat Exchange
(*f*) R. S. V. Paterson & Co. Ltd
(*g*) Zoological Gardens of Chester
(*h*) Chartered Institute of Transport
(*i*) Terry Mendoza (Photographics) Ltd
(*j*) Seamen's Society

Alphabetical filing rules II — indexing personal names

As already explained, the most important indexing unit, the surname, is placed first. Margaret Potter becomes Potter, Margaret, and J. V. H. Knott bexomes Knott, J. V. H.

Since K comes before P they would be arranged in sequence as follows:

> Knott, J. V. H.
> Potter, Margaret

Practical exercise 2   Arrange the following names in alphabetical order, correctly indexed (for the answers see p. 244).

(*a*) Peter Jones, Daniel Wheddon, Harry Hawke
(*b*) Samuel P. Larkin, Silas T. Lark, Ruby M. Lazarus
(*c*) A.J. Cronin, H. Melville, Rudyard Kipling, Charles Dickens

When the surnames have the same first letter, the second letter of the surname is used to decide the sequence, or if necessary the third letter of the surname.

Thus, Tom Driver, Roy Drover and Peter Dimbleby would be indexed in the order shown below:

> Dimbleby, Peter
> Driver, Tom
> Drover, Roy

Where the entire names are identical, the sequence is decided by the address. Thus David Jones, Cardiff; David Jones, Bramhall; David Jones, Stepney, would appear as:

> Jones, David, Bramhall
> Jones, David, Cardiff
> Jones, David, Stepney

Practical exercise 2a   Arrange the following names in correct sequence (for the answers see p. 244).

(*a*) R. Chambers, R. Chalmers, Eric Chalmers, Edith Chumleigh
(*b*) R. Fortescue & Sons Ltd, R. Fortescue, R. Forte, Peter Forth
(*c*) Howard Proctor Ltd, Peter Howard, P. T. Howard
(*d*) Gurr & Co. Ltd, Ben Gunn, B. Gunn Ltd, B. Gnu, B. Gnutsen
(*e*) R. Marshall & Co. Ltd, R. Marshall, Rosemary Marshall
(*f*) P. Lane, Penny Lane, Penelope Lane, Penelope P. Langdon
(*g*) Glover & Sons Ltd, Grover & Co., Glouceston Ltd, P. Grimes Ltd

(*h*) Murray, John Murray, John Martin, Joan Martindale
(*i*) Lyons of Dumbarton, Lyons of Doncaster, Lyons of Lyonnesse
(*j*) Armstrong (Dover) Ltd, Armstrong (Middlesex) Ltd, Armstrong (Manchester) Ltd

Alphabetical filing rules III − titles, degrees and decorations
Titles, degrees and decorations are *not* looked upon as indexing units. They are placed after the name, but are ignored. Thus the following would be listed in the manner shown:

Mrs Rose Godley, Sir George Godley, Rt Revd Thomas Godley

Godley, Sir George
Godley, Mrs Rose
Godley, Rt Revd Thomas

Practice exercise 3 List the following groups of names in correct alphabetical order (for the answers see p. 245).

(*a*) Mrs M. L. Gilbert, M. Gilbert, OBE, Professor Martin Gilbert
(*b*) Dr Howard Jones, MD, R. Jones, DFC, Mrs Rita Jones
(*c*) Mrs D. W. Heather, Lady Doreen Heather, Sir Dennis Heather, CH.

Alphabetical filing rules IV − names with a prefix
Many names have prefixes, such as O', Mc, Mac, Da, Du, Van and Von. With all such names the whole name is the first indexing unit, so that Peter van Tromp appears as

Van Tromp, Peter

and Leonardo da Vinci as

Da Vinci, Leonardo

Two different methods are used for Mac and Mc. Sometimes a special section in the files is given to these names. If so Mac and Mc are treated as if they were the same, and all names with these prefixes are filed in the special section under the letters that come after the prefix. Thus Macadam, Macnamara and McCardy would be filed as:

Macadam
McCardy
Macnamara

If there is not a special section then the names are filed as they are written, and the three names listed above would be rearranged as:

Macadam
Macnamara
McCardy

Another group that is often given a separate section is the group of names beginning with Saint or St. If there is a separate section, usually in the 'sa' part of the index, the names are treated as if spelled out in full, i.e. Saint, and this is treated as the first indexing unit. Some indexers put all the Saints together, followed by the Sts. Others mix them in together, treating them all as Saints and using the second indexing unit to determine the correct order.

Practice exercise 4 List the following groups of names in correct alphabetical order (for the answers see p. 245).

(*a*) Thomas O'Leary, Michael O'Loughlin, Peter Osgood, Mary O'Callaghan
(*b*) Peter Du Bois, Oscar Van Tromp, Pieter de Raat, Roger McCardy
(*c*) Thomas McEvoy, Peter MacIlven, Roger McInnes, the Right Honourable Hugh McGrath. (Assume that a special place is reserved for Mac and Mc.)
(*d*) Saint, A., St Andrew's School, St Aloysius College, St Trinian's, Saint James' Academy (assume a special section where all the Saints are together).
(*e*) Roberto da Costa, Rita de St Angelo, Irene d'Eye, Peter de Gout

Alphabetical filing rules V — hyphenated names
Where a name is hyphenated, it is usual to treat the two words which are joined as separate indexing units. There are exceptions to this rule, as shown below, but it holds good for the vast majority of names. Thus Peter Anson-Large, John Wilkes-Browne, John Lampeter-Smythe and Thomas Walker-Upjohn would be filed in order as:

Anson-Large, Peter
Lampeter-Smythe, John
Walker-Upjohn, Thomas
Wilkes-Browne, John

The exceptions to the rule are names which, although hyphenated, really make a single word, each part being incomplete without the other. Thus Ultra-sonics Ltd or Super-heaters Ltd, would be treated as having only two indexing units.

Practice exercise 5 Arrange these groups in correct order (for the answers see p. 245).

(*a*) Ian Forbes-Adam, Roberta Forbes-Robertson, Mildred Forbes-Poynter
(*b*) Peter Knapp, Roger Knapp-Fisher, Alan Knapp-Anderson
(*c*) Klockner-Knoeller Ltd, Arthur Klockner, Jane Klockner-Stubel
(*d*) Alan Ross, Peter Ross-Whyte, Clifford Ross-Whittingham, David Ross-White
(*e*) Ultra-electric Co. Ltd, Ultra-violet Ray Co. Ltd, Ultra-sonics Ltd

Alphabetical filing rules VI — separate words
Names where separate words occur are treated as if each word was a separate indexing unit, though here again there are exceptions. The rule may be illustrated by:

Make Your Own Board Co. Ltd
Making Merry Wine Co. Ltd
Mending While-U-Wait Co. Ltd

The exceptions are geographical names such as Isle of Man Gas Board. Here Isle of Man is treated as one indexing unit.

Practice exercise 6 Arrange these groups in correct order (for the answers see p. 246).

(*a*) J. R. South and Co. Ltd, South Western Gas Board, Southern Railway
(*b*) Harry South, South Hampstead Cricket Club, H. L. South
(*c*) W. D. Stewart, Stew and Simmer, Stewart Ward Coins Ltd
(*d*) Whiter Wash Co., White Sea Canal Co., R. J. White
(*e*) Sweeney Todd, Todd, S. J., Today's Wear, Toddlers' Wear
(*f*) Canvey Island Motors Ltd, J. R. Canvey, John Canvey, Peter Canvey.

12.11 Filing equipment

There is an enormous range of equipment available from hundreds of different business equipment manufacturers, many of which have become household names. It is impossible to illustrate the full range in a book of this size but some of the more specialized items are illustrated in the sections which follow. In describing the various methods of filing below, reference is made to these illustrations. The reader is urged to visit exhibitions like the International Business Show, held at regular intervals in Birmingham, and similar displays of office equipment and business systems.

Files

There are many varieties of files, including:

Box files. These have a solid box-like construction and a spring-loaded compression pad inside holds down the filed material firmly. Letters, leaflets, catalogues, etc., are simply inserted into the file and the spring-loaded arm is released to hold them in.

Lever-arch files. These are illustrated in Figure 12.9. They retain correspondence rather more safely than box files. Individual letters can be extracted without disturbing the file, by raising the lever to open the prongs. They are very useful for all sorts of correspondence and loose-leaf notes of various sorts. They are a 'best-buy' for students, being quite cheap and available at most stationery shops.

Many students and readers will find the following advice helpful:

(*a*) Purchase a lever-arch file and keep it as a subject file.
(*b*) Prepare an index, from brown paper or other suitable material based upon the table of contents of this book, i.e. one section for each chapter.
(*c*) File away in this index the following items:

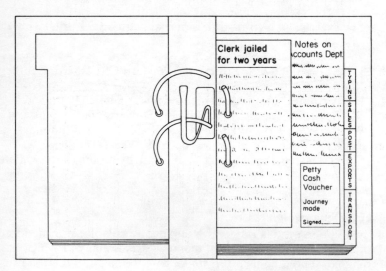

Figure 12.9   A 'lever-arch' subject file, with index pages

(i) Notes prepared while reading the chapter concerned.

(ii) Notes taken of lectures, conferences, etc., attended (if applicable).

(iii) Newspaper cuttings relevant to the subject.

(iv) Brochures and advertisements from firms.

(v) Specimen documents.

(vi) Personal souvenirs of visits made, etc.

The resulting collection is more interesting to revise than an ordinary notebook.

When in use in the office, lever-arch files can give very economical storage if they are arranged on circular platforms one above the other. As shown in Figure 12.10, up to twenty-four files can be stored on a single platform, and five such platforms mounted one

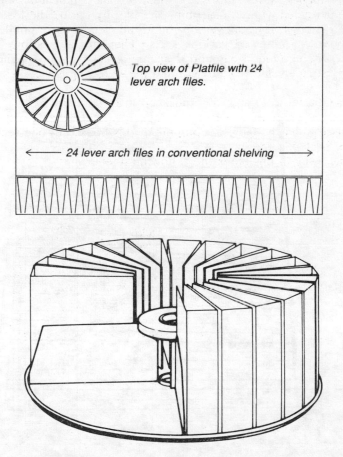

Top view of Platfile with 24 lever arch files.

←——— 24 lever arch files in conventional shelving ———→

Figure 12.10   A 'platfile' for up to 120 lever arch files

above the other on the central pillar of a free standing 'platfile' unit can hold up to 120 files. Such units are of all-steel construction, with a specially designed base to give the units the required strength to remain stable and rigid when filled to capacity. Maintenance-free, nylon bearings allow each platform to rotate independently and evenly, regardless of weight distribution. Castors are fitted to the base for mobility and dust cover tops are available as standard. Any number of clerks can have access to the unit to find the file they require. These platfiles are marketed by Rotadex Systems Ltd, 3—5 Fortnum Close, Kitts Green, Birmingham, B33 OJL. (Tel (021) 783 7411, Fax (021) 783 1876).

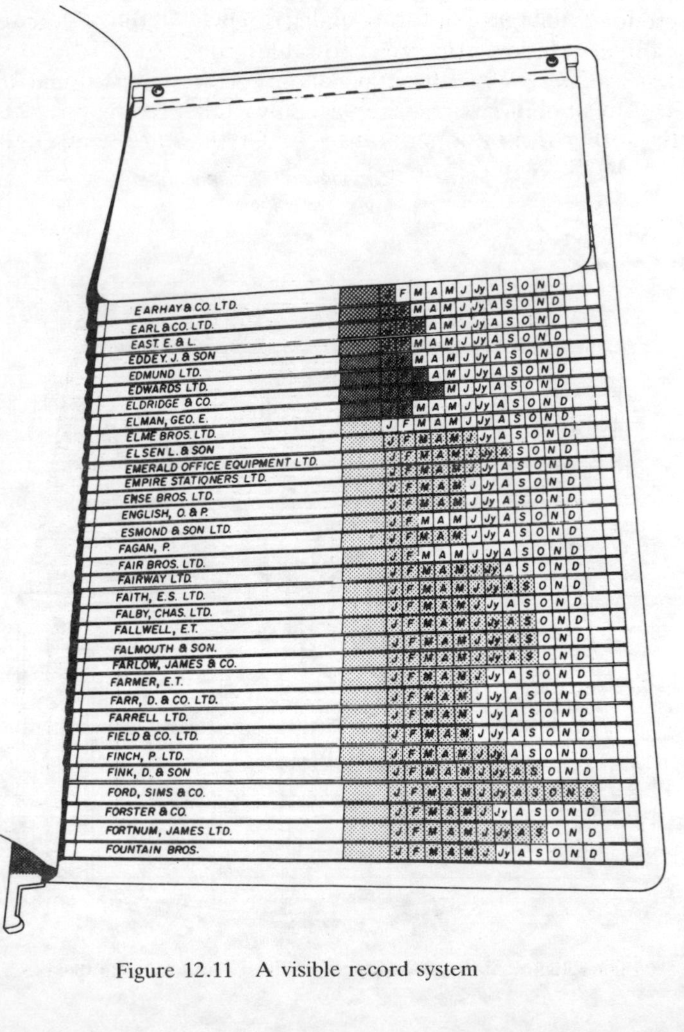

Figure 12.11 A visible record system

Concertina files. These are made up of a succession of pockets into which similar documents can be collected ready for processing. They are particularly suitable for items like petty cash vouchers.

Visible index files. These are particularly useful for ledger records, personnel records, membership records, sales records, attendance and marks registers in schools, etc. (see Figure 12.11).

Suspended horizontal files. With this type of filing, a metal framework is fitted into the top of each drawer of the filing cabinet, to give a raised rail from which pockets are suspended on metal rods. These rods may have nylon runners fitted to reduce noise as they move up and down the rails. Some are in concertina style, so that it is impossible to have documents or file folders inserted between the pockets. Documents and correspondence are filed in file folders, suspended vertically in the pockets, each of which will hold several file folders. Index strips give a visible index (see Figure 12.12).

Lateral files. With this type of filing the conventional three- or four-drawer filing cabinet is replaced by a taller, cupboard-like cabinet with neither front doors nor a back. The files are suspended, rather

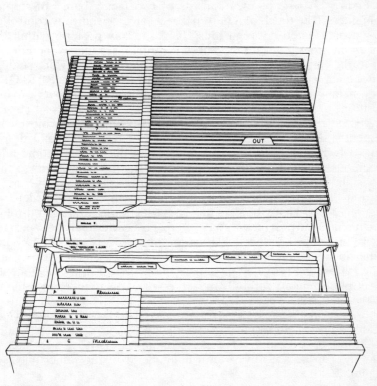

Figure 12.12   Horizontal suspension filing (courtesy of Expandex Ltd)

like clothes in a wardrobe, from rails fitted across the cabinet. As many as six ranks are possible at normal working heights, and since the files suspended in the pockets are accessible from both sides, it is possible for the filing clerks to work at the same cabinet from opposite sides. There is a considerable saving in floor space and the physical effort of opening and closing drawers is avoided.

Vertical files. This name is confusing, since today practically all filing systems are 'vertical' in the sense that documents are rarely stored flat with one document on top of another. Here it is used to describe a type of file supported by a plastic spine, in a vertical rack. The papers inside must be secured, either by a plastic thong or in pockets. The Anson vistafile is an excellent example, the spine being sufficiently wide to be used as an index and flash-board, where coloured flashes indicate certain types of information. When used, for example, in garages, it may indicate the type of car owned by the customer and the date the vehicle is due for the next service. A reminder can then be sent out with a booking for the service. (See Figures 12.13 and 12.14.)

Automated electronic filing. This type of filing system (illustrated in Figure 12.1 see p. 213) consists of two facing banks of storage containers. The touch of a button directs an electronically controlled conveyor situated between these banks to any position within the system in order to locate the selected container, which is then drawn on to the conveyor, and in seconds is delivered to the work station. After completing the filing activity, the operator presses a RESTORE button, and the container is automatically returned to its original position.

Ring, thong and post binders. Many documents are most conveniently stored in binders. **Ring binders** have spring-loaded split rings which may be opened to release the documents. Some have ingenious mechanisms for moving documents up and down, so that a visible index can be opened to admit a further visible index card at the correct place for its insertion in alphabetical order (see Figure 12.15). **Thong binders** have a plastic thong to thread through documents, and **post binders** have metal posts which may be separated off to insert further sheets. These are most widely used in accounts departments where **day books** are not kept – since they require much effort and provide only a permanent record of the documents. A set of documents carefully preserved in a post binder can itself act as the 'day book'.

Circular rotary filing. There are many types of rotary file, which enable a great many records to be filed in wallets or pockets around a central vertical pillar. They are economical of space, very accessible and can be used by several filing clerks at the same time (see Figure 12.16).

Safety first and filing cabinets. Since filing cabinets are accessible

REG.
NO.

1900 TU

EGISTRATION
UMBER

JAN
FEB
MAR
APR
MAY
JUN
JLY
AUG
SEP
OCT
NOV
DEC

OLOURED SIGNAL
O INDICATE
EXT SERVICE DUE

JAN
FEB
MAR
APR
MAY
JUN
JLY
AUG
SEP
OCT
NOV
DEC

OLOURED SIGNAL
O INDICATE
OT TEST DATE

NAME

STOMER'S NAME

OLOURED TITLE
RIP CAN BE
SED FOR COLOUR
ODING.
TO INDICATE
ODEL OR YEAR OF
HICLE

CHAS.
NO.

LOURED SIGNAL
SHOW 1st
RVICE REMINDER
S BEEN SENT

THE SYSTEM

The Anson Vehicle History System provides a folder for each vehicle.
The folder is suspended by means of a carrier bar which is recessed to accommodate a PRINTED SYSTEM STRIP.

THE SYSTEM STRIP

Key to the successful operation of the Anson Vehicle History System.
The system strip opposite shows the information necessary to operate the system successfully.
Title strips can be added to provide colour coding e.g. to indicate year or model of vehicle.
Also attached to the carrier bar are the coloured sliding signals.
These can indicate

1 Date when next service is due.
2 MOT test date.
3 Rustproof check.
4 Service reminder card sent.

Title strips and sliding signals are utilized by Service Management to meet their individual requirements.

In operation the system is simple yet extremely effective in generating extra business, enhancing the image of your Service Reception, and impressing your Customers. Minimal training of personnel is required thereby ensuring the continuity of your procedures.

**Let Ansons Vehicle History System Work
for YOU**

Figure 12.13   The Anson vistafile (courtesy of Blakeley Business Forms, Dewsbury
(Tel: 0924 461665, Fax: 0924 455050))

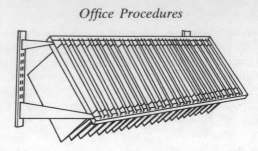

Figure 12.14 Anson vistafiles for vehicle history, suspended on a garage wall rack

only when drawers are open, there is always a danger that they will fall forward if more than one drawer is opened at once. This is particularly likely to happen if the lowest drawer is filled with light objects, such as handbags, boxes of paper handkerchiefs, etc. Such objects should always be stored in the top drawer rather than the bottom drawer.

12.12 Indexes

An index is a device for finding the position of records in a system quickly and easily. Several references to indexes have already been made, but a full list includes the following:

(*a*) *Page indexes*, such as are found in the back of a book. It is often helpful to include items more than once. For example, in this book the index not only shows Filing − with many subheadings under that entry − but also each of the individual entries in its own

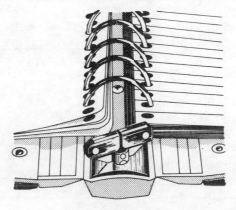

Figure 12.15 An ingenious ring binder with visi-index records (courtesy of Twinlock Ltd)

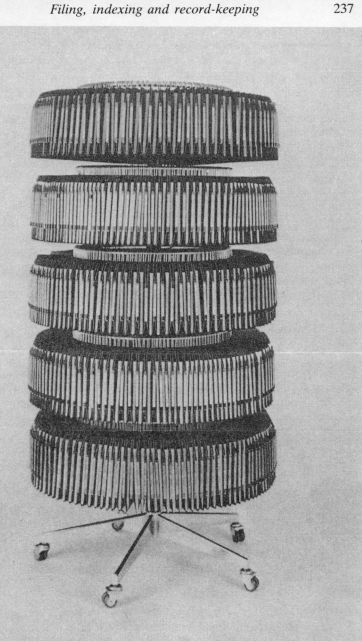

Figure 12.16   Circular rotary filing (courtesy of Flexiform Ltd)

place in the index, e.g. concertina files appears under C. Page indexes may be used in ledgers, sales departments, etc.

(*b*) *Card indexes.* These have already been referred to (see p. 219).

(*c*) *Visible card indexes.* These have again been referred to (see above and p. 232).

(*d*) *Wheel indexes.* These are a form of rotary card index which enable a very large number of records to be found very speedily by rotating the wheel until the card required is found (see Figure 12.17).

(*e*) *Strip indexes.* These have already been referred to (see Figure 5.3, p. 96).

(*f*) *Vowel indexes.* These indexes are used to split up a group of names into six columns, to make each name easier to find in the lists. Thus a list of names beginning with 'P' would be divided up into columns according to the first vowel in the name. 'Palmer' would come under the 'a' and 'Potterton' under the 'o', as shown in Figure 12.18. Y is regarded as the sixth vowel. The small numbers against the names in Figure 12.18 are the numbers of the file in the cabinet to which the vowel index applies.

12.13 Microfilm filing

Photographic processes enable the size of stored records to be reduced very considerably. An ordinary letter of A4 or quarto size can be reduced to thumb-nail size, and over 8000 sheets can be reproduced on a small spool of film. This method is most appropriate

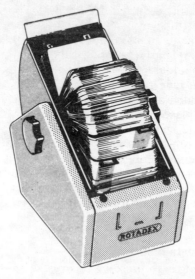

Figure 12.17 A wheel index (courtesy of Rotadex Systems Ltd)

A	E	I	O	U	Y
Palmer, P[11] Patterson, T[16]	Penrose, R[73] Pemberton, Q[1] Peterson, S[94]	Pilsner, S[147]	Potterton, H[72] Posy, R[89]	Phurrey, R[71] Plume, T[15]	Pyrford, H[5]

Figure 12.18 A vowel index

for storing records which must be kept for many years; it is particularly valuable for historical and museum records, for official government records and court records, etc. The cost of the initial equipment is high, and only worth while if extensive records are to be kept in this way. The process requires the following:

(*a*) *A camera*, usually using 35 mm film, which may have an automatic feeding device. Documents in batches are inserted into the feeding device, which passes them forward to be filmed in correct sequence. The camera may be able to photograph both sides of a document at the same time. Exposed film is sent to the manufacturers for processing.

Indexing the documents is a time-consuming but important process. Each batch may be given a batch number, followed by an individual number for each document. Alternatively, captions can be added to a document to indicate its contents.

(*b*) *A scanner unit*. This projects the filmed documents onto a screen where they may be read by the clerk or official consulting the records. A print of any required document can be supplied by some machines enlarged sufficiently to be read by the naked eye.

Recent developments in microfilm filing have made it much more versatile for ordinary business use. 'Jackets' have been developed which can hold photographs of sixty documents in a packet of 150 mm × 100 mm. One rarely has more than sixty live documents in any particular batch of correspondence. When anyone requires a file the 'jacket' is placed in a 'jacket duplicator' and photocopied. The whole duplicate jacket is sent to the person who requested it, and the original is refiled. No need for 'out' markers here. A file is never 'out'. The person requesting the file reads it in a 'file reader' and when he/she has finished with it, the copy is placed in the waste-paper basket, or destroyed if it is a security file.

Two photographs of a camera and viewer respectively, for microfilm filing may be seen in Figure 12.19.

12.14 Electronic data banks

The purpose of filing is to preserve records where they can be used again when required. The electronic systems available today are of

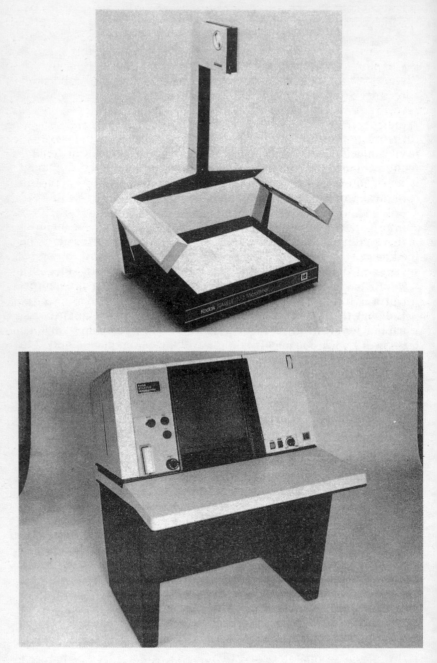

Figure 12.19   A microfilm camera (top) and viewer-prints (below) (courtesy of Kodak Ltd)

course superb systems for preserving records, and the speed at which computers operate (about 900 million operations every second) enables computerized records to be made available instantaneously. The activities of computers are dealt with later in this book (see Chapter 14) but we must just refer at this point to their ability to store records and make them available. Any such collection of records is called a **data bank**. On such a data bank the computer can record not only names, addresses, telephone numbers, etc., but also entire records of transactions with the person named. By interrogating the computer through a keyboard, one can summon the records for viewing on a visual display unit (VDU) similar to a television screen, or the computer will print out the information required.

An interesting aspect of such computerized records is the technique known as 'CD ROM', which stands for 'compact disc read-only memory.' A compact disc is a disc on which a huge quantity of information can be stored. We are all familiar with compact discs that play 'pop' or classical music, but they can equally store a huge collection of information – such as the full details of a particular range of diseases. If such a disc is made available to doctors, they have everything they need to know about a particular disease. They can 'read' the disc at any time, but they cannot change it and add new information to it because it is a 'read-only memory'. They cannot 'write to' the disc. If they are doctors who can add to the body of knowledge available, they must approach the medical library that issued the disc and make arrangements to add this new material to it for the benefit of the medical profession.

Security and the Data Protection Act, 1984

All records have a security aspect, whether they are computerized or not. To take a simple example, most people are sensitive about how much they earn, and do not wish others to know the details of the pay they earn, or the profits they make in their businesses, etc. Therefore wages records are one type of record that has a security aspect. Similarly personnel records often contain personal details that should not be available to other members of staff. It so happens that computerized records are particularly sensitive, if only because computers store so many details and produce them in seconds to anyone who knows what codes give access to the data bank. Of course we even have 'hackers' who know enough about computers to 'hack' their way in to other people's systems. For these reasons parliament has passed a Data Protection Act, 1984, which requires all those who keep computerized records to register with an office called the Data Protection Registry. Those who register are obliged to state why they need the records, and what use will be made of them, and to operate a secure system. The Act lays down certain 'data protection principles', which are listed below. Failure to observe them will lead to the registered person's name being removed from the register, and it will then be an offence for him/her to keep records on a data bank. The principles are:

(*a*) Only information which has been obtained lawfully and fairly may be recorded.

(*b*) It may only be held for the reasons given on registration.

(*c*) It may not be used, or disclosed, for any other reason, or in any way that is incompatible with the reasons given on registration.

(*d*) The data must be adequate, but not excessive, and must be kept up to date.

(*e*) It must not be kept longer than is necessary for the purpose stated.

(*f*) An individual shall be entitled to know what records are kept on him/her, and to have access to it without undue delay or expense.

(*g*) The system must be secure to prevent unauthorized access.

The Act does not apply to (*a*) payroll records, (*b*) pension records, (*c*) accounting records, (*d*) records of purchases or sales and (*e*) matters of national security.

Document Image Processing (DIP)

The development of document image processing (DIP) makes available another computerized filing system for storing huge volumes of paper records in a very small space, e.g. the contents of ten filing cabinets can be stored on one 5.25 inch optical disc. The system is of greatest use to those who have huge libraries of records – councils, which have dealings with every household in the area, say – and need to be able to answer telephone calls about problems at a moment's notice. If the documents relevant to a particular house-holder have been scanned by an 'image scanner' and stored on optical discs in such a way that all the information can be called up on a VDU (visual display unit) by anyone who needs it, the total records of any householder are available for discussion. One council has sixty-four work stations where those answering queries can access the computer and extract the full correspondence from the file for viewing within seconds of the call coming in. The relevant discs can be played rather like a jukebox, and in total they have 50 000 million pieces of information on file.

A document to be added to the filing system has to be marked with the correct filing marks and fed into the document scanner that can read the marks through OMR (optical mark recognition) or OCR (optical character recognition). It scans the document to store it in the correct place. The average cost of such a system is about £200 000, but if we imagine, for example, that it has all the fingerprints of all the criminals in the world stored on it, we can see that it might easily repay its cost very quickly. This kind of file may be used for all sorts of purposes, not just business documentation, and it is believed that in the 1990s this kind of filing system should attract between £500 million and £1000 million of business each year.

12.15   Selecting a suitable system

Filing will be most efficiently carried out if a system that will achieve the aims of the firm is adopted from the very beginning. All systems become out-dated, and need reviewing, preferably with the help of a specialist adviser from the supplier whose systems are being considered. Once a system has been installed, it is expensive and wasteful to change it, but up-dating of procedures is always helpful. Some of the commonest types of filing problems are mentioned in Table 12.1.

Table 12.1

Matter to be filed	Suggested methods
(a) Correspondence	Horizontal suspension filing, vertical suspension filing, lateral suspension filing, conventional filing cabinets.
(b) Invoices, credit notes and other documents	Post binders, lever-arch files, box files — for small businesses, concertina files.
(c) Ledger cards — sales and purchases	Visi-index files, posting trays supplied by systems manufacturers.
(d) Confidential staff records	Vertical vistafiles with thonging and pockets for documents. For security reasons the cabinet must be lockable.
(e) Computer print-out	Special racks and binders
(f) Dictating machine belts	Special storage racks from dictation machine manufacturers
(g) Data-processing paper tapes and magnetic tapes	Special storage racks from specialist suppliers.
(h) Large drawings and charts	Special chart-storing devices from specialist manufacturers.

12.16   Points to think about and discuss

(a) Firm A has its filing carried out in the departments, each of which has a single filing clerk. Firm B has its filing handled centrally. The staff consists of a filing supervisor, a chief filing clerk and eight filing clerks. Discuss the likely difficulties to be met with in Firm A that will not be met in Firm B, and vice versa.

(b) Miss A says 'Filing is tedious work, I am bored to death half the time'. Miss B says 'I find it fascinating to control this enormous collection of documents, each of which is important in some way'.

Discuss these two attitudes to filing. Prepare a two-minute speech by each young lady justifying her point of view.

(c) Sue Dawlish has plans to set up on her own account as a fashion designer.

She evisages having the following things to file:

(i) Sketches and patterns, both of garments she has actually put into production and ideas and designs which may come in useful later.
(ii) Suppliers' records for bills payable, invoices and statements.
(iii) Suppliers' catalogues, samples, etc.
(iv) Customers' records, including enquiries, quotations, orders, invoices, credit notes and correspondence.

What types of filing would you recommend to her?

12.17 Answer section
The answers to the practice exercises are given below:

Practice exercise 1 The first indexing units are:
(*a*) Marshall, (*b*) Cummings, (*c*) Daniels, (*d*) Potterton, (*e*) Liverpool, (*f*) Paterson, (*g*) Chester, (*h*) Transport, (*i*) Mendoza, (*j*) Seamen's

Practice exercise 2
(*a*) Hawke, Harry
Jones, Peter
Wheddon, Daniel
(*c*) Cronin, A. J.
Dickens, Charles
Kipling, Rudyard
Melville, H.

(*b*) Lark, Silas T.
Larkin, Samuel P.
Lazarus, Ruby M.

Practice exercise 2a
(*a*) Chalmers, Eric
Chalmers, R.
Chambers, R.
Chumleigh, Edith
(*c*) Howard, P. T.
Howard, Peter
Howard Proctor Ltd

(*b*) Forte, R.
Fortescue, R.
Fortescue, R. & Sons Ltd
Forth, Peter
(*d*) Gnu, B.
Gnutsen, B.
Gunn, B. Ltd
Gunn, Ben
Gurr & Co. Ltd

(*e*) Marshall, R.
Marshall, R. & Co. Ltd
Marshall, Rosemary

(*f*) Lane, P.
Lane, Penelope
Lane, Penny

(g) Glouceston Ltd
Glover & Sons Ltd
Grimes, P. Ltd
Grover & Co.

(i) Lyons, Doncaster, of
Lyons, Dumbarton, of
Lyons, Lyonnesse, of

Langdon, Penelope P.
(h) Martin, John
Martindale, Joan
Murray
Murray, John

(j) Armstrong (Dover) Ltd
Armstrong (Manchester) Ltd
Armstrong (Middlesex) Ltd

Practice exercise 3

(a) Gilbert, M., OBE
Gilbert, Mrs M. L.
Gilbert, Professor Martin

(c) Heather, Mrs D. W.
Heather, Sir Dennis, CH
Heather, Lady Doreen

(b) Jones, Dr Howard, MD
Jones, R., DFC
Jones, Mrs Rita

Practice exercise 4

(a) O'Callaghan, Mary
O'Leary, Thomas
O'Loughlin, Michael
Osgood, Peter

(b) De Raat, Pieter
Du Bois, Peter
McCardy, Roger
Van Tromp, Oscar

(c) McEvoy, Thomas
McGrath, the Rt Hon. Hugh
MacIlven, Peter
McInnes, Roger

(d) Saint A.
St Aloysius College
St Andrew's School
Saint James' Academy
St Trinian's

(e) Da Costa, Roberto
De Gout, Peter
De St Angelo, Rita
D'Eye, Irene

Practice exercise 5

(a) Forbes-Adam, Ian
Forbes-Poynter, Mildred
Forbes-Robertson, Roberta

(c) Klockner, Arthur
Klockner-Knoeller, Ltd
Klockner-Stubel, Jane

(b) Knapp, Peter
Knapp-Anderson, Alan
Knapp-Fisher, Roger

(d) Ross, Alan
Ross-White, David
Ross-Whittingham, Clifford
Ross-Whyte, Peter

(e) Ultra-electric Co. Ltd
Ultra-sonics Ltd
Ultra-violet Ray Co. Ltd

Practice exercise 6

(a) South, J. R. and Co. Ltd
Southern Railway
South Western Gas Board

(b) South, H. L.
South, Harry
South Hampstead Cricket Club

(c) Stew and Simmer
Stewart, W. D.
Stewart Ward Coins Ltd

(d) White, R. J.
Whiter Wash Co.
White Sea Canal Co.

(e) Today's Wear
Todd, S. J.
Todd, Sweeney
Toddlers' Wear

(f) Canvey, J. R.
Canvey, John
Canvey, Peter
Canvey Island Motors Ltd

12.18 Rapid revision − filing

Cover the page with a sheet of notepaper and uncover one question at a time.

Answers	Questions
−	1 What is filing?
1 Filing is the storing of correspondence in a retrieval system, whence it may be obtained for reference.	2 What happens to the correspondence?
2 It is placed in a file folder, which is given a title and is then stored in one of the five systems.	3 What are the five systems?
3 (a) Alphabetical. (b) Numerical. (c) Alpha-numerical. (d) Subjects. (e) Geographical.	4 Suppose there is only one letter from a particular correspondent?
4 Place it in the miscellaneous file.	5 How are letters in a miscellaneous file filed?
5 Alphabetically, with the As on top.	6 In a busy file how are the letters filed?
6 With the most recent letters on top.	7 What do we call this order?
7 Chronological order.	8 What are the essentials of a good filing system?
8 (a) Simplicity. (b) Security. (c) Compactness. (d) An appropriate classification. (e) Clear cross-references. (f) Adequate tracing of out-files. (g) Adequate follow-up of out-files. (h) A properly laid down document retention policy.	9 List the chief types of filing system.

9 (*a*) Box files, (*b*) lever-arch files, (*c*) concertina files, (*d*) visible index files, (*e*) card files, (*f*) horizontal suspension filing, (*g*) vertical suspension filing, (*h*) electronic filing.	10 What restrictions are placed on electronic filing?
10 The *Data Protection Act, 1984* requires all those who keep computerized records (other than routine records of accounts, wages, etc.) to register their reasons for keeping records with the Data Protection Registrar.	11 What is a CD ROM?
11 A compact disc 'Read-only Memory'.	12 What are such discs used for?
12 To contain a body of knowledge, e.g. medical facts on a particular class of diseases, or legal facts on a branch of the law.	13 Why 'read-only'?
13 Because the user can read all the facts on the disc but cannot 'write to' the disc, i.e. change it in any way.	14 What is DIP?
14 Document Image Processing. It is a way of filing documents by scanning them with an electronic eye and storing the image on an optical disc. The image can then be viewed on a screen to see exactly what the document said.	14 Go over the page again until you feel you are sure of the answers.

Exercises set 12

1 Write down the letters (*a*)−(*j*) in a column on the left-hand side of a sheet of paper. Then write against each letter the correct word or phrase, taken from the word list, which best fits the gaps in the sentences below.

(*a*) The body of rules laid down by management about the length of time documents are to be kept is called a ......

(*b*) ...... is defined as the storing of letters and documents in a systematic way, so that they may be retrieved later.

(*c*) When a document has two possible places where it could be filed, it is usual to file it in the most likely place and put a ...... in the less likely place.

(*d*) A mass of records available on a computer memory bank is called a ......

(*e*) Alphabetical filing is ......; we can go straight to the files and find the item we require.

(*f*) Where a number of commercial travellers are controlled by a sales manager from head office, and each has a sales area allotted to him/her, files are often kept in ...... order.

(*g*) A numerical system is indirect, because we cannot go straight to the file we require but must first refer to an ......

(*h*) A card used to show at a glance that a file is not in the system, because someone has borrowed it, is called an ......

(*i*) A 'tickler system' is one that tickles our memories about jobs to be done in a particular ...... or on a particular ......

(*j*) A ...... file is one that retains documents punched with a two-hole punch, and gives ...... to the filed papers at any point.

Word list: cross-reference, filing, direct, out-marker, month, data base, index, day, lever arch, geographical, access, document retention policy.

2 Describe (*a*) vertical filing, (*b*) horizontal (flat) filing.

3 (*a*) What is (i) a strip index, (ii) a vowel index, (iii) a visible card index? (*b*) Design a visible card suitable for indexing the customers of a firm. Make use of a signalling device to show the kinds of product sold.

4 (*a*) Describe the uses in filing of three of the following items of equipment: (i) folders, (ii) posting tray, (iii) suspension file, (iv) transfer case. (*b*) What is meant by three of the following: (i) a cross-reference sheet, (ii) an outguide, (iii) document retention, (iv) a follow-up system.

5 (*a*) List the following names in the order in which they would appear in an alphabetical filing system: (i) Department of Education and Science, (ii) John Smith & Sons Ltd, (iii) Dr A. P. Sherbert, (iv) United Nations Organization, (v) The Playboy Club, (vi) De la Rue Ltd, (vii) ABC Co. Ltd, (viii) David Aaronson, (ix) J. McDougall & Co., (x) J. MacFarlane & Co.
(*b*) Explain the essential features of a numerical system of filing and mention which organizations would be likely to use the system.

6 (*a*) What are the essential requirements of a good filing system? (*b*) List the following names in alphabetical order for indexing purposes: (i) K. White & Co. Ltd, (ii) R. Atkins Ltd, (iii) Dolman Ltd, (iv) Dr W. O'Brien, (v) R. McBride, (vi) Hotel Metropolitan, (vii) Department of the Environment, (viii) British Rail.

7 Explain the uses and advantages of visible card indexes.

8 The following terms are used in filing; explain fully what they mean. Give examples of diagrams where appropriate and explain their uses: (*a*) out or absent card, (*b*) guide card, (*c*) cross-reference, (*d*) chronological order.

9. (*a*) Describe a suitable system of filing and classification for use by an international company with branches in large cities in many parts of the world. The company manufactures disinfectants, fertilizers and detergents; (*b*) draw and complete a primary guide card and a secondary guide card to be used with this system.

10 'A good filing system is essential in an efficient office.' Comment on this statement and outline the factors which must be taken into account when devising a filing system.

11 (*a*) Arrange the following names in order for alphabetical filing: (i)

Morgan Groceries Ltd, (ii) The British Council, (iii) 5-Star Supermarket Ltd, (iv) The CBC Gas Appliance Co., (v) Dr T. B. Ruston, (vi) G. O'Connor, (vii) The Halifax Building Society, (viii) The YWCA, (ix) National Council of Women, (x) Hotel Supreme, (xi) Elder Dempster Ltd, (xii) The Prime Meat Co., (xiii) BBC, (xiv) British Oxygen Co. Ltd, (xv) Dawson and Cook Ltd.

(*b*) You have two files with identical surnames. Show by two different examples how you will decide which comes first in the alphabetical method.

(*c*) What rule governs the alphabetical placing of the name McAndrews?

12   There are six departments in your firm and each keeps its own files in its own way. There is talk of a central filing system but several departments object. Draw up in two columns a list of arguments for and against a central filing system.

13   (*a*) What system of filing requires the use of a card index? (*b*) What information would you include on a card? (*c*) Which part of this information must be easily visible? (*d*) Explain how and why these cards are used.

14   Describe in detail two filing systems. Mention their advantages and their suitability for certain businesses or departments.

15   Describe the construction and employment of: (*a*) lever-arch files; (*b*) box files; (*c*) concertina files.

16   Why do we file documents? What are the requirements of a filing system?

17   What system would you use or install so that files could be removed from the filing system and their return could be ensured after a reasonable time?

18   State what you regard as the essential requirements of a good filing system.

19   Explain briefly the following filing systems: (*a*) alphabetical, (*b*) geographical, (*c*) numerical, (*d*) subject.

20   (*a*) Why is the filing of documents indispensable in a large firm? (*b*) List the following names in alphabetical order for filing or indexing purposes: (i) Urban District of Wakefield, (ii) Albert Johnson, (iii) Sir Samuel Miles, (iv) The Ritz Hotel, (v) BIC Ltd, (vi) John Smith, (vii) London Co-operative Society, (viii) Professor Hugh Redman, (ix) Royal Northern Hospital, (x) School of African Studies.

21   (*a*) What is the purpose of filing? Answer as fully as possible. (*b*) When is it best to do the filing? Give your reasons. (*c*) What is the purpose of a miscellaneous folder?

22   Alphabetical and numerical filing sytems are used widely. Write fully about them, suggesting for which kind of business organization or department each may be best suited. Give your reasons.

23 Explain fully the meaning of the following expressions: (*a*) lateral filing, (*b*) an 'out' or 'absent' card, (*c*) a miscellaneous folder, (*d*) a secondary guide card. Give examples or diagrams where suitable.

24 Draft some 'hints on filing' for an inexperienced filing clerk. Answer fully.

25 What do you understand by (*a*) suspension filing, (*b*) alphabetical order, (*c*) guide cards, (*d*) 'nothing' comes before 'something'? Answer fully, giving examples or diagrams where suitable.

26 (*a*) Arrange the following names in order for alphabetical filing: (i) Hoyland Urban District Council, (ii) Ministry of Transport, (iii) D. R. Donnison, (iv) Corona Soft Drinks, (v) Grants of St James's (Northern) Ltd, (vi) Frank Coker (Contractors) Ltd, (vii) Dr T. J. O'Connor, (viii) Royston Parkin & Co., (ix) Royal Insurance Co. Ltd, (x) Old Denaby Motors.
(*b*) Why are index cards necessary in numerical filing? Give an example of the layout of the card you would use.

27 (*a*) Say what you understand by a cross-reference and give an example, (*b*) make an observation about the bottom drawer in a filing cabinet, (*c*) what are 'dead' files and how should they be treated?, (*d*) what is an 'out' or 'absent' card and how is it used?

28 List the methods of filing (including the type of equipment and system) you would use for (*a*) petty cash vouchers, (*b*) stock record cards, (*c*) dictating machine belts, (*d*) correspondence with suppliers; (*e*) large-size drawings and photographs in the publicity department. Give reasons for your answers.

29 (*a*) Why is it necessary to follow a set of rules when filing? (*b*) What does date order mean? (*c*) When is it useful to pre-sort correspondence for filing?

30 Which method of filing would you use for the sales department of the following: (*a*) a small cutlery business, (*b*) a large concern with 1 000 credit customers, (*c*) an exporting firm, with agents in many overseas countries? Give your reasons for your choice.

31 Why is a card index necessary with numerical filing? Draw up two sample cards and fill in the details. When would you use this system of filing?

32 Write a description of a filing system with which you are familiar. You should make reference to the following: (*a*) the type of cabinets used, e.g. vertical, (*b*) the system of classification, e.g. alphabetical, (*c*) the nature of the documents handled, (*d*) the method of controlling files taken away from the cabinet, (*e*) the method of transferring documents no longer required, (*f*) any additional information about the system that you consider important.

33 The filing clerk complains that he is short of space for storing current correspondence and that the files are becoming very bulky and difficult to handle. He also experiences difficulty in locating papers in the files

(indexed under subject headings) after other members of the staff have been engaged on filing. Examine the filing clerk's complaints and prepare a report to the office manager setting out your findings and making recommendations to improve the efficiency of the filing system.

34 The head of your department has asked you to examine some new systems of filing and recording information with the object of saving office space and at the same time having the records available for quick and easy reference. In a memo to your head of department explain the features of (*a*) microfilming, (*b*) lateral filing, (*c*) one other method you consider should be introduced.

35 (*a*) It is claimed by some people that a good filing system for correspondence does not need a separate index. Give your views on the truth or otherwise of this claim and illustrate your answers by reference to the various methods of filing.
   (*b*) What method and equipment would you use for filing (*i*) sales ledger cards, (ii) stock record cards?

36 In order to record details of several thousands of customers, your office has a card index system that consists of rather small cards stored upright in wooden drawers. Explain the disadvantages of this arrangement and give your suggestions for converting it to a modern visible system.

37 What effect is computerization having on filing procedures? Select any one procedure to illustrate your answer.

38 (*a*) You are short of space in your office, which is used to house the firm's filing cabinets, and you no longer have room to accommodate all the old records. Reference to the information on some of these old records will, however, need to be made periodically in the future. Suggest how you would deal with this problem. (*b*) How would you record and control the files that are temporarily removed for reference from the central filing room?

39 Describe the methods of filing, type of equipment, and indexing (if any) you would use for keeping any *four* of the following: (*a*) invoices received from suppliers, (*b*) confidential staff records, (*c*) catalogues received from wholesalers, (*d*) minutes of meetings, (*e*) petty cash vouchers.

40 (*a*) Place the following names in the correct form and order for indexing: (i) Walter Jones & Co. Ltd, (ii) The Beverley Mills Ltd, (iii) J. Robert Skinner, (iv) Smith and Robinson, (v) De La Rue and Co. Ltd, (vi) Thomas Slater, (vii) The Borough Council of Bigtown, (viii) P. R. McGrath, (ix) Department of Employment, (x) Dr John Peters, (xi) F. B. O'Sullivan, (xii) 20th Century Supplies Ltd.
   (*b*) Describe in detail two 'follow-up' systems that could be used to ensure that replies are received to letters sent from your office.

41 Your employer tells you that he has asked a friend who is a computer programmer to write a program on which it will be possible to record a mass of facts about persons, firms, rival products, potential customers,

etc. He tells you he wishes you to take charge of this work once the program is written, but it will be confidential information and not available to junior staff. Write a report for him about such records, bringing out any reservations you have.

42 What is document image processing? How could it be useful to an education committee answering frequent questions from parents on all sorts of matters?

13   Typing and word-processing

13.1   Text production – typewriters

In the nineteenth century most letters were handwritten and the chief requirement of a clerk was – in W. S. Gilbert's words – the ability 'to copy all the letters in a big, round hand'. Today the typewriter, in the hands of a competent typist, produces letters of good appearance: neat, legible and well displayed. It is not the work of a moment to achieve competence as a typist, and to learn to display material well and at speed requires patience, perseverance and intelligence on the part of the typist.

Today's typewriters show tremendous advances since the days of the 'manual' typewriter, when all the power and energy had to be provided by the secretary's own hands, and a long day's work in a busy typing pool left a secretary not only mentally but physically exhausted. Today most machines are electric, and also electronic. Instead of the keys being forced against the paper by the power supplied by the typist's fingers, the depression of a key merely completes an electrical circuit and the power needed to produce the text comes from the local power station. The electronic components perform miracles of ingenuity, such as automatic centring, underlining, automatic carriage return, automatic justification, which means the right-hand edge of the text provided is adjusted into a neat, flush, right-hand margin, etc. Some of the features of a typical electronic typewriter are described below.

- Interchangeable daisy-wheel typefaces with up to 100 characters in 10, 12 or 15 pitch, which enable you to vary your presentations with various typefaces, bold, roman and italic, etc.
- Line-display facilities which store the material typed in a buffer memory so that it can be checked and if necessary corrected before being typed. Depression of a single key types the whole line or paragraph if a screen-display is added.
- A spell-check facility with around 50000 of the most commonly used words in its memory, together with 300 words of your own choice. It bleeps when a spelling error is made.
- Adjustable impression controls to give the right power for different kinds of work.
- Automatic centring, underlining and carriage return.

- The drawing of vertical lines as well as horizontal lines so that display work, tabulations, etc., can be framed if required.
- Correction keys on some models, which will, with the help of a lift-off ribbon, remove an incorrect character from the paper for retyping.
- Automatic justification to give a flush right-hand margin.
- Codes to stop the machine for automatic insertion of variables such as addresses, special contractual terms, etc.
- Ribbon cartridges, which are easily inserted and give a high-quality appearance to correspondence.
- Space expand devices for accurate positioning of tabulated material or display material.
- Relocate keys, which enable corrections to be made elsewhere on the page and then give automatic relocation to the previous typing position for continued typing.

The list could be extended, but would need continual revision for developments occur rapidly in this area of office practice.

The term 'text production' used as the heading to this section needs some explanation. It covers the whole range of activities and procedures used in offices to produce good quality correspondence, reports, brochures, pamphlets and even books. The most sophisticated 'text production' facilities amount to 'desktop publishing', a term widely used.

Beyond the electronic typewriter we move into the field of word-processing, with a computerized system that places a wide variety of facilities at the service of the keyboard operator. For example, the ability to 'read' into the text charts, diagrams, logos and illustrations, the ability to change text and still recover the original text if it proves to be the preferred version, and many similar miracles.

A secretary is only as good as his or her typewriter. You must have a top-quality electronic typewriter or a word-processor. Traditional manual and electric machines are of course adequate for many routine activities, and for student use may be all that the student can afford. By contrast, in the real office situation there is everything to be said for the most sophisticated electronic machine or word-processor. Such a machine raises productivity and product quality.

Manual typewriters

As their name implies, manual typewriters are operated by hand, the typists striking the keys so that the typeface strikes the ribbon and prints the required character on the paper. It is essential to develop an even touch so that the text is printed uniformly on the paper. It is not the purpose of this book to teach typewriting, which is a specialist study in its own right. Many readers will be introduced to the typewriter as part of their office studies, and it is indeed desirable that everyone should learn to type. Manual typewriters are so cheap today that almost everyone can afford to own a typewriter for personal use, and readers are strongly recommended to take time to learn this useful skill.

The two main typefaces are 'pica' and 'elite'. Pica is the traditional typeface for office work. It gives a standard ten characters to the inch, and is bold in appearance. Elite gives twelve standard characters to the inch but for special purposes both these styles can be obtained with more or less characters to the inch.

Standard machines have six lines to the inch and may usually be set either to single, double or triple line spacing. Half line spacing is also possible on some machines. Figure 13.1 shows pica and elite typefaces.

Typestyles for electronic typewriters and daisy-wheel printers

On manual machines one has only a single typeface, the keys being permanent features of the machine's construction, and, once decided upon, the typeface stays with the machine for its working life. In the last 25 years all this has changed. It is now possible to have many different typefaces, because the typefaces are interchangeable. For example, a golf-ball machine has interchangeable heads that have a complete typeface on each head. We can change from one golf-ball-sized head to another, and completely change the typeface. Thus we could do all headings in italic print if we liked by changing to an italic typeface whenever we need to do a heading. Another type of

```
            Pica Typestyles

        This paragraph has been typed on a
    'Pica' machine.  Pica typestyles are
    designed with 10 characters to the inch
    (10 pitch).  They give a clear, legible
    typescript and are used for the vast
    majority of business correspondence.


            Elite Typestyles

        This paragraph has been typed on an 'Elite'
    machine.   It has 12 characters to the inch
    (12 pitch).   Elite typestyles give a smaller, more
    personal  appearance to the typescript.


        Although manufacturers have now designed
    many interesting typefaces, all typefaces are
    based on 'pica' or 'elite', with 10 or 12
    characters to the inch.
```

Figure 13.1 'Pica' and 'elite' typestyles

machine has interchangeable 'daisy wheels' instead of golf balls. A daisy-wheel is a circular metal plate with petals sticking out all round it, each of which has a letter, number or other character on it. As the typist types, the daisy wheel is rotated quickly to bring the correct character opposite the paper, and stop it while the character is impressed. Some idea of the variety of typestyles is shown in Figure 13.2, but the chart from which this was taken actually showed fifteen different typefaces. The ones not shown were called:

(*a*) Bookface Academic
(*b*) Courier 10
(*c*) Orator
(*d*) Prestige Pica
(*e*) Prestige Elite
(*f*) Script
(*g*) Symbol
(*h*) Gothic Mini
(*i*) Modern
(*j*) Bold face
(*k*) Essay

Most adaptable of all are the laser printers of computerized machines, which can call upon a vast memory of different typefaces and present text in any form the typesetter or secretary requires. By converting text with a particular typeface into an alternative typeface, the printer enables the two presentations to be compared.

Portable typewriters

These are lightweight models, which are very convenient for typists who travel about a great deal. Thus journalists, authors and others who travel in pursuit of news stories or background information essential to their craft use a portable machine. These usually have carriages 9 inches or 12 inches long, which is adequate for most ordinary purposes. Since the framework is less robust than standard machines, they are more suitable to experienced typists than to learners, and many parents who buy their teenage children a portable typewriter would do better to supply them with a standard model. The extra expense is offset by reduced servicing charges eventually.

Electric typewriters

These have many advantages over manual machines, of which the following may be noted:

(i) The typist does not tire so easily, since the merest contact on the keys is enough. The powered machine then drives the key

OCR-B

Not printers, EZ series or EP10

```
ABCDEFGHIJKLMNOPQRSTUVWXYZ
abcdefghijklmnopqrstuvwxyz
1234567890\-{}¤'+-=[]()
!@#$%^&* '"";?/|><,.
```

The Silver Reed line of fully electronic
typewriters and printers, featuring
the interchangeable type wheels, are
unsurpassed in performance, versatility
and dependability.

COURIER 12

* All models

```
ABCDEFGHIJKLMNOPQRSTUVWXYZ
abcdefghijklmnopqrstuvwxyz
1234567890!"£$%&'()=-#µ
[]°@¿+*:;³²±<>|/?,..
```

The Silver Reed line of fully electronic
typewriters and printers, featuring
the interchangeable type wheels, are
unsurpassed in performance, versatility
and dependability. Silver Reed Electronics - the state of the art in solid state.

LETTER GOTHIC

* All models

```
ABCDEFGHIJKLMNOPQRSTUVWXYZ
abcdefghijklmnopqrstuvwxyz
1234567890!"£$%&'()= -#µ
[]½@°32*++:;?/|<>,..
```

The Silver Reed line of fully electronic
typewriters and printers, featuring
the interchangeable type wheels, are
unsurpassed in performance, versatility
and dependability.

LIGHT ITALIC

All models excluding printers

```
ABCDEFGHIJKLMNOPQRSTUVWXYZ
abcdefghijklmnopqrstuvwxyz
1234567890!"£$%&'()= -#µ
[]½@°±+*:;³² ,.<>|/?
```

The Silver Reed line of fully electronic
typewriters and printers, featuring
the interchangeable type wheels, are
unsurpassed in performance, versatility
and dependability.

Figure 13.2 Some modern typefaces (courtesy of Silver Reed Business Machines Ltd)

forward to strike the ribbon, and as it drives all the keys uniformly, the typescript is even and easy to read.

(ii) Automatic carriage return saves the typist time and effort, automatically operating the line spacer at the same time.

(iii) 'Repeat characters' are provided, if not on all characters at least on certain ones. Thus the underscoring of words is carried out automatically, and the space bar can be operated automatically. These features save the typist much physical effort.

(iv) A carbon copy control enables the machine to be adjusted when several carbon copies are required. The physical effort required to take, say, ten carbon copies on a manual machine is very great, but by increasing the power behind the keys of an electric machine as many as twenty copies may be prepared.

Golf-ball typewriters

Some years ago a revolutionary type of electric typewriter, which has been extensively copied, appeared on the market. This was the **IBM Selectric machine**. Here the characters are moulded on to a spherical 'golf-ball' head. When a key is depressed, the machine selects the shortest path for the head to rotate and tilt so that the correct character strikes the ribbon. The machine is capable of typing up to fifteen characters per second, which is about twice as fast as most typists can type.

Because of the single typing element, the carriage does not move, the golf-ball typeface travelling across the stationary paper sliding on a guide shaft. The machine is therefore quiet, uses little desk space and operator-effort is minimal. The golf ball may be changed to give different typefaces, which enables variety of presentation to be incorporated into the typescript. Figure 13.3 shows one of the interchangeable 'golf-ball' typing elements, for which different typestyles are available.

Electronic typewriters

Electronic typewriters have recently replaced the golf-ball typewriter as the latest thing in typewriting. The more complex machines become part of a full word-processing system, which is described later. The chief features of an electronic typewriter have already been listed.

Figure 13.4 shows a typical electronic typing system, and Figure 13.5 shows the daisy-wheel print-head widely used in electronic machines. They are capable of typing seventeen characters per second, which is much faster than most typists can type.

A particular feature of typewriters today is the concept of modular upgrading, i.e. the ability to buy a basic machine and then add on extra facilities by plug-in, low-cost electronic modules. Such a typewriter is illustrated in Figure 13.6.

ماشین تحریرکارت مغناطیسی فارسی شکل تازه ای به کار شما خواهدبخشید .

پس از این لزومی ندارد نگران اشتباهات خود بشوید . اکنون تمام کارهای تحریری خود را میتوانید بصورت پیش نویس ، یعنی آسان ترین نوع ماشین نویسی تهیه کنید . اگر اشتباهی کردید کافیست به عقب برگشته و دوباره روی آن ماشین کرده و بکار خود ادامه دهید . در پایان یک نسخه بدون

Figure 13.3 A golf-ball electric typewriter — with Arabic typeface (courtesy of IBM (UK) Ltd)

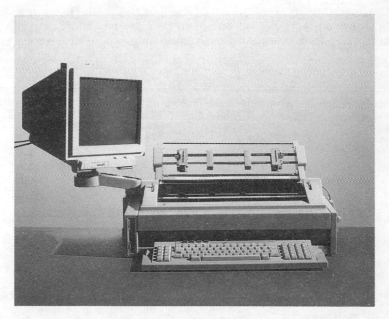

Figure 13.4 An electronic typing system: the Olivetti EVT 4000 S (courtesy of British Olivetti Ltd)

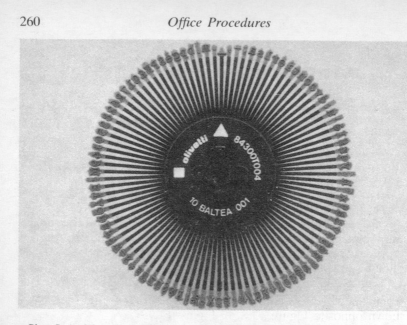

Plate 7. A 'daisy-wheel' printhead (reproduced by courtesy of British Olivetti Ltd).

One interesting feature of the electronic typewriter today, and this is also true of word-processors, is that all the traditional features of a manual typewriter have had to be reproduced in electrical (or electronic) form. For example, the mechanical space bar on a manual

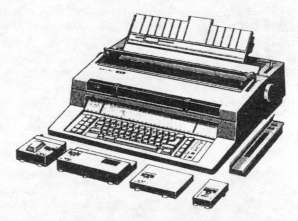

Figure 13.6   The Silver Reed EZ50 electronic typewriter. (courtesy of Silver Reed Office Systems Ltd)

Note: The EZ50 is a modular typewriter, with 'component packs' whereby the user can convert the basic machine into one with more sophisticated features just by adding an optional component pack.

typewriter is now replaced by a space bar key, which moves the cursor (the device on the screen telling the typist where the next letter will appear) one space ahead. If held down, the cursor will move ahead to give repeat spacing.

Figure 13.7 shows the key functions of a recent electronic machine, the Nakajima AE-800, and explains their purposes.

13.2 Word-processors

Word-processors are sophisticated electronic typewriters linked to some sort of memory system. Often these days the memory is provided by floppy discs, which can be read into the word-processor via a built-in disc-drive unit. This gives an infinite storage capacity of memory, since new floppy discs can be added at any time. The miniaturization of computer technology means that all the features of an advanced word-processor are available even to a small portable machine. For example, the Carrera word-processor illustrated in Figure 13.8 has all the features and advanced editing functions of larger machines, yet is easily portable. The features of the machine are shown opposite Figure 13.8, in Figure 13.9.

While the word-processor is the natural choice for the top secretary who wishes to produce impeccable correspondence, its many features include some that are of enormous help to lesser mortals, and put an end to much of the time-consuming and tedious work copy-typists have previously done. Among these we may list:

(*a*) *Standard form letters*. A letter frequently sent to many customers can be stored in the memory and recalled whenever it is required. The word-processor will stop at the date, reference section, internal address, etc., and enable the console typist to type in these variable details. The machine will then print the letter at speeds up to 400 words per minute.

(*b*) *Repetitive typing*. Standard paragraphs from contracts, leases and similar legal documents can be called forward and printed to save the typist typing them out.

(*c*) *Revision typing*. Reports and similar documents can be recalled from the memory to the visual display unit and corrected, updated or changed. The extra material will be accepted and the following material reshuffled to take account of the insertion. This puts an end to much of the tedious work of retyping. For example, suppose an executive writes a long and detailed report that is eventually to be distributed to 10 000 shareholders. The first thing is to type a 'draft' report, which will be passed to a senior executive for comments. This may result in several alterations. Formerly the amended report would call for renewed typing of any page with corrections. With the word-processor the text is simply recalled from the memory on to a VDU screen, the corrections are made or the paragraphs

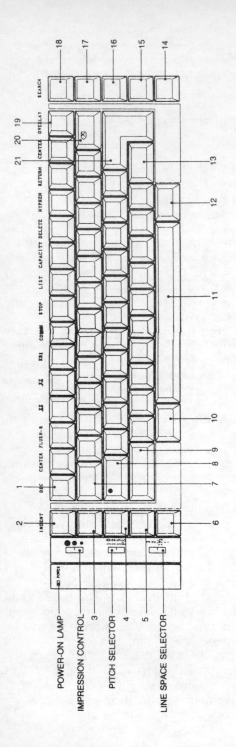

1 MARGIN RELEASE KEY
Releases the margins to type beyond them or set new ones.

2 LEFT MARGIN KEY
Sets the left margin.

3 RIGHT MARGIN KEY
Sets the right margin.

4 TAB SET/CLEAR KEY
Sets/clears tabs.

5 MODE KEY
Changes the modes.

6 CODE KEY
Activates special functions in conjunction with other keys.

7 TAB/BACK TAB KEY
Moves carrier or cursor to a tab forward or backward.

8 SHIFT LOCK KEY
   Locks the Shift key to type a series of capital
   letters. The red lamp on the key lights up when
   it's locked. Release it by touching either Shift key.

9/13 SHIFT KEY
   Enables typing a capital letter or a symbol on the
   upper half of a key.

10 REPEAT KEY
   Repeats typing one character or such key
   functions as spacing and correction.

11 SPACE BAR
   Moves carrier or cursor ahead one space. Hold it
   down for repeat spacing.

12 HALF SPACE KEY
   Moves carrier one half space to the right.

14 PRINT KEY
   Prints text on the display. Recalls (prints) a file
   stored in memory.

15 REVERSE INDEX KEY
   Retracts paper downward by the half-line (1/12")
   without moving carrier. Hold it down to retract
   paper continuously.

16 INDEX KEY
   Advances paper upward by the half-line (1/12")
   without moving carrier. Hold it down to advance
   paper continuously.

17 RELOCATION KEY
   Moves carrier one space after the last character
   in page.
   Moves cursor next to the last character in line or
   file on the display.

18 EXPRESS KEY
   Returns carrier to the left margin without line
   spacing.
   Moves cursor forward one space on the display.
   Hold it down for repeat spacing.

19 BACKSPACE KEY
   Moves carrier or cursor backward one space.
   Hold it down for repeat backspacing.

20 CORRECTION KEY
   Corrects characters. Hold it down for repeat
   correction.

21 RETURN KEY
   Returns carrier or cursor to the left margin on the
   next line.

Figure 13.7 The keyboard of an electronic typewriter and key functions explained (courtesy of Silver Reed Office Systems Ltd)

Figure 13.8   The Carrera word-processor (courtesy of Olympia (UK) Ltd)

reshuffled to take account of the criticism, and a new version is printed off.

13.3   The economics of text production

Today managements are faced with a dilemma about the most economical way of establishing the communication network, which is so essential with suppliers, customers and, in-house, between members of staff. Paper systems are expensive (the average letter is believed to cost most firms between £3 and £5). Today electronics makes it possible to replace much of the work formerly done in memo and letter form by e-mail − electronic messages distributed over a computer network to the terminals of key workers. Such messages arrive instantly and can be answered just as quickly simply by reversing a couple of codes.

Such systems are beyond the reach of many small firms, which must still rely on the more personal secretary−executive relationship, with the executive using a mixture of methods to make work available to the secretary. Thus, where the secretary has shorthand skills, letters, memos, etc. may be dictated direct. For such a secretary the day might start with him/her opening the mail and sorting it into various categories, some of which will be routine matters that can be dealt with at once without bothering the executive. Others will require executive attention, but the matters can be dealt with at once in a short executive−secretary meeting. The file of letters is read one at a time, and brief replies are dictated, or in many cases the secretary will simply be told what to do. For example:

'Brown & Co, Northampton − I think we'll say a definite "No" to that one, but tell them if they want to keep us informed of their

FEATURES

Printing system

Printing element	Drop in daisywheel
Print speed	12 cps
Print pitch	10 / 12 / 15
Hammer force	Low, medium, high
Ribbon	Correctable
Correction tape	Lift-off
Bi-directional print	
Pause print	
Background print	
Delayed print	

Paper handling

Max paper width	305 mm (12")
Max print width	229 mm (9")
Line spacing	1, 1.5, 2
Automatic paper insert	
Paper adjust up/down	

Display

14 line x 80 character LCD Display
5 position tilt adjustable

Memory

32K internal memory with battery back-up
3.5" 720K built-in disk drive

Spell check

Main dictionary	70,000 words
User dictionary	120 words

Word-processing functions

Block move, copy, delete
Search & replace
Column layout
Line draw
Header/footer
Page layout & view
Line format memory
Help function
Stop codes
Go to page
Forms management
Page numbering
Mailmerge
Appointments calendar

Editing functions

Line correction
Word erase
Full justification
Right margin flush
Automatic centring
Automatic underline
Indent margin
Tabulation
Decimal tabulation
Caps lock

Typewriter mode

Backspace
Repeat
Margin set/release
Micro adjust up/down

Technical specifications

Height	129 mm (5$^{1}/_{16}$")
Width	414 mm (16$^{5}/_{16}$")
Depth	400 mm (15$^{3}/_{4}$")
Weight	6.5 kg (14.3 lbs)
Voltage	240 V / 50 Hz

Figure 13.9 Features of the Carrera word-processor

range of products in the future we will consider them as we expand our own services to customers'.

The more important correspondence would then be dealt with, the secretary using his/her secretarial skills to take dictation and assist the executive by providing copies of past correspondence, drawing up rough drafts of reports, etc. This type of executive– secretary relationship is relatively economical – the secretary doing many useful things apart from the production of final correspondence, so that his/her salary cost is spread across a range of activities.

We may list the advantages of the 'personal-secretary' type of arrangement as follows:

(*a*) The secretary gets to know the whole range of the executive's work and can offer considerable back-up to the executive in all sorts of situations, e.g. at holiday times or when the executive is away on business trips.

(*b*) The quality of the correspondence and other text production is high, and great accuracy is achieved. For example, a secretary to a chemical engineer will soon learn the special technical terms used in his/her particular field, which an occasional typist would not know. Similarly the medical secretary gets to know the specialized medical vocabulary that doctors and surgeons use.

(*c*) The personal secretary often does his/her own filing, and consequently can locate correspondence without difficulty.

(*d*) The variable pace of the executive's day leaves time for the secretary to deal with many routine matters while being available to meet any urgent situation that may arise. This is an economical use of labour, with periods of high stress relieved by other periods of routine activity.

The second method of generating text is by the use of dictation machines, which are discussed more fully in Section 13.4. The system can be personal (as where an executive active elsewhere on company business dictates memos and correspondence on a portable tape-recorder, using a mini-cassette, which is posted in to the secretary for action. Alternatively, it can be impersonal, as where anyone who wishes to dictate correspondence is linked up over the telephone with an available tape-recorder, dictates a small batch of letters and disconnects. This enables the supervisor to extract the cassette containing that correspondence and pass it to a typist for typing. The executive with more correspondence simply reconnects and will automatically be given another available machine. Such a system is very useful where correspondence is only a sideline to the executive's main activity, e.g. lectures in colleges do need secretarial help, but it need not be personal, and full-time secretarial help would be prohibitively expensive.

Some correspondence may be prepared in manuscript form and passed to the secretary. Sometimes called 'longhand', the method is chiefly used for non-routine matters, where careful choice of words and phrases is important. Often the executive needs to clarify the material in his/her own mind, and writing does assist such a process. 'Writing maketh an exact man' says one philosopher. The manuscript material is then typed up on a word-processor, the memory facility for which enables the report or letter to be called up again for revision at a later date. This prevents tedious retyping.

Many firms hesitate to go to the expense of installing a local area network (LAN), and must continue with a system that is largely dependent on paper: memos and correspondence passing to and fro. There is a traditional conflict of ideas between those who advocate a personal service (a personal secretary serving a particular executive) and those who believe in an impersonal service, where work is submitted to a typing pool. Let us consider the advantages and disadvantages of each.

The typing pool

Under the typing-pool system most of the typists in a firm are collected together in a central office where they type the vast majority of the correspondence required. Probably only the senior executives, with their personal secretaries, will not have their correspondence prepared by the pool. Everybody else, either by manuscript (hand-written copy) or audio-tapes or by dictating to one of the pool typists who can do short-hand in one or other of its forms will make their requirements clear to the typing-pool supervisor, who will allocate the work to the typists and audio-typists in the pool. The advantages of this system may be listed as follows:

(*a*) It makes economical use of typist labour, since the idle time inevitable in departmental organization, e.g. while managers are at meetings, is filled by other work.

(*b*) Sickness and holiday difficulties are easily overcome, since the absence of a typist can be met by allocating work to others.

(*c*) A broader experience of the work of the office is given to the typists in the pool. This particularly improves the training of young staff, who can be employed on less essential activities such as routine envelope addressing, etc., as they learn the keyboard. They can then be raised to better levels of work as they acquire competence.

(*d*) Interruptions to the work are avoided — telephone queries can be intercepted and dealt with by the supervisor, and a body of trainee staff is available for taking messages, conducting searches, etc.

(*e*) More correct work results, not only because the supervisors check work before returning it to departments but also because greater skill results from specialization in a particular class of work.

(*f*) Less time is wasted – in departmental offices there is a tendency to lose typing time owing to a variety of interruptions.

(*g*) Noise is confined to the typing pool, and goes unnoticed, whereas departmental typists disturb their departments.

Against these advantages may be set the disadvantages of most centralized systems, which include a lack of personal contact between typists and executives, an increased need for messenger and collection services and the dissatisfaction of staff segregated from the general and wider activities of the enterprise to perform a limited, if useful, specialist activity.

13.4 Audio-typing

Audio-typing has developed rapidly in the last 20 years since the tape-recorder has been perfected. Its name implies that the typist types what he/she hears. Since most people speak faster than a typist can type (the late President Kennedy was reputed to speak at 400 words per minute) the audio-typist needs a machine that can be interrupted with a foot switch. The typist listens, memorizes a phrase, stops the machine and types the phrase. A variety of dictating machines is marketed, and the choice is therefore very wide.

Advantages of audio-typing systems

Audio-typing systems separate the executive from the typist. The executive can dictate to the machine at any convenient moment. Portable dictating machines enable the executive to dictate correspondence when travelling or when absent from the office. Multibank installations enable an executive to connect up to one of a central bank of dictation machines and dictate letters immediately the mail is opened or immediately after a telephone conversation or interview with a client or customer. There is a considerable saving in labour costs, since audio-typists are usually paid less than shorthand typists and may do more work because of the specialist nature of the activity. The shorthand typist must be absent from his/her work station to take dictation for much of the time. The audio-typist can work only at the installation provided by the management and therefore tends to produce a greater volume of finished work. Work is more fairly shared between typists, who do not work for a particular executive but for a group of executives. It is also easier to take over a spool of magnetic tape when a typist is absent than to take over a dictation book, which is full of personal 'short forms' the secretary has invented to speed up note-taking.

Qualities of the good audio-typist

The audio-typist must have the following qualities:

(*a*) The ability to type at a good basic speed.

(*b*) The ability to spell and punctuate properly. Since typing is carried out direct from what is heard on the stethophones, it is very important that the typist can turn this directly into a properly spelt and punctuated letter.

(*c*) The ability to display material properly.

It follows that an audio-typist should already be a trained typist, and should convert to audio-typing by a short conversion course. Resentment will be reduced if the typist is not a shorthand typist but has previously been engaged as a copy-typist only.

Disadvantages of dictation machines

Secretaries tend to resent dictation machines, which render their shorthand unnecessary and reduce freedom to move about the office taking dictation from executives. The secretary loses the sense of personal service that is so valuable in a firm, and becomes instead a clock-watcher who is anxious only to escape from the tyranny of the machine.

Whereas shorthand typists never break down or suffer from power failures, this is not uncommon with electronic machines, and considerable inconvenience and delay may result, e.g. at times of industrial unrest in the power industry.

Using the dictation machine

An executive dictating letters for the first time has to grow used to the impersonal nature of the system. It is essential to speak distinctly and give clear instructions about requirements, the number of copies needed, the type of paper to be used perhaps and the distribution of any copies within the firm.

In dictating to a shorthand typist, the executive who ponders what to say next gives the secretary a chance to read through and improve the notes. The executive who dictates to a dictation machine stops the machine when not actually speaking, since this saves tape. As a result the typist receives a continuous spool of dictation material.

The latest machines overcome many of the defects of earlier machines. For example, if the executive pauses for more than 4 seconds the machine will automatically cut out to save tape time. When tape is being replayed, the machine senses the material being replayed and cuts out immediately at the end of the replay. If the users releases the machine when it has been replaying, it automatically tracks forward to the end of the dictation and stops ready for any further dictation by the user. An automatic privacy lock on multi-user equipment prevents anyone back-tracking on to another user's dictation. Portable machines have quick-release cassettes that can be posted in for attention by secretarial staff or the typing pool from travellers and executives working on location.

Corrections can also be indicated on modern machines. A co-ordinated correction sheet, divided into sections, enables the user to mark in the point where corrections have been made, and where the new wording is to be found on the tape. With magnetic machines it is possible to re-record the correct wording over the top of the old wording.

Types of installation: centralized systems

(*a*) *Multi-bank system*. Here there are a number of recording machines in a central bank, to which executives are connected through the ordinary telephone circuits. The number of recording machines is commonly one for six executives. Executives are auto-matically connected to a free recorder. A supervisor distributes dictated recordings to the members of the typing pool. Each typist has a transcription machine for playing back the recordings, varying the speed by a foot pedal control. The system is very impersonal but relatively cheap, because the ratio of recorders to transcribers is 6:1 or even 8:1, which is economical.

(*b*) *Tandem system*. Here the executive calls a control panel on the ordinary telephone and is automatically routed to the next available secretary, who has a 'tandem' system. This consists of two dictation machines, each of which is available for recording or playing back. The executive dictates the letter to the machine that is recording, while at the same time the typist is transcribing a previously recorded piece of work. When this is completed, a switch is thrown, the roles of the machines are reversed and the typist transcribes the letter just recorded while the tandem machine is available for recording purposes.

A refinement on this system permits the executive to rewind and play back letters. Once again a confidential lock prevents one executive listening to a recording made by another executive. A phone link enables the typist to check details with the supervisor, or with the executive.

Figure 13.10 shows some typical office dictation appliances. They are (*a*) a pocket-size cassette recorder, (*b*) a disc recorder and (*c*) an office playback machine. The latter machine can also be operated by a foot pedal to avoid the need to interrupt the typing process while requiring the machine to play the next part of the tape.

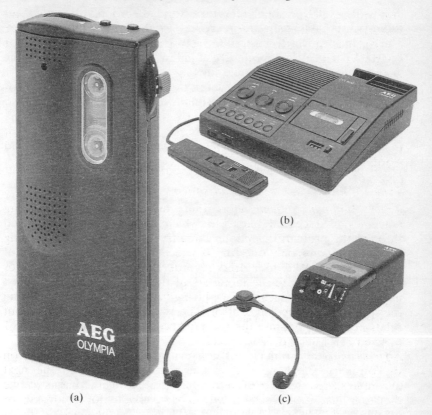

Figure 13.10 Audio-typing equipment: (*a*) portable cassette recorder, (*b*) disk recorder, (*c*) playback machine (courtesy of Olympia (UK) Ltd)

13.5 Points to think about and discuss

(*a*) Mary, a personal secretary to the managing director of a small firm, has been asked to speak to the students of her local technical college about the advantages and disadvantages of the small firm as an employer. What advantages and disadvantages do you think she might mention?

(*b*) Peter, who is having to leave school at 16 owing to family circumstances, is about to accept an office post as junior clerk. One of the reasons he was chosen was his excellent typing ability. He vows that one day he will be chairman of the board. What stages can you envisage in his progress towards successful achievement of this ambition.

(*c*) A firm is considering rearranging its work to meet changing requirements. The changes will have the following effects: (i) The dismissal of 100 personal secretaries and their replacement by 60 audio-typists. All staff are recruited locally, (ii) a reduction of 5 per cent in prices to customers, and (iii) an increase in profits of £600 000 per year is expected, estimated to represent a 1 per cent increase in dividend to shareholders.

The firm is the largest employer in the area in a highly competitive international field. What are the implications of these changes?

13.6   Rapid revision − typing and word-processing

Cover the page with a sheet of paper and uncover one question at a time

Answers	Questions
−	1 What is the typewriter used for?
1 To bring the correct characters to the paper and impress them to produce a legible text.	2 What is an electronic typewriter?
2 A typewriter that supports the usual typing activity with a number of additional functions. These functions add to the appearance, correctness and speed of delivery of the text in production.	3 List some of these extra functions.
3 (*a*) Line display, or paragraph display so that text can be checked for correctness before being printed, (*b*) right-hand margin justification, (*c*) impression controls to ensure all strokes are typed with the same force, (*d*) automatic centring, underlining and carriage return.	4 What are the advantages of the personal-secretary method of text production?
4 (*a*) A knowledgeable and fully qualified secretary controls and supervises every aspect of an executive's text creation work, (*b*) he/she knows all about the executive's work and can offer back-up support in all sorts of situations, e.g. holidays, sickness, foreign trips, exhibitions, etc., (*c*) the quality of text production is high and uniform.	5 What is a typing pool?
5 A group of typists working under a supervisor to prepare the vast majority of a firm's correspondence either by audio-typing methods or from manuscripts produced by executives˜ to whom personal	6 What are the advantages of a typing pool?

secretarial help is not available. It is a centralized service.

---

6 (*a*) Higher typist output, (*b*) cheaper labour used than the personal secretary type of employee, (*c*) greater variety of work received and hence wider experience for the typists, (*d*) improved training and supervision possible, (*e*) less noise in other offices.

7 List the disadvantages of a typing pool.

---

7 (*a*) Loss of personal convenience to departmental executives, (*b*) reduced use of their skills by some trained shorthand typists, (*c*) increased messenger and collection services required, (*d*) high cost of audio systems.

8 What is a word-processor?

---

8 A machine producing an electronic record of typed material that can be amended at will and reproduced faultlessly. The machine can accept revisions and alterations, adjusting the stored text to fit in afterwards, with justified right-hand margins.

9 What is a golf-ball machine?

---

9 A machine with interchangeable typing units, mounted on a moving typing element, which traverses across the paper. There is no moving carriage to this type of machine.

10 What are the advantages of audio-typing systems?

---

10 (*a*) They free the executive from the secretary, so that dictation may take place at any time, (*b*) they raise productivity, since the audio-typist can work only at the machine, and is under constant supervision, (*c*) peaks of work in particular departments are smoothed over the whole organization, (*d*) cheaper labour is used.

11 What are the requirements from a good audio-typist?

---

11 (*a*) The typist must be able to type at a good speed, (*b*) it is essential to spell, punctuate and display work properly.

12 What are the chief types of centralized dictation service?

---

12 (*a*) Multi-bank dictation systems to which executives are connected by their desk telephones, (*b*) 'tandem' systems.

13 What is a 'tandem' system?

---

13 A system where each audio-typist has two machines, one of which is recording while the typist is transcribing from the other.

14 Go over the page again until you feel you are sure of the answers.

Exercises set 13

1 Complete the sentences below by selecting the correct word or phrase from the word list.

   (a) A non-electric typewriter possessing the usual characteristics (ten or twelve characters to the inch and six lines to the inch) is often spoken of as a ...... machine.

   (b) A typist who types directly from a tape-recorder is called an ......

   (c) Variety can be introduced into correspondence, reports, etc., if our typewriter is supplied with ......

   (d) A room in which many typists work from shorthand notes, manuscript copy or from dictation machines is known as a ......

   (e) Portable typewriters are less ...... than standard machines and are therefore easily strained by inexperienced typists.

   (f) Electric typewriters save typist effort by features such as ...... return.

   (g) Electronic typewriters that permit the recall of text for additions or alterations, which can be accepted at any point, the disturbed material being automatically moved to accommodate it, are called ......

   (h) Where a typewriter can vary the space between words to make every line end at the same point, it is said to produce a ......

   (i) When an audio-typist has two machines, one of which records while the other is transcribing, she is said to have a ......

   (j) It is vital for an audio-typist to be able to ......

   Word list: audio-typist, robust, standard manual, typing pool, justified right-hand margin, spell and punctuate, automatic carriage, word-processors, tandem system, interchangeable typing heads or daisy wheels.

2 List the advantages and disadvantages of having the vast majority of the correspondence of a firm typed in a central typing pool.

3 It is proposed to establish a typing pool, using a central bank of dictating machines to which executives are connected through their ordinary desk telephones. Jenny, a shorthand typist, opposes the idea. Anne, a copy-typist, is in favour. Suggest reasons for their opposing views and discuss the possible advantages and disadvantages of the scheme.

4 In what ways does a word-processor differ from a typewriter. Explain the advantages to (a) a skilled secretary offering a top quality correspondence service to clients, (b) a routine copy-typist in a typing pool.

5 During the day you have typed the following: (a) twenty-four invoices for goods sold to customers on credit, (b) an agenda for the monthly industrial relations meeting between shop stewards and management (twenty copies), (c) a memo to the head caretaker about a heating appliance that is not working (two copies).
   Explain what processes will follow in each case before the efforts you have made are brought to final fruition.

6 Describe briefly the use of (*a*) a tandem dictation machine system, (*b*) a word-processor, (*c*) a portable typewriter.

7 The question of replacing shorthand typists by audio-typists and of purchasing appropriate machines is under consideration by your firm. Write a memorandum to the head of your department giving your views on this matter and setting out the advantages and disadvantages of recorded dictation.

8 Draft a standard letter to accompany brochures about your firm's products and price lists to send to all firms or customers who write in for information.

9 'Impeccable correspondence on well-designed stationery is essential to the success of any firm.'
   'It is better to contact 10 000 potential customers with a cheap leaflet than 100 people with an expensive-looking letterhead.'
   Contrast these two approaches to advertising your products.

10 Draw up a list of features available to a word-processor operator but not available to a typist using a standard manual typewriter.

14 Computers and data-processing

14.1 The importance of computers today

In the last 30 years computers have revolutionized office practice. Computers are electronic machines that can be made to carry out very simple activities at enormous speeds, roughly 900 million operations per second. Each of these operations in itself is a very simple event – you can compare it to switching on an electric light. But when the operations are organized (a process called **programming**) so that they perform a succession of operations, one after the other, the computer can be made to do quite complicated jobs in what seems to be only an instant. An often-quoted example is checking stolen credit cards. Suppose an American tourist presents a credit card in a London shop in order to purchase a souvenir of his visit. The computerized system can get through to America, compare the number of the credit card with every stolen credit card in the United States and send a message back to the shop confirming that the card is genuine and that the shop is safe in accepting the card in payment. This only takes about 6 seconds and only costs about 10 pence.

Since computers are best at doing very routine things, it follows that many simple jobs formerly done by junior staff can now be done by computers, and the junior staff used for other work. Some of this 'other work' has to do with the computer itself. For example, putting information into the computer to keep its records up to date, and learning how to write programs telling the computer what to do.

Since computers are so widely used, there is much to be said for everyone having a nodding acquaintance with the general workings of a computer. It is impossible to describe the actual applications fully, because they are very complex and detailed, but one or two examples are given later in this chapter. First we need to consider the principles behind computerization.

14.2 The basic rules behind the computerization of office procedures

These rules are as follows:

(*a*) Decide what you want to do and the best way to do it.

(*b*) Decide what data are needed, how to capture them and how to **input** them.

(*c*) Write the programs that will enable the computer to carry out the **data-processing** required.

(*d*) Decide what **output** you want, and how to deliver it to the end-user.

(*e*) If some of it is likely to be needed again, decide how to **store** it.

(*f*) Deliver the output that is required to the end-user.

Some idea of this complex collection of activities is given in Figure 14.1. Study it now.

Looking at these various activities in more detail we find as follows:

(*a*) *Deciding what we want to do.* We can only computerize any activity if we know exactly what we want to do and have decided on the best way to do it. The first activity usually is to find out what is being done at present in the non-computerized activity. Who does what, and why? This may mean holding a full investigation of the department concerned and writing a full report on exactly what is done, who does it, and what improvements might be achieved by a computerized system. For example, since computers can make up and print out invoices, it may mean that all the invoice typists will need to be moved to other work or be made redundant.

(*b*) *Dealing with the raw data.* Having decided on the best way to do things under the new system, we then have to envisage what are the raw facts and figures (called the **data**) that have to be fed into the computer. For example, if the computer is to type out and send off invoices to our customers, it will need to know all their names and addresses, as well as all the names of the various goods we manufacture, the prices we charge, the numbers ordered by each customer, any carriage charges, insurance charges, special discounts, VAT charges, etc. Since the computer cannot deal with ordinary alphabetical and numerical information, it has to be fed all these details in language that is machine-readable. How are we going to change that information into machine-readable form?

(*c*) *Writing the programs.* Programs are sets of instructions that manipulate the data supplied. With a payroll program, for example, the data might be the hours worked, the rate of pay, the tax code number, and various deductions to be made from the employee's salary. The employee is represented by a personnel number. The program will itself perform the calculations, to produce the net pay to which the employee is entitled.

Figure 14.2 shows a small portion of such a payroll program, written in COBOL, a high-level computer language. It is the most commonly used language for commercial programs, and stands for Common Business Orientated Language.

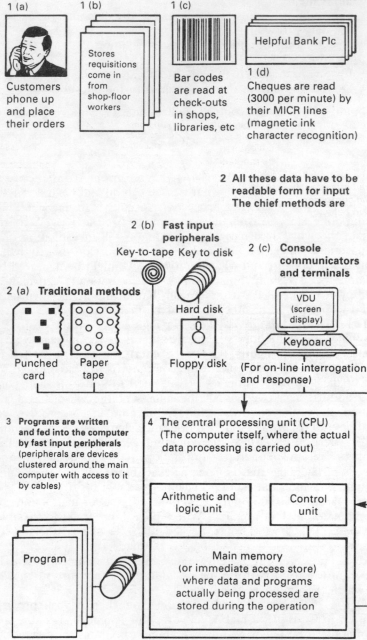

Figure 14.1 Computers and office procedures

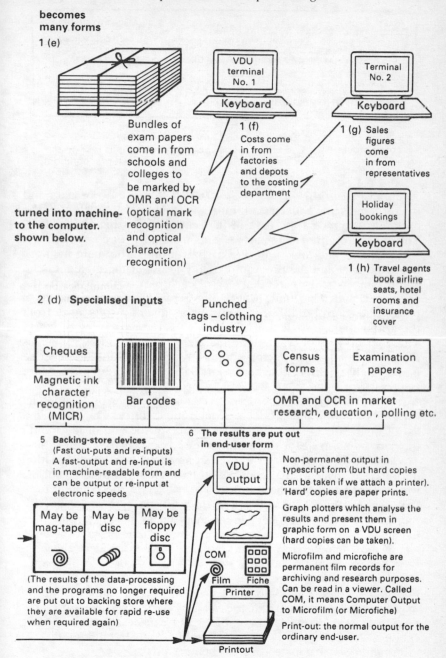

becomes many forms

1 (e)

Bundles of exam papers come in from schools and colleges to be marked by OMR and OCR (optical mark recognition and optical character recognition)

turned into machine-to the computer. shown below.

VDU terminal No. 1
Keyboard

1 (f) Costs come in from factories and depots to the costing department

Terminal No. 2
Keyboard

1 (g) Sales figures come in from representatives

Holiday bookings
Keyboard

1 (h) Travel agents book airline seats, hotel rooms and insurance cover

2 (d) **Specialised inputs**

Punched tags – clothing industry

Cheques
Magnetic ink character recognition (MICR)

Bar codes

Census forms

Examination papers

OMR and OCR in market research, education, polling etc.

5 **Backing-store devices**
(Fast out-puts and re-inputs) A fast-output and re-input is in machine-readable form and can be output or re-input at electronic speeds

6 **The results are put out in end-user form**

VDU output

May be mag-tape | May be disc | May be floppy disc

(The results of the data-processing and the programs no longer required are put out to backing store where they are available for rapid re-use when required again)

COM
Film Fiche
Printer
Printout

Non-permanent output in typescript form (but hard copies can be taken if we attach a printer). 'Hard' copies are paper prints.

Graph plotters which analyse the results and present them in graphic form on a VDU screen (hard copies can be taken).

Microfilm and microfiche are permanent film records for archiving and research purposes. Can be read in a viewer. Called COM, it means Computer Output to Microfilm (or Microfiche)

Print-out: the normal output for the ordinary end-user.

Figure 14.1 (*continued*)

```
CALC.
        MULTIPLY RATE BY HOURS GIVING GROSS-PAY.
        IF S-F-INDICATOR=1 SUBTRACT SUPERANNUATION FROM GROSS- PAY.
        ADD TAX, NAT-INS, HSA TO TOTAL-DEDUCTS.
        SUBTRACT TOTAL-DEDUCTS FROM GROSS-PAY GIVING NET-PAY.
PAY SLIP.
        MOVE PAY-DETAILS TO PRINT AREA.
        WRITE PAY-RECORD AFTER ADVANCING 2.
        GO TO FILE-UPDATE.
```

Figure 14.2   A portion of a payroll program

(*d*) *The Central Processing Unit (CPU)*. Once the raw data and the programs have been fed into the computer, it can use the programs to process the data in its **Central Processing Unit (CPU)**. This consists of three main parts — a main memory (or core memory), an arithmetic and logic unit and a control unit. The main memory holds the data and the program actually in use at the moment. The control unit organizes the delivery of each part of the work to the arithmetic and logic unit, where the actual **data-processing** takes place. The control unit also organizes the flow of results away from the arithmetic and logic unit to clear it for the next piece of work. These results may be wanted immediately by some end-user, such as the accountant or the factory manager. Those results not needed immediately can be held in some sort of backing store until they are required.

(*e*) *The backing store*. Suppose we have a number of commercial travellers who sell our products around the country. They send in a list of their expenses to us every week and at the end of the month they are reimbursed for the money they have spent. We enter these expenses as they arrive each week, but no one needs the information until payday, which is the 25th day of each month. In the meantime we just need to keep the records on the files in the computer. In that case we might as well leave them in machine language, for there is no point in storing them in ordinary language and then having to input them again. In the same way all the programs can be left in the computer in machine language. When needed, they can be called up from the backing store in a few seconds at electronic speeds.

Backing stores can come in three main forms. They can be on magnetic tape, on magnetic discs (called **hard discs**), or on **floppy discs**, which are not in the computer but can be stored in a filing cabinet. A single floppy disc can hold about 16 million bits of information (2 megabytes, a byte being 8 bits).

(*f*) *Data for the end-user*. Where an end-user wants the results of some data-processing, he/she usually wants them in readable form.

The machine language of the computer has to be turned back into words and figures and delivered to the end-user. The usual output will be in the form of a print-out or a 'hard-copy' — a photocopy of what appears on the screen of a visual display unit. We can also have screen displays (which are non-permanent) and microfilm or microfiche displays. These are photographed down to minute sizes — 270 pages, say, on a microfiche of 150 mm × 100 mm, i.e. 6 inches × 4 inches.

Now refer back to Figure 14.1 to see how these various activities take place to provide the final end-user with the information he/she needs.

14.3 The components of a computer configuration

When they were first built, computers were enormous machines, and generated so much heat that they needed special air-conditioned premises. Today they are so small that even enormously powerful machines can be packed into small suitcases to be carried wherever they are required and used on the operator's lap as he/she travels by air around the world — the so-called 'lap-top' computers. There are three main types of computer.

(*a*) *Mainframe computers.* Very large, sophisticated computers, with enormous capacities, able to do everything required by even the largest multi-national companies. They have large staffs of programmers able to write 'dedicated software', i.e. programs to suit the personal needs of the user-company. Because of the high costs of the systems, it became necessary to recover some of the cost by using the system for other firms' needs, and many mainframe users therefore act as computer bureaux, which will take on work, e.g. accounts work, for customers in return for a monthly payment.

(*b*) *Mini-computers.* These are smaller than mainframe computers but almost as powerful, and can do everything that most companies or firms require. They may employ their own programming staff, but more likely buy their programs as 'packages', gradually building up to full computerization as experience is gained. Very often a payroll package for doing the wages, or an accounts package for keeping the ordinary accounts of the business, will be the first packages purchased. Mini-computers cost between £15 000 and £50 000.

(*c*) *Micro-computers.* Often called PCs — personal computers — these are small machines that are still powerful enough to do most of the things required by the average small firm. They can be used in large organizations to carry out a particular section of the work, several micros being more convenient and adaptable than a mini-computer. They are also cheap enough and small enough to permit

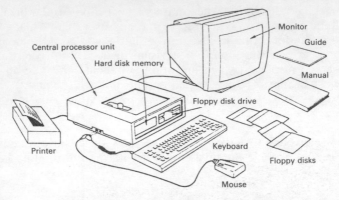

Figure 14.3 Components for a micro-computer

Notes

(i) The central processor occupies very little space in the main body of the computer, which also houses a hard-disc memory and a floppy-disc drive. If the user is storing most of the programs and data on floppy discs outside the computer, he/she must re-input them when required. This is the function of the floppy-disc drive, which loads the relevant program and data when instructed.

(ii) The monitor (visual display unit) is usually mounted on the central processor – in the illustration they have been shown apart.

(iii) The keyboard is used to give instructions to the computer. This is explained later.

(iv) The printer will give print-outs of any data required when instructed to do so.

(v) A mouse is a device for pinpointing any point on the screen of a VDU so that entries can be made very quickly and easily. It locates the cursor (the flashing point of light that tells us where the next entries will appear if anything is keyed in). This is explained later in the chapter (in the glossary of terms).

(vi) The manual and guide are reference books supplied with the micro by the manufacturers to help customers use the computer correctly.

their supply to every senior executive, or team leader, with sufficient software to cater for the particular activity he/she is supervising. A typical lay out for a micro-computer is shown in Figure 14.3.

Recent developments in the micro-computer field reflect the increasing miniaturization of components as micro-techniques enable whole computers to be built on silicon chips no bigger than a thumbnail. The result is that high-powered computers can now be built into a framework no larger than a briefcase. First we had the **lap-top computers**, so small that executives could use them on their laps as they flew around the world. Unfortunately some of them were also so powerful that they were suspected of interfering with the operation of the aircraft itself. The next development was the **notebook computer**, a super-compact, high-performance computer small enough to be carried in a briefcase and weighing only about 2 kg. Figure 14.4 shows a typical notebook computer from the Japanese Sharp Corporation.

Figure 14.4 A notebook computer (courtesy of Sharp Corporation)

It is helpful at this point to consider a simple use of a micro-computer. The most widely used applications are simple accounting, and the description given in Section 14.4 shows how the micro is used by a great many small firms in the United Kingdom. The system is called the Simplex Accounting System, and in this case the computerized version is called Micro-Simplex Plus.

14.4 Micro-Simplex Plus – a simple computerized accounting system

The advent of the micro-computer has put computerized accounting within reach of even the smallest businesses. Its great advantage is that the actual book-keeping entries are made instantaneously, often at the press of a single key. The tedious manual entry of single items, which are then carried to summaries, is replaced by keyboard entries of all items in the daily records. The VAT records and the summaries are then prepared automatically.

Information is fed into the micro-computer by a keyboard similar in layout to a typewriter keyboard except for one or two additional keys. There is also an extra number keyboard arranged in block form as with an electronic calculator. These keyboards allow all the accounting entries necessary for a firm to be entered into the computerized records as soon as the software package has been fed in from the program disc supplied by the software house. Schools and colleges that have a micro-computer and wish to obtain a demonstration tape (or better still the actual software, which is quite inexpensive) should write to the suppliers.

Micro Simplex is a Simplex System, owned by George Vyner Ltd of Huddersfield and licensed for sole use to Micro-Retailer Systems Ltd, 84 Mill St, Macclesfield, Cheshire SK11 6NR Tel: 0625 615375.

The Micro-Simplex system works off a series of programs stored on floppy discs, which, when inserted into a disc drive, will load the first program into the computer. The first thing we see is a menu of activities, called the main menu. Other subsidiary menus appear later.

The word 'menu' is important in computerization. It simply means that all the various activities the user (in this case the accountant) might require are listed like the options on a menu in a restaurant. The main menu of Micro-Simplex reads:

1   Enter and view information.
2   Print information to screen/printer.
3   Prepare VAT return.
4   Prepare profit and loss account.
5   System housekeeping.
6   Retail sales ledger.
7   Restart Micro-Simplex Plus.
    Select menu option. Esc to exit.

We respond to the invitation to select a menu option by pressing one of the keys 1–7.

By pressing Key 1 we select the 'Enter and view information' option. This is of course the most frequently used option, because every day we must enter the relevant details of each aspect of our business, the takings, payments for business stock, payments other than for stock, etc. If we press Key 1 the following menu appears.

The Enter and View Menu reads:

1 Enter sales and bankings.
2 Enter payments made by cash/cheques.
3 Enter unpaid bills.
4 Pay some unpaid bills.
5 Enter other transactions.
6 View bank accounts.
7 View cash account.

We are then invited to select the option we require. A touch on the 1 key will request the option for entering sales and bankings.

Every one of these menu items requires its own program of instructions to the computer, so that any piece of software is not a single program but a whole suite of programs. As soon as we touch Key 1 the computer screen shows 'Loading sales and bankings program'. This is what we call a 'user-friendly' computer. It tells us from moment to moment what is happening. As soon as the program is loaded, the screen will start to take us through the activity, step by step. Every entry we make will be held in a buffer memory until it is ready to go into the computer's records. Thus if we are giving the computer our sales figures for the day and we have five tills, it will invite us to key in the figures for Till No. 1, Till No. 2, etc., until all the figures are available. It will then add up the five figures and say 'Your total takings are ......', 'Are there any more takings', etc.

Finally the computer asks

'Is this entry correct?' Y/N

A touch on the Y key produces a further question.

'Are you sure?' Y/N

A further touch on the Y key convinces the computer it is safe to make the entry, and the computer will not only add the sales for the day to the computer's records but will also up-date the quarterly sales figure and the annual sales figure to take account of today's sales.

14.5 Computers and the binary system

One of the difficulties of computerization is the need to give the computer everything it needs in a form it can use with its rather limited intelligence — it can only recognize two situations, on and off, or, to give them a numerical value, 1 and 0. Fortunately there is a way in which any number and any letter can be represented with only 1 and 0. It is called the binary system. Consider the ordinary decimal system of numbers, using thousands, hundreds, tens and units. We have numbers such as 1 7 2 4 (one thousand, seven hundred and twenty-four). In this system the first column is called the units column. There are ten possible figures in the units column: 0, 1, 2, 3, 4, 5, 6, 7, 8, 9. As soon as we get to 10 we need a new column, the 'tens' column, and this enables us to continue 10, 11, 12, 13, etc., but when we get to 99 we shall reach 10×10s if we go any further and that leads us on into the 'hundreds' column: 100, 101, 102, etc.

Now if we apply the same idea to the binary system, which is a system where the columns are moved to the next column as soon as they reach 2, we have:

Decimal		*Binary*
0	=	0
1	=	1
2	=	10 (one, two, and no more)
3	=	11 (one, two, and one more)
4	=	100 (one two^2 and no more)
5	=	101 (one two^2 and one more)
6	=	110 (one two^2 and one two and no more)
7	=	111 (one two^2 and one 2, and one more)
8	=	1000 (one two^3 and no more)

Can you work out what 9 would be? It is 1001 (one 2^3 and one more). And what 10 would be? The answer is 1010 (one 2^3 and one two).

Clearly some numbers are going to be very large, and all letters and punctuation marks must be allocated a code in binary form if the machine is to be able to understand them and use them. What an input device does is take ordinary data, whether in alphabetical or numeric form, and turn it into binary form, so that it is machine-readable. What an output device does is take the results of the data-processing, which is in the form of a flood of machine-readable data, and turn it back into ordinary language and decimal figures.

14.6 A network of computers

Although a computer has many uses for a business as a stand-alone facility for such records as accounting, stock-keeping, payrolls, etc., it can of course be developed into a more sophisticated communication network. The essential features of a network arc illustrated in Figure 14.5. The essential points are the following.

First, the host computer is the central computer, which may be at head office or at a main access point somewhere in the system. For example, an airline which has a computer that may be accessed by many travel agents to book seats on planes will probably base the host computer at the hub airport (the one from which its services radiate).

Second, this host computer has all the main files in computerized form. These may be accessed by any number of remote terminals, all of which are given access (seemingly instantaneous). In fact the human operators keying in a booking, or asking a question, go so slowly compared with the computer's 900 million actions a second that it has time to take them all separately one after the other and yet appear to be instantaneous.

Third, each remote terminal can access the computer for a number of different purposes, e.g. to make an inquiry of some sort, to place an order, to notify a payment received, or for any other purpose for which a program has been written.

Fourth, all data input is validated (checked for correctness so far as the computer can tell). For example, if an account no. was given and the computer did not have an account with that number, it could not accept the entry, which would be returned to the terminal for immediate correction. Perhaps the operator miskeyed. Perhaps the account number on the document was incorrect. Perhaps the whole thing was fraudulent.

Fifth, valid data will be accepted and will be used to up-date the master file. With some records (said to be on-line) the up-date can be made at once. For example, with airline or hotel bookings we must up-date the records at once to reserve the seats and show them as not being available any longer − otherwise we shall have double bookings. On-line communication is instantaneous. With less urgent records − say an order for raw materials − the orders can be queued in an orderly sequence on a memory file (usually a magnetic disc) for off-peak booking when the computer has a spare moment.

Sixth, the up-dating of master files may simply leave them in a better state for the next day's work, but it may also generate all sorts of records. For example, we might generate orders (for those raw materials, or anything else that has reached its re-order point, as notified to the computer). It may alert people to particular problems (aircraft No. 2704 is due for a major overhaul and must be withdrawn from service). It may generate any number of management reports − sales by volume and value, overdue accounts, etc. It will certainly generate an audit trail − which keeps a record of every entry made, which terminal made the entry, at what time, on which date, and exactly what the entry was.

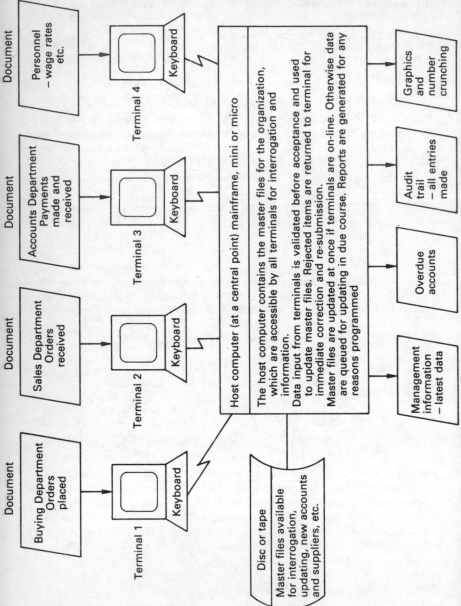

This is a different kind of business communication from the sort of correspondence mentioned in earlier chapters, but it is a very efficient use of electronic media in all sorts of useful situations.

14.7 A glossary of computer terms

This is not a textbook on computerization, but this introductory reference to computers is required because so many aspects of office procedure call for the use of computers today. The following list of computer terms is likely to be useful as a reference section to those who are studying computer appreciation.

All items in *italics* within an entry refer to other entries in the glossary.

Address. The location of an item in the computer's *memory*.

Algorithm. A set of logical rules for solving a problem in a finite number of moves.

Arithmetic and logic unit. That part of the *central processor unit* that carries out specific instructions assigned to it by the *control unit*. The instructions tend to be arithmetical in nature, e.g. 'Add one number to another' or 'Subtract one number from another number'.

Array. A series of storage locations in a computer arranged in a continuous pattern, like pigeon-holes in a hotel lobby for correspondence for guests. These storage locations can be accessed using index values.

Backing storage. A storage device to hold *programs* and *data 'off-line'* from the computer when they are not required by the *central processor unit*. For example, after entering a batch of purchases invoices affecting a number of contract accounts, the up-dated contract accounts would be put out to backing store until required again. Backing storage is always in machine-readable form. The usual backing-storage devices are *magnetic tape* and *magnetic disc*, but many small businesses use *floppy discs*, which can hold a complete set of programs and a year's data.

Bar codes. A specialized *input device* that can be read with a light pencil or wand, or by passing the strip over a light-sensitive window. The computer then searches its *memory* to name the item, record its price and adjust stock records. Computerized stock records increase the rate of stock turnover, since re-ordering only takes place when existing stocks reach an agreed low point, and only the optimum order is placed—often on a just-in-time basis.

BASIC. A simple computer language − the Beginners All-purpose Symbolic Instruction Code.

Batch. A collection of documents or other computer work collected together and coded prior to running in sequence. Where a computer gives *real-*

time access to users from remote *terminals*, it is usual for batches to be run in the background — interrupted by real-time users seeking access — so that a highly efficient use of computer time is achieved.

Batch total. The total of a *batch* used to check that all amounts to be entered have been accepted.

Binary code. This is the representation given by the *binary system* to any numeric or alphabetical character, using only the digits 1 and 0. Each character is represented by a different combination of ones and zeros to give it a unique code. An *input device* gets information into the computer by translating the information into its binary coded form, which the machine can recognize, accept and process.

Binary number. The representation of a character in numerical form using the *binary system*.

Binary system. A number system based on two, where each place value is not ten (as in the decimal system) but two, i.e. when we get more than one unit we move into the next place. Thus the numbers 0-7 in binary code are respectively 0, 1, 10, 11, 100, 101, 110 and 111. Any number or letter, punctuation mark, etc., can be allocated a *binary code*.

Bit. An abbreviation for binary digit. Each position, i.e. each place value, in a *binary number* is called a bit. Thus the decimal number 7, which in binary is 111, has three bits: 1 unit, 1 two (the second place in the binary system is a two, not a ten) and 1 four (the third place in a binary system is 2^2 (four) not 10^2 (one hundred) as in the decimal system). So 111 is a 4, a 2 and a 1, which is 7.

Blank. A space; a character where nothing is printed. As in printing, in a computer *memory* the space takes just as much room as any other character.

Buffer. A storage device where information arriving too fast from another device can be diverted until the slower device can absorb it.

Bug. An error in *coding* that causes a *program* to fail, or perform incorrectly.

Bus. A *data* highway; a number of transmission lines along which data are moved.

Byte. A byte is 8 *bits*, and may be used to hold two small numbers (because any number up to 15 only needs four bits — for example, decimal 15 is 1111 in the *binary system*) or one alphabetic or special character.

Cassette. A storage medium for *micro-computers* and personal computers, with narrow tape only 0.15″ wide. *Data* are written along the length of the tape, not across it, so the speed of reading and writing is slow.

Central processor unit. The CPU, the central unit of a computer, consisting of three elements: *(a) control unit, (b) arithmetic and logic unit* and *(c) main storage* (sometimes called main '*memory*' or 'immediate access memory'). The function of the CPU is to process *data* according to a *program* of instructions.

Chips. Small portions of a wafer of silicon on which photograph-like images have been printed and developed to give integrated circuits of great complexity; virtually a computer on a chip.

COBOL. Common Business-Orientated Language: a programming language (see *Program*) that is designed to be used to solve business-based problems.

Coding. A system of symbols that enables costs and similar items to be allocated a place within the costing system so that entry, processing, allocation or absorption, retrieval, etc. can be easily managed.

COM. Computer *output* to microfilm or microfiche: specialized outputs used for archiving vital records − 2 000 pages on a 30-metre roll of film; 98 or 270 pages on a 150 mm × 100 mm microfiche. The main uses are in insurance companies, banks, libraries and public record offices. They are not widely used in accounting activities.

Compiler. A *program* that translates statements made in a high-level language into *machine code*, so that the machine can actually execute the program.

Configuration. A grouping of components around a central processor to provide a complete system suitable for a particular firm or range of activities.

Console. A typewriter *keyboard* used by a computer operator to interrupt the computer and feed in further instructions. It will have a *VDU* attached to assist the process of inputting instructions, and to receive responses from the computer.

Control unit. That part of the *central processor unit* which accesses the *program* instructions held in *main storage* one at a time, and in the correct sequence. It interprets the coded instructions and assigns one of the other elements in the CPU to carry out the instruction, whatever it may be. Control units operate at a great speed, measured in *mips*. Common speeds are 5−12 mips.

Core. Another term for *memory*; where *data* can be stored for immediate access.

CPU. The *central processor unit*.

Cursor. A blinking light, which draws the operator's attention to the point on the screen where entries will appear if keyed in. It may be moved by pressing appropriate keys and in other ways.

Daisy-wheel printer. A *printer* that works from a daisy-wheel − a circle of metal or plastic with the characters embossed on 'petals' sticking out from the edge of the circle. The wheel rotates to bring the correct character to the ribbon, where a hammer strikes it to print the character through the ribbon. This can be done at about 90 characters per second (cps). This type of printer is mainly used in word-processing (see *Word-processor*) because of the high-quality output.

Data. Any items of information in machine-readable form − the basic material that computers process.

Data administrator. The person in charge of a database who may alone authorize changes in the *data* since the integrity of the data for one type of user might be adversely affected if another user, with different needs, was allowed to make changes which did not reflect the needs of all.

Data checking. See *Data validation*.

Data-processing. The automatic performance of operations on *data*. A *program* of instructions to the computer tells it what operations to perform, e.g. 'Compare Q with 200; if Q is less than 200 print out an urgent re-order memo to stock controller for the EOQ (economic order quantity)'.

Data transfer. The action of transferring *data* from one unit to another within the computer (for example, from storage into main *memory*). Other movements include the input of data to computer from an *input device* or from the computer to an *output device*.

Data transmission. The communication of *data* from one location to another. It may be local (within the computer, or between the computer and a *peripheral input device* or *output device*), or it may be from one remote *terminal* to another over dedicated telephone lines (usually direct-connect lines at present but eventually over a full network of fibre-optic lines or by satellite).

Data validation. A system for checking *data* to ensure they are within a permitted range of values, e.g. a percentage must be within the range 0−100. Works numbers for personnel may lie within certain limits. If we insert an account number the computer may be able to check that such an account does exist. Data outside the limits will be rejected and a *print-out* of rejections will be produced.

Degrees of integration. The number of transistor circuits on a silicon *chip*, e.g. SSI − small-scale integration; MSI − medium-scale integration; VLSI − very large-scale integration.

Digital device. A device where the *data* are represented by numerical quantities. For example, the wave of an ordinary telephone message is sampled 8000 times a second to measure the amplitude of the wave and these measurements are turned into a *binary code* of numerical data. The original wave is reconstituted at destination by a device called a *modem*.

Direct access. Any system of storage enabling a particular body of *data* to be located and consulted irrespective of where it is in the system.

Disc drive. A device that can read from and write to a disc, so that *data* or *programs* can be read from the disc into the computer's main *memory*, where the programs can be used to carry out operations on the data, adding new data or deleting data no longer required.

Document image processing. A system of scanning documents and recording them in miniature on an optical disc. This can be read by a laser and the document can be reproduced on a screen when required. The contents of ten filing cabinets can be stored on one 5.25″ optical disk.

Dump. The transfer of the contents of a *memory* or a *file* to another device, such as a *printer*.

EFTPOS. Electronic funds transfer at point of sale: a system that permits a bank customer to pay for goods by means of a bank card. The computer is accessed by the banker's card to check that funds are available in a customer's account and, if they are, it sanctions payment. The customer is debited (s/he has received back some of the funds on deposit) and the store credited with the amount paid.

File. A store of information on a particular topic which can be read into the computer at any time to accept *input*, answer queries, show the state of the system and keep a log of events as an audit trail.

Floppy disc. A single disc of plastic coated with magnetic oxide, and protected by a thin card envelope. They may be 8″, $5\frac{1}{4}$″ or $3\frac{1}{2}$″ in diameter with a capacity of up to 2 *megabytes*. The *read-write head* of the *disc drive* operates in a slot in the protective envelope to access the *data* or *programs* on the disc.

Flowchart. A stage in the development of a *program*. It is a graphical representation of the steps involved in a procedure or program.

FORTRAN. FORmula TRANslator: a high-level programming language designed to deal with mathematical computations.

Generation. A term used to describe the development of computers. First generation computers used valves, second generation used transistors, third generation used integrated circuits, fourth generation use VLSI (very large-scale integration: see *Degrees of integration*).

Gigo. Garbage in, garbage out: a computing maxim which reminds us that no computer can produce good *output* from bad *input*. Any results cannot be better than the input supplied, since they are based upon it.

Graph plotters. Devices which produce graphs, maps, charts, etc. They consist of a pen, or several pens, driven by a computer *program*. There are two types, drum plotters and flat-bed plotters.

Hard copy. A permanent record on paper of *output data* or of a *program*. Often taken from what appears on a *VDU* screen, by attaching a *printer*.

Hard disc. A method of storing *programs* and *data*. Unlike a *floppy disc*, which can be stored in a filing box or cabinet and only read into a computer from a *disc drive* as required, a hard disc is a more permanent piece of *hardware*, with very large capacity, able to operate at high speeds and permanently *on-line* to the computer.

Hardware. The durable mechanical, electrical and electronic components of a computer configuration e.g. the *central processor unit*, *terminal*, *printer disc drive*, etc.

Immediate access memory. The main *memory* in the *central processor unit*, where *data* and *programs* are held while awaiting processing. The first stage of any processing operation is to load the program required and the *file* of data into the immediate access memory.

Ink-jet printers. A non-impact *printer*, which sprays characters on to the paper at about 150 characters per second. Since these printers are silent, they are often used in hospitals, offices, etc.

Input. *Data* from an external source fed into a computer from an *input device* for processing.

Input device. A means of passing information into a computer. The information is passed in machine-readable form and may be *data* or instructions about how data is to be processed – the *program*. The chief input devices today are terminal *keyboards*, *magnetic tape*, *magnetic disc* and *floppy disc*, *bar codes*, *magnetic ink character recognition* (MICR), *optical mark recognition* (OMR), *optical character recognition* (OCR), tags and *magnetic strips*. The original input devices were *punched cards* and *paper tape*.

Integrated circuit. A very small electronic circuit on a *chip* of semi-conducting material such as silicon.

Joystick. An attachment that allows an operator to move the field of view on a screen, and draw a line or a curve, or store a position.

K. An abbreviation for 1 000 (actually 1 024) and used to denote the number of transistors on a silicon *chip memory*. Thus 1 k = 1 024 *bits* per chip, and we have 4 k, 16 k, 64 k and 256 k bit chips available.

Keyboard. A communicating device used to *input data* and commands to the computer. In many ways it is similar to a typewriter keyboard.

Key-to-disc system. A system whereby large volumes of *data* can be keyed by *VDU* operators directly to a disc *file*. When all the data have been keyed, the data on the disc can be input into the computer.

Lap-top computer. A micro-computer small enough to be held on the user's lap — as when travelling etc. Despite the small size, the computer is very powerful and can deal with the complete records of most small and medium-sized businesses.

Laser printer. Top-quality *printer*, printing a page at a time and up to 200 pages a minute, i.e. 26000 characters a second. As the machines are very expensive and the *output* is of the highest quality, the main users are companies with *mainframe computers*.

Light pen. Also called a sensing wand: a photosensitive detector housed in a case that can be held in the hand, and connected to the *VDU* controls by a cable. The computer can detect the position of the pen on the screen and display the details on record of the particular item pointed at, e.g. customer's address if a list of names is displayed.

Line printer. A fast *printer* for the commercial field printing a line at a time at speeds of 4000 lines per minute, on continuous stationery. Normal line width is 132 characters.

Listing. The printed *output* from a computer.

Loop. The repeated execution of a *program* instruction. It is a fault in the program and can only be stopped by aborting the program.

Machine code. The basic code on which a machine actually operates, a low-level numeric format. Early *programs* were written in this format. Today they are written in higher-level languages, but these languages have to be converted to the machine code applicable to the computer before the programs can be operated.

Magnetic disc. A pack of discs (or platters) coated with magnetic oxide on which *data* can be recorded in 800 tracks per disc, with about twenty recording surfaces in each pack. Access is by a *read-write head*, which can access about 2500 *megabytes* on a fixed disc unit, or about 200 megabytes on an exchangeable disc drive. It takes about 50 milliseconds (thousandths of a second) to locate data on the disc, which can then be read at 2 megabytes per second.

Magnetic ink character recognition. A system for reading documents such as cheques, paying-in slips, etc., at speeds of 2500 documents per minute. The vital details are printed on the cheque with magnetic ink in special typefaces. The magnetic ink character reader can detect the electric field created by each magnetic pattern as the characters pass under the read-head. Some of the information is pre-printed, but other information, e.g. the amount to be paid on the cheque, written in by the customer, has to be encoded before the documents are fed into the reader.

Magnetic strips. A specialist *input device* used by some major retailers to record *POS data* for stock taking and customer billing. They act rather similarly to *bar codes*.

Magnetic tape. A tape coated with ferrous oxide, chiefly used as a *backing storage* medium but also as an *input* (and *output*) *device*. It is usually $\frac{1}{2}''$ wide and 2400 feet long. Characters are recorded across the width of the tape and are read in sequence along the tape. Tape can hold either 1600 characters per inch or 6250 bpi (*bytes* per inch). A full tape at 1600 bpi holds 46 million bytes (46 *megabytes*). The tape is read, or written to, at speeds of 112.5″ per second (about 180000 bytes per second).

Mainframe computers. Very large computers; direct descendants of the original valve computers, with great power and many functions, but expensive to build, *program* and operate. They have at least 100 K *bytes* of primary (main) storage.

Main storage. The short-term storage medium, part of the *central processor unit*, in which *programs* and *data* are stored temporarily while they are being processed. This also includes data that have been processed and are waiting to be put out to a particular *output device*.

Management information system. A system designed to supply managers with all the *data* they need to plan, organize, staff, direct, control and report on all the operations required of any major company or institution.

Matrix printer. A *printer* that prints by building up characters from sets of dots made by firing needles at a carbon paper, which makes a dot on the print paper below it.

Megabyte. A million *bytes*. Used as a measure of capacity for any storage medium.

Memory. That part of a computer capable of storing *programs* and *data* for manipulation (see also *Main storage*).

Menu. A list of alternative procedures from which a user may select one particular activity. This will result in the loading of the required *program* for viewing, up-dating, interrogation, etc.

MICR. See *Magnetic ink character recognition*.

Micro-computers. Small computers, available at very low cost, flexible in application and adequate for most small businesses and for home use. Low-cost secondary storage is provided by *floppy discs*.

Microfiche. See *COM*.

Microfilm. See *COM*.

Microprocessor. A complex set of integrated circuits on a silicon *chip*, which is therefore virtually a computer on a chip of silicon. Introduced in 1971 by the Intel Corporation, of California's 'Silicon Valley'.

Mini computers. Medium-size computers — competitors for *main-frame computers* at a medium size and functionality.

Mips. Millions of instructions per second: the speed at which the *central processor unit* operates. Most *mainframe computers* work at speeds between 5 mips and 12 mips.

Modem. Modulator-demodulator: a device that codes or decodes computer *data* from digital to wave form and vice versa so that they can be transmitted accurately over telephone cables.

Mouse. A device that can direct the *cursor* very rapidly to any point on the screen of a *VDU* so that entries can be made quickly and easily. In many applications, e.g. filling complex forms, the box pinpointed can be enlarged to permit completion, say the address of the consignee, before being reduced down to screen size again while other boxes are completed. The final document will be printed full size.

Nanosecond. One thousand-millionth of a second.

Network. An interconnected pattern of communications that permits access to computers with large databases from anywhere in the network on a many-to-many basis. One such system is DIANE (Direct Information Access Network for Europe). British Telecom is developing System X as a network which will handle all communications in digital form. The minimum size of a network is two computers interlinked.

Notebook computer. Similar to a lap-top computer, but even smaller, and easily carried in a briefcase.

Number crunching. The calculation of useful ratios and other complex *data* using the ability of the computer to calculate at enormous speeds.

OCR. See *Optical character recognition*.

Off-line. A term used to describe any device, such as a *backing storage* disc, which is not *on-line* to the *central processor unit* but is in reserve until required.

OMR. See *Optical mark recognition*.

On-line. Describes equipment connected to and controlled by the computer. Such equipment is available for immediate use and can access the computer, interrogate it and receive responses immediately. (See also *Real-time*.)

Operating system. A collection of *software* controlling the basic computer operations.

Optical character recognition. Similar to *optical mark recognition*, but the computer can recognize alphabetical and numerical characters printed in one of the special type styles. The light reflected by a character creates a special pattern on the detector unique to the character concerned.

Optical mark recognition. A specialized *input device*, used on pre-printed questionnaires and other documents. The respondent fills in a box, or joins a pair of dots, to show his or her choice of answer. The documents are fed into a hopper, where light beams are shone on to each document and reflected back to a detector. The selected answer reflects back less light and can be detected. 10 000 copies per hour, with a failure rate of 1 per cent, can be processed. Unreadable forms are rejected into a special stacker and must be checked manually.

Output. Computer results or information ready for transfer to an *output device*.

Output devices. Devices that will pass on the processed results of the computer's calculations to the computer user, or to a storage device for further use when required. Until sufficient *data* have accumulated, results from the *central processor unit* are held temporarily in main *memory*. The chief output devices are *VDUs*, *printers* of various types, *graph plotters* and *COM*.

Paper tape. A method of inputting *data* and outputting data, by punching characters across paper tape with a pattern of holes. Ten characters per inch can be punched on the tape. They are read by a paper-tape reader at about 1 000 characters per second. The punching is a much slower operation, because the punch is mechanically operated.

Parity channel. A channel on *paper tape* that enables the computer to validate each character, to detect any failure in the punching method.

Peripheral device. The collective name for any device that is not part of the *central processor unit* itself, but is in the surrounding area to *input data*, or *output data*, or store it in some permanent way until required.

POS. Point-of-sale: a POS device can read *bar codes*, credit cards, etc., and call up *data* from the *memory* to give customer activity in each trading area, the price of the goods, etc. (See also *EFTPOS*.)

Printer. An *output device* that produces the results on paper; the most common form of computer output especially in the commercial field, where bank statements, wage slips, invoices, etc., are the end products after processing. The common types of printer are *line printers*, *matrix printers*, *daisy-wheel printers*, *laser printers* and *ink-jet printers*.

Print-out. The listing from a computer.

Processor. The part of the computer actually performing the computing.

Program. A set of instructions in correct order that tells the computer how to carry out the task it is being asked to perform.

Programmer. A person who designs, writes, tests and up-dates *programs*.

Punched card. An early *input device*, still in use, which is punched with eighty columns, with twelve punchable rows in each column. A character is punched so as to give a unique pattern in a column, and there can therefore be eighty characters per card. They are read by photo-electric cells at speeds of 1 500 cards per minute, but punching the cards is a slower process. Their use is declining because of their slow speeds and bulky nature when stored.

Punched tags. *POS* tags used in clothing stores to identify garments, sizes and prices. The codes are punched into the tag in two places. One half is torn off and these tags are sent at the end of the day to the central computer, where they give a daily update of sales from all stores, and the stock position. They are a way of capturing POS *data*.

RAM. Random access memory: the components of a *memory* that can be accessed at any point and both read from and written to. A computer advertised as 64 k (see *K*) has $64 \times 1\,024$ *bytes* of random access memory. (See also *ROM* and *Random access*.)

Random access. The ability to access a *file* and find a record independently of all the other records in the file.

Read. The process of transferring information from an *input device* or a *backing storage* device into the *central processor unit*.

Read-write head. The essential element of a *disc drive*, which can find and read any *program* or item of *data* stored on a disc, and take it into main *memory* for processing. When the processing is complete, the program, or revised data, will be returned to disc storage, i.e. it will be written back on to the disc by the read-write head.

Real-time. Any *on-line* system that can feed *data* directly into a computer and use the resulting *output* to control a system (such as a railway network, oil refinery or airport landing operation).

ROM. Read only memory: the components of a *memory* that can be read from but not written to. It is used among other things for holding the operating system and utility *programs* of a computer. ROM discs are also used as data-bases for all sorts of areas, such as medical information, educational courses, etc. (See also *RAM*.)

Semi-conductor. Any device that restricts electron flow to one direction only, e.g. a valve, transistor or silicon *chip*.

Silicon chips. See *Chips*.

Software. The operating system and application *programs* that organize the computer's resources and make the whole set of separate elements operate together to function as a computer.

Systems analysis. The process of examining documents and systems of work to detect what has to be done, what is the best method of doing it, and how can it be computerized. It leads eventually to a *program* of procedures the computer will follow.

Terminal. A device made up of a *keyboard* and a *VDU* that has become the standard means of communicating with a computer. *Input* is achieved via the keyboard, and *output* appears on the VDU screen (or in some earlier terminals it was typed out on a typewriter to give a hard copy). What appears on the screen can be produced as a hard copy if a *printer* is attached. Used more generally the term can mean any device at the end of a transmission of *data*, such as a VDU, tele-printer, cash-receipting machine, badge or credit card reader, *modem* or *mini-computer*.

Time-sharing. The interleaved use of the computer by two or more end-users so that each appears to have the computer's entire attention. Made possible by the fantastic speed of the computer.

Thermal printer. A non-impact *printer*, which makes characters appear on a special heat-sensitive paper by means of heated wires in the print head. They are silent and therefore useful in hospitals, but their speeds are slow (100 characters a second).

Transistor. A *semi-conductor* device, smaller than the original device (the thermionic *valve*). It restricts electron flow to one direction. Transistors are more efficient than valves, since they do not require heat to stimulate electron flow, and replaced valves in computers about 1960.

Validating. The process of proving the correctness of a piece of *data*.

Valve. The thermionic valve was the original *semi-conductor* device, which restricts the flow of electrons to one direction. In America it is called a vacuum tube. It can act as an amplifier of electrical signals and as an on/off switch. Valves were used in the earliest computers, but are bulky and use a lot of energy.

VDU. A visual display unit, or monitor, usually part of a *terminal* and giving instantaneous displays of *output* from the computer. Hard copies may be taken if a *printer* is attached. The VDU also acts as an *input device* either *on-line*, e.g. having direct access to the *central processor unit* as in air-line bookings, or *off-line*, e.g. the *key-to-disc system*.

Visual display unit. See *VDU*.

Volatility. The capacity of a component to lose its *data* if switched off or if there is a power failure. Loss of data must always be guarded against by having back-up records, and by having sound layouts that are clear so that wrong plugs will not be pulled out, wrong switches turned off, etc.

Winchester discs. *Hard discs* for *micro-computers*, either single platter or multi-platter (see *Magnetic disc*), and either integral parts of the computer or 'stand-alone' versions as separate units. More expensive than *floppy discs*, they have faster performance and larger storage capacities (5–40 *megabytes*).

Windows. A software package developed by the Microsoft Corporation, which acts as a high-level operating system for the management of files, the running of computer programs and the analysis of data. It permits split-screen displays of required information, graphics, etc., and there is a wide range of compatible programs available for many applications.

Word-processor. A computerized system for producing all types of written correspondence, reports, etc., with enormous advantages over the ordinary typewriter, and usually available as packages today. The text that results appears on a screen for instant checking is stored in the computer *memory* for recall (to up-date drafts, for example) and can be printed out at high speeds with many of the features of printed text.

14.8 Rapid revision – computers and data-processing

Cover the page with a sheet of notepaper and uncover one question at a time.

	Answers		Questions
	–	1	What is a computer?
1	It is an electronic machine that can be made to perform many routine activities at very high speeds.	2	What are its basic activities?
2	(*a*) The acceptance of data in machine-readable form, (*b*) data-processing, (*c*) the output of results, the machine-readable results being converted back to alphabetical and numerical form.	3	How is the data-processing organized?
3	By a detailed program of instructions for each type of activity the computer is required to perform.	4	Who writes the programs?
4	Special trained staff, called computer programmers.	5	List the main methods of inputting data

5 (*a*) Punched cards, (*b*) punched paper tape, (*c*) key to tape and key to disc, (*d*) keyboards (with a VDU facility), (*e*) MICR (magnetic ink character recognition), (*f*) bar codes, (*g*) OMR and OCR (optical mark recognition and optical character recognition), (*h*) punched tags.

6 What is the main part of the computer?

---

6 The CPU (central processor unit).

7 What are its component parts?

---

7 (*a*) The main memory, (*b*) the arithmetic and logic unit, (*c*) the control unit.

8 What is a backing store device?

---

8 It is a method of storing data and programs in machine-readable form so that they can quickly be recalled into the CPU if they are needed.

9 Name five methods of outputting data.

---

9 (*a*) Screen display on a VDU, (*b*) screen display in graphic form, (*c*) COM (computer output to microfilm or microfiche), (*d*) print-out, (*e*) hard copies (of a screen display).

10 What is meant by a 'user-friendly' system?

---

10 It is a system that (*a*) keeps the user advised what is happening, usually by a line of writing on the screen 'Please wait. I am calculating the percentages'. (*b*) Prevents errors by asking 'Are you sure?' questions. For example, 'You are asking me to delete Smith's debt of £665.63. Is this correct? Y/N'. If I touch the Y key, the machine will ask 'Are you sure? Y/N'. If I touch the Y key again, it will clear Smith's debt.

11 Go over the page again until you are sure of all the answers.

Exercises set 14

1 Write down the letters (*a*)-(*j*) in a column and against them write the word from the word-list given below that is needed to complete the sentences (*a*)-(*j*).

(*a*) The most important element of a computer is the ......
(*b*) The programs and data actually being used for data-processing are stored in the ......
(*c*) Programs and data not required immediately are put out for storage into the ......
(*d*) Data that become available from documents, inquiries, censuses, etc. have to be input into the computer in ...... form.
(*e*) COBOL stands for ......
(*f*) The writing in magnetic ink on a cheque is part of the system known as ......

(*g*) The commonest form of output from a computer in permanent form is called ......
(*h*) The original large computers were called ...... computers.
(*i*) A mouse is a device for locating the ...... on the screen of a VDU.
(*j*) The number 13 in ...... would be 1101 (one 2^3, one 2^2 and 1 more.)

Word list: main memory, printout, MICR (magnetic ink character recognition), central processor unit, Common Business Orientated Language, backing store, binary code, cursor, mainframe, machine-readable.

2 In the following questions choose the correct answer to the question from either (*a*), (*b*), (*c*) or (*d*):

(i) The most convenient computer for business staff travelling for sales purposes is (*a*) the mainframe, (*b*) the lap-top, (*c*) the mini, (*d*) a micro.
(ii) The easiest way to itemize customers' purchases at points of sale (check-outs) is by (*a*) punched tags, (*b*) MICR, (*c*) key to disc, (*d*) bar codes.
(iii) The number 15 in binary code would be (*a*) XV, (*b*) 1111, (*c*) 10001, (*d*) 1011.
(iv) The most popular 'end-user' output from a computer is (*a*) print-out; (*b*) magnetic tape, (*c*) microfiche, (*d*) microfilm.

3 Explain the following computer terms:

(*a*) user-friendly   (*b*) COBOL
(*c*) output device   (*d*) menu
(*e*) BASIC   (*f*) MICR

4 Explain the part played by each of the following in a computer configuration:

(*a*) Key to disc   (*b*) graph plotter
(*c*) VDU   (*d*) printer
(*e*) punched card   (*f*) backing-store disc

5 Work out the binary code for the following numbers: 1, 2, 3, 5, 6, 7, 8, 11, 13, 15.

6 Work out the binary code for the following numbers: 16, 17, 20, 23, 24, 25, 27, 29, 30, 31.

15 Reprography

15.1 Introduction

Reprography is the art of reproducing writing and illustrations, in other words the art of making copies. The earliest copies were made by clerks, who simply 'copied all the letters in a big, round, hand'. How to make copies without all this laborious copying work proved to be a problem that was not easy to solve, but in the 1990s we may say we have solved the problem after 200 years of intensive work. Not only can we copy an A4 page in less than a second, but we can send it 10 000 miles in less than 20 seconds as well, so that copies of important documents, such as bills of lading (which represent the ownership of goods on the high seas) and air waybills (which represent the ownership of goods in the cargo holds of aircraft) can reach our foreign customers before the ship even sails or the aircraft takes off.

There is little point in describing the historical development of reprography, but we could mention one famous name, David Gestetner (1854–1939), who succeeded in devising a quick way of making little holes in stencils, so that ordinary handwriting could be produced as a series of punctures through which ink could be squeezed to make a copy of the written words. The original toothed wheel was improved to give a neo-cyclostyle, (a new, wheeled stylus), which pricked the paper as the wheel revolved. Gestetner is still a famous name in reprographics but the art has moved on enormously since the neo-cyclostyle first appeared in 1890. See Figure 15.1.

Almost all offices today use one or other of the many plain-paper copiers on the market. The name 'plain-paper copier' is important, because if we have to have special paper for copying, e.g. photographic paper, which is sensitive to light, or hectograph copy paper, which is heavily inked with rather messy copying material, then we not only have to tie up our capital in special stocks of paper but we usually have to store it carefully, and it may have a limited shelf-life, which means waste. With the plain paper copier all we need is a supply of the paper, and the image needed is built up on the paper by an electro-static charge.

However, the old ideas of David Gestetner have not been entirely dispensed with. The idea of duplicating by forcing ink through perforations made in a stencil is still available for cheap copying,

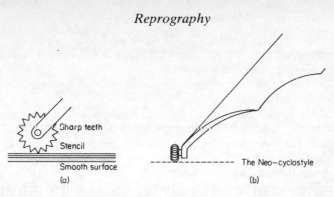

Figure 15.1   David Gestetner's stencil cutter (courtesy of Gestetner Ltd)

but today the stencil is designed and cut by digital methods, in a **digital duplicator**, explained below. In addition, for high quality, long-run printing (more than 1 000 copies) the **offset printer** is still the cheapest and best. This is explained in Section 15.8 below.

Before considering this we must refer to the general problems of choosing a copying system.

15.2   Choosing a copying system

It is easy to decide that we need a copy, or a number of copies, of a document, letter, newspaper article, photograph or diagram. It is more difficult to know which is the best device to purchase to produce the copies needed, and a machine that would be suitable for one particular purpose might be totally unsuitable for another. Contrast the managing director, who wants to send a single copy of a very secret document to the chairman of the board, with the Scotland Yard detective requiring 5 000 copies of a 'Wanted for Murder' poster. It is unlikely that the process used to produce the single copy would be equally appropriate for a run-off of 5 000 copies.

All copying requires is a system that can be used over and over again. Before purchasing such a system, it is necessary to evaluate the copying requirements that arise over a period of several months, and to decide the most likely needs of the department or firm. It is a matter of **cost-benefit analysis**, setting the costs of any particular system against the benefits to be obtained, and thus deciding on the best buy. The following considerations would need to be taken into account:

(*a*) Does the office need one-off copies or long production runs? Some machines are suitable for long production runs and are robust enough to stand up to hour after hour of work. Others are intended only for occasional copies, and cannot work for long periods without over-heating or breaking down.

(*b*) Is speed necessary? Some machines produce a copy in seconds.

Others take time to produce the first copy but then run off many copies more quickly. Clearly such machines are unsuitable for a firm needing one-off copies very quickly.

(*c*) Do we need to copy one side only or do we need to copy double-sided originals?

(*d*) Many machines cannot be purchased but only hired from the manufacturers, who usually charge on a 'usage meter'. Usually the first copy is very expensive, the next few copies fairly expensive, and subsequent copies very cheap. It follows that before hiring such a machine we should estimate how many short-run, medium-run and long-run copies we are likely to want per week, month or year. This will enable us to evaluate the machine, and whether it is wise to hire it.

(*e*) What is the nature of the material to be copied? Some copiers work only if there is carbon in the ink. A ballpoint pen with blue ink will not 'copy' on such machines. Students who regularly photocopy their notes will find it helpful to use only black ink ballpoint pens.

(*f*) What are the likely running costs of any particular system? For example, how much are the masters, how much is the paper, do we need only one size (say A4) or are A3 and A5 also necessary. How many copies per month or year will be required?

Another consideration is whether coloured copies are required. Copiers that produce colour copies of photographic quality are available, but they are expensive and relatively slow. However, the demand for colour on advertising leaflets, brochures, etc., as a means of producing a lively, vigorous and memorable leaflet or poster is increasing, and the ability to offer up to six colours by having interchangeable cartridges of colour toner is now an attractive feature of many machines.

A further consideration is the ecological one. These days many customers and many employees are 'green conscious', and quick to reject a system that is harmful to the environment, wasteful of energy, or excessively greedy for paper − a natural product. For example, many copiers need to be adequately ventilated, and care should be taken when disposing of spent toner material. A copier that senses the approach of a member of staff and switches itself on is better than one that is left on all the time. A copier with a quick warm-up time is economical compared with one with a slow warm-up time, which tends to encourage us to leave the copier on all the time.

Once all these considerations have been taken into account, a few simple calculations will help management choose a system that is appropriate to a company's needs and as economical as possible.

The chief copying methods in use today are therefore:

(*a*) Carbon copying and NCR copying (no carbon required).

(*b*) Plain-paper copying (electrostatic copying).
(*c*) Digital duplicating.
(*d*) Offset printing.

A Resource Centre. Perhaps the best idea of all when choosing a copying system is to set up a centralized resource centre. This will enable a variety of the most suitable machines to be purchased for the general use of the whole office or institution. Staffed by trained technicians who quickly master the peculiarities of different machines, and know the most appropriate process for a particular requirement, such resource centres can give an economical and efficient service. The capital equipment purchased is more fully utilized, so that better value is obtained for the money expended.

The controller of such a resource centre also acquires the knowledge and expertise to carry out the evaluation of equipment suggested under (*a*) to (*f*) above. By visiting the business equipment firms and exhibitions like the International Business Show, the supervisor will represent the firm as an informed and knowledgeable buyer, not buying on impulse, or after listening to a salesman's glib tongue, but buying that selection of proven equipment which meets the firm's requirements.

Sometimes the objection is raised to a resource centre that it often delays a department's work because it closes for lunch or for a tea-break; often these are times when an individual requiring copies of a document, etc., can come to the centre and use its facilities. While it cannot be too strongly emphasized that departments should think ahead about their requirements, it is also true of all centralized services, but particularly reprography, that rota systems should ensure that the centre is manned at all times, and that a 'walk-in' service is always available.

15.3 Carbon (and NCR) copying

Carbon paper is paper coated with a layer of carbon, either on one side or on both sides. It used to be a very messy method of copying, but modern carbon paper, which is usually single-sided, is treated so that the carbon does not come off until actually written upon or typed upon. It produces simultaneous copies, and where several copies are produced, this is called 'manifolding'. Usually, four good copies can be obtained, but with special thin carbon paper and an electric typewriter up to twenty copies can be obtained.

However, the labour involved in interleaving paper and carbons is tiresome. Many stationers prepare business documents in prepacked sets, which can be inserted into a typewriter conveniently without the need to interleave carbon paper. The documents have a carbon surface wherever necessary on the back of each sheet, so that the necessary information will be copied on to the copy below it. This carbon will never be used more than once, so it is a cheap 'one-off' type of carbon coating. Furthermore, a document lower down in the pack may not need to have all the information stated, and the manufacturers arrange for these details to be omitted − by leaving out the carbon above that copy. For example, a delivery note does not need to have the prices on it − it is often better if the carman does not know how valuable the packages are that he is carrying. By leaving out the carbon at that point, the information does not appear on the carman's copy.

NCR paper

A system that eliminates the need for carbon paper is that known as NCR paper (No Carbon Required). Here the paper is coated with chemicals that are themselves colourless, but when combined they form a coloured liquid. The surface is coated with millions of microscopic globules of chemical. The pen − preferably a ballpoint pen − or the typewriter key fractures the globules on the paper, producing a visible copy on the pages below. There is one difficulty with such paper. If the user is not aware of the nature of NCR paper, he/she may waste a whole pad of forms by writing on the top one. They must be torn off the pad in sets before using them. It is even sadder when someone uses the pad as a resting place for a piece of scrap paper. The message 'Please phone Mr Smith before 2.30 − very urgent', will appear on all the forms below·it, and will make that telephone message a very expensive one. NCR forms are very useful for any document where two or three copies only are required, and save time in busy offices, since carbon paper does not have to be interleaved.

Simultaneous records and NCR paper. Carbon paper and NCR paper are widely used in various types of records where we only need two or three copies of something. These systems are called 'simultaneous record systems' because the two or three copies are made out at the same moment, the top copy being copied directly on to the other two records. For example, the Kalamazoo Wages System is widely used to pay wages in the United Kingdom, and about 3 million employees are paid every week, or month, by this simultaneous records system. To keep proper records of wages three things are required:

(*a*) A **pay advice note**, which shows the employee exactly how the pay has been calculated. This is used to make up the wage packet, and enables the employee to check the pay on receipt. Sometimes the packet has small holes in it so that coins can be counted, and the notes can be checked, before opening the packet.

(*b*) A **payroll**, which lists all payments made for the week or month, and which is the firm's record retained in a special loose-leaf binder.

(*c*) An individual **employee's record card**, which lists all the employee's pay for the year. In any query about pay we can produce this record to discuss it with the employee. We do not want to produce the payroll, for this would enable the employee to see what other staff earn.

The way in which the records are laid out is illustrated in Figure 15.2. First, a layer of ten pay advice slips is laid on a stiff board supplied by Kalamazoo and is held steady by a row of studs. These ten advice slips will eventually go into ten wage packets. Second, the payroll sheet is laid on top of the pay advice slips, covering them exactly. Third, the first of the employee's wages records is taken from a storage case and placed over the top of the other two records. It is positioned so that this week's record, which is about to be made out, covers the first column on the payroll sheet, and therefore the first wages slip. As the entries are made on the employee's record sheet, the pressure bursts the globules on the lower pages and makes the necessary copies. The same procedure is followed with the next nine employees' record cards, each one being positioned over the next clean wages slip. We then have:

(*a*) An up-dated record card for each employee.

(*b*) A payroll sheet showing the full details of payments made this week to ten employees.

(*c*) Ten completed wage slips for the cashier to use when making up the wages envelopes. If the employees' wages are paid directly into their bank accounts, the slips are simply put in an envelope and given to the employee. An example of a typical Kalamazoo slip is given in Figure 15.3

15.4 Plain-paper copying (electrostatic copying)

When this system was invented it was originally called **xerography**, and the company that developed it became famous as Rank Xerox.

The word 'xerography' really means 'dry-pictures', and distinguished this process from photocopying, which was a process using wet developer. Today there are other dry copiers besides the Rank Xerox, for this type of copier is manufactured by other firms. However, the name 'Rank Xerox' is synonymous with the electrostatic copying process, and the author is indebted to this firm for some of the source material for this section.

Most readers will be familiar with static electricity, which charges up many articles in everyday life, such as a fountain pen rubbed upon a coat sleeve or a glass rod rubbed with silk. Such static

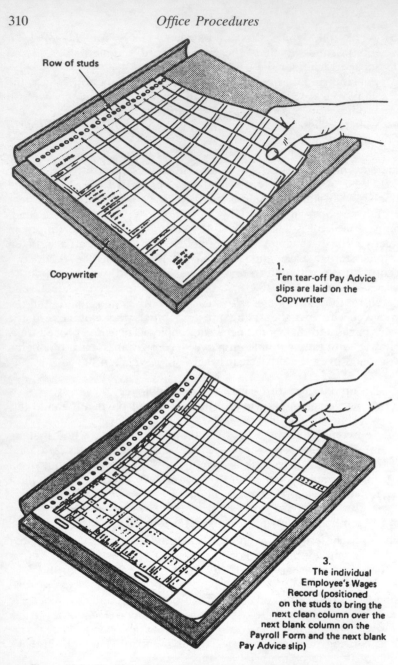

Row of studs

Copywriter

1.
Ten tear-off Pay Advice slips are laid on the Copywriter

3.
The individual Employee's Wages Record (positioned on the studs to bring the next clean column over the next blank column on the Payroll Form and the next blank Pay Advice slip)

Figure 15.2   The Kalamazoo wages system (courtesy of Kalamazoo Ltd, Birmingham)

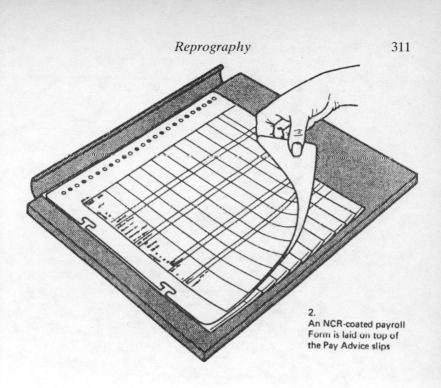

2.
An NCR-coated payroll
Form is laid on top of
the Pay Advice slips

4.
The torn-off Pay Advice slips
folded once to go into the
pay packets. If paid in cash
the money is inserted in the
same envelope

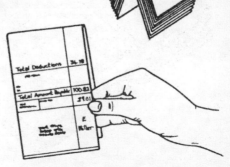

Figure 15.2 (*continued*)

Pay Advice

Week or Mth. No.	Date	14	10/7

	Details	
Earnings	A	187 50
	B	15 00
	C	
	D	
	E	
	SSP	37 76
	SMP	— —
	Gross Pay	240 26
	Superannuation	— —

K Code	Gross Pay less Superannuation	240 26
	Gross Pay to date for Tax Purposes	2800 00
	less Tax Free Pay	691 74
	plus Additional K Code Pay	— —
	Taxable Pay to Date	2108 26
	Tax Due to Date	527 00
	Tax Refund	— —
K Codes	Tax Due this Period	
	Regulatory Limit	
	Tax not collected due to Reg. Limit	

Deductions	Tax	47 75
	*N.I. Contribution (Employee)	17 72
	1 Xmas Fund	1 00
	2 Trade Union	1 00
	3 Dr. Barnardo's	1 00
	4	
	5	
	Total Deductions	68 47
	Net Pay	171 79
	F Lodging allowance	31 50
	Total Amount Payable	203 29
	N.I. Contribution (Employer)	25 01
	N.I. Total (Employer and Employee)	42 73
	G	
	*Contracted-Out Contbn. incl. above	
	Earn. on which E'ees contbn. pyble.	
	Earn. on which E'ees contbn. at CO Rate pyble.	

Your Pay is made up as shown above

Miller
K.E.

charges may be used to hold minute powdery particles of developer on paper. This may then be heated so that the developer melts and fuses into the paper, reproducing whatever shapes and patterns the static charge had taken. The Xerox copier arranges the static charge as an image of any document that is to be copied. Figure 15.4 shows how the system works.

This entire process takes only a few seconds, and can be arranged to take place repeatedly so that copies are delivered at the rate of one every second. The original Rank Xerox 3600 machine took its name from its ability to deliver 3600 copies every hour. A later version, illustrated in Figure 15.5, works faster, and has a sorter device attached at the end which will arrange up to fifty copies of a succession of pages so that they are in correct order ready to be stapled into booklet form. A report can thus be prepared, e.g. for every member of the board of the company, in a very short time indeed once an initial copy is typed for use as a master.

The Xerox Docutech Publishing Series

These are the latest product range from the Rank Xerox Company. They combine three advanced technologies, digital scanning, laser imaging and xerography. Used in the 'in-house' publishing field and in document-managing, these machines can scan any document and store it in its memory. The resulting stored digital master can then be reproduced as a clear image, which can be manipulated by a graphical user interface. Thus a part of the stored picture only could be used, and captions, explanatory material, etc., could be produced around it (a process called 'cutting and pasting', but of course it is all done electronically). The resulting revised version can then be printed by the xerox process. Linking such machines into a firm's computer network allows a huge range of material to be provided

---

Figure 15.3   A Kalamazoo pay advice slip (courtesy of Kalamazoo Ltd, Birmingham)

Notes

(i) The week or month number is shown and the date it commences.

(ii) There are seven lines for types of earning, such as basic wage, overtime, commission, etc. One of these lines is for statutory sick pay and another is for statutory maternity pay. The total of these gives the gross pay.

(iii) Superannuation is then deducted, because it is not taxable.

(iv) The gross pay for tax purposes is then used to find the tax payable - using the tax tables provided by the Inland Revenue. Note that to find the tax to be deducted, we have to look at the employee's last weekly or monthly record. In the case illustrated the tax paid up to last week was £479.25. This means that as the tax due to date is £527.00, we must deduct £47.75 this week.

(v) The deductions are then listed, which gives the net pay.

(vi) There is then one line for any addition to net pay − such as refunds of tax overpaid or expenses incurred. This gives the total amount payable.

(vii) The employer also needs to know what the total cost was for National Insurance − in this case the employer had to pay £25.01, making £42.73 in all.

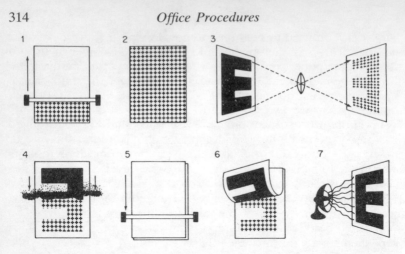

Figure 15.4   How xerography works (courtesy of Rank Xerox Ltd)

Notes

1 The surface of a coated plate (or drum) is sensitized by an electrically charged grid, which moves across it.

2 The coating of the plate is now fully charged with positive electricity.

3 The original document (E) is projected on to the coated plate. Positive charges disappear in areas exposed to light. A pattern of charges is left on the coated plate of exactly the same shape as the dark part of the original document.

4 A negatively charged powder is dusted over the plate and adheres to the positively charged image.

5 A sheet of paper is now placed over the plate and receives a positive charge.

6 The positively charged paper attracts powder from the plate, forming a direct positive image.

7 The print is fixed by heat for a few seconds to form the permanent image.

for all parts of the business and for clients and customers. See Figure 15.6.

Other plain-paper copiers

Today there is a huge range of copiers available and even the smaller and least expensive models are very reliable and have a usefully long life if serviced regularly. They bring plain-paper copying within the reach of even the smallest organizations, such as clubs and societies, charities, etc.

Larger machines offer a full range of facilities. For example the Olympia Omega 8600 ZD (see Figure 15.7) offers the following facilities:

- It senses the size of the original to be copied and feeds the correct-sized paper from one of four stacks of paper held in cassettes. Up to 4 850 sheets can be stored in these cassettes.
- If the copy is to be magnified or reduced, the operator specifies

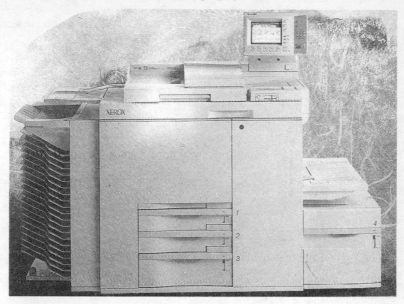

Figure 15.5 The Xerox 5380 with sorter (courtesy of Rank Xerox Ltd)

the size of final copies, and the machine calculates the exact ratio of enlargement or reduction. Copies can be anywhere in size between 50 per cent and 200 per cent of the original size.

- The display panel is clearly laid out, enabling anyone to operate the machine on a 'walk-up and use' basis.
- There is an accurate two-hole punch, so that all copies are correctly aligned when bound for distribution.
- Copies can be made of photographs by using the photo-mode key, which gives good clarity.

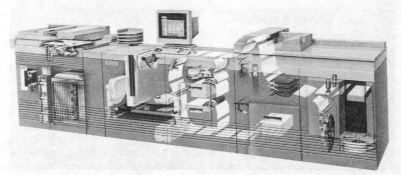

Figure 15.6 The Xerox Docutech Publishing Model 90 (courtesy of Rank Xerox Ltd)

Figure 15.7   The Olympia 8600 ZD (courtesy of Olympia (UK) Ltd)

- Double-sided copying is achieved automatically with this copier, the original being turned over by a 'reverse document feeder'. This is called 'copying in the duplex mode'.
- Continuous copying is possible up to 999 copies.
- The toner supply is sufficient for 62 500 copies.
- 86 copies per minute can be obtained (67 if A3 size).
- A management panel enables control to be exercised over the use of the copier by various departments.
- A long run can be interrupted, by a copy-interrupt function, to give someone waiting for a single copy the chance to run it off.
- A foot-switch is available.

One very important point in dealing with all methods of reprography is the need to check the master copy and ensure it is completely accurate and nothing has been omitted before the run begins. It is always worthwhile letting one or two other people 'proof-read' it first. There is little point producing 86 copies per minute if they all have errors in them. It just means that 86 people will know your work is slipshod. Spelling, punctuation, paragraphing, etc., all come in for appraisal and criticism — and the criticism will fall upon the person whose signature appears on the document even if someone less important has actually prepared it.

Asking others to proof-read the document will help detect errors, and lets you share the blame if errors still go through unnoticed. One firm of the author's acquaintance printed a wages book with 'Net Insurance' instead of 'Nat. Insurance' — an abbreviation for National Insurance. Not only was the phone board jammed with customers asking what 'Net Insurance' was, but as the firm had printed 40 000 copies packed in packs of 20 copies each, they had to open 2 000 parcels and put a letter of explanation in every book. It cost a fortune, and was a very boring job for the staff who had to do it.

Similarly, check master copies for completeness. To leave out the date or time of a meeting, or the venue, means a follow-up letter will need to be sent.

15.5 Using the plain-paper copier

Although these machines are very simple to use, and are intended to be available for use by all staff on a 'walk-up' basis, a few words about them may still be helpful. Useful rules are:

(*a*) Always ask for help if you are new to an office and are not familiar with the particular machine in use. Some of the electronic displays are quite complex and difficult to work out by a trial and error process. Ask to be inducted into the use of the machine, and if there is a manual tucked into the back of the machine or lying around near it, don't be afraid to read it through and study the illustrations.

(*b*) Switch the machine on as soon as you get to it in case it has a lengthy warm-up period. Some machines switch themselves on as you walk up to them. Some are left running all the time, especially in busy departments or in resource centres.

(*c*) Make sure your master copy is perfect, and position it carefully. Always take a single copy as a first run to see whether the result is properly positioned on the paper. You may be enlarging the original or reducing it. The glass plate on which you lay the master may be dirty, or have little spots of toner on it, which will reproduce on every copy. Clean it up before doing a major print run.

(*d*) Specify the number of copies you require if the first copy is satisfactory, and proceed with the first run. Do not leave the machine to 'get on with it' unsupervised. Keep an eye on it, as paper jams can occur, paper can run out in the cassette, or toner can run out, etc. These usually result in a flashing electronic sign on the control panel. Take steps to rectify the fault, or call someone who can.

(*e*) The use of the copier is a great temptation to staff, who may be tempted to run off copies for non-business purposes. Most firms take a poor view of such practices, because most machines are leased from suppliers at a charge that may be fairly nominal (about 1.2 pence per copy is common, but some machines are more expensive for short runs). If firms do sanction the use of the machine, they often specify a charge which will be collected by the petty cashier. As a general rule, do not use a copier without permission for private work.

There is a huge range of plain-paper copiers available and the whole field is very competitive. There is little point in buying any machine just because it is there. It is best to 'shop around' and weigh up the machine's ability to do the types of copying you require at a price you can afford. Those who regularly purchase such items for a large organization should get themselves on the mailing list of such 'freebie' magazines as *Business Equipment Digest*, IML Group PLC, Blair House, High St, Tonbridge, Kent, TN9 1BQ. Such magazines will draw to their attention every new development in the whole range of business equipment.

15.6 Digital duplicators

The term 'duplicator' refers back to the early methods of reprography developed by David Gestetner, which were known by the general name of 'ink-stencil duplicators'. The system was for a waxed stencil to be typed, or drawn upon with a cyclostyle pen, so that it was perforated with the text, diagrams, etc., which were to be reproduced. The stencil was carefully checked and any corrections could be made by means of a rubbery solution to seal the error, which was then retyped or otherwise corrected. The stencil was then fitted face downwards on to an inked drum, which could be rotated. As the paper was drawn in a sheet at a time, pressure on the stencil forced ink through the perforations on to the paper, producing a satisfactory copy at each revolution of the drum.

Today the digital duplicator is a sophisticated development of this original idea, without the messiness of the original process. The digital duplicator is similar in appearance to a plain-paper copier, with a similar control panel. The document to be printed is first scanned digitally. As we saw in Figure 6.2 about digital transmissions of telephone messages, the word 'digital' means 'in number form', and the numbers concerned were the amplitudes of the wave pattern of the caller's voice. If the same ideas are applied to scanning a document, every point on the document can be measured to give its exact position on the document. The signals thus produced are then processed by a thermal imaging system. Thermal imaging means 'heat' imaging. Where the document has a piece of text or a diagram, the heat makes minute holes in a 'master' to give a faithful representation of the scanned document. The printing process can then proceed, with ink being forced through the tiny holes to give a copy of the original document on each sheet of paper fed in; and 120 copies a minute can be printed, at a cost of much less than the plain-paper copier, and with very long print runs. Colour drums, red, blue, green, yellow, brown and black are interchangeable in seconds, and if a personal computer is attached, the duplicator can scan and copy forms, charts, letters and graphs generated by the computer. Figure 15.8 shows the Gestetner 5375 'Copy Printer' − the firm's current digital duplicator.

15.7 Faxes as copiers

There are several fax machines on the market that double as plain-paper copiers at speeds of about ten copies per minute. Therefore an office with only a small copy volume but needing a fax machine may find it is sufficient to buy one of these dual-purpose faxes.

Figure 15.8   The Gestetner 5375 'copy printer' − a digital duplicator
(courtesy of Gestetner Ltd)

15.8 Offset printing

Where a firm or company is a fairly large organization and wishes to produce a whole range of forms, publicity material, in-house journals, etc., it will probably find it pays to use offset printing.

The offset process is a duplication system offering very high quality reproduction on hard papers. It is capable of excellent colour work, great accuracy and high speeds. It enables even the small office to produce most of its own handouts, advertising circulars, statistical and factual reports, and documents for office use.

Principles of offset

(*a*) *Oil and water don't mix*. The process depends upon the well-known principle that oil and water − or, more truthfully in this case, grease and water − don't mix. A greasy image of the printing, artwork, etc., which is to appear on the copies is produced on the offset litho plate. This may be done with a special greasy ribbon, or with special offset pens, pencils, brush ink, stamp pads and ruling and writing ink, using a paper plate. Alternatively, a photographic plate may be prepared. The whole plate is then damped and the water covers the plate, except where it is repelled by the greasy image. Then the ink is rolled across the plate. This ink is also greasy and is repelled by the damp parts of the plate but accepted by the greasy image. We now have a greasy, inked picture of the original matter.

(*b*) *The offset process*. This inked picture is now transferred from the plate to a rubber-covered cylinder called the blanket cylinder, which picks up a reverse picture of the original material. In any printing process the print comes out back to front. Ordinary printers spend a long apprenticeship learning to set type back to front, so that when it is pressed down upon the paper by the printing press, the printed matter will be the right way round. The ordinary reader can then read it. The offset process overcomes this setting difficulty by offsetting the print on to a blanket of rubber. The typist who prepared the plate prepared it with an ordinary typewriter. This will be reversed on to the offset blanket, and reversed again on to the copy paper as the offset blanket comes into contact with it. This double reversal gives a readable copy. Figure 15.9 illustrates these offset principles.

Making plates

The master plates for offset duplicating may be prepared on paper plates, which have a life span of up to 2 000 copies. The manufacturers can prepare metal plates with a very long life for customers who require long reprographic runs. Photographic plates may also be made by customers on their own premises, using their own electrostatic equipment.

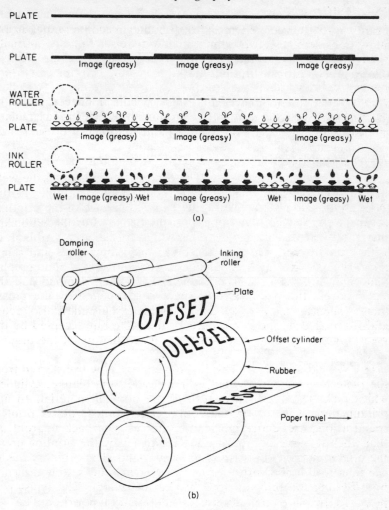

Figure 15.9 The principles of offset reprography: (*a*) grease and water won't mix; (*b*) a reverse print of a reverse print is legible (courtesy of Gestetner Ltd)

15.9 Points to think about and discuss

(*a*) Jones, the manager of the sales department, is anxious to establish a unified resource centre which would be able to afford the most expensive reprographic equipment, and would supply the advertising material he considers essential. Bloggs, in charge of production, maintains that the Sales Department's inability to produce the copies it needs is due to inefficiency, and failure in the past to buy wisely with the budget of money allocated to Jones. His own department is well supplied with reprographic equipment and he regards a centralized system as too remote from the actual work areas. Consider these two points of view.

(*b*) In what ways would a reprographic service be of use to the following people or institutions?

(i) An infants' schoolteacher.
(ii) The secretary of a residents' association.
(iii) An estate agent.
(iv) The Ministry of Housing.
(v) A bank manager.
(vi) An inwards mail clerk.
(vii) A 'multiple shop' organization.
(viii) A building society.

15.10 Rapid revision − reprography
Cover the page with a sheet of paper and uncover one question at a time.

Answers	Questions
−	1 Why is the copying and duplicating of documents so important today?
1 Because businesses are large, and everyone must be kept informed if all are to function efficiently as a team.	2 Who first perfected a copying process?
2 David Gestetner, 1854−1939.	3 Why has plain-paper copying largely replaced other methods in recent years?
3 Because the machines are easy to use; give dry copies at speeds of one copy per second or faster and do not need special supplies, except toner in handy containers.	4 Why is carbon copying still useful in some situations?
4 It is cheap and convenient where only one or two copies are required.	5 What is NCR paper?
5 Paper where no carbon is required.	6 Why is no carbon required?
6 Because the sets of documents are coated with globules of invisible ink which becomes visible when the pressure of a ball-point pen breaks the globules.	7 What do we call an office that prepares copies for other departments?
7 A resource centre.	8 What problems must be overcome in setting up a resource centre?
8 (*a*) The work of the firm must be analysed to decide the types of document brochures, etc, required, (*b*) the most suitable and economic	9 What is digital duplicating?

ways to meet these requirements must be decided upon, (c) the necessary equipment must be purchased or hired, (d) staff procedures must be laid down to ensure efficient operations.

9	It is a method of ink stencil duplicating in which the document to be copied is scanned electronically to produce a digital measurement of every point on the document, which is then turned into a set of holes in a master copy by thermal imaging. Copies can then be run off very cheaply from this master.	10	What is offset printing?
10	A sophisticated duplicating system that gives very cheap copies from very long runs. The master is a greasy image of the text or document to be copied. This master is then damped.	11	What are the principles of offset printing?
11	(a) Grease and water don't mix. (b) An offset print of an original gives a reverse image, but an offset print from this reverse image gives a legible copy. The image is offset on to a rubber blanket and then offset again on to copy paper.	12	Go over the page again until you are sure of all the answers.

Exercise set 15

1 Write the letters (a)–(j) on to a sheet of paper and write against them the correct word or phrase from the word list to complete the following sentences:

(a) The earliest form of reprography was David Gestetner's stretched wax paper on which the text was written with a ...... pen.

(b) Today the usual type of copier in most offices is a ......

(c) A special department devoted to the production of handouts, display material and advertising circulars is a ......

(d) Before purchasing reprographic equipment, it is best to consider carefully the ...... of your firm or institution.

(e) NCR paper is paper that produces copies but ...... is ......

(f) Since any errors on a master will be reproduced on every copy that it produces, it is essential that masters are ......

(g) ..... gives dry copies.

(h) If a copy is produced from an electrically charged plate, it is called an ...... process.

(i) To ...... a reprographic machine is to attempt to judge its suitability for your office.

(j) The material used to give the actual print in a plain-paper copier is called ......

Word list: toner, requirements, cyclostyle, plain paper copier, electro-static, no carbon, required, resource centre, carefully checked, xerography, evaluate.

2 List some of the chief reasons for a copying service in (*a*) an architect's office, (*b*) a technical college. How would a resource centre help each of these establishments? What are the advantages and disadvantages of a resource centre?

3 What is reprography? List at least five reasons why we might need to make copies in an office. In your answer you may refer to any office with which you are familiar. Students may refer to a school or college office if they wish.

4 What are simultaneous record systems? Why are carbon copies or NCR copies usually satisfactory for such systems?

5 What materials are required for a plain-paper copier? Why are they such popular copiers today?

6 It is proposed to set up a resource centre in a busy college to handle all the copying requirements of every department. What preliminary study should be undertaken if such a proposal is to be successful?

7 You are asked to draw up ten rules for the use of a plain-paper copier by junior staff. What points would you include in your list?

8 What is offset printing? Why would a large company that regularly circulates instructions, advertising material and an 'in-house journal' to its ninety-five branches find this method of reprography helpful?

9 Your small office has for years regularly turned out its advertising material for mail slots on a stencil duplicator. It usually mails 500 customers and potential customers at a time. You are asked by the manager to advise him which of the following would be suitable for the future:

(*a*) A fax machine that doubles as a plain-paper copier.
(*b*) A plain-paper copier.
(*c*) A digital duplicator.
(*d*) An offset printer.

List the points in favour of each of the above and the points against.

16 Communication in business

16.1 Selecting appropriate media for communication needs

In Figure 4.1 (see p. 70) we have a chart showing the various methods of communication today. The types of communication are divided into two groups, spoken communication and written communication, and each of these groups is then divided into two further groups — personal methods of communication and mass-media methods. It is useful at this point to look back at Figure 4.1 and remind ourselves of the wide range of methods available to us.

Most of these methods of communication are described somewhere in this book, and the reader should use the index at the back to find an appropriate account of each method. The size of an organization often decides which methods of communication are available to us. For example, even the smallest firm has a telephone, which will reach almost any corner of the earth, but only large firms have computer networks with e-mail messages flashing to and fro at electronic speeds. Not everyone has a fax machine, but those who have know how useful they are and how quickly the fax messages reach their destination.

In selecting the best balance of facilities for communicating with our customers, our suppliers, government agencies and our depots, warehouses and branches, we shall choose those facilities that make economic sense. The size of our business, the nature of the industry we are in and the wealth we are creating, which enables us to afford the things we need, will all be powerful influences. We shall then use these facilities to advance the success of our firm or company, and to maintain the intricate network of links which alone can promote our property.

16.2 The formality of business relationships

In general it is desirable to maintain a formal relationship with staff, customers, clients and suppliers. This does not mean that informality does not have some part to play in business, for we must all relax at times, and social, cultural and recreational activities develop inevitably from business relationships. The point is that when we turn to the serious business of creating wealth and, to use a modern term, adding value to the goods and services in which we trade, we need to don a cloak of formality. This formal communication reminds us all that business is a serious matter, and that it depends upon fair treatment of one another. The proceeds of business activity must be shared in some agreed fair ratio, not always equally, for some parties may be stronger than others, but to the satisfaction of all parties. Any unfairness exercised against one party to the benefit of the other in the end diminishes the amount of business carried on. It destroys the trust in one another that is essential if bargains are to be honoured.

As examples of this formality we may mention the following:

(*a*) In business correspondence there is a 'correct' way to write, and we do not lapse from this formality until we have established enduring links with a firm or company. Even when a more informal way of communicating has developed over the years, any sign of a change in the relationship – a failure to pay bills when due, rumours of a take-over, or anything else to disturb the established pattern of trading – causes us to revert to a more formal approach.

(*b*) At any business meeting the chairperson sets the tone of the meeting and conducts it according to the formal rules for meetings. These are explained in great detail later in Chapter 19, but briefly the rules are that only one person may speak at a time and all remarks are made 'through the chair'. We do not address individuals personally, or criticize them directly. Instead we say to the chairperson that we feel the policy proposed by ...... is an undesirable one, in view of ...... and ...... The discussion is about the agenda item under consideration and not about any particular individual's attitude to it. People can disagree strongly about policy and yet preserve a mutual respect for one another, in the absence of any criminal or anti-social behaviour.

16.3 Writing business letters

The writing of business letters calls for two classes of skill. First, we need to know how to lay out a business letter in acceptable form, and be thoroughly familiar with it, so that in practically every letter we write we use the standard layout. There will always be the odd letter that for some reason is non-standard, but in general we should write naturally in the well-tried, standard way, so that our correspondents will feel at ease with the letter when it arrives. The other skill is the ability to write in good English, with the letter's subject matter falling into clear paragraphs, each of which is written in lucid sentences. The ability to write in sentences, both simple sentences and more complex sentences, ensures that each part of the letter expresses a complete thought, or a group of related thoughts. This enables our correspondent to follow the points we are making, in logical steps, and to arrive at the end of the letter with a clear understanding of our point of view on the matter, or matters, that we have raised.

These two aspects require a great deal of explanation, and we shall learn the skills best if we understand the reasons behind the various practices that have been adopted over the years. We will therefore start by considering the legal aspects of business correspondence.

The legal aspects of business correspondence

Almost all business activity is contractual in nature. This means that the two people engaged in any particular transaction are undertaking certain obligations to one another and at the same time acquiring certain rights. Thus the furniture manufacturer who agrees to supply some of his/her products to a wholesaler is entering into a transaction by which he/she accepts an obligation to supply the goods specified in return for a right to receive a monetary payment called 'the price'. Where a service is to be supplied, the arrangement is just the same. For example, a security company agrees to protect premises with its security guards and specialist devices, in return for an agreed contractual fee.

Should any dispute arise, it can be settled by going to court, with the aggrieved party suing the other party. To sue someone is to summon them to court, to show why you should not have the justice you are seeking. The judge will look at the correspondence that has passed between you (including any documents such as contracts, invoices, memos, etc.) and will pronounce judgment in the matter.

It is this legal nature of correspondence that requires us to set out our correspondence in a standard form or layout. The chief points are:

- The names and addresses of both parties to the contract must be stated on all correspondence.
- All correspondence must be clearly dated.
- To assist in tracing correspondence, it is usual to give references at the top of the letter. These references will be file references to let each party know where the chain of correspondence, of which this letter forms one link, is to be found in its filing system. The references usually read:

    Your Ref. ....
    Our Ref. ....

- To make the subject matter of the letter clear, it is usual to give a subject heading at the start of the letter. In large organizations correspondence is opened by a group of middle managers, who sort it into the trays of the person most likely to deal with it. For example, a letter with the subject-heading **Overdue account of**

your Salisbury Depot will at once be put into the accountant's tray, while one headed **Insurance claim – Road accident at Wembley** will probably be dealt with by the transport manager.

- To start the letter itself, we need some sort of greeting. This is called the salutation, and may be a general greeting, such as Dear Sir or Dear Madam, but may be more personal, such as Dear John or Dear Lucy.

- We then have a number of paragraphs that deal with the matter in hand. Useful points about these are given later.

- Finally we need a concluding section. This is called 'the complimentary close' or 'subscription'. It usually consists of a farewell remark, followed by a handwritten signature, supported by the typewritten name of the signatory and the position held in the company. Many people have illegible signatures and the typewritten name identifies the signatory.

- Finally, if copies are being sent to other departments, there may be a list of their names, headed CC (copies circulated). If enclosures are to be sent with the letter, a list of the items enclosed will be given, headed Enc.

If all these details are included, the court will have no difficulty understanding what the parties have done. Clearly we do not expect to finish up in court when we start to deal with a supplier or customer, but in case we do, the formal layout described above and illustrated in Figure 16.1 will serve as evidence.

16.4 The layout of a business letter

Business letters may be laid out in various styles, and a large organization will usually specify a 'house style' to which all secretarial staff are required to conform. The most popular style today is the 'fully blocked' style, which is illustrated in Figure 16.1. It is the easiest layout to achieve on modern typewriters and word-processors. Each line begins at the extreme left-hand margin, there being no indentation of any sort to hold up the typing of the next line of text. We thus have the full block of type down the left-hand edge of the page, which gives the style its name.

Other styles are illustrated later, but it is helpful to mention here the one problem with the fully blocked style. When the letter is filed away with many other letters, all the details are given on the extreme left-hand edge, which is inconvenient when searching for a particular letter, because the file has to be fully opened before we can see the date of each letter and the references. Some people prefer therefore to use the semi-blocked style (see p. 387), in which the references and the date are brought over to the right-hand side, where they are more easily seen when filed away. A third style of letter is the indented style (see p. 389), which has a more open, pleasing appearance, and incidentally has the date, the references

Linacre House, Jordan Hill, Oxford OX2 8DP
Tel: (0865) 310366. Telex: 83111 BHPOXF G. Fax: (0865) 310898

17 September 19..

Our ref. MB/OJ
Your ref. CTC 31 August 19..

AIR MAIL

Inter-Gulf Textbooks Ltd
Bahrain Island
Arabian Gulf

<u>Attention of College Textbook Coordinator</u>

Dear Sirs

MADE SIMPLE TEXTBOOKS

Thank you for your enquiry about textbooks suitable for first
year students. There are a number of titles which are
appropriate.

In the Business Studies field the titles which are most
popular include Book-keeping, Business and Enterprise Studies,
Statistics for Business, Teeline Shorthand, Information
Technology, Office Practice, Economics, Law, Business and
Commercial Law and Typing.

In languages, English, French, German, Italian, Spanish,
Russian and Latin are in great demand.

I note that you do not sell technical books so I have not
listed these titles.

We shall be delighted to supply books to you on favourable
terms, as shown in the price list attached.

Yours faithfully

Martin de la Bedoyere
Product Manager

Enc

Butterworth-Heinemann Limited, part of Reed International Books
Registered Office: 88 Kingsway, London WC2 8AB. Registered in England: 194771

Figure 16.1   A letter in fully-blocked style (courtesy of Butterworth-
Heinemann Ltd)

and also the signature on the right-hand side, where they are easily visible in a file of letters. The indented style takes slightly longer to type than the fully blocked style of Figure 16.1. Study this fully blocked letter now.

Some of the points we referred to earlier can now be explained in a little more detail.

The letterhead

One of the essential parts of any documentary evidence, whether it is a letter or a document such as an invoice, is that it should have the names and addresses of both parties to the correspondence. By having a printed letterhead, a firm ensures that the necessary details about its own name, address and telephone number are recorded on every letter. Then, when the typist types in the name and address of the addressee (see 'The internal address', p. 331), the letter will contain the names and addresses of both parties to the correspondence.

Since letterheads can be used in evidence as proof of a firm's contractual activities, they present a security problem. They should not be allowed to fall into the hands of outsiders – say visiting commercial travellers. The issue of headed notepaper should be closely controlled and if some new piece of legislation or change in the letterhead details renders stocks of stationery obsolete, the surplus stock should be cut up and used as scrap, or even shredded for packing material.

The date

Dates should always be typed with the month clearly stated in words. This avoids confusion, since in the USA it is usual to specify the month first. In the United Kingdom the day is usually specified first in an all-number date. Thus 4.12.94 means 4th December 1994 in the United Kingdom, and 12th April 1994 in the USA. Many firms have now dispensed with abbreviations like 'st', 'nd', 'rd', and 'th' after the number of the day, so that the date would usually be written in the style 17 September 1994. In Figure 16.1 the year has been shown as 19.. to save dating the artwork.

The references

As mentioned above, the letterheading often includes lines reading 'Our Reference' and 'Your Reference'. Depending upon the size of the organization concerned, references may simply pinpoint particular executives and their secretaries. WSG/AL would perhaps refer to the executive W. S. Gilbert and his secretary Alison Laker. Government correspondence often pinpoints the department and file number holding the correspondence, as those who correspond with the Inland Revenue authorities will know.

Mailing instructions

The name and address of the addressee must appear at the top of the letter, as explained in the section about letterheading. As this internal address is used in the preparation of the envelope, it is usual to include two other items — the mailing instructions and the attention line. They thus become part of the inside address and are incorporated on the envelope.

As regards mailing instructions, many letters are sent by special mail services, e.g. air mail, registered post, recorded delivery, special delivery, etc. It is usual for these instructions to be typed above the internal address, in block capitals. Because the envelope is usually prepared from the internal address, the mailing instruction can then be typed on to the envelope, or if a rubber stamp is available, the instruction can be stamped boldly on the envelope. Besides drawing attention to the special instructions when the envelope is being prepared, the inclusion of the mailing instruction on the letter in this way assists subsequent enquiries about the non-arrival of a letter by pinpointing the method of dispatch. Our file copy of the letter tells us which service was used.

Attention lines

Where a letter is addressed to a particular individual within a firm, it is more expeditiously handled when mail is sorted in the addressee's mail room. The address would therefore start with the individual's name. Where this is prevented by an instruction in the addressee's letterhead requiring all letters to be addressed to the firm, it is customary to mark the letter and the envelope 'Attention of . . . . . .' This attention line should be underscored, and may be adapted to direct the letter to a particular department. Typical attention lines would be

Attention of Mr David Lane
Attention of J. Senior, Esq., Sales Manager
CONFIDENTIAL: Attention of the Personnel Officer

Although a firm may reserve the right to open all mail, such a letter would almost certainly be put unread into the mail tray of the person required to attend to it, while the confidential letter would probably not be opened.

The internal address

The internal address serves the two purposes of (*a*) naming in the letter itself the other party to the correspondence, and (*b*) providing a guide to the secretary in the preparation of the envelope. If the internal address is correct, then the envelope prepared from it will be correct too.

The salutation and the complimentary close

The salutation is the greeting at the start of the letter, and the complimentary close is the closing remark before the signature. These two parts of the letter are related in that the degree of familiarity or formality shown in the salutation will conform with that in the complimentary close. For example, a letter beginning with a rather formal 'Dear Sir' will usually end with an equally formal 'Yours faithfully'. A letter where we are personally acquainted with the addressee might begin 'Dear Mr MacIntyre' and end with the more personal 'Yours sincerely'. When the letter begins with a very familiar 'Dear John', the secretary may not type the salutation at all, the executive writing 'Dear John' in his/her own handwriting and ending with a personal salutation such as 'Very sincerely, Alex'.

The complimentary close and the signature are sometimes referred to as 'the subscription', a word which means 'written below' (the body of the letter).

Subject headings

A subject heading has several uses. It is usually inserted just after the salutation. The subject heading assists in the distribution of mail when it is opened in the addressee's mail room. It also assists the executive to whom it is addressed by immediately disclosing the subject matter of the letter — recalling any earlier correspondence at once to his/her mind. It is also a useful reminder to a busy filing clerk, secretary or executive of the subject matter of the letter when searching through a file of correspondence.

The main body of the letter

This consists of a number of paragraphs dealing with the subject matter of the letter. The important points about the actual content of the letter are explained in Section 16.5

The signature

After the complimentary close it is usual to leave sufficient space (five single lines) for a handwritten signature, followed by the type-written name of the person who has signed the letter, and his/her official position. Some companies like to have the name of the company included in the subscription. It often happens that executives ask their secretaries to sign letters p.p. (per pro) themselves. The actual meaning of per pro is *per procurationem*, which means 'by the action of' and implies that the person signing has the authority to sign. The following styles of signature might therefore be appropriate:

Yours sincerely

P. Green
General Manager

Yours sincerely,
THE FARM EQUIPMENT CO LTD,

P. Green
General Manager

Yours sincerely,

Rosemary Squires,
p.p. Peter Green
General Manager

Enclosures

An 'enclosure' is a separate item from the letter that is to be sent in the same envelope. Sometimes the enclosures are kept in bulk in the Post Department, and it will be there that the letter is finally sealed.

It is usual to put details of the enclosures at the end of the letter. These are generally typed at the left-hand margin of the page, and may include the number of enclosures thus: Enclosures 4. Alternatively, this may be abbreviated to Encs. 4. It is possible that the enclosures will be enumerated to prevent any misunderstanding, so that the entry reads:

Enclosures: 1   price list
2   catalogue
3   order form
4   reply-paid gummed label

It is the responsibility of the person actually dispatching mail to ensure that the envelope is 'stuffed' with all the items it should contain, i.e. the letter itself and the correct number of enclosures.

Distribution

It often happens that a letter is intended to go to a number of people, either because they are all equally interested, e.g. the members of a committee, or because they must be kept informed of the contents of the letter. Usually the distribution list comes at the end of the letter, thus:

Distribution: Head of Department − Engineering
Head of Department − Sales
Head of Department − Production
Chief Accountant
Managing Director
Chairman

Where the distribution is limited to one or two people only, the abbreviation CC (copy circulated) would be used, say CC Mr Charles Smith. The addressee then knows that Mr Charles Smith has been acquainted with the contents.

Sometimes it is desirable to pass a copy to some other party without the addressee being aware of the fact. Thus if it was felt advisable to pass a copy to the legal department without letting the addressee know, a request to send a carbon copy to the legal department might be marked NOO − not on original. The top copy of the letter is removed before this is typed on to the second copy. Seeing the NOO sign, the legal department knows that, for the time being anyway, the addressee is not aware that legal action is being considered against him/her.

Continuation sheets

Letters on headed notepaper are continued on to sheets of plain bond paper. The word 'cont'd' leads on to the next page, where the page number, addressee's name, and date are typed at the top to assist in identifying a loose page, should it become separated from the body of the letter. This can be typed right across the top of the continuation page, thus:

Mr Thomas Cross −2− 23 December 19. .

16.5 The body of the letter

Although the layout of a letter is important and familiarity with the standard layout helps us to get down to work quickly and methodically, the actual letter we write is the most important activity. We have to say what we want to say as clearly and concisely as possible. If this is the first letter we have written on the matter, we want to start with the maximum impact. If it is one in a chain of letters, we want to recall to our correspondent's mind all that has gone before and update him/her by a further piece or pieces of information.

It is advisable before starting the letter to jot down the points to be made and to number them so they are in the best order. If the letter is to be dictated, it is particularly important to be well-organized, with all the bits of information you need to dictate. A secretary will not be impressed by an executive who does not know the surname of the correspondent, or his/her initials, or the address, and who hesitates over the dictation, searching for odd scraps of paper in pockets, handbags, filofaxes, etc. If dictation is to a machine, the machine has to be told everything, so that the audio-typist can get on with the letter without delay. While a secretary can perhaps look at past correspondence for missing details, the audio-typist is remote from the scene of operations and possibly in a completely different building.

Having collected your information, you are ready to start the letter.

The opening paragraph

The opening paragraph tends to be short and often continues the greeting begun in the salutation if we are on familiar terms with our correspondent. In more formal situations it outlines the subject matter of the letter, reinforcing the subject heading. It may refer to earlier correspondence, and it always sets the tone of the letter. Thus a letter that was intended to make the strongest possible protest about the products or services supplied by the correspondent would not begin in a light-hearted way, but would start seriously and formally. By contrast, a letter acknowledging a large order and anticipating a long and fruitful course of dealings with a customer would begin pleasantly and keep a friendly tone throughout.

The main subject matter

The body of the letter would consist of one or more paragraphs, each dealing with a topic that is an element in the subject matter to be dealt with. Paragraphs should not be too long, unless the subject matter is particularly serious and can sustain the reader's interest because of its urgent nature. If a series of important points is being made, they may be listed (*a*), (*b*), (*c*), etc., or if they have a paragraph each, the paragraphs may be numbered. It is in this part of the letter that the writer must explain what he/she feels about the matter, and what he/she feels the next step should be. If detailed recommendations are being made, they may be listed in the final paragraph so that the correspondent can deal with them item by item.

Within this framework we may list the following points:

1 *Be brief.* Everyone is busy and has dozens of things to do. A long-winded style is irritating. Get to the point straight away, or with the briefest of opening remarks if the correspondent is known to be new to the arrangements.
2 *Be positive.* State the facts. If there are alternative points of view, state them in turn with equal clarity. Then, if your opinion is important, state clearly what you believe and why. Management is about decision-making. Those who endlessly sit on fences only gain splinters in inconvenient places.

3 *Write simply*. There is no point in trying to show your erudition. The people who employ you probably chose you because of it. Use simple language, state plainly what you have to say, put out signposts indicating the direction of your thoughts (such as sub-headings) if necessary, and come to a clear conclusion.

4 *Be courteous*. Bluster is rarely effective in correspondence. You should always keep a rein on your statements even when you feel strongly about the matter in hand. To be courteous even in a serious matter adds force to your message, for your very restraint shows how seriously you view the subject.

5 *Summarize the matter in the final paragraph*. Generally speaking, a final paragraph that shows the way ahead (even if the best way ahead is to do nothing) leaves your correspondent with a clear guideline for the future.

16.6 Standard form letters

Correspondence costs money and anything we can do to reduce the cost is helpful. In most businesses the same sort of problem arises again and again, and if we devise a standard form letter and run off fifty copies of it on a plain-paper copier or a digital duplicator we can save a lot of time and money. Such a letter usually deals with more than one problem, but by filling up the blank letter with the name and address of the addressee and indicating which part of the letter applies on this occasion, we can quickly solve the problem. Figure 16.2 shows such a letter.

16.7 Standard form paragraphs

Most electronic typewriters and word-processors can accept standard paragraphs, which enable a variety of matters to be stored in the memory of the machine and called up into action by a simple code number when required. For example in Figure 16.3 there are ten paragraphs dealing with a number of possible problems in connection with George Vyner's Simplex Account Books. The ten paragraphs shown have been extracted from a full range of 100 paragraphs used by this firm when dealing with much of their routine correspondence. The manager dealing with the problem raised by a customer only has to write on the letter the numbers of the paragraphs needed to answer it. For example the codes, 3, 7 and 10 would be sufficient to respond to the type of letter which comes in every day from new entrants to business who wish to obtain Simplex Account Books. The secretary would simply head up the letter with the address of the applicant and the salutation, Dear Sir or Dear Madam as appropriate, type in the codes for the required paragraphs and the machine will produce the text from its memory.

```
To ............              The Ash Tree Theatre,
    ............              Wendover Hillside,
    ............              2174 Gogmagog Road
    Postcode .....           Cambridge
                             England
                             CB4 1PQ
                                  Our Ref .....
                                  Date
Theatre Admissions Dept

Dear ................,
```

Thank you for your letter enquiring about admission tickets. We cannot deal
with your request, for the reasons ticked below.

1. You failed to say which date you intend
    to visit us. Please send this information
    referring to the reference no. given
    above . A phone call quoting this
    reference will do.   ....

2. The theatre is fully booked on this
    date and until the end of the run.
    Your cheque must therefore be returned.   ....

3. We are fully booked on the date you
    suggest but can offer you tickets for
    ......   or ......   Will you
    please write, or phone, quoting the
    reference above, when we shall be
    happy to send you the tickets you
    need.   ....

4. We regret we cannot send tickets
    except on Cash with Order terms.
    Please send a cheque for £...... when
    we shall send your tickets by return.   ....

5. Your cheque cannot be presented
    because ....
    Will you please rectify this error
    and return it in the enclosed FREEPOST
    envelope   ....

Yours faithfully

Mary Tyler
Bookings Secretary
```

Figure 16.2   A standard form letter

## 16.8   Quick-reply letters

A quick-reply letter is used by many types of administrative offices,
e.g. central government departments and local authorities. They are
constantly faced with the need to open a file on businesses of
```

1. Thank you for your letter enquiring about *Simplex Account Books*. We enclose a brochure giving full details and a current price list.

2. Thank you for your letter enquiring about our free sets of material for use in United Kingdom schools. I enclose a 'Teacher's Set' of materials and if you let me know, either by telephone or letter, how many students you will be teaching this year, I will send you enough material for each student to try our practice exercise.

3. Thank you for your letter. We understand that, as you are commencing your own small business, you wish to take advantage of our special offer of *Simplex Account Books*. I enclose details of this offer and if you complete the form and return it, we will dispatch your books by return of post.

4. We thank you for your letter dated ... and as requested have pleasure in enclosing herewith an application for membership of the Simplex Club. This entitles you to free advice on any book-keeping problems you meet when using our *Simplex Account Books*.

5. We thank you for your letter dated ... and have pleasure in enclosing herewith our special notes in connection with the final accounts of partnerships.

6. We thank you for your letter dated ... and have pleasure in enclosing herewith our special notes in connection with the final accounts of a limited company.

7. We are also enclosing an application form for membership of the Simplex Club and leaflet/order forms about our two publications. *Simplified Book-keeping for Small Businesses* and *Self-Employment, Not Unemployment*, in which you may be interested.

8. Finally I wish you every success in your new venture and trust that you will be a Simplex user for many years to come. For your future convenience the *Simplex D Account Book* now includes a priced re-order form which appears between weekly pages 47 and 48.

9. If we can be of any further assistance to you please do not hesitate to let us know.

10. Yours faithfully,

Brian Senior
General Manager
GEORGE VYNER (DISTRIBUTORS) LTD
PO Box 1, Holmfirth, Huddersfield, HD7 2PR
(0484) 685221

Figure 16.3   A selection of standard paragraphs (courtesy of George Vyner Ltd, Huddersfield)

various sorts for control purposes. One of the many bodies of this sort is the Inland Revenue Department. Figure 16.4 shows the IR form 41G, which is included in its booklet *Starting in Business*. Many people who have been employees, and therefore appear in the UK tax records as employees, paying tax under the PAYE (pay as you earn) scheme, leave to become self-employed. This leads to a change in their tax records. It often means a refund of tax, which benefits the new business, because businesses sometimes take a little while to become profitable, and while they are not making profits, they cannot be charged tax. To make the change, and get their business file opened with the Inland Revenue, the quick-reply letter shown in Figure 16.4 must be completed.

Note that the chief feature of a quick-reply letter is that the page is divided in half by a centre line. Short, detailed questions are listed on the left-hand side, with space for a quick reply on the right-hand side. The design of such a form is usually a co-operative effort, the rough draft being passed around various people so that nothing is overlooked. When completed by the addressee, and returned, the file for the new business can be started up and will be kept as a current file for all the years that the business continues to run. It becomes a very detailed record of the business's tax affairs, and the various tax inspectors can see at a glance the profits made, the promptness of payments, the good times and the bad times, etc.

Such forms should be reviewed from time to time to see that they still meet the needs of the Department, and a named individual will usually be charged with the duty of collecting and collating points that arise during the lifetime of the form. Then when it comes up for review, account can be taken of any defects that have come to the Department's attention.

16.9 Circulars

A circular is a letter or leaflet to be distributed among a circle of interested people, such as potential customers. It will often be in letter form but may be in leaflet form. This means that it will not have any address of the sender (other than a 'published by ......' line, usually at the foot of the page). Nor will it have an addressee's address, since it is for general distribution. This kind of circular is used, for example, at election times by political parties. They are pushed through our letterboxes in the hope we will find the contents of interest, and will be influenced to vote for the policies proposed.

For business purposes circulars often take the form of open letters, addressed to all and sundry. Such a circular, written to accompany catalogues and price lists is shown in Figure 16.5.

The essential feature of a circular is that it should have maximum impact — conveying the information required in a crisp, businesslike, lively style rather than in a formal way. Such letters stand a great chance of being considered 'junk-mail', especially if the number of

ENQUIRIES	REPLIES
1. In what name is the business carried on, if not in your own name?	1.
2. (a) What is the business address if different from your private address?	2. (a)
(b) What is your private address?	(b)
3. What is the nature of the business?	3.
4. When did you start in this business?	4.
5. If you took over an existing business, from whom did you acquire it?	5.
6. Have you any partners? If so, please give their names and private addresses.	6.
7. To what date do you propose to make up your business accounts? If they are to be prepared by an accountant, please give his name and address.	7.
8. If you are not already operating PAYE as an employer, have you any employees earning—	8.
(a) more than £34.00 a week	(a)
(b) more than £1 a week who have other employment?	(b)
9. If in addition to running your business you are in paid employment, or are continuing an existing business, please give particulars.	9.
10. (a) If your have left employment, please state the name and address of your employer and the date you left. If you still have the leaving certificate form P45 handed to you by your last employer, please attach it.	10. (a)
(b) If you have discontinued another business please state the nature and address of that business and the date it ceased.	(b)
11. If you have previously made a tax return, please state—	11.
(a) the name of the Tax Office to which you made it.	(a)
(b) the reference number in that office.	(b)
(c) if the office was Centre 1, enter your National Insurance number in the box provided.	(c)

(If you are a married woman the answers to question 11 should relate to your husband. If you cannot give these particulars, state the name and address of your husband's employer or his business address).

Full Name.. **Date**.............. 19 ....
(In BLOCK letters)

If you are a woman state whether single, married, widowed, separated or divorced; if married give your husband's Christian or other Forenames

....

41G

Figure 16.4 A quick-reply letter for notifying commencement of a business (courtesy of the Inland Revenue Department)

Publishers for Commerce, Industry and the Professions

FORMECON SERVICES LIMITED
Gateway, Crewe, Cheshire, CW1 1YN

Telephone	•	**0270 500 800 (Customer Sales)**
	•	**0270 500 000 (Administration)**
Telefax No.	•	0270 500 505
Doc. Exch.	•	DX 20163 Crewe

Dear Sirs

EXPORT DOCUMENTATION - TO REACH THE DESTINATION!

In today's international business world it's more important
than ever to make sure that your export procedures are carried
out correctly and efficiently.

To achieve this, you need documentation which is simpler to
complete, guarantees the provision of all necessary
information and instructions, and is presented in an
internationally recognisable format.

The Formecon range of International Documentation fulfils
these requirements. The superior quality of our products also
promises you the benefit of a competent, professional image
being presented by your organisation to your contacts and
customers throughout the world.

We have pleasure in enclosing <u>eight new catalogues of Export
Documentation</u>. In addition to a full range of shipping
documentation published to the latest approved format,
including a complete set of 13 Incoterm forms, there are
products for internal use to help you to control and maintain
your export business.

Our documentation is designed for easy completion by hand or
typewriter, but if you are considering computerisation of your
export procedures, our Formfill Export Software will enable
you to make a smooth transition to automatic production of all
shipping documents - please see Catalogue No 18.

Why leave things to chance? You **know** that one small error,
ommission or misunderstanding can have disastrous and far-
reaching implications - for that shipment and for future
business.

Get the paperwork right first time, get the goods delivered on
time and <u>get paid on time</u> - Formecon products are designed to
help you achieve that, every time.

Yours sincerely

Wm J Thompson
Wm J Thompson
Managing Director

Registration Number No 1649187
England
Wm J Thompson, D M Townley, A B Reports
Members of
The Law Society Association The North Staffs
Chamber of Commerce and Industry The Institute of Export
BSI Quality Assurance BS 5750 Part 1 Registered No FM 19852

Figure 16.5 A circular for direct mailing (courtesy of Formecon Services Ltd)

addressees is large. One company the authors frequently deal with has lists of up to 300 000 addresses. A circular sent out to such a vast number of addressees must find many who are just not interested in the client's product. The circular is 'filed in the waste-paper basket'. A good response rate from such a mailing might be 1 per cent, which would be 3000 responses.

By contrast, if we reduce the mailing list to those more likely to be interested, the costs will be less and the response rate will be better. The circular from Castle Park Business Centre (see Figure 16.6) would be catering for a relatively small group – those wishing to set up business in the Cambridge area. One or two organizations would be interested in such a circular, e.g. the local Enterprise Agency would know all the budding entrepreneurs in the area, and might be willing to take a small stock of the circulars and give them out to all those enquiring about premises. Similarly, technical colleges running courses on 'How to run a small business' might be interested. The local authority, seeking to promote Cambridge as a centre for excellence in the business field, might be prepared to take copies and make them available, while the local tourist centre might be prepared to take supplies visitors would be able to pick up if they were interested.

16.10 Report writing

Countless problems arise in business, and a solution has to be found to them. Some problems arise in the form of emergencies such as accidents, natural disasters, strikes, environmental complaints, etc. Others are the result of the normal cycles of business activiy – a product losing its attraction for customers, or being rendered obsolete by new technologies. Government interference may render a product unprofitable, or require it to be modified to comply with regulations.

The solution to such problems is frequently found by appointing a small committee to look into the problem and report on its findings, with recommendations for an appropriate solution. The committee may be an **ad hoc committee** or a **standing committee**. An **ad hoc** committee is a committee appointed for a particular purpose, which collects evidence bearing on the problem, analyses it and reports back with recommendations. A standing committee holds a watching brief over the problem area, e.g. quality control. It collects its evidence as a routine matter from hourly, daily or weekly reports, and reports regularly to the board or an appropriate director.

The effective point of control is in all cases the report and the recommendations it makes. The writing of reports is therefore a very important role for middle management and senior staff, and it is essential to be able to write clearly and lucidly about the matter in hand. We may distinguish the following aspects of report writing:

**CASTLE PARK
BUSINESS CENTRE**

S H E R A T O N   H O U S E

The business address for :

* **Budding entrepreneurs**
* **Established smaller businesses**
* **Satellites of established companies**
* **EC companies seeking to enter the UK market**

**At Sheraton House we offer a complete office service at a
prestigious Cambridge address.** Close to the City Centre and the
Science Park, in the fastest growing area of the United Kingdom,
we are strategically placed for business with all EC countries.

Offices are available immediately, with no lease to negotiate, no
legal costs, no long-term commitment, no capital outlay. A
standard three or six month licence agreement gives your business
total flexibility. If your business grows you can move easily
within Sheraton House to larger premises.

Central staff are employed to operate telephone, fax, secretarial
and postal services. All premises costs are covered by your
monthly rental. We have photocopiers, meeting rooms, seminar
rooms, coffee and tea making facilities, car parking and security
cover. Your absence is covered by an efficient reception staff,
and your premises are available (but secure) 24 hours a day.

So we run the office, while you run your business!

For further details please contact :

> Nicky Stepanov
> Centre Manager
> Castle Park Business Centre
> Sheraton House
> Castle Park
> Cambridge
> CB3 0AX
> **Tel : (0223) 462244**

Sheraton House
Castle Park · Cambridge
CB3 0AX
Tel (0223) 462244
Telex 818436
Fax (0223) 460178

Castle Park Business Centre
is a division of
J T Developments Ltd
Reg. No. 737202 England
Registered Office
Bush House · 72 Prince Street
Bristol BS1 4HU

Figure 16.6   A circular about business premises (courtesy of Castle Park Business Centre)

(*a*) The statement of the problem.

(*b*) The appointment of a team leader and a team to investigate the matter. This confers upon them the right to collect information, etc., and to report back their conclusions.

(*c*) The gathering of information.

(*d*) The planning of the report, including the analysis of the information, the presentation of any data in suitable form and the marshalling of the evidence in good order.

(*e*) The conclusions to be drawn from the analysed information.

(*f*) The recommendations to solve the problem.

(*g*) Publication of the report.

Stating the problem and appointing the team

Problems arise for all sorts of reasons on all sorts of matters. It is the function of the managing director to be aware of all the problems that do arise, and the problem will move rapidly up the chain of command to managing director level. Usually some middle manager or supervisor will become aware of the problem and will raise it with his/her supervisor, who will raise it with a director, who will in turn raise it with the managing director. Emergency situations will of course be dealt with at once, but problems concerning company policy will usually begin by becoming an agenda item, at the next board meeting.

The chairman will call for an account of the problem from the most appropriate director; some discussion will take place and a resolution will be passed requiring either an existing committee, or an ad hoc committee set up for the purpose, to investigate the matter and report back. This resolution will be minuted by the minuting secretary and becomes the legal authority for the activities of the team leader and his team. Such a resolution might read:

22 June 19. . It is resolved that Mrs R. Jones, Deputy Accountant, shall choose three members of staff from the Audit Department and consider the policies at present in use to deal with the investment of the company pension fund. The portfolio of investments is to be considered from the following viewpoints:

(*a*) The proportion of funds directly invested in the activities of the company.

(*b*) The safeguarding of the portfolio, and whether any part of it is at present pledged against loans made to the company by banks and other financial institutions.

(*c*) The present market value of the portfolio and its adequacy for the pensions payable now, and in the future.

This resolution is said to set the *terms of reference* of the team, and the final report always begins by referring to the terms of reference and recapitulating why the team was appointed, what it was required to do, to whom it was to report and whether any time limit was set.

Planning the report

The enquiries made and the evidence collected may take some time, but gradually will accumulate into a body of knowledge that makes it possible to state what the present situation is, how it developed, etc. Gradually the team begins to think about the eventual presentation of this data, the conclusions to which the data are leading, and the recommendations it will need to make.

The analysis of the data is a process of selecting appropriate material for the report and bringing it into correct sequence for presentation. Team discussions will gradually lead to firm conclusions about the matter in hand, but the word 'gradually' is important. It is necessary for someone to play 'devil's advocate' and delay the decision process by arguing against the line of the argument that is in favour of a particular conclusion, so that the case in favour has to be fully justified and the possibility of error reduced. The balance of the evidence has to be clearly in favour of the conclusion arrived at, especially if someone's reputation is at stake.

Circumstantial evidence is evidence tending to support a particular conclusion because the train of known facts is difficult to explain in any other way. At the same time it is not clear proof, and it is always possible that later evidence will provide an alternative explanation. The report may need to give both sides of the argument, and any attempt to report without revealing the doubts that do exist in the matter is a form of bias, and wholly undesirable.

Arrangement of the evidence in a logical order for presentation is vital if the report is to be effective. The sequence might follow the outline given below:

(*a*) The terms of reference of the investigating team, and its composition.
(*b*) An outline of the problem.
(*c*) A detailed account of the way the problem was handled: what lines of inquiry were pursued, who took charge of each and what was the *modus operandi* in each case.
(*d*) The conclusions arrived at from each line of inquiry and the bearing they had on the whole problem.
(*e*) The general conclusions drawn, and the reasons why they were arrived at. The reasons why possible alternative conclusions were rejected.
(*f*) The recommendations made.

(*g*) The systematic arrangement of all the evidence in the form of appendices so that it is available for inspection and analysis by any interested parties.

All this requires quite careful planning, and leads on to the actual writing of the report, which may include statistical details, statements by interested parties, etc. In important investigations these may be presented as appendices of various sorts.

It is important to find the right balance of evidence, so that the committee can point clearly to it as the reason for its conclusions and recommendations. If there is any doubt in the matter, the adverse evidence should not be suppressed but highlighted. What the committee's recommendations are based on in such a case is a balance of probabilities, in which it rejects the evidence pointing the other way as being less likely than its preferred conclusions.

The next stage is to arrange the information in its most logical sequence, so that the report is well-constructed. The board wants a simple account of a complex matter, one which brings out the important points in correct order and reaches a set of logical conclusions.

This planning stage enables the actual report to be written convincingly and without hesitation. It has all been thought through and discussed in detail among the team to ensure that nothing has been overlooked. Someone has played 'devil's advocate' and presented arguments of a 'what if' sort — to enable the whole team to participate in discussing the evidence, and hammer out a common set of conclusions. If a report is steam-rollered through by a team leader who has a strong personality, it is highly likely it will eventually arouse controversy and may be accused of being a 'whitewash'.

The structure of the report
The usual structure of a report is as follows:

(*a*) The title page.
(*b*) The table of contents.
(*c*) The summary.
(*d*) The introduction.
(*e*) The body of the report.
(*f*) The conclusions.
(*g*) The recommendations.
(*h*) The appendices (if any).
(*i*) Acknowledgements.
(*j*) References and bibliography.
(*k*) An index.

Although this is the final structure, it cannot be written in this order. The title page, the table of contents and the summary are usually written at the end, because the main thing is to write the report — these other items are only part of the general presentation. It may seem strange to have a summary at the front of the report, but it is a fact that many people will not want to read the whole report. They will want a quick breakdown of the subject matter, the conclusions drawn and the recommendations made. The body of the report can be read by those (usually lower level) staff who have to implement the recommendations. The board of a company, for example, will only want to know the bare bones of the matter, on which decisions have to be made.

The introduction to the report

A report should always be formal in its approach, as befits any matter that is to be circulated to interested parties and become a matter of private, or even public, record. Many reports are made available to the press, and as such are liable to be commented upon by journalists, editors and the general public. It is easy enough for them to be misunderstood, or misinterpreted, or even misrepresented deliberately, as those who read the daily papers regularly will soon discover. The best way to avoid such problems is to be formal in one's approach, to write carefully, choosing one's words and proving the content of the report, stage by stage, to establish its authenticity.

The introductory stages are as follows:

(*a*) The report should have a clear title, which is self-explanatory.

(*b*) It should be addressed to the person or the body that commissioned the report, and if necessary say by what authority they appointed the panel giving the report.

(*c*) It should bear the name of the individual submitting the report or the chairperson of the committee responsible for its production. The names of other members of the committee should be listed and any special capacities shown.

(*d*) Unless it is a routine report, the terms of reference should be given. This is sometimes done as part of the salutation, as shown in the specimen introduction in Figure 16.7.

(*e*) It would be usual to date the report to fix its publication clearly at a particular point in time, since it will almost certainly be archived eventually, and referred to, possibly many years later.

A typical introduction might look something like the introduction given in Figure 16.7.

The body of the report

We now come to the main body of the report. It depends upon the subject matter of the investigation, but we may envisage the following possible components of the report.

Publication Date
1 November 19..

*The Company Pension Fund
Report*

To Mr H. Ratcliffe
Chairman of the Board
Thompson, Wild and Washbourne (Camside) Ltd.,
2495 City Road,
Wroxeter,
Shropshire,
WR1 2PQ

From Mrs R Jones, deputy accountant, on behalf of the *ad hoc*
committee appointed by the Board on 22 June 19..

Members of the Committee (Audit Department)
P. Martin   Accountant
R. Jones   Actuary
M. Larkin   Chief clerk

Sir,

We were appointed on 22 June 19.. to consider the policies in use
at present to invest the company pension funds, and to consider the
investments from the following points of view.

(*a*) The proportion of funds directly invested in the activities of the
company.
(*b*) The safeguarding of the portfolio and whether any part of it is at
present pledged against loans made to the company by banks and
other institutions.
(*c*) The present market value of the portfolio and its adequacy for
the pensions payable now and in the future.

The committee began by investigating the present portfolio, its
availability for scrutiny and the whereabouts of recorded investments
which were not immediately available. We then took statements from
all the present trustees of the fund, of which there are five. Our
enquiries were about the past decisions made both as to the purchase
of investments month by month as funds became available, and as to
the turnover of the portfolio as values changed over the years. We also
considered the spread of the portfolio. Mr R. Jones took on the difficult
task of valuing the portfolio and assessing its adequacy in accordance
with (*c*) above.

We also approached the three past directors, now retired, who were
at one time trustees of the fund, but the most influential of the former
trustees, Mr Peter Bird, died two years ago and could not be
questioned.

We have to report as follows:

Figure 16.7   A typical introduction to a report

(*a*) A description of the situation at the time the investigation began. Without going into enormous detail, we must set the scene by mentioning the most important features of the events. In the circumstances described in the introduction (Figure 16.7) we need a brief account of the present portfolio. This should list the stocks, shares and debentures in the portfolio and whether they are in fact available. If not the report should state where they are e.g. they may have been lodged as security for loans made to the firm by banks.

(*b*) We then move on to deal with the matters raised in our terms of reference. Part (*a*) of the terms of reference asks whether any of the funds are directly invested in the business. This may not be illegal, but it is probably undesirable, because if the company gets into difficulties the pensioners will probably be in difficulty too. The essence of a portfolio is that it should be a balanced portfolio and not have 'all its eggs in one basket'. Part (*c*) of the terms of reference call for a full actuarial report on the value of the fund, and the adequacy of the reserves to meet the pension requirements for the future. This is going to require a detailed report, with a clear analysis of all aspects of the portfolio.

Wherever possible a report should contain statistical data, diagrams and charts to support the conclusions of the committee. Some knowledge of statistics is extremely helpful and evidence presented in this way will be very informative to members of any board of directors, many members of which will be trained to understand such data.

A long and detailed report may confuse its readers, and it is wise to draw conclusions on each section as we go along. The use of 'bullets' pinpoints salient features of the section, e.g.:

Conclusions on the first part of our terms of reference (the proportion of funds directly invested in the company).

- We found that 52 per cent of the total pension fund was invested directly in the company.
- We also found that 31 per cent of the fund was used directly as working capital, without any official recognition by way of loan document or debenture, apart from an entry in the pension fund account transferring it to the company's bank account.
- The other 21 per cent was recognized by a debenture document, but this document gave the pension fund interest at about half the rate of interest usual on debentures in the general market. One trustee of the fund did protest at this unfair treatment but he was overruled by the other trustees.
- We conclude that this situation is unsatisfactory, the needs of

pensioners being subordinated to the current needs of the company, and an unwise proportion of the total funds being committed to a single investment.

Such a set of conclusions already begins to indicate that the Committee's report will be highly critical of the arrangements at present.

Working through the terms of reference

As we deal with each item in the terms of reference, we move on to the next, building up a clear account of each aspect. There may be some difficulty in phrasing particular sections of the report because it may be necessary to allocate blame or pinpoint some dereliction of duty. It is usual to express such conclusions in as moderate a way as possible, because one does not wish to be accused of libellous statements. Libel is the making of defamatory statements in a permanent form, i.e. in writing or in print, or perhaps in artwork or in the form of a statue.

Slander is the same sort of thing in non-permanent form, e.g. spoken defamation or a gesture. It is a less serious defamation than libel. However, if the spoken word is on radio or television, it is held to be libel, not slander, because of the bigger audience. Thus, the report should be toned down to do no more than refer to the regrettable lapse − whatever it was − leaving the party that commissioned the report to phrase more serious complaints or charges at some internal inquiry. Of course with a matter of public concern the Crown Prosecution Service may eventually pursue charges.

Where a report is not about a contentious matter at all, but is just investigating the best way for a particular activity to be pursued, e.g. the merger of two companies or a choice between various policies, then such considerations do not enter into the problem. At the same time every problem affects someone − a decision one way will affect some people adversely, and an alternative solution will adversely affect others. One can only do one's best, stating the *pros* and *cons* in each case. The *pros* are the points in favour of a particular case while the *cons* are the points against it.

Remember though that we do have to come to a decision. Those who state both sides but refuse to make a decision do no service to anyone and defeat the whole point of a committee to examine a problem. If the committee cannot come to a decision because its members cannot agree, then the report gives the majority opinion, and those who disagree may hand in a **minority report** explaining why they take a contrary view.

The conclusions

The conclusions (disregarding the possibility of a minority report) restate the conclusions arrived at in each sub-section, though perhaps in slightly less detail. They must be quite specific, if that is possible, relating the conclusions to each aspect of the terms of reference and giving the committee's clear view of the matter. If absolute proof of a particular point is not possible, the wording should state this, but give the committee's view of the balance of probabilities in the matter.

Figure 16.8 gives a set of conclusions for the imaginary scenario described in Figure 16.7. The reader will appreciate that it is difficult to write a report except on the basis of an actual investigation. Study these conclusions now.

The recommendations

The recommendations are the most important part of a report, because they suggest what should actually be done. It depends of course upon the subject matter of the report what they will be, but

---

Conclusions
  The committee's conclusions are as follows:

1 That the state of the pension fund is serious, and it is essential to revise the procedures used in the management of the fund without delay.
2 Part of the problem arises because the assets of the fund have come to be regarded as generally available for the financing of the company's affairs. There is no rule in the trust deed that this may not be done, but it is undesirable because it places the future position of pension holders in jeopardy should the trading position of the company deteriorate.
3 The principle of a balanced portfolio − that funds should be spread as widely as possible across a range of investments − have not been followed in recent years, and too high a proportion of the assets have been made available to a single borrower − the company itself.
4 The trustees of the fund have not conducted formal meetings on a regular basis for some years, but have relied on the fact that everyone knows what is going on and what use is being made of the funds. This lack of formality has prevented any real review of the state of the fund.
5 The actuarial report provided by Richard Jones reveals that the market value of the fund is lower than the book records would indicate, and the return to the fund from most of the investments lower than it should be. It is able at present to provide the funds to honour past pensions, but the situation is deteriorating and unless something is done a time will come when the fund is not adequate for the needs of the pensioners.

Figure 16.8 The 'conclusions' section of a report

Office Procedures

the essential point is that the individual or the committee carrying out the investigation is now more knowledgeable about the matters than anyone else. He, she or it has become the expert — knowledgeable about the matter and able to see the way ahead. The recommendations should follow directly from the conclusions reached, and should command respect. In the vast majority of cases in ordinary business activity they will be put into effect after discussion at senior management level. It is a sad fact that many reports at government level do in fact gather dust on ministry shelves, usually for financial reasons or because they are politically inexpedient.

The recommendations in our imaginary scenario outlined in Figures 16.7 and 16.8 might be as shown in Figure 16.9.

Recommendations
  We recommend as follows:

(a) That the trust deed for the pension fund be revised to set out more clearly the procedures under which it will be operated. In particular that not more than 10 per cent of the funds should be invested in the company itself, and not more than 5 per cent in any one company or investment.
(b) As part of this revision, the body of trustees should be changed to include (i) a representative of the pensioners, and (ii) a representative of the present staff, below the rank of director.
(c) The meetings of the pension fund trustees should be more regular, and more formal, and should include at each meeting (say 6 monthly) a review of the adequacy of the fund for meeting its present and future commitments.
(d) The company itself should make provision in its annual accounts over the next 3 years to reduce the amounts on loan to it from the pension fund, to the 10 per cent level recommended in (a) above. In addition, the sums at present on loan should be recognized formally as being an investment of the fund in the company, and a debenture deed should be drawn up for this purpose. The trustees, as revised (see (b) above), shall be the debenture trustees for this new deed.
(e) The funds released by (d) above shall be invested in a balanced portfolio spread across gilt-edged securities, blue-chip shares and growing companies on the unlisted securities market (USM).
(f) To allay anxiety a report about the future conduct of the pension fund should be made available to all staff and pensioners, outlining the action to be taken to restore the fund to good health, and an annual report should be issued for the future to keep interested parties informed of the success of the arrangements made.

Figure 16.9 The recommendations of the committee

The appendices

An appendix is an addition to a document, report or book that gives additional information of use to the reader. There are several reasons for having an appendix.

First, an appendix is useful as an **up-date to the document** itself. Many long reports take several months to write, and there will be a time interval between the decision to consider the investigation complete and the date of publication. During this time interval further data of interest may come in or perhaps some social or economic or political change may occur. An appendix would be an appropriate place to give the new information, or to refer to the impact of changes on the views expressed in the report.

Second, an appendix is a useful place to **keep information that is difficult to include in the main text**. For instance, statistical data is often given separately in this way. There will be many reports where the charts and diagrams can usefully be placed in an appendix. They would be referred to in the main text, and the reader would be urged to peruse them, but they would be a separate section.

Third, an appendix may also be used to **segregate off some useful background material**. For example, a legal report might include a glossary of Latin terms, or a book about computers might include a glossary of computer terms. The *Concise Oxford Dictionary* has appendices of weights and measures, monetary units, and Greek and Russian alphabets.

Acknowledgements

A report usually includes a list of acknowledgements, which mentions the help given by various people in the preparation of the report. Since this is usually a gesture of thanks from the person writing the report, it can appear at the front of the report following the table of contents.

References and bibliography

In many reports it is quite common to explain a point that is referred to in the body of a text in a note given in a reference section at the back of the book. For example, the reference in the Recommendations (see Figure 16.9) to 'blue chip' shares might call for a short explanation and a list of some of these important shares, deemed to be absolutely reliable. Similarly, if books or magazine articles are referred to, the name of the book should be given, with its author, publisher, etc. in the form:

Iman Wilkens, *Where Troy Once Stood*, 1st Edn., Rider Books, 1991, p. 49.

Two terms often used in bibliographies are *ibid.* and *op. cit.* The former is an abbreviation for *ibidem*, which is Latin for 'in the same book'. So '*ibid.*, p. 62' means 'in the same book as the one just mentioned, on page 62'.

Op. cit. is an abbreviation for the Latin *opere citate* and means 'in the work already quoted'. So '*op. cit.*, p. 279' refers to page 279 in the book already quoted.

The mention of books and articles in a bibliography serves two purposes. It enables the readers to obtain the work for themselves and read the opinions and ideas of the author. Secondly, it acknowledges that the author of the report did not think of the point made by himself/herself, but found it in the publication cited. The credit for the idea should not therefore be given to the author of the report, but to the original author.

Completion of the report

Usually at this stage it is desirable to have a report typed up if it is in handwritten form. The typed copy may be described as a first draft, and it may be subject to a certain amount of rewriting and improvement. If the first draft can be done on a word-processor, which stores the first draft in its memory, it will save a considerable amount of retyping later − a tedious chore for the typist. The draft stored in the computer's memory can be recalled to the screen of the visual display unit (VDU) and corrected on the screen. Whole paragraphs can be repositioned if necessary, while correct passages need not be retyped. The exact arrangements depend upon the software used, but the handbook of instructions will make clear exactly what is possible to revise and improve a draft.

16.11 Proofreading

Proofreading is a very important activity. The hope is that all correspondence sent out by an office will be impeccable; without error of any sort. Clearly some errors are easier to detect than others, e.g. spelling mistakes are fairly easy to detect, though we may have to refer to a dictionary to make sure of some spellings. Similarly errors in sets of figures can be checked against the original, and we should always check calculations carefully. If columns or rows of figures are totalled *always* check them. Not so easy to detect are errors of syntax − errors in the arrangement of words within a sentence, and their agreement with one another. Many middle-management staff, particularly those promoted to management because of their skills in non-managerial roles − (say shop-floor roles) − find business letters difficult because they do not know the rules of syntax. 'We was intending to do that' is a typical mistake. 'We' is a plural pronoun, but 'was' is a singular verb, so 'we was' is incorrect, and it should be 'we were'. The reader will notice many such mistakes.

There are useful signs that have been used in proofreading for many years. They are collected together in a publication called *Marks for copy preparation and proof correction: British Standard BS5261C: 1976*, published by the British Standards Institution. Copies may be obtained from the Institution at Linford Wood, Milton Keynes MK14 6LE, (Tel: 0 908 2211 66). The complete set of marks is printed on thick card, which is very durable, and the price is very reasonable. Telephone for the current price before sending 'cash with order'. Students are strongly recommended to purchase their own copies, since typesetters and printers appreciate copy that is correctly marked. To use the standard marks is economical both of time and effort, and other marks are often ambiguous.

To assist the reader the Institution has kindly permitted the reproduction of some of these signs in Figure 16.10. Study this illustration now, and the notes beneath it.

Note that 'copy' is the draft material to be set by a typesetter or printer. It will usually be typed and may have been produced on a word-processor, which, because of the ease of correction, usually means that the 'copy' will be fairly free of mistakes. On the other hand, it may be in manuscript form. This gives a greater chance of error, and possibly even problems caused by poor handwriting. The process of checking and correcting copy is called 'marking-up'. It consists not only in finding errors in the original but indicating to the printer what size type to use, the style of type (the font or fount), how to use capital and small letters (upper and lower case), etc.

Proofs are the product of typesetting. They are sent to the customer who has commissioned the work for proofreading before the completed work is sent to the printer for printing. There is usually a time limit set on proofreading, which must therefore be given priority, especially if the report or book is being prepared to meet a deadline. It is important not to change the text unduly at this stage – any changes by the author or editor should have been made at 'marking-up' stage. The British Standard Institution's document referred to recommends the use of coloured ink to distinguish the various kinds of correction. The suggestions are:

(*a*) *Green ink*. This is used by the typesetter's supervisor, who reads the proofs before they go to the customer. Green marks indicate that the supervisor has found errors which are the typsetter's fault and will be corrected free of charge once the proofreading stage is completed.

(*b*) *Red ink*. The proofs marked up by the supervisor are now sent to the customer, and possibly several sets are requested if there are editors, readers, authors and co-authors interested in seeing

Classified list of marks (Table 1 from BS 5261 : Part 2)

NOTE: The letters M and P in the notes column indicate marks
for marking-up copy and for correcting proofs respectively.

Group A General

Number	Instruction	Textual mark	Marginal mark	Notes
A4	Refer to appropriate authority anything of doubtful accuracy	Encircle word(s) affected	(?)	P
B1	Insert in text the matter indicated in the margin	�	New matter followed by ⎩	M P Identical to B2
B2	Insert additional matter identified by a letter in a diamond	⎩	⎩ Followed by for example ◇A	M P The relevant section of the copy should be supplied with the corresponding letter marked on it in a diamond e.g. ◇A
B3	Delete	/ through character(s) or ⊢——⊣ through words to be deleted	♂	M P
C21	Close up. Delete space between characters or words	linking ⌒ characters	⌒	M P
B7	Set in or change to italic	——— under character(s) to be set or changed	⊔⊔⊔	M P Where space does not permit textual marks encircle the affected area instead
B8	Set in or change to capital letters	≡≡≡ under character(s) to be set or changed	≡	
B12	Change capital letters to lower case letters	Encircle character(s) to be changed	≢	P For use when B5 is inappropriate
C1	Start new paragraph	⌐_	⌐_	M P
C2	Run on (no new paragraph)	⌒	⌒	M P
C3	Transpose characters or words	⊔⌐ between characters or words, numbered when necessary	⌐⊔	M P
B18	Substitute or insert full stop or decimal point	/ through character or ⎩ where required	⊙	M P

Figure 16.10 Marks for copy preparation and proof correction (courtesy of British Standards Institution)

copies. Only the top copy will have the green marks as the green corrections will appear in black on the photocopies. Red ink is used by these proofreaders to mark in errors in the typesetting which are to be corrected free of charge by the typesetter, because they are the typesetter's fault.

(*c*) *Blue ink or black ink.* These colours are used when an author wishes to change the original text. Such corrections have to be paid for by the customer, and may be expensive. They should therefore not be made unless they correct some clear error in the original wording, or where the law or some regulation has been changed in the time lag between authorship and publication. To change the wording just because the author could phrase the sentence better is undesirable at this stage.

When all copies have been proofread by the various readers one of the editors will collate the corrections of the rest on to the original set of proofs for the typesetter to work from when correcting the computer's stored copy in its memory.

Anyone who reads a set of proofs and then is given the job of collating their own and other readers' corrections on to the original set of proofs (the set that has the green-ink corrections of the typesetters' supervisor) soon discovers the following point. Anyone – absolutely anyone – can miss mistakes in proofreading. However careful one is trying to be it is still highly likely that errors will go through unnoticed, and even the tiniest mistakes can have very serious consequences. Mention was made earlier of a mistake where 'Nat Insurance' was printed as 'Net Insurance' and people all over the country phoned in to ask what on earth 'net insurance' was. Reading a set of proofs about a computer program the author of this book found an error which two other proofreaders had missed. The program was declared to 'stimulate the chemical activity in rivers'. Of course the word that should have been used was 'simulate'. The computer program was designed to show what would happen in a real river if, say, a sudden growth of plant life used up oxygen – how much extra plant life would cause the fish to die. The difference

---

Notes to Figure 16.10 opposite

(i) Each mark has been numbered by BS1, in one of three groups, A, B and C.

(ii) In the selection shown these numbers are given in the left hand column. There are 67 marks altogether.

(iii) The instruction to the printer is given in the second column. Note that this instruction does not have to be written on the paper being corrected. As soon as the printer or typesetter sees the textual mark (Column 3) he/she knows at once what has to be done.

(iv) A mark in the body of a long piece of text may be difficult to see and consequently may be overlooked. To avoid this the proof reader also puts a mark in the margin of the page at the same level as the correction. This catches the printer's eye and he/she locates the error that has to be corrected.

(v) Finally in column 5 there are some explanatory notes.

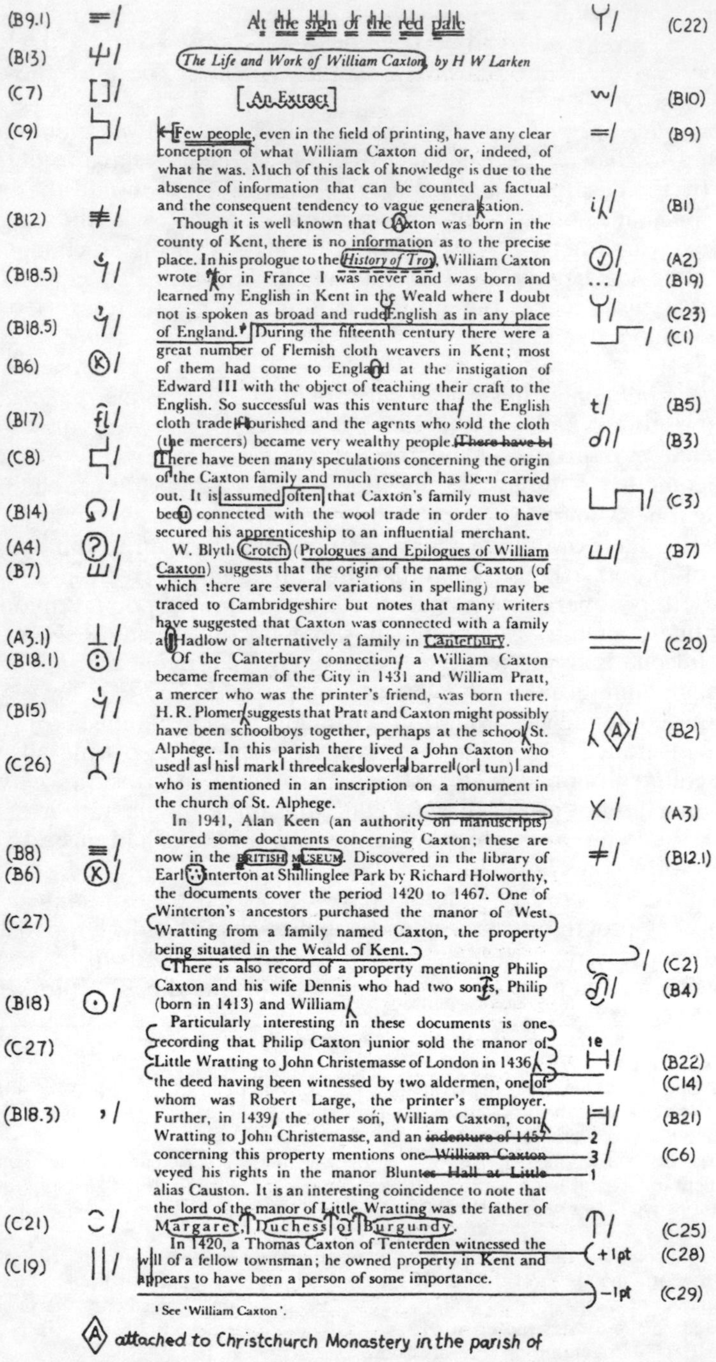

Marked galley proof of text

(B9.1)   =/

At the sign of the red pale:

(B13)   ⊣/

(The Life and Work of William Caxton) by H W Larken

(C7)   []/

[An Extract]

(C9)   ⅂/

Few people, even in the field of printing, have any clear conception of what William Caxton did or, indeed, of what he was. Much of this lack of knowledge is due to the absence of information that can be counted as factual and the consequent tendency to vague generalisation.

Though it is well known that Caxton was born in the county of Kent, there is no information as to the precise place. In his prologue to the *History of Troy*, William Caxton wrote 'for in France I was never and was born and learned my English in Kent in the Weald where I doubt not is spoken as broad and rude English as in any place of England.' During the fifteenth century there were a great number of Flemish cloth weavers in Kent; most of them had come to England at the instigation of Edward III with the object of teaching their craft to the English. So successful was this venture that the English cloth trade flourished and the agents who sold the cloth (the mercers) became very wealthy people. There have been There have been many speculations concerning the origin of the Caxton family and much research has been carried out. It is assumed often that Caxton's family must have been connected with the wool trade in order to have secured his apprenticeship to an influential merchant.

W. Blyth Crotch (Prologues and Epilogues of William Caxton) suggests that the origin of the name Caxton (of which there are several variations in spelling) may be traced to Cambridgeshire but notes that many writers have suggested that Caxton was connected with a family at Hadlow or alternatively a family in Canterbury.

Of the Canterbury connection a William Caxton became freeman of the City in 1431 and William Pratt, a mercer who was the printer's friend, was born there. H. R. Plomer suggests that Pratt and Caxton might possibly have been schoolboys together, perhaps at the school St. Alphege. In this parish there lived a John Caxton who used as his mark three cakes over a barrel (or tun) and who is mentioned in an inscription on a monument in the church of St. Alphege.

In 1941, Alan Keen (an authority on manuscripts) secured some documents concerning Caxton; these are now in the BRITISH MUSEUM. Discovered in the library of Earl Winterton at Shillinglee Park by Richard Holworthy, the documents cover the period 1420 to 1467. One of Winterton's ancestors purchased the manor of West Wratting from a family named Caxton, the property being situated in the Weald of Kent.

There is also record of a property mentioning Philip Caxton and his wife Dennis who had two sons, Philip (born in 1413) and William.

Particularly interesting in these documents is one recording that Philip Caxton junior sold the manor of Little Wratting to John Christemasse of London in 1436, the deed having been witnessed by two aldermen, one of whom was Robert Large, the printer's employer. Further, in 1439 the other son, William Caxton, conveyed Wratting to John Christemasse, and an indenture of 1457 concerning this property mentions one William Caxton conveyed his rights in the manor Bluntes Hall at Little alias Causton. It is an interesting coincidence to note that the lord of the manor of Little Wratting was the father of Margaret, Duchess of Burgundy.

In 1420, a Thomas Caxton of Tenterden witnessed the will of a fellow townsman; he owned property in Kent and appears to have been a person of some importance.

¹ See 'William Caxton'.

Margin marks (right column, top to bottom):
Ɏ/ (C22)   ⌇/ (B10)   =/ (B9)   i↓/ (B1)   ⊘/ (A2)   .../ (B19)   Ɏ/ (C23)   ⌐⌐/ (C1)   t/ (B5)   ∂∩/ (B3)   ⌐⌐/ (C3)   ш/ (B7)   ═/ (C20)   ⒜/ (B2)   ×/ (A3)   ≠/ (B12.1)   ⊋/ (C2)   ∂∩/ (B4)   1e ⊢/ (B22)   /(C14)   ⊢/ -2 (B21)   3/ (C6)   -1   ↑/ (C25)   (+1pt (C28)   )-1pt (C29)

Margin marks (left column, top to bottom):
(B9.1) =/   (B13) ⊣/   (C7) []/   (C9) ⅂/   (B12) ≠/   (B18.5) ⅄/   (B18.5) ⅄/   (B6) Ⓚ/   (B17) f̂l/   (C8) ⊐/   (B14) ∩/   (A4) ⑦/   (B7) ш/   (A3.1) ⊥/   (B18.1) ⊙/   (B15) ⅄/   (C26) Ⴤ/   (B8)(B6) ═ Ⓚ/   (C27)   (B18) ⊙/   (C27)   (B18.3) ⸴/   (C21) ∁/   (C19) |||/

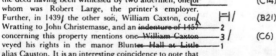

Ⓐ attached to Christchurch Monastery in the parish of

Figure 16.11   A marked up proof (courtesy of British Standards Institution)

Revised galley proof of text incorporating corrections

AT THE SIGN OF THE RED PALE

The Life and Work of William Caxton, *by H W Larken*

An Extract

FEW PEOPLE, even in the field of printing, have any clear conception of what William Caxton did or, indeed, of what he was. Much of this lack of knowledge is due to the absence of information that can be counted as factual and the consequent tendency to vague generalisation.

Though it is well known that Caxton was born in the county of Kent, there is no information as to the precise place. In his prologue to the *History of Troy*, William Caxton wrote '. . . for in France I was never and was born and learned my English in Kent in the Weald where I doubt not is spoken as broad and rude English as in any place of England.'

During the fifteenth century there were a great number of Flemish cloth weavers in Kent; most of them had come to England at the instigation of Edward III with the object of teaching their craft to the English. So successful was this venture that the English cloth trade flourished and the agents who sold the cloth (the mercers) became very wealthy people.

There have been many speculations concerning the origin of the Caxton family and much research has been carried out. It is often assumed that Caxton's family must have been connected with the wool trade in order to have secured his apprenticeship to an influential merchant.

W. Blyth Crotch (*Prologues and Epilogues of William Caxton*) suggests that the origin of the name Caxton (of which there are several variations in spelling) may be traced to Cambridgeshire but notes that many writers have suggested that Caxton was connected with a family at Hadlow or alternatively a family in Canterbury.

Of the Canterbury connection: a William Caxton became freeman of the City in 1431 and William Pratt, a mercer who was the printer's friend, was born there. H. R. Plomer[1] suggests that Pratt and Caxton might possibly have been schoolboys together, perhaps at the school attached to Christchurch Monastery in the parish of St. Alphege. In this parish there lived a John Caxton who used as his mark three cakes over a barrel (or tun) and who is mentioned in an inscription on a monument in the church of St. Alphege.

In 1941, Alan Keen (an authority on manuscripts) secured some documents concerning Caxton; these are now in the British Museum. Discovered in the library of Earl Winterton at Shillinglee Park by Richard Holworthy, the documents cover the period 1420 to 1467. One of Winterton's ancestors purchased the manor of West Wratting from a family named Caxton, the property being situated in the Weald of Kent. There is also record of a property mentioning Philip Caxton and his wife Dennis who had two sons, Philip (born in 1413) and William.

Particularly interesting in these documents is one recording that Philip Caxton junior sold the manor of Little Wratting to John Christemasse of London in 1436—the deed having been witnessed by two aldermen, one of whom was Robert Large, the printer's employer. Further, in 1439, the other son, William Caxton, conveyed his rights in the manor Bluntes Hall at Little Wratting to John Christemasse, and an indenture of 1457 concerning this property mentions one William Caxton alias Causton. It is an interesting coincidence to note that the lord of the manor of Little Wratting was the father of Margaret, Duchess of Burgundy.

In 1420, a Thomas Caxton of Tenterden witnessed the will of a fellow townsman; he owned property in Kent and appears to have been a person of some importance.

[1] See 'William Caxton'.

Figure 16.12   The corrected proof (courtesy of British Standards Institution)

between 'simulate' and 'stimulate' is only a single letter, but it conveys a totally different meaning.

Figures 16.11 and 16.12 show a proof that has been corrected and the final version of the text after correction. Figure 16.13 shows a typical piece of manuscript marked up for typesetting.

Careers in publishing

Although proofreading is not an easy job (and Figure 16.11 on p. 358 shows just how difficult it can be) it is a skill that can be learned, especially by those who have a good command of the English language. While many top editors would have a degree in English, and most editors would have at least 'A Level' English the

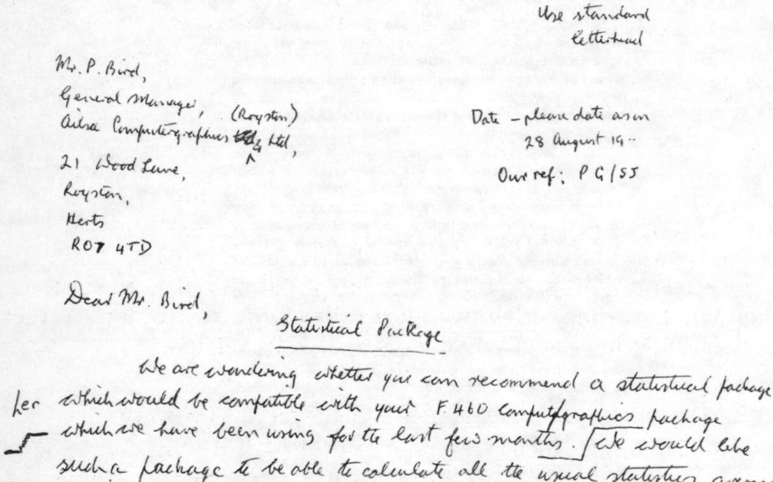
Use standard letterhead

Mr. P. Bird,
General Manager,
Ailsa Computergraphics (Royston) Ltd,
21 Wood Lane,
Royston,
Herts
RO7 4TD

Date – please date as on 28 August 19..

Our ref: PG/SS

Dear Mr. Bird,

Statistical Package

We are wondering whether you can recommend a statistical package which would be compatible with your F.460 Computgraphics package which we have been using for the last few months. We would like such a package to be able to calculate all the usual statistics, averages, quartile and standard deviations, etc from data generated in connection with our ordinary business affairs.

This data is fed into our host computer from terminals sited at various depots, factories, import reception areas and at Heathrow airport.

Any assistance you can give us in this matter would be appreciated.

Yours sincerely

P. Goodheart

Director of Communication

(A) It would help us greatly if you could give full details of the likely price, and the back-up facilities you can offer should we decide to purchase the package (including a 'hot line' facility if this is available).

Figure 16.13 A manuscript letter marked-up for typesetting (courtesy of Pitman Examination Institute) fact remains that qualifications can be acquired after leaving school or college. Quite a lot of editors do move across from other areas of work where they have good qualifications, and come into the publishing field some years after formal education. This is entirely desirable, because many of the books and learned journals which have to be proofread are about technical, scientific and sociological subjects, and it is a great advantage if the editor has a good background in the subject. Mistakes will not go unnoticed if the editor has a similar background knowledge to the author whose book is being proofread.

There are of course many other office procedures to be carried out in publishing firms, and a great many of them are quite routine. Any well-educated young person can get a start in the publishing field. A great change has come over the industry in recent years, and it has lost its dusty, rather Dickensian, image. Instead it has become an industry; with a huge turnover, a really remarkable technology, a warm, democratic place to work, simply buzzing with lively innovative writers, artists, designers – and the occasional glimpse of famous faces and great 'names'. There are good opportunities for promotion, and plenty of responsibility available for young, enthusiastic people who are prepared to work hard. It isn't just the writing and editing of books, but the marketing of them, the media presentation, etc., which is so helpful if a book is to succeed. When you have finished your Office Procedures course don't forget the publishing field as a possible user of your talents.

16.12 Organizing a business correspondence department

Communication is such an important part of business life, and affects so many people in so many different ways, that it is essential to think through all the necessary office procedures and arrive at a satisfactory (and economic) solution to the problems encountered. The basic problem is that we have a large number of people in any major firm or institution initiating correspondence (we will call them the 'authors') and sending it to appropriate destinations (the addressees). In between these two groups we have intermediaries who actually turn the authors' initial ideas into some form of correspondence; letters, circulars, copy for typesetting, telexes, faxes, etc. We will call these people the 'word-processors'. Any review of the business correspondence arrangements (and they should be reviewed regularly) must include a careful investigation of these three groups and how they interact.

The stages of such an inquiry might be:

(*a*) Discover who the authors are and what types of communication they are initiating (or likely to initiate).

(*b*) Discover who the addressees are, and whether they are within the firm or external. Which types of communication are best suited to them? For example, one firm marketing yoghurt in tubs and packs found that sending people a specimen order form and instructions on how to phone through a daily order, for next-day delivery, increased business fourfold. The addressees liked the simplicity of the arrangement and became steady, daily customers.

(c) Find out which types of equipment are needed to produce the necessary letters, memos, faxes, e-mail, reports, etc.

(d) Find out what numbers of 'word-processors' are needed and what skills they require.

(e) Draw up recommendations for management about all these matters and the reorganization, re-equipping of offices, retraining of staff, rewriting of manuals of procedures, etc.

(f) Implementing the changes once they are approved might include the following activities:

(i) Revision of the firm's letterhead to improve its appearance and give it a unique appearance, with a house 'logo', distinctive colouring and layout.

(ii) Specification of a house-style for correspondence and training of 'word-processors' to use it in a proper manner.

(iii) Training of management staff and supervisors to write business letters. Many such staff come to management late in life, having worked their way up through the ranks in some technical or service occupation, such as distribution, warehousing, etc. Their secretaries (the word-processors) are often better placed to write good letters than the 'authors' they serve. Managers and supervisors should be trained to recognize and use such talents, not insist on their own versions (even when they are wrong).

(iv) Developing a training programme for 'word-processors' to give every secretary or junior office worker a chance to develop. Moving such staff between jobs to broaden their activities and develop new skills encourages younger staff. It is part of that policy of 'grow your own' managers, which ensures that a broad range of talent is always available to move into higher levels of work as staff changes, retirements, etc, create vacancies.

16.13 Points to think about and discuss

(a) A new computerized typing system is programmed to count how many pieces of work are completed each day by the operator. It is claimed that this gives better management control of the staff producing correspondence. What problems do you think might arise in the adoption of such equipment?

(b) Figure 16.14 shows a memo circulated to all staff. Comment on the memo from the point of view of:

```
Memo to:  All clerical staff              Date:  1 July 19--
From:     Organization and Methods Department

_____

Following the memo from Mr Hughes earlier this week, the word-processing
investigation will start on Monday next.  All clerical staff are
required to take an extra copy of all memos, letters, reports etc pro-
duced in the two weeks commencing 4 July and 11 July.  These should be
placed in a file cover labelled WP Investigation and showing your own
name.  On each piece of work please add the following coding, as near
to the top right hand corner as possible.

A.................. This is the author's name i.e. who sent you the work.
P.................. This is the process used to produce the work   i.e.
                   copy typing, audio-typing, word processor, original
                   composition by yourself from notes etc
Rec................ Received at .......... time received
Ret................ Returned at .......... time returned

Any comments or notes may be added if you wish.

Please include all rejected or re-typed letters so that the full extent
of your work is appreciated.

Thank you for your cooperation.
                                     Rita Griffiths
                                     WP Project Teamleader
```

Figure 16.14   A memo from the Organization and Methods Department

(i) The total cost of the exercise.
(ii) Analysis of the resulting raw data.
(iii) Staff attitudes to the survey.

16.14   Rapid revision – business communication

Answers	Questions
	1 What are the main sub-divisions of business communication?
1 Spoken communication and written communication. Each of these can be sub-divided into personal methods of communication and mass-media methods of communication.	2 Why is it best to maintain a formal relationship in communication with staff, customers and clients?
2 Informality can be misunderstood, e.g. slang expressions may not be understood at all, or may be mis-interpreted by the person addressed.	3 What forms does this formality take?
3 (*a*) Business correspondence tends to follow a set pattern, with standard layouts, salutations, paragraphing and complimentary closures. (*b*) Business meetings follow standard rules of procedure, remarks are	4 List the elements in a business letter.

addressed formally 'through the chair' and an agreed agenda is pursued subject to 'points of order' (see Chapter 19).

4 (*a*) The letterhead, (*b*) the references to earlier correspondence, (*c*) the date, (*d*) the inside name and address, (*e*) the salutation, (*f*) the subject heading, (*g*) the opening paragraph, (*h*) the body of the letter, (*i*) the closing paragraph, (*j*) the complimentary close, (*k*) the signature, (*l*) the enclosures, (*m*) the circulation of copies.

5 What are the three common styles of letter?

5 (*a*) Fully blocked, (*b*) semi-blocked, (*c*) indented style.

6 What is a standard form letter?

6 A letter covering a number of difficulties that arise with customers. Such a letter can save time in correspondence. A tick to indicate which difficulty applies in the particular case under consideration is all that is required (see Figure 16.2).

7 What are standard paragraphs?

7 Short paragraphs held in the memory of a word-processor, dealing with particular difficulties that arise frequently. The author of a letter simply indicates which paragraphs are to be called up from the memory to compose the letter (see Figure 16.3).

8 What is a 'quick-reply' letter?

8 A standard letter divided down the middle into question and answer sections. Questions are asked on the left-hand side, and the correspondent is asked to reply opposite, on the right-hand side (see Figure 16.4).

9 What is a circular?

9 A letter for general circulation, without any inside address, and designed to be so striking and informative that it evokes a response from the reader.

10 How is a report called for?

10 Someone in authority appoints an individual or a committee to investigate some matter giving cause for concern, and lays down terms of reference as guidance.

11 What is the usual structure of a report?

11 (*a*) The title page, (*b*) the table of contents, (*c*) the summary, (*d*) the introduction, (*e*) the body of the report, (*f*) the conclusions, (*g*) the recommendations, (*h*) the appendices (if any), (*i*) any ac-

12 What is marking-up?

knowledgements, (*j*) references and bibliography, (*k*) the index.

12 It is the process of preparing copy for typesetting by marking any errors and giving instructions to the typesetter about layout, print size and style, etc.	13 What colours are used in proofreading?
13 (*a*) Green for the printer's corrections, (*b*) red for typesetter's errors, (*c*) blue or black for author's changes to the original text.	14 What are the main parties in the business of office communication called?
14 (*a*) the 'authors', who initiate the correspondence, (*b*) the 'word processors', who turn it into letters, memos, etc., (*c*) the addressees, who receive the correspondence and (it is hoped) respond to it.	15 Go over the page again until you are sure of all the answers.

Exercises set 16

1 In each of the following exercises pretend you are working for one of the following:

(*a*) Your own firm, if you are employed and are studying as a day release or evening class student.

(*b*) If you are in full-time education, write as if you were employed by your school or college.

(*c*) If neither of the above categories suits you, write as if you were employed by any firm that advertises in your local or national newspaper. In all cases it is a wise precaution to head each piece of work you submit *Educational Exercise Only*.

(*a*) You are interested in buying a fax machine which offers high quality printing and long life, without fading. You have been told that a firm called Whatfax Ltd, of 21 Hill Rd, Littlemere, Dorset, DH1 2SP, offers sound advice on the full range of fax machines. Write and ask them to recommend a suitable model and quote a price, including full details of warranties, service contracts, etc.

(*b*) Your firm has been asked by Balloons for Hire Ltd to sponsor one balloon for a charity balloon race from Lands End to John O'Groats. The cost is likely to be £1 250. Write expressing your sincere regret, inventing a sensible excuse, and enclosing a donation of £25 to the charity.

(*c*) Your firm is planning to run a seminar, for which it is hoped 300 top executives will enrol, on the subject of 'Safety in the Ports' – with particular reference to the ports of your own country. Write a letter to be circulated to six organizations that might have a hall, dining facilities and seminar rooms suitable for this event. Ask for the fullest details, including charges, menus for lunch and dinner, accommodation for out-of-town visitors, facilities available, etc.

(*d*) A firm has written to you offering to visit your premises and demonstrate their locking devices, which it says can be fitted to any type of equipment and prevent its theft. As your recent stocktaking reveals the theft of several items of office equipment and scientific equipment, you agree to a visit and give a choice of three dates in the near future. Ask for a prompt response, as your calendar is rapidly filling up.

(*e*) Your local Chamber of Commerce (see telephone directory) has expressed the view that too few firms and institutions are willing to complete its regular questionnaire on business trends and prospects. Write offering to appoint a senior member of staff to deal with this matter, and collect and collate opinions of managers in the various departments before completing it. Ask to be put on the mailing list for this project.

2 Draw up a standard form letter for use when returning cheques to customers. The following faults are the most likely to occur, and should be given a line or paragraph on the letter. Ask them in the opening paragraph to return the cheque once the correction has been made. Common faults:

(*a*) They forget to date the cheque.
(*b*) The cheque has been dated, but with last year's date.
(*c*) They forget to sign the cheque.
(*d*) The word 'pounds' is left out of the written part of the cheque, e.g. it reads 'Pay one hundred and twenty 59'.
(*e*) The amount in words and the amount in figures are not the same.
(*f*) They have altered the cheque, but the alteration has not been initialled.
(*g*) The cheque is postdated but you cannot accept a postdated cheque.

3 Draw up a standard form letter to be used by a fashion warehouse dealing with customers by mail order. The chief items to be mentioned in the order are as follows:

(*a*) They forgot to send the payment and you only deal on CWO (cash with order) terms.
(*b*) The cheque sent had some defect. Leave a space so you can tell them what is wrong with the cheque.
(*c*) The colour they requested is out of stock. You are sending the nearest to it.
(*d*) They forgot to send payment for the postage and packing. Ask them to send this at once, and leave a space to say how much.
(*e*) The goods were too large for the postal service and will be coming by rail on ...... (leave space for date). Will the customer please arrange to be in on that date.

4 You are appointed by a student body to supervise the money available in a charitable fund to relieve the distress of students who for some reason are not properly funded. Draw up a quick-reply letter to be completed by all students who seek help from the charity, asking such questions as you think would be necessary to establish that the applicant is in fact a student, and what his/her true financial position is. In the letter make it clear that there is a limit of £100 for any grant in any one term.

5 Devise a quick-reply letter to be completed by all tenants in a block of flats about the uses to be made of a surplus of £20 000 in the maintenance

funds to which they have all contributed. Various proposals have been suggested, including a refund *pro rata*, a reduction in next year's charges, and three or four improvements that could be adopted. Use your imagination as to what these might be. Remember that the completed form should have all the details you need to know about the tenants, as well as their views on the matters under discussion.

6   Write circulars for each of the following situations:

(*a*) Imagine you work for the publisher of this textbook and wish to send a direct-mail shot to all schools and colleges, drawing it to the attention of the teacher/lecturer i/c Business English. Tell them about the book, give all the details and offer inspection copies to those interested. Design an application form for an inspection copy, to appear in a tear-off section at the bottom of the circular.

(*b*) Draw up a circular to go to the chief administration officer of all large companies in an area, announcing a display of office furniture and equipment at a local venue. There are 320 manufacturers and wholesalers taking stands. Tell them you are enclosing two free admission tickets and further free tickets may be obtained by applying by telephone, letter or fax. Point out that the ticket details should be completed before arrival to avoid delay in entering the exhibition, and that children under the age of 14 are not admitted.

(*c*) Imagine you work for a charitable institution whose particular interest is to preserve links with prisoners in countries with oppressive regimes. Draw up a circular to be sent to all student unions at major educational establishments. You want to obtain the names and addresses of students willing to write on a regular basis to a particular, named prisoner. You also hope that the students will organize some event to raise funds for this work, or make some sort of donation from union funds.

7   You have been appointed chairperson of an *ad hoc* committee to consider the proposals for the use of a piece of waste land owned by your company. The possible uses are (*a*) as an extension to the car park, (*b*) as a site for a creche for nursery age children of employees, (*c*) as a leisure recreation centre for employees and (*d*) for a new pumping house.

Draw up the title page and introduction to this report, inventing such names or other information as seem necessary.

8   You are a security guard in charge of industrial premises. Last night you detained an intruder aged 14, who was leaving the premises through a broken window carrying one of the company's micro-computers. The 'boy', who proved to be a girl, was actually detained by your guard dog, who nipped her slightly. She had to have one stitch and some injections at the local hospital. Write an account of the incident, making up such details as you need.

9   You are a senior judge of the High Court who has been appointed to hold a public inquiry into parental charges of abuse of their rights by social workers acting on reports of child abuse by non-interested parties, i.e. neighbours, etc. Draw up a list of aspects of the problem about which you might feel it was necessary to collect evidence.

17 Personnel

17.1 The Personnel Department

Every organization needs a wide variety of personnel, i.e. a wide variety of human beings capable of performing the various activities which must be carried out if an enterprise is to be successful. Organizations must find people with the right skills, abilities and aptitudes, and, having found them, they must keep them loyal by a variety of incentives. Of course money is a great incentive, and an attractive salary goes a long way to finding staff in the first place, and keeping them once they have been found. Still, money isn't everything, and other features that go to make an attractive package to a potential employee include such items as a company car, recreational facilities, sickness benefits, favourable holiday arrangements, etc. Such items are often called 'perks', an abbreviation of the word 'perquisites', which is defined in our dictionaries as 'a casual profit additional to normal income'.

There is a popular misconception that the Personnel Department is a welfare department whose chief function is to take care of the employees. This is not really the case, although this may be part of the Department's work in keeping employees loyal to the organization. The true function of the Personnel Department is to ensure that the organization obtains such human resources as are needed in all its various activities, with all the necessary skills, abilities and expertise, so that the enterprise is never hampered from a lack of efficient workers. Unfortunately there are also times when an organization, through some ill-chance and possibly through no fault of its own, has too much labour. Then the Personnel Department has the unpleasant task of making people redundant and cutting the labour force, releasing on to the labour market those skilled people it has worked so hard to train over the years. One personnel officer wrote during a recent recession of the awful task of dismissing staff who were often personal friends, and of the relief he felt when, having got rid of them all, it was time to make himself redundant too. Clearly such a depressing activity does not sound much like the 'welfare organization' of popular imagination.

We may list the most important activities of the Personnel Department as follows:

(*a*) To recruit new personnel in such numbers as are required in all the various 'trades' and categories used in the organization.

(*b*) To induct these staff into the firm or company, making them feel at home and making them aware of any possible problems or hazards.

(*c*) Training them so that they acquire the skills and abilities they are going to need; and retraining them as they rise within the firm to higher and higher levels of responsibility. This is the policy of 'growing your own managers'. Over the course of years staff are raised to higher and higher levels.

(*d*) Setting standards throughout the organization by such devices as 'job descriptions', which lay down the qualities and skills needed at every level, so that those who get appointed to a particular post have the ability to do the job properly.

(*e*) Maintaining discipline throughout the labour force by following proper procedures for investigating incidents, warning those who are at fault, maintaining records of events that have occurred, etc.

(*f*) Dismissing staff where this is absolutely necessary, after giving the employee concerned adequate opportunities to explain or reform his/her conduct.

(*g*) Ensuring compliance of the firm or company with all the duties and responsibilities laid down by law in the personnel field. In particular these days it is essential to ensure that there is no racial or sexual discrimination in employment, and that the numbers of employees in the various groups correspond reasonably closely to the 'mix' of colours, religions and other groupings in the community at large.

(*h*) Dealing with welfare matters as they present themselves, e.g. bereavements, accidents, industrial injuries, sickness, nervous breakdowns, etc.

Table 17.1 gives some idea of the work of the Personnel Department, which draws its authority from the senior management (in the case of companies, from the board of directors) and influences what is done in every department.

17.2 Personnel records

A good system of personnel records is essential for any firm. It is unwise ever to discard personnel records, although eventually they do get 'archived' and stored away. One never knows when a request for back-dated records will arise, since often relatives approach us trying to trace a former employee, police arrive pursuing enquiries and former employees desperate to obtain clear evidence of employment may write in. Fortunately there are some really reliable sets of records available from firms that specialize in these areas, notably from Formecon Services Ltd, Gateway, Crewe, CW1 1YN, whose permission to use illustrations is gratefully acknowledged. They have

Table 17.1 The duties and interests of the personnel department

Board of Directors or other senior management
Personnel director or personnel officer (PO)
Range of activities

Attention to statutory details	Attention to boardroom or management requirements	Securing staff	Staff development
(a) Industrial relations	(a) Manpower objectives, as part of corporate objectives.	(a) Departments requisition staff	(a) Annual (or twice yearly) appraisal and merit rating
(b) Wages regulations	(b) Job descriptions	(b) PO provides job description	(b) In-house training
(c) Sickness and maternity pay	(c) Appraisal procedures	(c) Advertises for candidates	(c) Sideways movements to broaden experience
(d) Health and safety at work	(d) Disciplinary procedures	(d) Application forms sent out	(d) College-based training
(e) Sexual equality	(e) Grievance procedures	(e) Short-list drawn up	(e) Modular training for specialist jobs
(f) Racial equality	(f) Dismissal procedures	(f) Interviews	(f) Promotions as years pass
(g) Dismissal procedures	(g) Public relations	(g) Appointment of selected candidates	(g) Full professional qualification
(h) Redundancy arrangements	(h) Environmental relations	(h) Induction on arrival	(h) Prevention of wastage (unnecessary staff changes)
	(i) Trade union relations on cost and productivity	(i) Review at end of probationary period	(i) 'Grow your own' management programmes
	(j) Welfare arrangements	(j) Appointment confirmed	
	(k) Contraction of the labour force as required	(k) Contract of employment drawn up	

'thought through' all the procedures used in personnel offices and produced a range of forms to cover every eventuality. The full list is given in Table 17.2.

It starts with a **personnel requisition** form made out by the head of department concerned who wishes staff to be found to fill a particular vacancy. Naturally it requires the head of department to give clear instructions about the type of person to be recruited, the skills expected from a successful applicant, the likely experience such an applicant would have had and other factors that might be a recommendation. Such forms can be invaluable to any personnel officer and form part of an employee's records retained in the employee's data folder.

It ends with a leaver's folder, to be given to staff leaving the employer. This provides the leaver with a full record of his/her employment. There is a wallet for retaining documents supplied to the leaver, e.g. references, testimonials, a P45 for the next employer, etc.

Table 17.2   A list of personnel forms (courtesy of Formecon Services Ltd)

Ref.	Description
FS.30	Personnel requisition
FS.33	Application for employment (concise form)
FS.34	Application for employment (extended form)
FS.38	Pre-interview general test
FS.40	Job description
FS.42	Job applicant selection interview record
FS.43	Pre-employment telephone enquiry
FS.44	Pre-employment reference enquiry
FS.45	School leaver/pre-employment reference enquiry
FS.52	Induction checklist
FS.55	Training history record
FS.63	Statement of terms of employment
FS.66	Request for medical report and consent by employee
FS.80	Record of hours worked
FS.83	Attendance record
FS.85	Employee holiday record
FS.87	Employee job performance self-appraisal
FS.88	Employee performance appraisal
FS.101	Employee details
FS.102	Employee data folder
FS.103	Employee record up-date
FS.72	Employer's rules and procedures
FS.73	Dismissal/disciplinary investigative report
FS.74	Warning (record of)
FS.75	Interview notification
FS.76	Interview decision
FS.77	Termination summary (for employer)
FS.78	Termination summary (for employee)
FS.105	Leaver's folder

Specimen copies of these forms will be supplied to lecturers, teachers, etc., at a nominal charge. One point worth mentioning about such records is that paper records are still very much favoured by personnel officers because computerized records are subject to the restraints imposed by the Data Protection Act. The Act lays down certain principles, which have already been given (see p. 241). However, there are some exemptions. The Act does not apply to (*a*) payroll or pension records, (*b*) accounting records, (*c*) records of purchases and sales, (*d*) records aimed at financial or management forecasts, (*e*) matters of national security. But payroll records may not be disclosed except to an individual seeking his/her own records, or for purposes for which the person concerned has given his/her consent.

Such restrictions present difficulties for personnel records, which should ideally be kept for a very long time, and often contain personal details that should not be revealed to parties other than the personnel staff and the employees concerned. It is essential that those employed in the Personnel Department should be discreet and aware of the serious consequences that will follow any leakage of information about the personal affairs of any number of staff. Staff may take strong objection to public knowledge of facts revealed to an employer on a confidential basis. It is part of the induction process of staff moving into the personnel field for the personnel officer to make it absolutely clear that knowledge acquired from the personnel records must remain completely confidential. In general, paper records are more easily protected than electronic records.

A word or two about some of these forms is given below:

Personnel requisition forms

The recruitment of a new member of staff starts when a supervisor or manager somewhere in a firm completes a personnel requisition form and submits it either to his/her superior or to the Personnel Department. The form used may have been designed 'in-house', but Figure 17.1 shows the personnel requisition form from the Formecon series. It serves two purposes. First, it requires the department that needs an extra employee to give all the information necessary, so that a suitable advertisement can be drawn up, giving the qualifications and experience required. The form draws out from the manager seeking to appoint staff both the job description (we must be able to tell applicants exactly what we want them to do) and the person specification (we don't want to appoint someone who is totally unsuitable). The second use of the form is to serve as the original document for the personnel department in its attempt to fill the position. It enables the whole process to be started and opens the file on the vacancy. Figure 17.1 shows the two sides of the form.

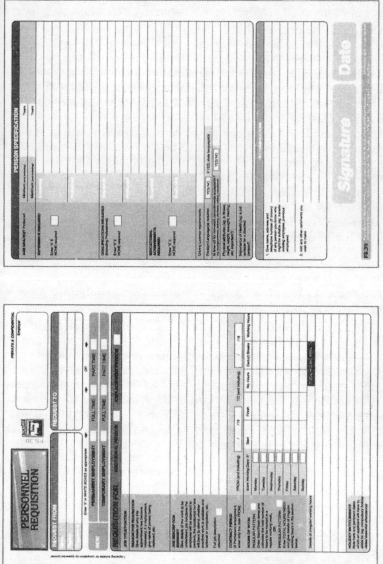

Figure 17.1 A personnel requisition form (courtesy of Formecon Services Ltd)

Application forms

The application form becomes the basis of the employer's consideration of the potential employee's situation. It calls for a list of the applicant's qualifications and experience, his/her previous employment record; his/her outside interests, etc. It may give the applicant a chance to demonstrate his/her interest in the job, and background approach to it, by asking general questions such as 'How do you think you can be of use to this company?' It may make the employer's situation quite clear on such matters as racial and sexual bias, with statements like 'This company is an equal opportunity employer and places no limit on the progress that can be made by any individual whose work merits promotion to higher levels'.

When completed by the applicant, the form facilitates comparisons between employees and enables them to be shuffled into a sequence of one sort or another. Thus the level of qualification might be one sequence, with the best qualified at the top and the least qualified at the bottom. However, it is just as common to reject people as being over-qualified for the post on offer as it is to reject them for being under-qualified. The question is how well do they fit the job specification for the post for which they have applied.

Employee data folders

An employee data folder is a device in wallet form to file all loose pieces of paper relevant to a particular employee while at the same time having on the front cover, where it is most accessible, all the main information about the employee. It forms the main element in an employer's personnel system, and has within it all relevant documents, starting with the application form, interview reports, induction record, contract of employment, etc. It encourages good practice and procedure, at trifling cost, and records such items as promotions, remuneration records, disciplinary procedures, sickness and punctuality records, career developments, etc. The front cover of a data folder, which is usually of such a size that A4 sheets can be filed away inside it, is given in Figure 17.2.

Induction checklists

The arrival of a new employee is a significant moment in the life of both the new employee and the employer. The employer becomes at once liable to the employee in all sorts of ways, e.g. to provide a safe system of work, to pay the agreed remuneration, etc. The employer also becomes **vicariously liable** for all the actions of the employee. The word 'vicariously' means 'through the actions of another person' – thus a van driver who drives recklessly while on the firm's business may enable an injured person to sue the employer, as well as the van driver.

It follows that the new employee should be carefully inducted into

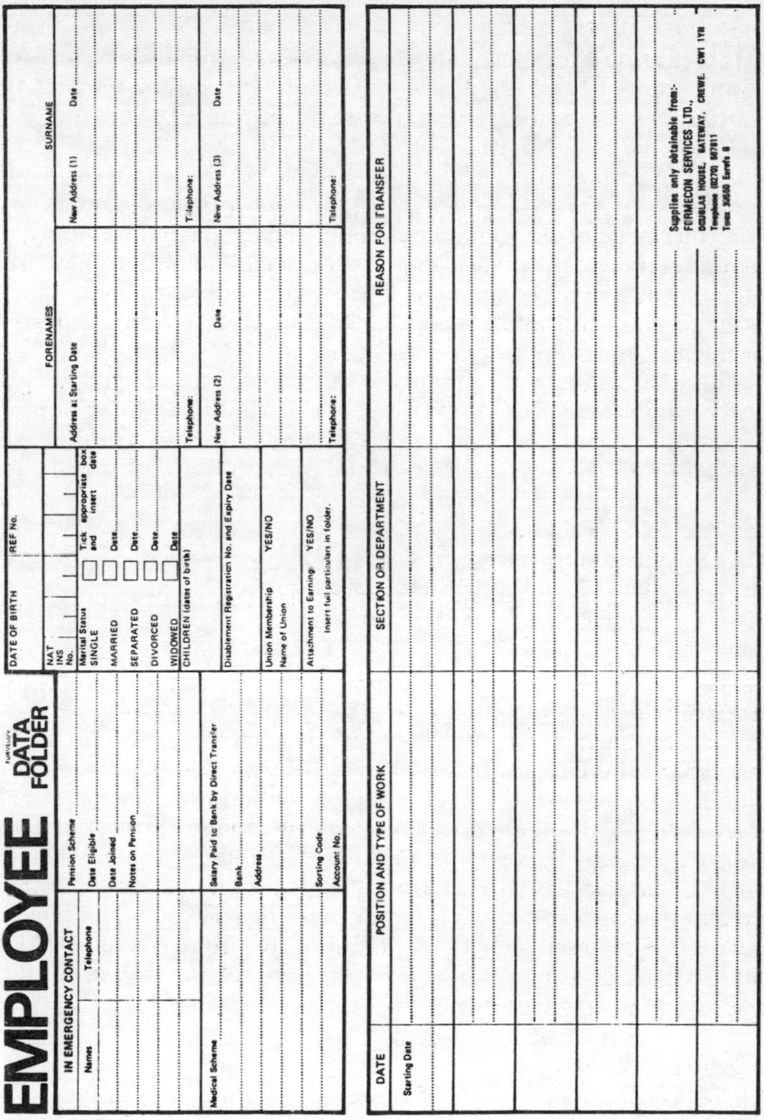

EMPLOYEE DATA FOLDER

IN EMERGENCY CONTACT
Names Telephone

Pension Scheme
Date Eligible
Date Joined
Notes on Pension

Medical Scheme

Salary Paid to Bank by Direct Transfer
Bank
Address
Sorting Code
Account No.

DATE OF BIRTH   REF No.

NAT. INS. No.

Marital Status
SINGLE
MARRIED   Date
SEPARATED   Date
DIVORCED   Date
WIDOWED   Date
CHILDREN (dates of birth)

Tick appropriate box and insert date

Disablement Registration No. and Expiry Date

Union Membership   YES/NO
Name of Union

Attachment to Earning   YES/NO
Insert full particulars in folder.

FORENAMES   SURNAME

Address at Starting Date   New Address (1)   Date
Telephone: Telephone:
New Address (2)   Date   New Address (3)   Date
Telephone: Telephone:

POSITION AND TYPE OF WORK   SECTION OR DEPARTMENT   REASON FOR TRANSFER

DATE
Starting Date

Supplies only obtainable from:-
FORMECON SERVICES LTD.,
DOUGLAS HOUSE, GATEWAY, CREWE. CW1 1YN
Telephone (0270) 587011
Telex 36660 Earth 8

Figure 17.2   An employee data folder (courtesy of Formecon Services Ltd)

all the special features of the new employment, possible hazards, restrictions on entry to particular buildings, etc. The induction check list in Figure 17.3. gives a useful list of points to be covered by the personnel officer or his/her deputy at the induction meeting, though it may also be common to call in certain specialists to handle part of

INDUCTION CHECK LIST — CHANCELLOR Employment Forms

EMPLOYEE — Surname / Forenames — DEPARTMENT — START DATE / /19

NOTE TO EMPLOYER — The object of good induction training is to reduce initial anxiety and enable the new employee to settle down into the job more quickly. Carry out induction on the first day. Tick each point when understood by the employee, ensuring that named personnel and location details are provided where necessary.

ON COMPLETION OF THIS FORM, GIVE COPY TO EMPLOYEE. ORIGINAL TO BE RETAINED BY:-

GENERAL INFORMATION

1. ENTER EMPLOYEE DETAILS (FS.101) ON DATA FOLDER (FS.102)
2. OBTAIN P45 AND SSP(L) LEAVER'S STATEMENT
3. PROVIDE WRITTEN OR VERBAL JOB DESCRIPTION
4. EXPLAIN RATES OF PAY (a) BASIC
5. (b) OVERTIME
6. (c) BONUS/COMMISSION
7. (d) HOLIDAY PAY
8. HOW, WHEN AND WHERE PAID
9. HOURS OF WORK (or shifts if any)
10. BREAKS
11. OVERTIME AVAILABILITY
12. DEDUCTIONS (a) SAVINGS
13. (b) CHARITABLE
14. (c) TRADE UNION (via Employer)
15. (d) OTHER (e.g. social club)
16. EXPLAIN PAYSLIP FORMAT
17. CONFIRM EMPLOYERS' HOLIDAY ARRANGEMENTS
18. EXPLAIN HOLIDAY QUALIFICATIONS
19. CHECK CONFLICTING HOLIDAY COMMITMENTS
20. PENSION ARRANGEMENTS FOR RETIREMENT
21. CANTEEN FACILITIES
22. SOCIAL AND RECREATIONAL FACILITIES
23. TRANSPORT AND PARKING
24. PERSONAL PROBLEMS Consult Ext.
25. TRADE UNION MEMBERSHIP
26. PRODUCTS AND/OR SERVICES
27. HISTORY OF FORMATION/DEVELOPMENT
28. STRUCTURE OF ORGANISATION
29. EDUCATION, TRAINING, PROMOTION AND TRANSFER
30. SUGGESTION SCHEME (give booklet if available)

RULES, HEALTH AND SAFETY

31. EMPLOYERS' RULES (give copy to employee)
32. DISCIPLINARY PROCEDURE AND APPEALS
33. LOCATION OF FACTORIES/OFFICE ACT
34. TIME-KEEPING AND RECORDING
35. LATENESS - EFFECT ON PAY
36. SICKNESS - REQUIREMENTS FOR NOTIFICATION AND SELF-CERTIFICATION/AGREED QUALIFYING DAYS FOR SSP
37. SICKNESS - EFFECT ON PAY
38. ACCEPTABLE REASONS FOR TIME OFF OR ABSENCE
39. ABSENCE: (e.g. maternity - SMP) EFFECT ON PAY
40. PROCEDURE FOR ARRANGING TIME OFF WORK
41. PROCEDURE ON RETURN FROM ABSENCE
42. SMOKING REGULATIONS
43. FIRE DRILL (a) WHAT TO DO
44. (b) EMERGENCY EXITS
45. (c) WHERE TO ASSEMBLE
46. (d) REPORT TO Name
47. (e) LOCATION OF FIRE FIGHTING EQUIPMENT
48. SPECIAL SAFETY PRECAUTIONS/HEALTH HAZARDS
49. WRITTEN SAFETY POLICY STATEMENT (give copy to employee)
50. YOUR SAFETY OFFICER/REP Name Ext.
51. SAFETY CLOTHING - SHOES, GLOVES, ETC.
52. EAR/EYE PROTECTORS, HELMETS, BARRIER CREAMS, ETC.
53. SAFETY CLOTHING Name Ext.
54. LIFTING AND HANDLING INSTRUCTIONS
55. HAZARDOUS SUBSTANCES, ACCIDENT AVOIDANCE AND TIDINESS
56. ACCIDENTS/DISEASES/DANGEROUS OCCURRENCES Report to Ext.
57. ACCIDENT BOOK/REGISTER Held by Ext.
58. MEDICAL/FIRST-AID ROOM Loca'n Ext.
59. YOUR FIRST-AIDER Name Ext.
60. GENERAL COMPLAINTS TO Name Ext.

61. TOUR OF PREMISES: Introduce to other members of department and ensure that they will help the newcomer to settle down. Explain each person's job. Point out location of toilets/washroom/lockers/cloakroom, emergency exits and fire equipment, first-aid points, medical room and canteen. Also, ensure that any special hazards and prohibited areas, etc, are identified to the new employee.

62. OTHER INFORMATION: (specify)

For Employer — Induction supervised by — Employee — I have received the above induction training:- — Date / /19

FS.52 R.4 Reproduction of this form in whole or in part requires the written consent of the Publishers and Suppliers. ©FORMECON SERVICES LTD, 1983,1984,1986,1987,1989 FORMECON SERVICES LTD. GATEWAY CREWE CW1 1YN Telephone 0270 500800 Fax 0270 500505 Telex 36550 Eurofs G

Figure 17.3 An induction checklist (courtesy of Formecon Services Ltd, Crewe)

the proceedings. This gives variety to the meeting and introduces key personnel. Thus the chief accountant might speak about pay procedures, statutory sick pay, statutory maternity pay, overtime rates, lodging allowances, etc. He/she will also collect the P45 form from those who have been in a previous employment. This form enables the Wages Department to collect tax at the appropriate rate.

It is not unusual to finish the induction meeting by a tour of the building or site, introducing further key personnel, and showing some of the products the firm makes and how it operates. On return to the original induction room, the new employees are given an opportunity to ask questions before being asked to sign their induction slips as proof that they have been inducted in a proper manner. A duplicate copy will probably be given to them for their own records.

Visible records

Where large numbers of staff are employed, a visible record system is desirable, and many firms which market business systems offer simple folders and binders that can be used for displaying records quickly and easily. The essential feature of such a system is a card for each employee with the name written along the top edge. The visible edge of the card contains room not only for the names of the member of staff but also for a range of visible marker 'flashes', which pinpoint particular information. Thus various qualifications could be 'flashed' by different coloured signals: supervisors in red, pensionable workers in yellow, registered disabled personnel in green, etc. A file of such cards is easily carried to a meeting with the managing director or the union negotiating panel, or the Staff Association annual general meeting.

17.3 Job descriptions

Part of the procedure for filling in a personnel requisition form is the drawing up of a suitable job description. Actually job descriptions have more than one function. When we first decide to appoint someone to a particular post, we must have a clear idea of the work required, and a job description is the management's attempt to describe as clearly as possible the type of work an employee will be required to do. However, we cannot specify in detail every type of task to be performed, and new tasks arise all the time. It is therefore wise to include in the job description some phrases that require the employee to be generally co-operative and helpful in any type of work assigned to him/her. One of the worst things from an employer's point of view is to have staff down tools and say 'I'm not doing that, it's not my job.' Such phrases as 'and will co-operate with Mrs X at busy times with mail shots and other publicity' draw attention to the need to play a full role in the department.

Equally it is unsatisfactory to an employee to be suddenly burdened with a number of tasks not envisaged as being within the classes of work that would be required when employment began. Some firms therefore, when job descriptions are under review, ask the employee to fill in a job description form too. This will include all the work that the employee is called upon to perform. It can be used as a basis for discussion with the member of staff and for comparison with the job description as drawn up by management. It will soon be clear that some areas of work are not included on one of the forms. These will be the subject of negotiation. For example, management may want the employee to take on an extra task, and it may be a matter for debate as to whether the time is available to do it. Equally management may detect that the employee has been burdened with work that some other member of staff should be doing. Some people love to delegate their work to others and have an easier life as a result. Correction of such unfair behaviour resolves the difficulty.

Job descriptions are not only used when recruiting staff, but once prepared are on file as valuable reference points for a number of activities. For example:

1 They may be used at the periodical review of an employee's work, when merit awards and pay increases are under consideration. Both the member of staff and his/her supervisor may be asked to comment on the employee's performance and whether the full job description is being carried out.
2 They are useful when training replacement staff. It is always essential to have staff trained to take over another person's work at a moment's notice. Holidays, sickness, promotions, staff giving notice, retirement and premature deaths cause vacancies all the time. The job description enables staff to be trained up to take over aspects of other people's work and thus ease all such difficulties.
3 In any dispute with a member of staff the job description is the reference point for judging performance. If performance is poor, this is made quite clear, in writing. An employee will then have a chance to correct his/her performance, and failure to do so may lead to dismissal. An employee who alleges unfair dismissal will find it less easy to succeed at an industrial tribunal in the face of several clear warnings in writing.

Listed below are some of the headings on a typical job description form. The layout of the form gives enough space for each of these points to be fully explained.

1 *Job titles*. A good job title accurately conveys the nature of the work the jobholder is required to perform.
2 *Purpose of the job*. A brief outline of the main reasons why this job is needed by the employer.
3 *Job location*. This states where the job is principally located, whether travel forms a part of the job, and details of any territory for which the jobholder is responsible.

4 *Responsibilities*. A description of those aspects of the job that require judgement, common sense and the use of personal technical skill(s), qualifications, etc., e.g. negotiating prices or making personal decisions regarding health and safety, directing the work of others, etc.

5 *Duties*. Details of the fundamental tasks the jobholder must do, e.g. operating a machine, taking sales orders, etc. Since most jobs involve a wide range of duties, it may not be practical to list them all here. This box concludes with the words, 'The employee must also perform any other duties the employer might reasonably expect'.

6 *Authority and discretion*. The limits of the jobholder's authority should be defined under this title, making clear, particularly in financial terms, the level at which expenditure requires approval from a supervisor.

7 *Liaison*. Many jobs include direct and indirect contact with other people (including persons other than employees) and this requires a description as to the scope of contact, the classes of employees whom the jobholder supervises and to whom the jobholder is responsible.

8 *Targets*. With some jobs the provision of work targets or 'goals' is a useful addition to the job description. These may relate to quantity, e.g. sales or production levels, or quality, e.g. reject rate.

9 *Conditions*. Many jobs have special conditions attached, such as requirement for the jobholder to be mobile or to have colour vision. Such conditions should be described in this section.

17.4 The recruitment of staff

Recruitment presents a number of problems. Not only has the personnel officer to find people of the right quality, knowledge and experience, but it is essential to do so at the least cost, and in line with legal and social restraints imposed by a variety of Acts of Parliament. Before considering the avenues of recruitment we must consider these aspects.

Cost

An average display advertisement in a large circulation national newspaper costs several hundred pounds. A similar advertisement in a local evening newspaper may cost as much as £100. A small classified advertisement costs between £20 and £35. If we use a local employment agency to find us staff of a particular type, we can expect it to cost us at least 1 week's pay for that member of staff, and if the person concerned is at all skilled, e.g. a fashion designer, it would be nearer 1 month's pay, perhaps as much as £2 000. Such agencies do save the personnel officer a great deal of time and expense, for much of the preliminary work of selection is done in the agency, and only one or two high-flyers are actually interviewed for the position. Certainly the costs are high if this method of recruitment is used.

Probably the cheapest way of recruiting staff is to ask existing staff who know of friends or relatives in need of a job to give their names and addresses to the Personnel Department, or bring them along one evening for an interview. There are no costs associated with this type of recruitment, and the existing employees, without knowing it perhaps, do a good deal of the selection process. For example, an existing employee is not likely to introduce a person who is a known troublemaker, or who has personality defects that make him/her unable to work and succeed in that kind of firm or company. The existing employees will have the possibility of adverse repercussions on their own careers in mind when they propose a new member of staff. Equally the new members of staff will have a sense of loyalty to the persons proposing them and will be keen to avoid embarrassing them in any way. The trouble is that there are racial and sexual overtones to this method of recruitment.

Racial and sexual balance in personnel

The UK has undergone some important changes in recent years, particularly the increased number of citizens from the Caribbean, Africa and Asia. Another change is the greater part played by women in the labour force and their needs for equality of opportunity. The trouble with asking staff to introduce relatives and friends for employment is that these introductions will tend to be biased, both as to ethnic origin and sex, towards the status quo. Thus those at present employing predominantly white staff will tend to be introduced to applicants who are also white, and male staff are more likely to introduce a male friend when expansion occurs, rather than to think of female staff seeking to break into an area of work previously largely staffed by males. The adoption of such a recruitment policy could even be viewed officially as a form of veiled discrimination, if it results in the personnel of any firm not corresponding in pattern to the ethnic pattern of the community or the sexual pattern within a profession or trade. In some industries it might be desirable to have a bias in favour of underemployed groups to redress the adverse balance in employment within a firm or company.

17.5 Filling a vacancy – the sequence of events

From the moment that a department sends in its personnel requisition form to the personnel department a sequence of events is put in train to fill the vacancy. We will presume that a job description is already available, so that we know what the job is, what grade it is, what skills will be required, etc. The chain of events may be listed as follows:

(*a*) Is there anyone on the staff who is already looking for this type of post?

(*b*) If not, is there anyone who would regard this post as a promotion, or an interesting sideways move?

(*c*) If not, what is the best way to fill the vacancy? Do we need to contact an outside agency, or do we need to advertise the post?

(*d*) If so, how should the advertisement be worded?

(*e*) The routine of sending out applications, considering the replies, drawing up a short list for interviews, interviewing and appointing the most suitable candidate gets under way.

We must now consider each of these ideas in turn, and view them from two points of view − the point of view of the firm and the point of view of the aspiring applicant.

(*a*) *Appointing from within the firm.* It is essential to consider appointment from within the firm, because if it is company policy to 'grow your own' managers, we must keep our word and at least consider everyone who has registered an interest in promotion or a sideways move. Even people who have not registered such an interest may have the necessary qualifications, and, especially if they have had good merit ratings in recent months, should at least be told that a vacancy is available before the post is opened to all comers. If there is a house journal, the vacancy could be mentioned in the next issue, and thus be drawn to the attention of all staff. If particular individuals are believed to be 'self-starters', and to deserve consideration, they could be sent a personal memo giving details of the post and setting a deadline by which they should apply, if interested.

From the point of view of staff, particularly younger staff, let us say this. You need to look ahead and think where you are going and what sort of position you envisage yourself filling in the firm in say 1 year, 5 years and 10 years from now. If an opportunity arises, one that is a logical step in your plan for self-advancement, do not hesitate to put in for consideration for the post. It may be others will have a better claim on this occasion, but you will at least have thrown your hat into the ring. Similarly, if you fail to hear of the opportunity until too late, it is worthwhile registering a protest − however mildly − drawing the personnel officer's attention to the fact that this post would have interested you. When the next opportunity arises, you will not be passed over, and in the meantime you may have acquired the further skills and experience to make you a more valuable applicant.

The appointment of someone from within the firm of course creates a vacancy in the post he/she has previously occupied, and gives someone at that lower level from outside the firm a chance to come in. Sometimes a small chain of moves results as people are moved sideways (to broaden their knowledge) or are promoted, before eventually the vacant post is filled from outside.

(*Note: waiting lists.* It is a sad fact today that many people who would dearly like a particular job are not accepted − after all, only one applicant can be appointed. It is a good idea if you are a disappointed candidate and feel the job would have suited you, to write and ask to be put on a waiting list, saying why you particularly regret being passed over on this occasion. The next time a vacancy occurs, the personnel officer may call you in before advertising the post just to see if you are still interested.)

(*b*) Using an outside service. There are a number of bodies charged with the responsibility of helping unemployed people or school- and college-leavers to find employment. Examples are the Youth Employment Service, the local job centres and specialist organizations like NACRO (the National Council for the Re-settlement of Offenders). Such bodies may not charge for their services, or even if they do charge for them, they will have done quite a lot of sorting out of the candidates to reject those who do not have the correct qualifications, or the wrong physique, or are unsuitable for any reason. This is therefore an economical way to find staff.

Other organizations have specialist knowledge about staff in particular fields, and will find staff with the right skills and experience, or the right flair (in the design field, for example). They do charge quite considerable sums, but they do have fairly expensive overheads to cover. For example, a 'head-hunting' firm scouring the world for a chemical engineer with knowledge about the extraction of oil from tar sands may spend a lot of money on long-range telephone calls before it finds a suitable candidate.

Many personnel officers use the services of local employment agencies to find low-level staff. To some extent these local offices specialize in particular fields, e.g. accountancy and book-keeping, secretarial and word-processing posts, etc. Their charges are reasonable, and they select suitable people for the post under consideration, thus saving you much time and expense on posting out application forms, vetting the forms when they arrive, interviewing, etc. Since they handle many staff acting as temps (temporary employees), they may have on their books people they know to be reliable, and who will be glad to accept a permanent post. Such organizations also have regular weekly advertisements in local papers and will advertise for a suitable person to help a personnel officer with a problem. They then handle all the applications that come in and send the best one or two applicants only for interview.

(*c*) *Advertising a vacancy.* A number of considerations enter into such advertisements. First, we must choose the best medium for the advertisement. Lower level posts are usually advertised locally, often in the 'freebie' press, copies of which are delivered free of charge to every house in most towns and cities today. The charges are not cheap: £100 is quite common for a small boxed advertisement, such as the one shown in Figure 17.4. It is usual to give the following information:

(i) The name of the firm or company.
(ii) A brief outline of its work, and its situation in the industry.
(iii) A brief job description and the qualifications hoped for from applicants. This reduces the number of applications from unemployed people who have no chance of succeeding because they do not have the necessary skills or experience.
(iv) Some idea of the salary payable, or at least a reference to the fact that the salary is negotiable.

Elliott Power Tools (Camside) Ltd

QUALIFIED BOOK-KEEPER OR JUNIOR ACCOUNTANT

We are a growing firm in the power-tools field. We need an assistant book-keeper or accountant to help with our accounts to Final Accounts level. Some knowledge of computerization would be a recommendation, as we are about to change to computerized accounting. This position would suit a young person, already part-qualified but intending to pursue his/her studies to full professional level.

Full details of the post, salary payable, etc., on application in writing to Mrs E. Langtry, The Personnel Officer, (Dept. E.S.) Elliott Power Tools (Camside) Ltd, 5173 Camside, Ely CB7 9QD. Or ring for an informal discussion on 0312 000715. Ask for Elizabeth Langtry.

Figure 17.4   A typical advertisement for recruiting staff

(v) Details of how to apply and an address for all correspondence. In urgent situations a telephone number and named contact may be given to encourage applicants to phone for an informal discussion. The advantages of such a discussion are that it reduces the number of unsuitable applications. A few minutes' conversation may reveal to the caller that he/she just could not do the job required. By contrast, it may reveal that the job is just the sort of post he/she needs, while the personnel officer may also sense this and urge the caller to apply, since there is a good chance of success.

(vi) A coded insertion in the address, e.g. Dept ES, may enable the advertiser to identify which advertisement produced the response. For example, the reference ES may indicate *Evening Standard*. This is useful in choosing newspapers for future advertisements.

Other points about advertising are that the wording must be carefully chosen so as to recruit on a fair basis; then allegations of racial or sexual discrimination cannot be made. For example, to advertise for a 'Girl Friday' (a term that relates back to Robinson Crusoe's helper 'Man Friday' on his desert island) appears to exclude male applicants, and a requirement to include a recent photograph has been held to be veiled discrimination, since it gives the firm a chance to exclude the applicant on the grounds of race and colour without actually revealing the true reason.

(*d*) *Drawing up a short list*. Applicants responding to an advertisement usually send a brief letter of the type shown in Figure 17.5, requesting an application form. From the forms returned the most suitable applicants will be selected for a short list. They will then be called for interview, and requested to bring with them such documents as are necessary to prove their qualifications listed in the application form, and the original copies of any testimonials sent. References should be taken up − preferably before the candidates are invited for interview − and a summary of the chief points for and against a candidate should be drawn up for the benefit of the interviewing panel.

Interviewing

The purpose of an interview is to assess the personal qualities of the applicants, to assess their character and test their knowledge of the field of activity they are intending to carry out. A more detailed description of the work will be given to the applicants at the interview, and any reservations they have about the post can be heard and answered. More is said about interviewing, from the candidate's point of view, later in this chapter (p. 386). From the firm's point of view it is usual to appoint a small panel to attend the interview if it is an important position. Usually the head of department that filled out the original personnel requisition will attend, and assume the responsibility for picking a person who can do the job that is required. He/she knows the technical details of the post, the equipment to be used, the level of work required, etc. Another member of the panel might be interested in the sort of co-operation that is essential between top level people. Is the applicant a stable personality? Is he/she honest? Will he/she co-operate with other staff and 'go the extra mile for the good of the firm'? Such a panel member might take the line, 'Why are you prepared to leave your present firm?' Is he/she not happy for some reason? If not, what is wrong? There are many difficulties in appointing new staff, and one of the worst is applicants' failure to take the job after all even when they have been selected. It is usual to ask outright 'If we decide to appoint you, will you definitely take the post or have you reservations about it?' 'Do you envisage any difficulties about the family, changing schools for the children, etc.?'

17.6 Job applications (the applicant's approach)

If we view job applications from the applicant's point of view, it is clear that the purpose of the exercise is to secure the job, and it is essential to show some degree of enthusiasm to be successful. At times of business depression this is not always easy, because it may be necessary to make several dozen applications. Every application goes through a number of stages, which may be listed as follows:

1 A brief letter requesting an application form for a post you have seen advertised.
2 The drawing up of a *curriculum vitae* (CV) to be sent with the application form when it arrives.
3 A covering letter, to cover the return of the application form.
4 A letter acknowledging the receipt of an invitation to an interview and confirming your intention to attend.
5 Preparatory work for the interview, including a serious attempt to anticipate the questions that may be asked and to plan the responses you will make.
6 A letter acknowledging the receipt of a letter of appointment, and confirming your intention to start work as requested.
7 Alternatively, a letter expressing your disappointment at not being selected, and asking that your name be borne in mind should a further vacancy occur, or should the person actually selected not take up the appointment.

As an alternative to 1 and 2 above, we could have a letter written to a firm whose activities we are interested in and which we should like to work for, although so far as we are aware no vacancy exists at present. This is a slightly more adventurous activity than the routine application, but it does have the advantage that it is probably the only application the firm will be receiving, and the person who deals with staffing will therefore give it undivided attention.

This group of letters seems a fairly daunting prospect, but once you have written a rough draft for each, they will soon become routine, and will present few problems, except the rather tedious chore of writing or typing them out each time they are required. Don't get depressed about this. You have to keep at it with cheerful enthusiasm. A draft is a rough guide both to the layout and the content of a letter, which you will then adapt to suit the particular letter you are writing. A set of draft letters is given in Figures 17.5–17.10.

If we consider a young person responding to the advertisement given in Figure 17.4, the letter might be something like Figure 17.5.

Returning the application form

Application forms vary, but are usually fairly detailed and give you an opportunity to list the qualifications you have already acquired and the previous posts you have held (if any). There is a document called a CV (*curriculum vitae*), which we can all draw up; it gives an account of our qualifications and experience. The words *curriculum vitae* mean 'course of my life'. It is well worth while drawing up a CV to cover your own qualifications and experience, and having it typed so that it is really presentable (see Figure 17.6). Run off a dozen copies of it at the local copy shop so that you always have a copy available. From time to time it is useful to update it as you gain further qualifications and experience. A CV is chiefly used when an application form is not supplied by the employer.

Since we only have one application form and it is easy to make a slip or two on it, there is much to be said for writing our answers on a sheet of plain paper first, before we complete any line on the form. Alternatively, photocopy the form at a local copy shop, and fill up this copy first in pencil. When you are satisfied with your effort, copy it out on to the original form and post it off with a covering letter. A draft of this covering letter is given in Figure 17.7.

Interviews

From the applicant's viewpoint an interview is a face-to-face opportunity to influence an organization in his/her favour, with a view to appointment. After perhaps years of hard work in acquiring a basic education, and some specialist skills, the opportunity so keenly desired may be thrown away by a shrug of the shoulders or a momentary sign of disapproval, e.g. of a firm's products. The approach to an interview should be as careful as the revision period

Mrs. E. Langtry,
The Personnel Officer,
Elliott Power Tools (Camside) Ltd,
5173 Camside,
ELY
CB7 9QD

Lucy Ann Jones
27 Canary Walk,
Wildflower Way,
Milton,
Cambs.
CB7 3TU
23 July 19..
My Ref. Job application No. 7

Dear Madam,
  Qualified Book-Keeper — Evening Standard 23 July 19..

  Would you kindly send me the application form and job description for the post referred to in today's advertisement in the *Evening Standard*.

  I am an 18-year-old college leaver who has just completed a course for National Vocational Qualifications Levels I and II. The subjects covered included Economics, Accountancy, Statistics, Business English, British Constitution, Secretarial Studies and Computer Appreciation — all at Level II standard. I also have nine passes at GCSE level, including Mathematics, Physics, Chemistry, Domestic Science and Needlework. The other subjects are covered by those already mentioned.

  I enclose a SAE for reply and thank you for your help.

                                        Yours faithfully,

                                        Lucy A. Jones

Enclosure:
1 SAE for reply.

Figure 17.5 A draft letter requesting an application form

Notes

  (i) Those already familiar with the writing of business letters can see that this is not in fully blocked style but in semi-blocked style. This means that the date, the references and the subscription are on the right-hand side of the page. This is more easy for filing purposes than the fully blocked style, because as you open the file to find any filed letter the references, etc., are more easily seen.

  (ii) Note the subject heading, which is underlined. It tells us the subject matter of the letter, and saves the personnel officer's time.

  (iii) The first paragraph, though short, is the vital one.

  (iv) The second paragraph is to convince the personnel officer that you are a genuine prospect for the post on offer. Whatever job you are applying for, it is always advisable to highlight the qualifications that are most appropriate for the post.

  (v) Offering a stamped addressed envelope (SAE) for a reply is expensive but worth the effort. It shows that you appreciate the costs of recruiting staff. Make sure the envelope is a suitable size — A4 is best, but A5 will do at a pinch.

Curriculum Vitae
  Name: Lucy Ann Jones
  Address: 27 Canary Walk, Wildflower Way, Milton, Cambs, CB7 3TU
  Telephone No: (0000) 412956
  Marital Status: Single
  Date of birth: 17 March 19. .
  Education: (i)   Milton Comprehensive School
             (ii) Cambridge Technical College

Qualifications: GCSE		Maths (C), English (B), Physics (D), Chemistry (C), Economics (A), Principles of Accounting (A), Domestic Science (B), Needlework (D), Computer Appreciation (C)
	NVQ	Level II Economics, Accountancy, Statistics, Business English, Secretarial Studies, Computer Appreciation Level I British Constitution
Employment experience		Part-time posts in shops, restaurants and travel agents. Six-week secondment to Industry course in keyboarding – Helpful Bank PLC, Cambridge (classified 'Superior')
Non-vocational interests		Travel, rock-climbing (Happy Venturers' Rock-Climbing Club). Amateur dramatics (Cambridge Playmakers)
Posts of responsibility		Member of Cambridge College Road Safety Committee Member of St John's Ambulance Student Section

Figure 17.6   A curriculum vitae

before an examination. One should prepare for the interview thoughtfully, trying to anticipate what the employer is looking for in an applicant, and anticipating the questions that might be asked.

The whole process starts with the arrival of the interview letter, which gives the date and time of the interview. Unless it has been arranged in a hurry, with a very short interval between the arrival of the letter and the interview, it is best to acknowledge the letter in writing. If the time period is shorter, phone and confirm that you will be attending the interview. Firms like to know what is happening. There are often three or four senior people on an interview panel, all of whom have set their ordinary work aside to deal adequately with applicants. If you intend to be there, at least let them know. Even more important, if you have already accepted another post, or

```
Mrs. E. Langtry,                        Lucy Ann Jones
The Personnel Officer,                  27 Canary Walk,
Elliott Power Tools (Camside) Ltd,      Wildflower Way,
5173 Camside,                           Milton,
ELY                                     Cambs.
CB7 9QD                                 CB7 3TU
                                        27 July 19. .
                                        My Ref. Job application No. 7

Dear Sir,
       Completed Application Form — Qualified Book-Keeper

    My completed application form for this post is enclosed. It is exactly
the opportunity I am hoping for, so I hope you will find my application
satisfactory and will feel able to grant me an interview.
    Would you please acknowledge the application's safe receipt by
returning the slip at the bottom of this letter in the enclosed SAE.
    Thank you for your courtesy and I hope to hear from you in due
course.


                                    Yours faithfully,

                                    Lucy A. Jones



Enclosures:
1   Completed application form
2   SAE for acknowledgement
----------------------------------------------------------------------------
                                    Personnel Dept,
                                    Elliott Power Tools
Date  . . . . . . . .               (Camside) Ltd,
                                    5173 Camside
                                    Ely
                                    CB7 9QD


    We acknowledge receipt of your completed application form, which
is receiving attention.

                            Signed . . . . . . . . . . . . . . . . . . . . . .
```

Figure 17.7   Returning an application form

Notes

(i) There is much to be said for the slip at the foot of the letter asking them to acknowledge the form's safe arrival. It is always frustrating to wait several weeks not even knowing whether your form has arrived — let alone whether it is being considered.

(ii) Such an inclusion also alerts them to the fact that you are well-organized and businesslike. It may impress them enough to put you on the short-list for interview.

have changed your mind about this particular application, let them know of this decision. There may be someone else they can invite along instead. Firms that are not informed tend to blame the college or school for failing to tell students how to behave in such matters.

A typical letter of acceptance is shown in Figure 17.8.

Preparing for the interview

Having acknowledged receipt of the interview letter, you must prepare for the interview. Firms usually take a good deal of trouble over interviews, and there may be three or more people present, which can be a little intimidating. Very often the personnel officer will begin by some words of welcome and an invitation to you to tell them a little about yourself. This is really inviting you to repeat the information you have already supplied on the application form, and which they have already read, but it does have some point. It will put you at your ease, because at least you know all about your own level of achievement and can speak about it confidently. It helps them assess your ability to communicate and your self-esteem. Some people have too high an opinion of themselves, some take an unduly

---

The Personnel Officer,   Lucy A. Jones
Elliott Power Tools (Camside) Ltd,   27 Canary Walk,
5173 Camside,   Wildflower Way,
ELY   Milton,
CB7 9QD   Cambs.
        CB7 3TU
        1 August 19. .
        My Ref. Job application No. 7

Dear Sir,

Interview 8 August 19. . 11.00 a.m.

Queen's Offices

Thank you very much for inviting me to this interview. I confirm that I shall attend as requested, and will bring with me the original certificates for the qualifications mentioned in my application form.

Yours faithfully,

Lucy A. Jones

Figure 17.8 Accepting an interview

pessimistic view of their achievements, while others have a nicely balanced assessment of their own abilities.

These preliminaries also enable them to test you out to a small extent. Thus, if you have weak grades in mathematics, and mathematics is important to them, they may try to find out a little more about you. Do you really dislike mathematics? What is the real reason for the low grades? Try to anticipate what you could be asked about your qualifications. Tell them the facts (not some covered-up version of the facts). Tell them clearly what you are enthusiastic about, what you are hesitant about and any real weak spots. Then if they say that they are really disappointed about your weak spot in one subject, tell them you'll work hard at it to raise your standard. Don't sink into despair, but say you'll do your very best to solve the problem.

They may then ask you one or two general questions, which gives you a chance to show a bit more than mere qualifications. Anticipate these questions before you go to the interview. Take a sheet of paper and write out a possible question and the answer you might make to it. Suppose they say 'You're applying to work for us here at Symonds Electronics. What do you know about the sort of things we do here?' This might be quite a problem, if you know very little about the firm. Find out what you can about the firm − if it is local, go down and have a look at it. Perhaps a receptionist or a security doorman might give you a little help.

Another popular question is 'In what way do you think your services could be of use to us here?' Most young people are so anxious to find a job and solve their own problems that they don't realize that the firm or company is interested in solving its problems, not theirs. They will look more kindly upon your application if you seem to be more interested in them than in yourself. At the very least you can reply that you are hard-working, cheerful, enthusiastic, punctual in attendance and unlikely to be absent.

You should also stress the level of attainment you have reached in certain subjects and that you hope these will prove to be of use to them. Emphasize that you expect some degree of in-house training will be necessary, and you hope to repay this by hard work and conscientious effort. Speak positively, not negatively. Assess your good characteristics and mention them modestly. Don't dwell on your weaknesses, but if they mention them, let them know that you are aware of them, and are doing what you can to overcome them.

It is usual to ask the applicant whether he/she has anything to ask the panel, and although there are some obvious things you do want to know (if they haven't already covered the points), such as the wages or salary payable, the hours of work and perhaps the holiday arrangements, there are other things that make a better impression. For example, almost every business activity leads on to some sort of professional qualification. There is a professional body in almost every walk of life. If you phrase a question along the following lines it may open up a useful train of thought.

> I am just a little bit in the dark as to where this post that I'm applying for could eventually lead me. I'd like to carry my education on in my own time once I've started work, and I wonder if you do give any sort of career guidance to employees. Is there a professional qualification that I should aim for, or anything like that?

They won't be able to give you a very clear answer unless you are applying for a position that leads clearly into a particular profession. So many people start off in one direction but eventually find their niche in another area of work. For example, you might start off as a cost clerk but move into the buying department and end up qualifying in the Chartered Institute of Purchasing and Supply. Commerce and industry today have dozens of specialist areas, each of which is a lifetime's study in its own right. The point is that asking such a question switches their minds entirely away from your inexperience and naivety. Instead they are already thinking of you as a serious prospect for eventual promotion.

17.7 Acknowledging the letter of appointment (or writing a letter of regret)

A letter of appointment is often couched in terms that constitute an offer of employment, and as such it is always desirable to accept the offer by acknowledging the letter and confirming that you will in fact take up the appointment on the date suggested. In any case it is only courteous to reply to the letter and express your thanks at this successful conclusion to the application you made, no doubt some time ago. Accepting the offer does of course make a binding contract, but in the United Kingdom a formal contract of employment is not issued at once − a little time is allowed to elapse so that if the employee should terminate the employment fairly quickly, having decided that the work was not what he/she had hoped for, the expense and effort of making out a contract would be saved. Figure 17.9 shows a typical letter acknowledging a letter of appointment, and accepting the appointment.

While it is always good to be offered an appointment, for every successful applicant there will usually be five disappointed job-seekers, for most 'short lists' consist of six people. It is possible that you will feel fairly indifferent if you are not accepted, because, on thinking it over, for example, you may have realized that the job wasn't really the one for you. If you do feel very disappointed, it does absolutely no harm (and it only costs a stamp) to tell people how you feel. All sorts of situations arise where the selected applicant

Mrs E. Langtry,
The Personnel Officer,
Elliott Power Tools (Camside) Ltd,
5173 Camside,
ELY
CB7 9QD

Lucy A. Jones
27 Canary Walk,
Wildflower Way,
Milton,
Cambs.
CB7 3TU

12 August 19. .
My Ref. Job application No. 7
Your ref: TJB/DL 10 August 19. .

Dear Mrs Langtry,

Letter of appointment

Thank you very much indeed for this letter of appointment. I confirm that I shall attend on 1 September to take up the appointment as requested. I am most grateful for this opportunity and look forward to working in the Accounts Department very much.

Yours sincerely,

Lucy A. Jones

Figure 17.9   Acknowledging a letter of appointment

gets a better offer, or is prevented from taking up the appointment for some other reason. If you write a dignified letter telling them of your disappointment, they make take you on anyway, and if there is any difficulty over the selected applicant, you will almost certainly get the position. Someone who really wants to work in that situation is worth ten applicants who are indifferent about the job (see Figure 17.10).

17.8   The welfare of employees

Most firms feel some sense of obligation to employees, and assist those who get into difficulties, especially if it is through no fault of the employee. Certain basic welfare facilities are provided in offices by law, e.g. first-aid facilities and canteen facilities. Many firms exceed their strict legal obligations by paying employees while they are sick and absent from work because of accidental injuries. Many provide insurance policies to cover their employees against death, so that some basic sum will be available to dependants. Many provide recreational facilities, sports grounds or entertainment for children at festival times.

This type of welfare provision is not motivated solely by generosity.

Mrs E. Langtry,   Lucy A. Jones
The Personnel Officer,   27 Canary Walk,
Elliott Power Tools (Camside) Ltd,   Wildflower Way,
5173 Camside,   Milton,
ELY   Cambs.
CB7 9QD   CB7 3TU

                                          12 August 19. .
                                          My Ref. Job application No. 7
                                          Your ref: TJB/DL 10 August 19. .

Dear Mrs Langtry,

Post as Qualified Book-Keeper

   I cannot tell you how very sad I feel that you are unable to offer me
the post as Qualified Book-keeper. I had such a good interview, and
have done so well in my examinations, that I did feel I had every
chance of success.
   While I appreciate that you must have had a better applicant than
me, I wonder if you would keep me on your books as someone who
really does want to work for your firm. There is always the chance that
the applicant you did select will have other offers and may eventually
not accept the appointment. Alternatively, some other vacancy which
you could offer me may occur. I really felt at the interview that I could
work well in your firm and prove to be a very useful member of your
staff.
   With apologies for troubling you further.

                                          Lucy A. Jones

Figure 17.10   A letter that refuses to give up hope

Such facilities reduce labour turnover, and therefore save money in
securing new staff and training them until they are competent. They
encourage staff loyalty, so that extra effort will be forthcoming at
peak periods of activity. Industrial unrest is reduced, sickness and
absenteeism may decline when such services are provided, and the
employee will consequently be more productive. The personnel
officer will play a considerable part in this type of activity, often
acting as management representative on canteen, recreational, or
staff association committees.

17.9   The Health and Safety at Work Act, 1974 (HSW)
However solicitous some employers are of the welfare of employees, it
is also the case that others are less caring, and over many years

some measures to ensure that systems of work were at least reasonably safe have been introduced. Regulation began with the Factory Acts of the nineteenth century, and became more detailed in the twentieth with the enactment of such measures as the Offices, Shops and Railway Premises Act, 1963. Today the major Act is the Health and Safety at Work Act, 1974. This is a wide-ranging Act, which underpins all previous Acts and reinforces them with requirements imposed upon employers. Some of these requirements are:

(*a*) A requirement on employers to ensure, so far as is reasonably practicable, that the system of work is safe and healthy, and that the welfare of employees is assured.

(*b*) This requirement covers many matters, such as the proper maintenance of industrial plant, the safeguarding of machines, and careful supervision of the use, handling, storage and transport of goods and materials. It requires proper training to be given to staff moving to new jobs in new areas, and the proper cleaning and maintenance of working areas.

(*c*) Those with over five employees must draw up and make available to employees a written statement of the firm's general policy on 'Health and Safety at Work'. This statement must include not only the general policy but the organization to back it up and the arrangements to carry it out. This will often include the appointment of a designated safety officer and safety committees, which will meet regularly to consider current developments. Often the personnel officer is an appropriate person to assume the role of safety officer and take the chair at the safety committee meetings.

EC law and health and safety at work

UK Acts of Parliament have always tended in this sort of field to enact general requirements, which could then be implemented in ways best suited to the particular firm or company concerned. By contrast, European Community law tends to be more prescriptive, and to lay down the format to be followed in implementing the regulations. The Directive 89/931, which deals with this subject of health and safety, has been called the 'Framework Directive', because it lays down a fairly close framework within which EC firms must ensure adequate health and safety controls. This framework has been brought into UK law by the *Management of Health and Safety at Work Regulations, 1992*. The 'Framework Directive' also says that detailed regulations for a particular set of circumstances must be introduced as 'daughter' directives. These will usually require governments to enact them into domestic law. The requirements about the safety of employees using visual display units and keyboard apparatus are an example of 'daughter' regulations, and they have serious implications for employers using electronic equipment.

17.10 The dismissal of employees

Dismissal of an employee is sometimes necessary. The circumstances may arise because of dishonesty, or other sorts of scurrilous behaviour. It may be that the employee is incompetent, or unco-operative to such a degree that he/she interferes with the smooth running of the organization. Redundancy can also be the cause of the dismissal. Under the *Trade Union and Labour Relations (Consolidation) Act, 1992*, an employee who claims unfair dismissal can appeal to an industrial tribunal. For this reason it is important for personnel officers to keep adequate records of any incidents in an employee's service that might at some later date accumulate into sufficient reason for dismissal. In particular it is essential when dealing with employees to observe the rules of natural justice. These are:

 (i) No man should be a judge in his own case.
(ii) *Audi alteram partem* (hear the other side).

As an example of (i) above, we may imagine an employee being dismissed summarily by a director on the grounds that the employee was insolent. In such a situation the director has been judge, jury and executioner, all in the course of 5 minutes. That is a clear breach of natural justice. Had a little time been allowed to elapse, the employee might have had time to apologize, and explain that he has a reputation as a bit of a wit and he let himself go too far. As examples of (ii), we may instance many cases where, by holding a formal meeting and permitting the employee to be represented if he wishes by a more mature person, the employee's side of the story could be heard. The director may be picking on the employee, or he/she may have troubles at home, and consequently be a bit temperamental.

An employer may always dismiss an employee who admits dishonesty, without notice, and may refuse to give a reference. If a reference is given, the true reasons for the dismissal may be stated without fear of an action for defamation. Bad behaviour of other sorts may also justify instant dismissal. Incompetence in that particular work would not usually justify dismissal without notice. A written notice to the employee that his/her work was deemed unsatisfactory might be better as a first step.

A reference is given by an employer as a gesture of kindness to an employee. An employee cannot demand a reference as a right – no legal obligation exists to give a reference. Where an employer is dissatisfied with the work of an employee, he/she is entitled to say so, and so long as malice is not present, the statements made or written are not defamatory. Malice is an improper motive. It would be malicious to make a false statement out of a wish to harm the employee, and this would entitle the employee to sue for defamation.

Personnel officers are naturally very careful to avoid statements that defame ex-employees. On the other hand, they have a duty to other employers to disclose circumstances such as dishonesty or scurrilous behaviour. There is some danger that they will be held to be negligent in the courts if they give glowing references when they know of some reason why that person should not be employed. A common practice is to insert a disclaimer in references. This disclaims responsibility for losses suffered by anyone placing reliance on the statements made. However, there is some doubt in law as to whether such a disclaimer will excuse an employer from liability if a deliberately false reference is given.

Testimonials and referees

Application forms often ask for the names and addresses of one or two people who can speak for the applicant, and support the application by their willingness to give some account of his/her past employment record, or school and college record. Young people often find it difficult to provide such references. It is a point worth bearing in mind in the last years of education, when students often take part-time jobs with employers and agencies who can provide just such evidence. Be solicitous of your own good name in all such situations and at the end of the employment ask the employer whether you may use his/her name as a reference should that be necessary. By naming such a person as referee, you do give the referee the right to tell the truth about you and cannot sue the referee for defamation if what is said is adverse comment upon you (so long as it is true). Where there is some chance that the person may change jobs or move from the area, an alternative solution is to ask whether the referee would provide a testimonial. This is an open letter, usually beginning 'To whom it may concern'. It gives a statement about the person named, his/her qualities and weaknesses, honesty, etc., and is supplied to the applicant in an open envelope to be used as he/she thinks fit. Usually a photocopy is sent with application forms, and the original is taken to any interview that is arranged.

17.11 The rights of employees

The rights of employees may be divided into two parts, personal rights and collective rights. These two sets of rights have been the cause of much controversy in recent years, and almost every year has seen some new piece of legislation about them. Even today the attitude of the European Community towards such matters tends to be different from the UK government's views, and further modifications of the law may be expected. The rights of employees are a major branch of law, and too big a subject to go into here, but a short list of the rights under each of the sub-headings mentioned above is as follows:

Personal rights

The controlling Act is the Employment Protection (Consolidation) Act, 1978, as amended. The chief rights are:

(*a*) A right to written particulars of the terms of employment (provided the employee works at least 16 hours a week and has been in employment for at least 13 weeks). These particulars must specify such matters as the date of commencement; the rate of pay; the hours of work; the entitlement to holidays; rules on sickness, injury, etc.; details of pension arrangements; the period of notice; and the employee's job title.
(*b*) A right to an itemized pay statement.
(*c*) Women have certain statutory rights to maternity leave.
(*d*) A right to a written notice of dismissal in certain circumstances.
(*e*) A right to redundancy payments in certain circumstances.

Collective rights

The controlling act is the Trade Union and Labour Relations (Consolidation) Act, 1992. The basic rights are (*a*) to belong to a trade union of the employee's choice, and (*b*) a right not to be harassed for refusing to belong to a trade union. Many collective rights will be exercised through a trade union, including the right to participate in an official strike, and to picket peacefully.

17.12 Staff training

Staff training may be divided into four main sections:

(*a*) *Induction training.* This enables the new employee to know about the firm, its products, its organization and his/her place within that organization. It also draws attention to any hazards in the working situation.
(*b*) *Job training.* This will teach apprentices and other new employees the particular skills they require and the routines and business systems used.
(*c*) *Long-term craft training, or professional education.* Over a period of years young employees will be assisted to master their own trades and professions, often by day-release courses at local technical colleges. For office staff full professional qualification in the chosen field of work is highly desirable.
(*d*) *Supervisory and management training.* This is designed to prepare the experienced worker for employment at higher levels. It emphasizes decision-making, self-reliance, self-restraint and an

awareness of the intricacy of business life and life in general. We do not expect simple answers to difficult problems.

17.13 Points to think about and discuss

(*a*) Charles Brown is starting work today straight from school. What types of training might be necessary: (i) immediately, (ii) in the first few years of employment, (iii) in later years (say 10 years or more after joining the firm)?

(*b*) Two members of staff are being considered for dismissal. Tom Smith is unsatisfactory in most ways, has a poor attendance and punctuality record, watches the clock and is off home as soon as his hours of work are over. Bill Jones is a union enthusiast who has brought sections of the work force out on strike several times recently.

What should be the correct management approach in these cases?

(*c*) A proposal that a staff swimming pool should be provided has been made by the staff association. Consider the suggestion, and suggest arguments for, and against, proceeding with the project.

17.14 Rapid revision — the Personnel Department

Cover the page with a sheet of paper and uncover one question at a time.

	Answers		*Questions*
	–	1	List the functions of the personnel office.
1	(*a*) To recruit staff, (*b*) to train and develop staff, (*c*) to devise adequate job descriptions, and a ladder of promotion, (*d*) to devise and operate welfare schemes, (*e*) to prepare contracts of employment, (*f*) to prepare redundancy schemes, (*g*) to dismiss employees, (*h*) to give references and testimonials.	2	What professional body is active in the field of personnel?
2	The Institute of Personnel Management.	3	What is job grading?
3	Job grading is a system of classifying jobs to define the skills needed, the qualities required by the employee, and the promotion prospects.	4	What forms should be sent to a person enquiring about a particular post?
4	(*a*) An application form; (*b*) a job description; (*c*) an information sheet about the firm, its products and the locality.	5	What documents should a new employee take along on the first day of employment?

5 (*a*) A letter of appointment, (*b*) a P45.

6 It is a programme, usually drawn up by Personnel Department, to introduce new employees to the firm and help them to understand their position in the organization.

7 The *Employment Protection (Consolidation) Act, 1978.*

8 (*a*) Employees who have worked for at least 4 weeks – 1 week's notice, (*b*) after two years' employment – 1 week's notice for each year of employment, (*c*) not less than 12 weeks' notice if employed for 12 years or more.

9 A folder in which an employee's service records can be kept over the years so that they form a complete dossier on the employee.

10 (*a*) The application form, (*b*) the interview record, (*c*) the induction record.

11 (*a*) Possibly the dismissal notice, the redundancy notice or his/her letter of resignation; (*b*) any testimonial supplied to the leaver.

12 (*a*) If all are to enjoy equal opportunities, it is essential to avoid racial bias and sexual bias in employment. Generally speaking, the range of personnel employed should reflect the range of races in the surrounding locality, and an unfair balance between male and female staff should be avoided.

13 Partly for humanitarian reasons, but also because such concern reduces labour turnover and reduces training costs, recruitment costs and the disturbances in customer relations that result from staff changes.

6 What is an induction programme?

7 What Act of Parliament controls the employment of staff today?

8 What notice is an employee entitled to?

9 What is an employee data folder?

10 What should be the first few documents of such a dossier?

11 What would be the final documents in such a record?

12 What is meant by (*a*) racial balance, and (*b*) sexual balance in the personnel of a business?

13 Why is the welfare of employees of concern to employers?

14 Go over the page again until you are sure of all the answers.

Exercises set 17

1 The company for which you work wishes to adopt a standard form of application that could be completed by all applicants for employment in its offices. Draft a suitable application form.

2 The personnel officer wishes to notify all departments of the firm that

Monday, 21 June, will be the occasion of a day's outing to Stratford-on-Avon in celebration of the firm's centenary.

Draft an internal memorandum from the personnel officer notifying all departments of the outing and the fact that the factory will be closed on that day.

3 In connection with staff appointments, write brief notes on (*a*) application forms, (*b*) testimonials, (*c*) referees, (*d*) P45.

4 Discuss the ways in which an organization may provide for the safety, health and welfare of its office employees.

5 Design a visible record card suitable for student records in a college office. Information is required concerning a student's address (including the local authority in whose area he/she resides), date of birth, course, department, examinations passed, name and address of employer, together with other relevant personal data. Your illustration should also indicate (*a*) the information conveyed on the visible edge, (*b*) the use of a signalling device.

6 A firm employs the following personnel:
There is a managing director to whom the general manager and two senior executives are accountable. Each of the senior executives has a secretary. There are three managers.
Personnel, with a shorthand typist and two clerks.
Production, with a staff of one shorthand typist and two clerks.
Company secretary, with a staff of three filing clerks, three copy-typists, three shorthand typists and two wages clerks.
The personnel manager reports to one senior executive.
The production manager reports to the other senior executive.
The company secretary reports to the general manager.

Make out an organization chart, showing clearly the lines of authority.

7 You are a member of the Personnel Department of a large industrial organization. What information would you want the head of another department to give when asking you to find a new employee?

(*a*) Design a record card for use in a personnel department, with provision for the following information:

Employee's name	Date left
Employee's address	Date of birth
Department	Education and qualifications
Date joined	Job title
	Salary

Fill in the relevant information as for a junior clerk.

(*b*) What means can you suggest for quick recognition of cards of a particular department?

8 What do you regard as the main personal qualities and abilities necessary for (i) a receptionist, (ii) a copy-typist, (iii) a filling and records clerk?
You are employed in the personnel department of a large concern:

(*a*) Draft an advertisement to appear in the press for a vacancy for a telephonist.

(*b*) What qualities, knowledge and skill do you consider the successful applicant should possess?

(*c*) Why is it important for an organization to have a competent telephonist?

9   You are asked to draw up a holiday rota (2 weeks' holiday each) for the ten members of your staff covering the months of July, August and September. They are as follows:

Yourself	Manager in charge
Mr A	Your deputy
Miss B	Telephonist
Miss C	Typist-telephonist
Mrs E	General clerk (with past wages experience)
Mr D	General clerk
Mr F	Wages clerk and book-keeper
Miss G	Typist
Miss H	Personal secretary
Mr J	Junior accountant.

Miss B is to be married on Saturday, 1 July, and will be on honeymoon for the next 2 weeks. Mr J's wife is a nurse and has had to book her holiday from 5 August to 19 August. Mr F prefers a September vacation.

10   The four chief aspects of your department's work are (*a*) staff recruitment, (*b*) staff training, (*c*) staff records, (*d*) wages.

Topman and Deputy supervise staff recruitment and also assist with training. Training is carried out chiefly by Knowall, Knowhow and Adviser. Records are kept by Loggitt and wages are prepared by Cashman. Adviser at one time was in charge of records and Knowall was at one time wages clerk. In the 5-week period commencing on 4 April all seven of these staff have to attend a 1-week course on computer appreciation at the staff training college. Devise a rota which will ensure that all aspects of the department's activities are kept going during this period.

11   Wild, Brown and partners, solicitors, of 2174 High St, Lowport, LD7 2HB, require a school-leaver to train for general office duties and legal work concerned with local court procedures. They require a good general educational level, with examination passes in Mathematics and English. Secretarial or keyboard skills will be a recommendation. The salary is negotiable, depending on age and qualifications. Help with travel expenses is possible, or, to someone prepared to move to the locality, help with lodgings may be possible. Applications to K. Newbold, or telephone Lowport 217656. Draft a suitable advertisement for the *Lowport Advertiser*.

12   Engineering PLC seeks a trainee management accountant, preferably someone with experience of the engineering industry and a basic knowledge of book-keeping. Computer experience would be a recommen-

dation. The applicant would have the chance to begin a career in the costing department, with student membership of the Chartered Institute of Management Accountants. The entry requirements of the Institute must be met before this can be arranged. Salary negotiable according to age, qualifications, etc. Applications to the Personnel Officer, at The Blackberry Industrial Site, Coventry, CV2 7SP. Draft a suitable advertisement for the *Coventry Freebie News*.

13   In the following exercises you are asked to do certain things connected with job applications. It depends upon your circumstances how you can best arrange to deal with these questions. Ideally you should attempt them all.

(*a*) You want to get an application form for a job advertised at Crow Ltd for a junior accounts assistant. As the time is short, you decide to telephone for an application form. With a fellow student, act out the part of the applicant at one end of the call, and the receptionist (and anyone else) at the other end of the call.
   Your fellow students might like to comment on your performance. Perhaps someone else could do it better.

(*b*) Write a letter applying to Richmont PLC at St Peter's Place, Crosby Court, London, EC2 1DP, for the application form for the post of trainee sales agent (computer databases). Give the company details of your own educational background, emphasizing any that appear to relate particularly to this type of post.

(*c*) Write a letter to the Countryshire County Council, asking for details of a post advertised in your local newspaper for a trainee social worker. Give some details of your qualifications to date to persuade them that you are a worthwhile applicant for the post.

(*d*) Make a telephone call to John Brown, the personnel officer at Countryshire County Council, to say that the form you have been sent refers to residential posts only. Explain that as you have family responsibilities (caring for an invalid sister), you cannot take up residential work, and ask whether there is any point in filling out the form. (Let us imagine in fact that the CCC has sent the wrong form.) One person should play the applicant, and another the receptionist and other people at the county council end. Other students present should appraise the speakers' abilities to communicate by telephone.

(*e*) Write a letter to accompany your completed application form for the post of Transport Clerk at XYZ Freight Forwarding Ltd, Oxford Way, Ely, Cambs, CB19 3DP. In your letter refer to the fact that you have not enclosed your original certificates as you are uneasy about losing them, but say you have sent photocopies of them instead, and will produce the originals at any interview to which you should be called.

(*f*) Write a letter of thanks to Mastercare-Services Ltd for the interview offered you on Friday 28 May 19.. at the Old School House, Chelderbury, Oxon., OX10 9QE. The interview is at 9.30 am. Confirm that you will attend and will present, at the interview, the certificates the company requires to see.

(*g*) Phone Peter Thompson, the personnel officer at the Superior Press Ltd, on 0000 429510, to thank him for the appointment at 2.30 pm on Friday 22 June 19.. Explain that you will be unable to attend that interview as you have an appointment with another employer at that time. Can he offer you an alternative appointment please? One person should play the applicant and another the receptionist (and other people) at Superior Press Ltd. Other students present should appraise the speaker's abilities to communicate by telephone.

(*h*) Phone Emma Wright, the personnel officer at Heighly Engineering Ltd, to express your regrets that you will not be attending the interview at 10.30 am on Friday 17 May 19.. as you have already accepted an offer of employment elsewhere. At the same time tell her you do have a friend with very similar qualifications to your own who would really like to be interviewed. Is there any chance that he could take your place? Give the friend's name and address, and tell Ms Wright that you will arrange for him to send a CV by recorded delivery today addressed to her personally. (In the meantime will she please send him an interview letter.) Don't forget to thank her for her courtesy. One person should play the part of the applicant, and one the parts of the receptionist and the personnel officer. Other students should appraise and criticize their efforts.

14   With each of these questions write down what you would say in replying to a member of an interview panel:

(*a*) You seem to have done quite well in a range of different subjects. Which subjects do you think are your best subjects? And which subjects would you say are your worst?

(*b*) To some extent we like all new employees to start at the bottom, even though they may be quite well qualified, as you are. How do you think you would react if a certain amount of quite routine, humdrum work was allocated to you in the first few months?

(*c*) We have had cases in the past where well-qualified people have adopted a superior tone when dealing with lower level staff, such as receptionists, porters, shop-floor staff, car-park attendants, etc. What is your own attitude to such staff? Do you think you would be likely to have any difficulties of that sort?

(*d*) We have a no-smoking policy at all times, except in the car-parking areas. Is that likely to be a problem to you?

(*e*) The post you are being offered is one where you may, on the firm's behalf, develop devices and systems that will be patented and be a source of major revenue for the firm. The legal position is that what is developed in the firm's time, using the firm's facilities, belongs to the firm and not the employee. Naturally an employee who is particularly successful in such matters gets well rewarded – but do you have any problem with the underlying principle?

(*f*) If you come to work for us, we shall spend, over the course of the years, a great deal of money on training you and teaching you many things. If you leave us as soon as you are trained and go to some other employer, we have of course wasted a great deal of money. How loyal do you think you are likely to be to the company if we offer you a position?

(g) Forgive me for asking this question, but we do have to ask it. Have you at any time been the subject of investigation by the police, or charged with any offence?

(h) You are applying for a post that requires you to handle finances. It is usual for employers to ask such people to take out an insurance policy called a fidelity bond. This requires you to fill up a proposal form, which you must answer honestly, and one of the questions asks whether you have ever been charged with an offence about financial matters. It also asks whether you have been made bankrupt in any country. Would you have any objection to completing such a proposal form? I should explain that what this policy means is that if you should at any time abscond with funds, we could claim for the loss, provided the theft had been notified to the police.

(i) This does not apply to the post you are applying for at present, but if you gain promotion, it is sometimes helpful if you can drive a car. Do you drive at present? Are you likely to learn to drive a car in the near future?

(j) You say you drive a car. Do you have a clean licence?

(k) Do you have any family circumstances you wish to reveal to us?

(l) Are you disabled in any way? (This does not necessarily affect our ability to offer you employment, but we are obliged by law to employ a certain quota of disabled people and if you do have a registered disability you should reveal it to us for inclusion in our returns to the disablement officer.)

(m) Who is your next of kin? (In case of sudden illness, etc., we need to know whom to contact.)

(n) It is sometimes necessary to move staff around the country and even to destinations abroad, though we try to limit this to those aged 21 and over. What is your view of such a requirement, given that help with accommodation, moving expenses, etc., would be given?

(o) If we offer you employment, do you think you will accept the appointment?

(p) If we find we cannot offer you a post at present, we might like to keep you as a reserve candidate. This is because we sometimes get let down by our first choice, and then we might be able to offer the position to you. Would you like to be kept as a reserve candidate or not?

18 Accounting and payment procedures

18.1 The functions of the Accounts Department

The Accounts Department is one of the most important departments in any firm, and the accountant is always a senior member of staff, often with a seat on the board of the company. In earlier times accounting was chiefly concerned with keeping a record of the transactions between the firm and other firms. Debtors' and creditors' accounts were kept, using a system of **double-entry book-keeping**. Although these records are still very important, the work of the accountant has extended to cover every aspect of the enterprise. The accounts department will account to the following:

(a) The individual employee for wages, expenses, commission, etc.

(b) The supplier for goods and services supplied.

(c) The management for the profitability or otherwise of the enterprise.

(d) The government for its share of the profits (corporation tax or income tax) and for value added tax, national insurance contributions, payments from employees under the pay as you earn scheme, etc.

(e) Outside institutions, where it collects funds on their behalf, e.g. contributions to charitable bodies like Dr Barnardo's Homes are often deducted by firms from employees' salaries.

Within the firm the **management accountant** will prepare costing figures that not only show what units of production are costing but also show future **cost estimates**. As production proceeds, a check on actual costs against estimated costs can be made. If actual costs are greater than estimated costs, an enquiry can be made into the reasons for the difference, and corrective measures can be taken. This procedure is called **variance analysis**.

Similarly, the financial accountant will prepare **budgets** for each department's expenditure and will watch to see whether a department is overspending. An urgent memo to the head of the department exceeding its budget will lead to a reduction in expenditure in line with the budget of money available.

18.2 Double-entry book-keeping

The accounts department keeps its records by a system known as double-entry book-keeping. This system was developed in the Middle Ages by the merchants of Lombardy in northern Italy, who later gave their name to Lombard Street, the banking centre of the City of London. Figure 18.1 illustrates the system, and although it is a complex diagram, the reader will find it repays close study, using the notes below as a guide. Of course today the double-entry system would usually be computerized, with the computer receiving batches of information about invoices received or dispatched, payments in and out, etc., but the computerized system still adheres to the basic entries indicated in Figure 18.1.

(*a*) *Every transaction has an original document.* These documents, many of which are described in this book (for a full description, see *Book-keeping Made Simple*), may be:

(i) Invoices.	(v) Statements.
(ii) Debit notes.	(vi) Receipts.
(iii) Credit notes.	(vii) Petty cash vouchers.
(iv) Cheques.	(viii) One of many other documents.

Whenever any business transaction that requires an accounting record takes place, a document will be prepared and passed to the accounts department.

(*b*) *These documents are then entered in the books of original entry.* Books of original entry are often called **day books**, because we enter items in them day by day in chronological order. The French word for a day book is *journal*, so some firms call them journals. The most common in use are:

   (i) A purchases day book.
  (ii) A sales day book.
 (iii) A purchases returns day book.
 (iv) A sales returns day book.
  (v) A journal proper (this is used for all the rarer entries, like dishonoured cheques, bad debts, purchases of assets, etc.).
 (vi) Cash books.
(vii) Petty cash books.

Where a computerized system is being used, the documents of a particular type (say the purchase invoices) would be batched up and encoded for the key operator, who would then be able to key the information into machine language for processing by the computer. Later, if required, a print-out of the appropriate day book would be run off, and held on file for reference as and when required.

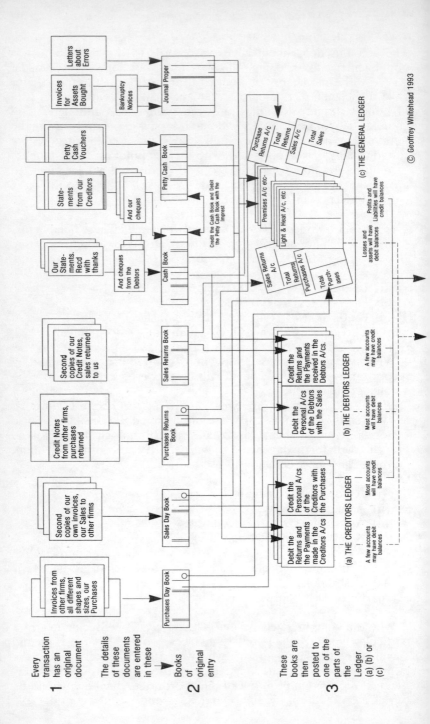

© Geoffrey Whitehead 1993

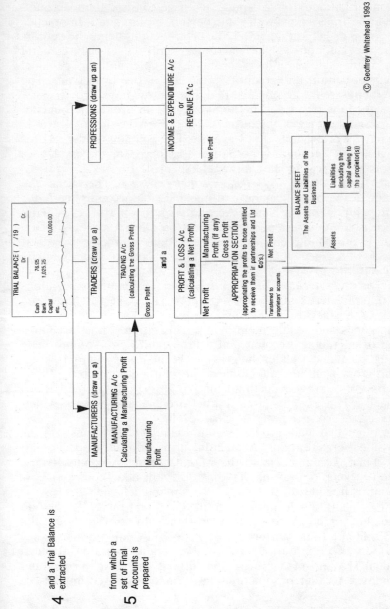

4 and a Trial Balance is extracted

5 from which a set of Final Accounts is prepared

Figure 18.1 Double-entry book-keeping

© Geoffrey Whitehead 1993

(*c*) *The day books are then posted to the ledger*. The ledger is the most important book of account. Each page consists of an 'account' of the firm's transactions with some person, firm or good. In practice the ledger is usually sub-divided, the chief sections being the debtors ledger, the creditors ledger and the general ledger. The general ledger houses all the other accounts that are not the personal accounts of debtors and creditors. They are of two main types. The **real accounts** are the accounts of real things owned by the business — the assets of the business. The **nominal accounts** are the accounts of the losses and profits of the business. The word 'nominal' means 'in name only'. For example, the wages account contains all the records of wages paid, but there is nothing really there, for the employees have taken the real money home and spent it.

(*d*) *A Trial Balance of the ledger is then extracted*. This checks the accuracy of the book-keeping and marshals the accounts ready for the preparation of the Final Accounts of the business. A Trial Balance is simply a list of the balances on all the accounts in the ledger. If the double entries have been done correctly, the debit balances will exactly balance the credit balances, and the Trial Balance is said to 'agree'.

(*e*) *The Final Accounts are then drawn up*. Different organizations have different types of 'Final Accounts'. The largest of the three groups of businesses is the one engaging in trade (commerce), buying goods and selling them again. This group's 'final accounts' consist of a Trading Account and a Profit and Loss Account. The Trading Account calculates the **gross profit**, i.e. the profit on trading, but this gross profit figure then has to be whittled down in the Profit and Loss Account by deducting from the gross profit all the various overhead expenses. This gives the **net profit** of the business. 'Net' means 'clean', so 'net profit' is clean profit.

The other two main groups are the manufacturing firms and the professional organizations. A manufacturing firm has a special part of its 'Final Accounts' called the Manufacturing Account. It then goes on to keep the normal Trading Account and Profit and Loss Account as it trades in the goods it has manufactured.

Professional firms do not engage in trade, and therefore they do not need a Trading Account. Similarly, they do not usually use the term Profit and Loss Account, since a surgeon would not like to say 'I made £5 000 profit out of Mrs Jones' appendix operation'. Instead the 'final account' of a professional firm is called an **Income and Expenditure Account**, or sometimes the term **Revenue Account** is used.

18.3 The computerization of double entry

Chapter 14 of this book gives a detailed account of the use of computers in office procedures, and in that chapter some reference has been made to the computerization of book-keeping procedures in particular. A whole range of programs is available, and a variety of choices presented to the accountant. From start to finish we may list the following different ways to proceed; some of them are more suitable for very small businesses and some are only possible for the very largest organizations, such as multinational corporations and nationalized industries. The list reads:

(*a*) Choose a very simple system such as Micro-Simplex Plus already described in Chapter 14.4 (see pp. 284−5).

(*b*) Make arrangements with an organization such as The Accounting Centre, Elscott House, Arcadia Ave, Finchley Central, London, N3 2JE. They receive the data of other firms and process it.

(*c*) Buy from a local dealer a full set of accounting software such as 'Sage Sterling'. This software is typical of the very best software packages available, and is distributed through 1 600 local dealers. There is a free hotline available for the first 3 months after purchase, and this hotline is then available at any time for a modest annual fee. You may write to The Sage Group Ltd, Benton Park Rd, Newcastle upon Tyne, NE7 7LZ.

There are of course other software houses, and the most reliable guide to the market is Section Z of the *Reference Book for the Self-employed and Smaller Businesses*, published by Croner Publications Ltd, which is available in most libraries.

(*d*) For those with very specialist needs it is of course possible to have dedicated software written by a software house, to suit a firm's particular requirements. However, this is hardly ever necessary today for accountancy purposes, as there are so many packages available and they meet almost every need.

How computers have changed book-keeping

Figure 18.1 shows how the double entry book-keeping system works. If we wish to see how computers have modified book-keeping it is useful to redraw this chart, in computerized form, and this is done in Figure 18.2. The chart is largely self-explanatory. It features sales procedures in particular, other procedures are similar.

It is not usual for computers to prepare final accounts, although they can be programmed to do so. The point here is that the cost of a program to make decisions at the Final Accounts level is greater than the cost of the work saved. Generally speaking, the preparation of Final Accounts from the print-outs of the ledgers supplied by the computer is a straightforward task easily carried out manually. If there are a good many decisions to be made at 'Final Accounts' stage the accountant will usually do the accounts on a 'spreadsheet' program, but simpler systems may actually have a standard arrangement computerized. For example, Micro-Simplex Plus, the com-

(1) Every transaction has an original document

(but now most of these documents will be produced by the computer automatically Instead of manually)

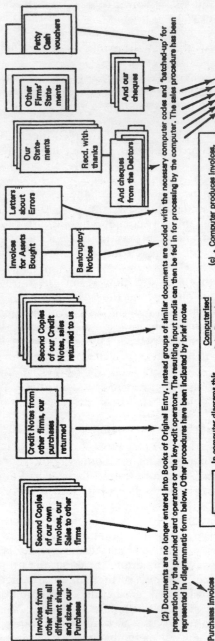

Petty Cash vouchers

Other Firms' Statements — And our cheques

Our Statements — Recd. with thanks — And cheques from the Debtors

Letters about Errors

Invoices for Assets Bought

Bankruptcy Notices

Second Copies of our Credit Notes, sales returned to us

Credit Notes from other firms, our purchases returned

Second Copies of our own Invoices, our Sales to other firms

Invoices from other firms, all different shapes and sizes, our Purchases

(2) Documents are no longer entered into Books of Original Entry. Instead groups of similar documents are coded with the necessary computer codes and 'batched-up' for preparation by the punched card operators or the key-edit operators. The resulting input media can then be fed in for processing by the computer. The sales procedure has been represented in diagrammatic form below. Other procedures have been indicated by brief notes

Other documents such as debit notes, credit notes, journal documents for journal entries are treated similarly according to their own requirements and lead to inputs, data processing and updating of all ledger accounts. The computer will thus hold the entire ledger system on its files, or as much of the system as the management decide

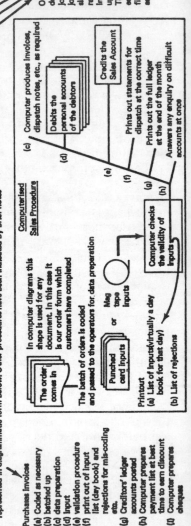

Computerised Sales Procedure

(c) Computer produces invoices, dispatch notes, etc., as required

(d) Debits the personal accounts of the debtors

Credits the Sales Account

(e) Prints out statements for dispatch at the correct time

(f) Prints out the full ledger at the end of the month

(g)

(h) Answers any enquiry on difficult accounts at once

In computer diagrams this shape is used for any document. In this case it is our order form which customers have completed

The batch of orders is coded and passed to the operators for data preparation

Punched card Inputs or Mag tape Inputs

Computer checks the validity of inputs

Printout
(a) List of Inputs(virtually a day book for that day)
(b) List of rejections

The order comes in

Purchases Invoice
(a) Coded as necessary
(b) batched up
(c) data preparation
(d) Input
(e) validation procedure
(f) print out of Input list (day book) and rejections for mis-coding etc.
(g) Creditors' ledger accounts posted
(h) Computer prepares payment list at best time to earn discount
(i) Computer prepares cheques

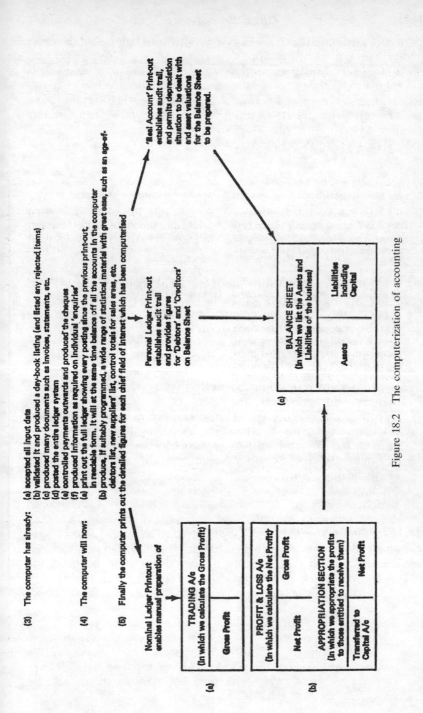

(3) The computer has already:
  (a) accepted all input data
  (b) validated it and produced a day-book listing (and listed any rejected items)
  (c) produced many documents such as invoices, statements, etc.
  (d) posted the entire ledger system
  (e) controlled payments outwards and produced the cheques
  (f) produced information as required on individual 'enquiries'

(4) The computer will now:
  (a) print out the full ledger showing every posting since the previous print-out, in readable form. It will at the same time balance off all the accounts in the computer
  (b) produce, if suitably programmed, a wide range of statistical material with great ease, such as an age-of-debtors list, new suppliers' list, control totals for sales areas, etc.

(5) Finally the computer prints out the detailed figures for each chief field of interest which has been computerised

Nominal Ledger Printout enable manual preparation of

Personal Ledger Print-out establishes audit trail and provides figures for 'Debtors' and 'Creditors' on Balance Sheet

'Real Account' Print-out establishes audit trail, and permits depreciation situation to be dealt with and asset valuations for the Balance Sheet to be prepared.

(a)

TRADING A/c
(In which we calculate the Gross Profit)

	Gross Profit
Gross Profit	

(b)

PROFIT & LOSS A/c
(In which we calculate the Net Profit)

	Gross Profit
Net Profit	

APPROPRIATION SECTION
(In which we appropriate the profits to those entitled to receive them)

Transferred to Capital A/c	Net Profit

(c)

BALANCE SHEET
(In which we list the Assets and Liabilities of the business)

Assets	Liabilities Including Capital

Figure 18.2 The computerization of accounting

puterized version of the Simplex system illustrated on p. 284, has this facility, and will ask the trader at a certain point. 'Would you like me to do a set of final accounts now? Y/N'. A touch on the Y key will then prepare a set of final accounts. This does mean that the trader can have a set of final accounts every month (or even every day) if he/she wants it. Micro-Simplex is available from Micro Retailer Systems Ltd, 84 Mill St, Macclesfield, Cheshire, SKL1 6NR. Tel: 0625 615375 Fax 612546.

18.4 Credit control

While new customers are essential to every business, especially a business that is trying to grow, there is no point in starting to deal with a risky business, e.g. one that has already established a reputation as a poor payer, with unreliable or inefficient management procedures. The following points are worth listing in this respect:

(*a*) It is not usual to deal with a complete stranger on credit terms – in other words, on terms where he/she can have the goods and services now, and need not pay until later.

(*b*) If they are asking for such terms, it would not be usual to accept without good references from reliable people.

Credit reference agencies specialize in collecting information on such matters, and will, for a relatively modest fee, report anything they know. For example, they verify the trading title of firms and companies, their registered addresses, etc. They check records at Company House and report, for example, on whether a company is borrowing so widely that it appears to have cash-flow problems. They also check the financial records of company directors, partners, etc., and the county court judgments against debtor firms.

Other goods references come from trade creditors in the same trade as yourself. Don't just accept a letter of recommendation, actually phone the firm or company concerned and ask if the letter is genuine and whether they have any reservations at all about the potential customer. Banks will often give an opinion but they are usually of the 'believed to be good for their ordinary business transactions' variety, which means very little. The firm's accountants or auditors (if they have any) may be better.

(*c*) The usual first step is to ask for cash-on-delivery (COD) or payment by pro-forma invoice. This means you send them an invoice showing the value of the goods and if they pay the invoice, you dispatch the goods. This means they have to trust you – which is always better than you trusting them, because you know *you* are reliable, so they are not at risk.

(*d*) If you do agree to give them credit terms, set a credit limit that is reasonable − say twice the value of their first order − and don't let any future order exceed it. Some firms place one or two small orders and pay promptly, but then send a massive order for which they do not intend to pay.

(*e*) You have specified a credit period − say 30 days from invoice date. If you don't get the money by that date, phone them and ask why. Insist on payment according to the agreed terms. If they don't pay on time but still place further orders, don't send the goods. Put them on a pro-forma basis and ensure that the first invoice you send includes all the outstanding amounts.

(*f*) Finally, when you have tried (i) a phone call and (ii) a letter requesting payment, and still have no response, ask your solicitor to write and demand payment within 7 days on pain of legal action. Most solicitors have a system for chasing bad debts that goes through a set procedure. Early on in this procedure legal action is commenced and a writ is served. Suing for payment does not mean we expect to go to court. What we intend to do is to put the debtor under pressure. The threat of court action, if pursued to the end, would lead to the court ruling that an act of bankruptcy (non-payment of a debt) had occurred. Under this threat the debtor pays up. People usually pay the creditor who is worrying them the most.

The full chain of correspondence on credit matters is therefore:

(i) Pre-contract negotiations about the supply of goods or services and the method of payment.

(ii) A request for references (and perhaps, simultaneously, inquiries via a credit reference agency).

(iii) The setting of a credit limit and its monitoring whenever a further order is received.

(iv) A telephone request for payment of an overdue account.

(v) A formal written request for payment, coupled with notification that the customer will be reduced to pro-forma invoice terms for future orders.

(vi) A solicitor's letter, followed by the commencement of legal action.

Do not be frightened of using a solicitor because you fear a big legal bill. The profession is highly competitive, and a frank discussion of your situation beforehand will ensure the bills are kept low. Using a solicitor puts the customer under pressure, and ensures the late payer pays up.

18.5 Internal and external audits

Auditing is the systematic checking of accounting activities. Internal audits are those conducted within the firm by employees of the Accounts Department called auditors. External audits are those carried out by an independent firm, appointed as required by Section 159 of the *Companies Acts*. This requires all companies to appoint auditors, and pay them an adequate remuneration for checking that all aspects of the firm's accounts have been properly kept, and that they comply with the accounting requirements of the *Companies Acts*, 1985−9.

A basic principle of auditing is that a thorough check of all aspects of the firm's accounting should be made from time to time, without prior warning being given. This makes it impossible for staff to cover up improper practices before the auditors arrive. Often, where a firm is large, investigations are made on a 'random sample' basis. This means that some sampling method, e.g. drawing names out of a hat, will decide which departments are subject to rigorous checks, and which to less thorough investigations.

18.6 Methods of payment

Above all, in business, we hope to get paid for what we do, and if we don't get paid, we shall go out of business because we cannot pay our own debts. 'Bethink you of my own poor honesty' wrote one medieval businessman to his debtor. If our debtors do not pay us, we cannot pay our own creditors. There are a number of methods of payment. The chief ones are:

(a) Payment in legal tender − notes and coins of the realm

In every society, except the most primitive, some form of money is in use. In earlier times the majority of goods were bartered, i.e. exchanged for one another. Money was reserved for important matters like 'bride price' and 'blood price'. 'Bride price' is self-explanatory. 'Blood price' was paid by a man who had been so unfortunate as to kill another man; otherwise the 'avengers of blood' would pay his family a visit and exact vengeance by killing someone of equal status to the unfortunate deceased. In advanced nations these practices have long since ceased, but prices are fixed every day for countless products and services. To enable these prices to be satisfactorily paid, the law-making body designates what is known as 'legal tender' i.e. a method of payment that it is agreed satisfies all debts.

Legal tender in the United Kingdom consists of coins of the realm and Bank of England notes. Some Scottish banknotes are also legal tender. The denominations are as follows:

		The fifty-pence piece	= 50p
The penny	= 1p	The £1 coin	= £1.00
The twopenny piece	= 2p	The £5 note	= £5.00
The five-pence piece	= 5p	The £10 note	= £10.00
The ten-pence piece	= 10p	The £20 note	= £20.00
The twenty-pence piece	= 20p	The £50 note	= £50.00
		Other higher notes are also issued.	

If a creditor is offered payment in legal coins or notes, he must accept them. If he refuses to do so, the debtor is not discharged from payment, but he is discharged from having to tender payment. He has offered once and that is enough. The creditor must now come and request payment.

There is a further restriction on legal tender. Imagine a customer who offered to pay a bill for £50.00 in pennies. This would be a great imposition on the shopkeeper forced to count so many tiny coins. To prevent this sort of payment, a limit is set on each coin's use as legal tender. The limit for bronze coins is 20 pence. A shopkeeper offered more than twenty pennies may refuse to accept them. For decimal silver the limit is £5.00, except for 50-pence coins. These are legal tender up to £10.00, and £1 coins and notes are legal tender for any amount. If offered coins or notes within the limits of legal tender, the shopkeeper or other creditor must accept them in settlement of the debt owed.

One sometimes hears, at times of financial crisis, of tourists and other visitors being in difficulty because hotel-keepers will not accept their foreign notes in settlement of hotel bills, etc. This is because the rate of exchange is upset by the financial panic. An hotel-keeper hesitates to take foreign currency for fear it will decline in value. One does not hear of such difficulties as far as home nationals are concerned − legal tender is always legal tender. Only very rarely, as when an entire nation's currency collapses, does legal tender in that country cease to be valuable. This happened in Germany at the end of the Second World War, for example.

Cash handling. The handling of cash is one of the most difficult activities to control. The best guarantee of success in cash handling is the absolute honesty of the cashier and assistant cashiers, who should be chosen for their integrity and paid a salary commensurate with their responsibilities. The use of sophisticated cash registers is very advantageous, and enables the class of staff employed at the tills to be reduced, but even the most advanced machines are not proof against a cunning and determined cashier resolved to divert cash or stock into his/her own pocket. It is estimated that in the United Kingdom alone between £150 million and £300 million is pilfered every year by cashiers in the retail trade. Collusion between cashiers and managers of retail outlets is difficult to detect and, when discovered, often merely results in dismissal. The thief moves on to take employment elsewhere.

Figure 18.3 shows a modern cash register and coin dispenser, which displays most of the features that make a modern till so advantageous wherever money is collected. It illustrates a machine that not only calculates the change for the customer, but also dispenses it in a conveniently placed cup. The cashier handles only the amount tendered, and any notes to be given as change. The coins are dispensed automatically and need not be counted out by the cashier.

The features of these tills contributing to the security of cash are as follows:

(*a*) Every item purchased is registered both on the visible scale as it is 'rung up', on the till receipt that is eventually given to the customer, and on the **audit roll** in the cash register.

(*b*) The total bill is displayed for the customer's benefit and is also printed on the till receipt (Figure 18.4), and the audit roll.

(*c*) The amount tendered by the customer is recorded.

(*d*) The change due is automatically calculated, printed on the till receipt for the customer's benefit, and, in the case of the coin-

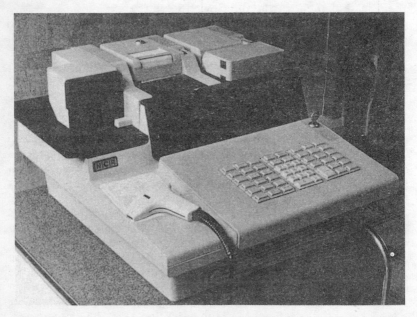

Figure 18.3   An NCR point of sale terminal for retail trade (courtesy of NCR Ltd)

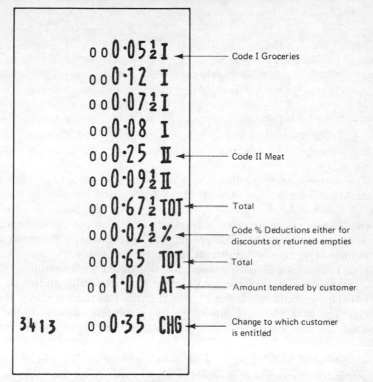

Figure 18.4 A till receipt

dispensing machines, is automatically dispensed as far as coins are concerned.

Naturally the cashier's department will be very concerned with cash receipts and payments, but there are certain serious inconveniences about 'legal tender' that have reduced cash payments enormously in recent years. The chief one is that cash that is legal tender has the characteristic known as **negotiability**. A £5 note is a negotiable instrument. This means that, when passed on to someone else who takes it in good faith and for value, it gives a perfect 'title' or right of ownership. This perfect right of ownership cannot be destroyed, even by the true owner. An example will illustrate this.

London Bank Ltd send £5 000 of soiled banknotes by van to the Bank of England. On the way they are stolen. The thief uses some of the money to buy a car from Sunshine Garages Ltd. He insists on paying in cash, and tenders £4 350 in notes. The garage proprietor counts them out and banks them after the thief has driven off.

London Bank Ltd are able to prove that the notes are the stolen notes, but can do nothing about it. Sunshine Garages Ltd took the notes in good faith, for value given (the car), without notice of any defect in the thief's title. They therefore receive a good title to the notes, which are now their property. All London Bank Ltd can do is to carry on looking for the thief and have him convicted.

It follows that theft of money is very common, and all too easy in many cases. To prevent it we often pay in other ways, notably by cheque, by credit transfer, by direct debit and by credit or debit cards.

(b) Payments by cheque

Cheques are by far the commonest method used for settling indebtedness, and about 3 million are cleared every working day. A cheque is an order to a banker to pay a sum of money to a named person, or to his order. This means that if the named person orders the banker to pay someone else, the banker will pay that person instead. Cheques may be written on any piece of paper, or even on an object like a tablecloth, but bankers prefer them to be on standard-sized pieces of paper which fit their machines. A cheque book is issued free of charge to everyone who opens a current account.

It must be clearly stated who is going to sign cheques, and specimen signatures must be lodged with the bank. This helps to ensure that forgeries do not go undetected. Quite often two signatures are required, thus making it more difficult for employees to embezzle money.

A full account of the legal position of the cheques is not needed here. Those who are interested might like to read a companion volume, *Commerce Made Simple*. We should perhaps mention two Acts of Parliament. Under the Cheques Act, 1957 (which deals with the legal situation of cheques) one of the provisions is that if a person pays by cheque, the fact that the banker has stamped the word PAID on the cheque constitutes a receipt for the money paid. It is not therefore necessary to send people a receipt for the payment, although under the Act they may insist upon having a receipt if they wish. The point about this at the time the Act was passed was that all paid cheques were returned by the bank to the drawer of the cheque – the person who paid the money. He/she therefore had the receipt that was needed. It doesn't make quite so much sense now that the funds are paid through the banking system electronically, and the cheque does not return to the drawer.

The second Act is the Cheques Act, 1992. This was passed because of a growing dishonesty in the handling of cheques in recent years. Many stolen cheques were paid into the accounts of thieves who had endorsed the cheques to themselves. Although the thieves were caught and punished for the offence, the original owner could not reclaim the money from the bank if it had paid the cheque in good faith, honestly believing the endorsement to be valid.

The 1992 Act recognized that if a cheque was crossed 'A/C Payee', it could only be paid into the account of the payee – and no one else's account. Many banks now issue cheques crossed 'A/C Payee', and this has reduced the dishonest use of cheques. Banks will only accept such cheques if handed over the counter to be paid into the account of the person named as payee. Any attempt to pay such a cheque into a different account will be refused, and the person seeking to do so will be told of the new law.

(c) Securing payment by standing order

Where a firm has many small debtors who are paying the money they owe by instalments out of ordinary weekly or monthly income, it is usual to ask for payments by standing order. If a cheque is an order to a banker to pay money, a 'standing order' must be very similar to a cheque. In fact it is an order to pay a sum of money regularly on a given day of the month. This is the easy way of settling regularly recurring payments such as mortgage repayments, hire-purchase transactions, rent and rates, etc. Most large service organizations such as the electricity and gas boards will accept standing orders for a reasonable sum towards electricity bills and gas bills. They usually have an arrangement whereby they will settle any under- or over-payment once a year.

The advantages of the standing order system are clear. Instead of our debtor having to go to the trouble to write out a cheque each month, and post it to us so that we can pay it in to our bank, the standing order is made out when the original hire-purchase transaction or mortgage transaction is arranged. It is then paid automatically by the bank, so long as the debtor has left funds in his/her account to cover it. The sensible debtor deducts such sums every month on payday from his/her cheque book stub, so that he/she is clear that these funds are not available for use. They have already been spent (or will be as soon as the due date arrives). As far as the office of the hire-purchase finance house or mortgage company is concerned, entries become credit transfers into the firm's bank account, and are picked up from the bank statement. Firms with many such payments probably have a weekly bank statement, so that all the entries from the good payers can be recorded. The bad payers will then be revealed and letters, probably computer generated, will be sent to the debtors warning them that their payments have not been received. A word about this 'credit transfer' system, sometimes called 'bank giro', is helpful at this point.

(d) The bank giro, or credit transfer system

The bank giro system is a credit-transfer system, in other words, money is transferred into a customer's bank account on the credit side without him/her actually being told about it, though he/she probably knows it will happen. The term 'bank giro' was adopted a few years ago by the banks at a time when they were facing competition from a government-sponsored bank called National Girobank. This bank has now been privatized. The term implies that the money goes round and round, like a gyroscope − so it is a rather silly term. Credit transfer is really the better name.

The principle of the credit-transfer system is payment directly into the bank account of the payee. The transfer may be executed by a standing order, a trader's credit or a counter credit. The payee is not informed about it immediately but discovers it when he/she asks for a bank statement.

A growing use of this system is in the payment of wages. The procedure is to present the bank with a list of employees and the sums due to them. For each employee a credit-transfer slip is prepared and sent to the bank. The sums due are transferred to the credit of the employees' accounts. The total of these payments is debited to the employer's account, one cheque being written for the whole sum. Sometimes the credit transfer is referred to as a 'direct-credit', a term which has come into use recently as being the opposite of a 'direct-debit' (see below).

(e) The direct-debit system

The direct-debit system was developed in the 1970s and 1980s as an answer to inflationary problems. In many situations standing orders used to be appropriate but they are not so now, because prices rise every year, owing to inflation. The author can remember when his subscription to a certain motoring organization was £3 per annum. Over the years this has risen to £97.50, though, granted, the services on offer are now much more extensive. The point is that a standing order is no help if the subscriptions to organizations rise year by year. Under the direct-debit system the firm or organization requiring the payment may now ask for it instead of the customer ordering it to be paid. Naturally this needs the customer's general agreement, but it is helpful in inflationary times. The organization requests the bank for a direct debit, removing the correct sum for the present year from the member's account. Banks will only do this if the member has signed a 'direct-debit mandate', which agrees that the organization may request this type of payment from time to time.

(f) Banker's draft facilities

A banker's draft is like a cheque drawn by the bank on itself. It enables customers to offer persons or firms to whom they are in debt a cheque that has the absolute authority of a big bank behind it. These drafts can be used when a trader deals with a wholesaler for the first time, or when offering payment in a foreign country. Whereas a personal cheque would probably not be acceptable to a foreigner, a draft backed with the authority of one of the 'Big Four' probably would be. A 'traveller's cheque' is therefore a special type of banker's draft. There is one difficulty about banker's drafts. The situation is somewhat risky in that, if the draft is stolen and used before the owner reports the loss, it may be impossible to recover the money from anyone except the thief, who is usually not available as a target for legal action.

(g) *Payments through the Post Office system*

There are 24 000 post offices in the United Kingdom, and many of the non-banking members of society use this network to pay accounts. The chief arrangement is through the giro-system (see below). Post office services do change from time to time, but firms who deal with many customers (such as mail-order firms) need to know about these services, which are:

(i) The Transcash system means that any bill may be paid at the post office counter so long as the organization asking for payment has a Girobank Account. The customer simply completes a Transcash form at the counter and pays over the money (sometimes with a small handling charge as well). The cash is transferred to the account of the organization, and the post office counter clerk gives a receipt to the customer as proof of payment.

(ii) *Postal orders* are sold in values ranging from 50p to £20. A small charge called 'poundage' is made according to the value of the order. The payee's name should be filled in on the order and the name of the post office where it is to be cashed. If it is crossed by the sender, it cannot be cashed, but must be paid into a bank account. It can still be passed on to another person and be banked by him/her.

The counterfoil is used (*a*) to make claims if the postal order is lost, but these will not be honoured if it has already been cashed, (*b*) to enable the purchaser to get his money back − even if the name of a payee has been filled in. To do this he presents both halves.

A postal order is not negotiable, but it may be passed on and cashed through a bank.

(iii) *Payments using National Savings Bank deposits*. Where a person has a National Savings Bank account and wishes to pay bills such as telephone bills, gas bills, electricity bills, rates, etc., it is possible to make a withdrawal from the account in favour of the firm or public authority concerned. The money is technically drawn out in cash form, but is at once paid over for transfer to the payee, where it is paid into his/her Giro account. Giro accounts are explained below.

(iv) *The Girobank system.* The Girobank started as the UK National Giro in the mid-1960s, although many other countries had used giro systems for many years. The explanation is that giros are more suitable for countries that lack a sophisticated banking system, and even in Britain the vast majority of those recruited to giro have proved to be from the non-banking sector of the community. The giro system is particularly useful to firms such as mail-order houses, whose home agents (mostly housewives from the non-banking section of the community) are now able to pay their weekly payments in to their local post offices for the credit of the mail-order house's account.

Although originally run as a nationalized corporation, Girobank has now become a wholly owned subsidiary of the Alliance and Leicester Building Society. Besides transactions being made at 24 000 post offices, it also operates 'banking by telephone' and 'banking by post' services.

A full range of services is available, including chequebook services, and a cheque guarantee card, which also operates cash machines and acts as a debit card for payments in shops. Direct debits and standing orders are acceptable, interest is paid on the balances in current accounts and a monthly statement is available. Overdrafts are permitted up to £200 without prior arrangement − but larger amounts will be considered on request. There is an overdraft protection scheme and a scheme to safeguard credit cards. The system operates from an advanced computerized organization at Bootle in Lancashire.

(v) *Cash-on-delivery.* COD services are a way of securing payment for goods when the consignee is not known well enough to be given credit by the consignor. The consignor fills up a form at the post office stating the value of the goods, called the 'trade charge'. This sum of money will be collected by the postman on delivery, and if it is not forthcoming, he will retain the packet and return it to the post office. The addressee can then collect the parcel from the post office on payment of the trade charge, which will be remitted by Giro cheque to the consignor. If not collected by the consignee in a reasonable time, the packet will be returned to the consignor. The packet must be sent as a registered letter, and the trade charge to be collected must not exceed £350. For safety, amounts in excess of £50 will not be collected by postal staff, and the consignee must bring the money to the post office to collect the packet. The charge is £1.20 plus normal postage to contract customers (who use this method of collection regularly). It is £1.60 plus normal postage to other customers.

(g) Payment by inland bill of exchange

A bill of exchange is a method of payment used between businessmen that has certain advantages over other methods of payment. It has a very precise definition, which is given below, from the Bills of Exchange Act, 1882. An illustration is given in Figure 18.5 and explained in the notes below it. It is best to read the definition first, and then look at Figure 18.5 and notice how it fits the definition. This is:

> A bill of exchange is an unconditional order in writing, addressed by one person to another, signed by the person giving it, requiring the person to whom it is addressed to pay on demand or at a fixed or determinable future time a sum certain in money to or to the order of a specified person, or to bearer.
>
> (Bills of Exchange Act, 1882)

The following points will help your understanding:

(*a*) The one who writes out the order to pay is called the **drawer**.

(*b*) The one who is drawn upon, i.e. ordered to pay, is called the **drawee**.

(*c*) Later this person (the drawee) may 'accept' the bill. This is a special use of the word 'accept', because it means 'accepts the obligation to pay expressed in the bill'. If I accept the duty to pay I write 'accepted' across the face of the bill and sign it (even just signing my name on it will do). From that time on I am known as the **acceptor** of the bill and have absolute liability on it − I must honour the bill on the due date. If I dishonour it, that is an utterly disgraceful act and may lead to bankruptcy (unless I make other arrangements).

(*d*) The amount of money must be absolutely clear. 'A sum certain' − this is not the same as 'a certain sum'. For example, I cannot make out a bill requiring someone to pay the value of my horse Dobbin. That is an uncertain sum. It must say 'Three thousand pounds' or 'Four hundred pounds'.

(*e*) The time must either be fixed or at least determinable. For example, '90 days after date' is determinable if the bill is dated 1 July. It is 29 September.

(*f*) The person who is entitled to be paid is called the 'payee', but it is usually the same person as the drawer, since − as we shall see − it is usually the drawer who is supplying goods to the value of the bill, and wants to be paid for them. If the drawer decides he wants the acceptor to pay someone else, he can always order him to pay that person by endorsing the bill (writing on the back of it) 'Pay J. Smith' or whoever it is. That is why the definition says 'to pay . . . . . . to, or to the order of, a specified person'.

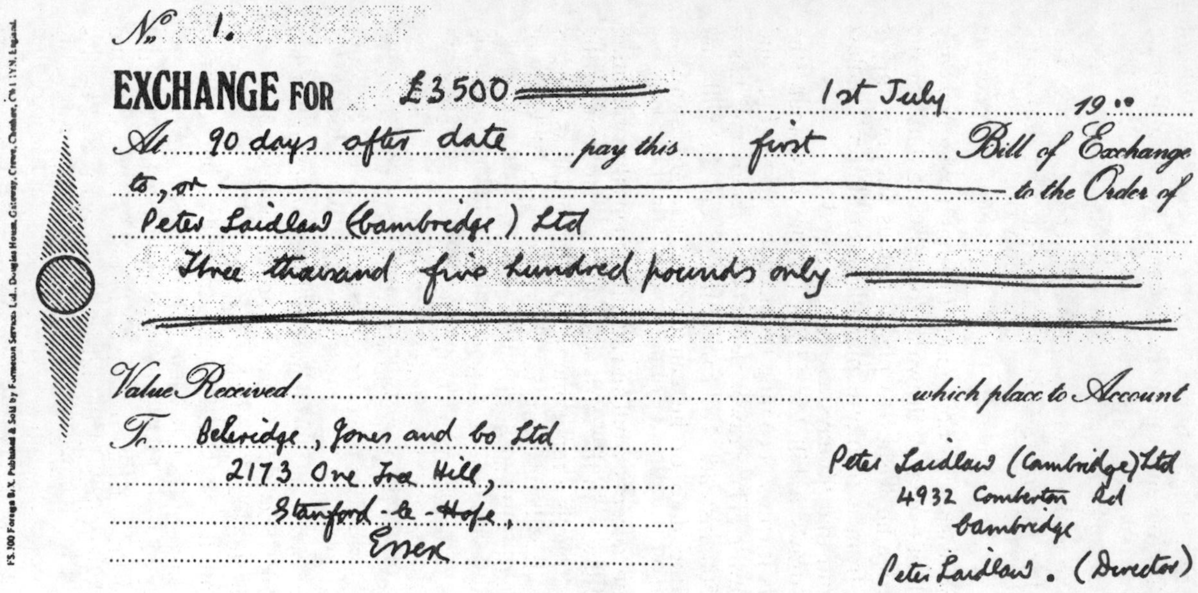
No. 1.

EXCHANGE FOR £3500 ——— 1st July 19..

At 90 days after date pay this first Bill of Exchange

to, or ——— to the Order of

Peter Laidlaw (Cambridge) Ltd

Three thousand five hundred pounds only ———

Value Received which place to Account

To Beleridge, Jones and Co Ltd

2173 One Tree Hill,

Stanford-le-Hope,

Essex

Peter Laidlaw (Cambridge) Ltd

4932 Comberton Rd

Cambridge

Peter Laidlaw. (Director)

Figure 18.5 An inland bill of exchange

Notes

(i) The drawer of the bill is Peter Laidlaw, a director of Peter Laidlaw (Cambridge) Ltd.

(ii) The drawees are Beleridge, Jones and Co. Ltd. They have not yet accepted the bill, and so have no liability on it at all at present.

(iii) The bill is an unconditional order in writing. It says 'Pay three thousand five hundred pounds to Peter Laidlaw (Cambridge) Ltd.' It does not say 'provided you are in funds at the time' or any condition. It just says 'Pay!'.

(iv) It is addressed by one person (Peter Laidlaw) to another (Beleridge, Jones and Co. Ltd) and is signed by the person giving it (Peter Laidlaw).

(v) The date is determinable, it is 90 days after 1 July, which is 29 September, 19...

(vi) The sum of money is certain, three thousand five hundred pounds.

(vii) The bill is payable to, or to the order of, Peter Laidlaw (Cambridge) Ltd

(*g*) A bill can be made payable to bearer, but this is risky, since any finder of the bill, or any thief, could claim the money, and the acceptor would be free of debt if he paid the wrong person, even if that person had no right to the bill.

Now read the definition again and study Figure 18.5 carefully.

The use of bills of exchange

It is very important to understand how bills of exchange work. The process is illustrated in Figure 18.6(*a*) and (*b*), but first notice the following points.

(*a*) A person who wishes to buy goods but has no money may agree to accept a bill of exchange drawn at some future date for the full value of the order he wishes to place. Let us suppose this is £3 500 of furniture from a furniture manufacturer. Peter Laidlaw (Cambridge) Ltd, and that 90 days' credit is agreed.

(*b*) The drawer draws a bill for £3 500 on the customer (the drawee) who accepts it (thus becoming the acceptor of the bill) and returns it to the drawer. The drawer delivers the goods and has a 90-day bill for £3 500 instead. He can either keep the bill and present it on the due date or he can cash it straight away, as explained below.

(*c*) When a drawee 'accepts' a bill and acknowledges the obligation in it, he is bound by law — in the most solemn way — to honour the bill on the due date. If he is a reputable person, the bill is as good as money, and any bank will discount it. There are special kinds of bank that do little else but discount bills of exchange — they are called discount houses. What they will do is cash the bill by giving the drawer the *present value* of the bill. This is the face value less interest at an agreed rate for the number of days it has to run. So the drawer who discounts the bill with the bank gets less than the face value — in other words a discount is deducted by the discount house.

(*d*) The bill is endorsed by the drawer with a signed and dated order to pay the bank. The bank is now a 'holder in due course' of the bill, and owns it, having given value for it.

(*e*) On the due date the bank will present the bill to the acceptor, who honours it by paying the full value. The bank has earned the amount of interest it deducted when it discounted the bill, and the 'loan' it made to the drawer had been paid in full. Where does the acceptor get the money to honour the bill? The answer is that he has had 90 days to sell the furniture at a profit, and can therefore honour the bill and have something left over for himself.

We can now follow what is happening in the two diagrams, Figure 18.6(*a*) and Figure 18.6(*b*).

The conclusion is that bills of exchange are a useful instrument to

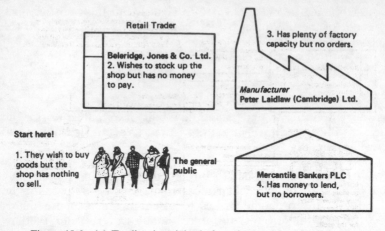

Figure 18.6 (a) Trading inactivity before the use of a bill of exchange
Notes
(i) Business cannot proceed because the retail trader has nothing to sell and no money to buy stock.
(ii) What is needed is a mechanism by which the retailer can order supplies without paying for them at once, but which enables the manufacturer to be paid immediately.
(iii) Since a bill of exchange from a reputable trader is almost as good as money, it will be as acceptable to a bank as money. They have plenty of money to lend out to reliable customers, so they do not mind oiling the wheels of commerce by advancing money to the holder of a bill of exchange.

encourage business activity, and are mutually beneficial to all parties so long as no difficulties arise and the bill is honoured on the due date. If a bill is dishonoured on the due date, it is a serious matter for the acceptor of the bill, because to fail to honour an agreement entered into in such a formal manner constitutes an act of bankruptcy, which could lead to the business being unable to trade any more. In fact it is possible to renew a bill, so long as there is every prospect that the arrangement will be honoured, but further interest is payable and any legal charges are also payable by the acceptor of the dishonoured bill.

18.7 Securing payment from overseas customers

When dealing with overseas customers, there is always the problem 'Shall we ever be paid for the goods and services we supply?' It is essential to devise a system of payment acceptable to both parties and offering each the security required, i.e. the exporter has to be sure payment will be received without undue delay and the importer has to be sure the goods or services will be supplied, and will be up to specification.

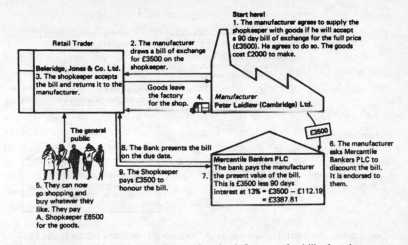

Figure 18.6 (b) Active trading under the influence of a bill of exchange

Notes

(i) How did everyone do out of the various activities sparked off by the drawing of this Bill of Exchange?

(ii) The manufacturer sold goods costing £2 000 for £3 500, but actually only realized £3 387.81 after discounting charges. Profit – £1 387.81.

(iii) Beleridge, Jones & Co Ltd sold goods costing £3 500 for £6 500 Profit £3 000.

(iv) Mercantile Bankers PLC loaned £3 387.81 for 90 days and earned £112.19. This is actually 13.4% interest.

(v) The general public enjoyed the pleasures of the consumer society; comfortable furniture costing £6 500.

There are five main methods of proceeding. They are:

(*a*) Cash with order.
(*b*) Documentary letter of credit.
(*c*) Documents against payment.
(*d*) Documents against acceptance.
(*e*) Open account terms.

They are arranged in the order that reflects the degree of trust we can place in the foreign customer. If he/she is quite unknown to us, we might demand 'cash with order'. If we can trust them as much as any other known and reliable customer, we usually offer 'open account' terms. We must now consider these in turn.

(*a*) *Cash with order.* With this method we expect the customer to pay in full when placing the order. Naturally not many customers will wish to do this, but it is quite common when the amount is small, e.g. foreign students ordering textbooks from publishers.

(*b*) *Overseas transactions paid for by documentary credits.* A documentary letter of credit is a device for arranging export trade with the maximum security for the exporter. When approached to supply goods, the exporter agrees to do so provided the foreign customer opens an *irrevocable letter of credit* in his favour with a reputable bank. The word 'irrevocable' means that the customer cannot cancel it without the exporter's permission. The letter of credit is sent to the exporter by a London bank, which is known as the 'correspondent bank' because it acts on behalf of the foreign bank holding the funds. The letter of credit tells the exporter exactly what he must do to obtain the money. For example, it will tell him exactly what goods to supply, where to ship them, what documents to produce and other details. Provided the exporter fulfils every requirement of the letter of credit and submits the necessary documents to the bank after the goods have been shipped, the credit will be released and the exporter paid.

The best arrangement is a *confirmed irrevocable letter of credit*. Here the credit arranged by the customer's bank is *confirmed* by the London bank, so that it actually makes itself responsible for the payment to the exporter. When the exporter presents the documents, and it is found that they conform fully with the letter of credit, the London bank releases payment at once. If the credit is unconfirmed, the London bank takes the documents lodged with it and sends them to the foreign bank, which releases the credit as soon as it has checked the documents.

(*c*) *Documents against payment and* (*d*) *documents against acceptance*. Both these methods of payment make use of bills of exchange, which have already been explained. However, since we are now dealing with foreign customers, we are dealing with foreign bills of exchange. There is no real difference between inland and foreign bills except that, when something goes wrong, the foreign bill is treated in a more formal way. The bill has to be 'protested', a legal procedure requiring a lawyer in the country concerned to certify that the bill has been presented to the debtor, who either refused to honour it or was unable to honour it. Leaving that aside, how do these two methods help the exporter to secure payment?

Consider a British company, Engineering Ltd, which receives an order from Australia for twenty bus engines, valued at £10 000. Having undertaken the purchase of raw materials, etc., and made the engines, Engineering Ltd ships them on the SS *Southern Star* to the Australian Bus Co. Having kept their part of the bargain, Engineering Ltd would now like to be paid for the engines. On the other hand, the Australian firm has not yet received them and is unwilling to pay until they arrive. The document representing ownership of the goods while on the high seas is the bill of lading, or, if the goods go by air, it is the air waybill. If this document is held back from the foreign customer, he/she will be unable to obtain the goods even if they arrive safely. In our present case the bus engines will be held until the bill of lading is presented to the master of the SS *Southern Star* on arrival in Australia. If we attach a bill of exchange to the documents (there will usually be an insurance policy and possibly an import licence as well as the bill of lading), the bank acting on our behalf will call the importer in. If the bill of exchange is a sight bill — payable on sight — the documents will be released as soon as payment is made. This is D/P (documents against payment). If the bill of exchange is a 'usance bill' — one offering a period of time to pay, according to the customary use of the trade concerned — the bill of lading, etc., will be released as soon as the importer has accepted the bill, i.e. written 'accepted' on it and signed his/her name. This is D/A (documents against acceptance).

The whole procedure is illustrated in Figure 18.7. However, there is one further point shown. When the 'documents against acceptance' procedure is being used, the exporter may obtain almost all the money he/she hopes to receive eventually by virtually borrowing it from the UK bank. By making out an inland bill of exchange and asking the bank to accept it — in other words add its good name to the bill — the exporter can discount this bill at once on the money market and obtain the funds. The tenor of the bill (the time before it falls due for payment) is the same as the Australian bill, and when it becomes due for payment, the funds received from Australia will provide the money to honour the bill.

(*e*) *Open account terms*. Countless movements in overseas trade are from head offices of multinational companies to overseas branches, or from an exporter to his/her agent abroad. In such cases the parties do have complete faith in one another and therefore 'open account' dealing is the logical way to trade.

18.8 Value added tax procedures

On 1 April 1973 a new taxation system was introduced in the United Kingdom, replacing two other forms of taxation, purchase tax and selective employment tax, which were abolished on that date. The new tax was designed partly to bring the United Kingdom taxation system into closer alignment with European Community systems, but it has also spread taxation over a wider range of consumer products, making taxation fairer than in the past. The disadvantage of the new tax system is that it requires about 1 500 000 businesses, many of them quite small, to keep VAT records. This has meant that VAT routines have become part of office practice for every firm in the country.

The principle of VAT is that tax is levied on the value added to goods at every stage as they pass from the natural raw material stage to the finished product, and then onwards to the final consumer. All

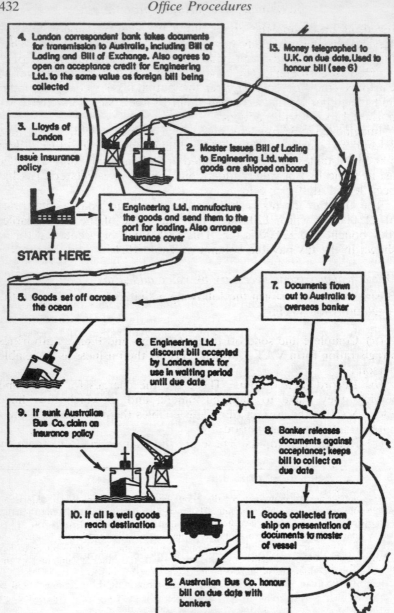

Figure 18.7   Financing overseas trade with a bill of exchange (see notes opposite)

the firms processing the goods along the way buy goods and use services that have already had some tax levied upon them. When they in turn sell goods or provide services, they levy tax on the price charged to customers. The amount they are liable to pay over to Customs is the difference between the 'output tax' levied on customers and the 'input tax' levied upon them by their suppliers. It is proportional to the value added.

Imagine an oak tree cut down in a farmer's field, taken to a sawmill and cut into planks, sold to a manufacturer and turned into 500 coffee tables eventually retailed at £44 each including tax. The list in Table 18.1 of values added, etc., might be calculated. Tax has been levied at 10 per cent.

The effect of the tax is that the final consumers pay a total price of £22 000, of which £20 000 is the true value of the coffee tables they bought and £2 000 is tax. This £2 000 will be accounted for as shown in the tax payable column of Table 18.1.

Office activities made necessary by value added tax
Businesses must perform the following activities to comply with the regulations for VAT:

(*a*) Complete and send off to the Customs and Excise authorities a registration form VAT 1, which registers the business as a 'taxable person'.

(*b*) Record their outputs. These are the charges for goods and services they make to their customers, and to which they have added VAT at the correct rate. This enables them to calculate their output tax for any tax period.

(*c*) Record their inputs. These are the charges made to them by

---

Notes
(i) Engineering Ltd manufactures the goods and delivers them to the shipowner with a copy invoice and a bill of lading. The master returns the bill of lading signed to acknowledge that the goods have been shipped in good order and condition.

(ii) Engineering Ltd has also arranged an insurance policy at Lloyd's to cover the shipment. It now draws up a bill of exchange requiring the Australian buyer to pay for the goods on the due date, and present it (with the other documents) to the London correspondent bank named by its overseas customer.

(iii) The London bank agrees to help Engineering Ltd by accepting a bill of exchange for the same amount as the foreign bill lodged with it for collection. Engineering Ltd can discount this bill at once and use the money.

(iv) The London bank sends the documents of title to Australia and releases them to the Bus Co. when it accepts the original bill of exchange. It holds the bill until the due date and collects the money.

(v) If the goods arrive safely, the Bus Co. collects them at the docks.

(vi) If they are lost at sea, the Bus Co. claims the insurance money.

(vii) On the due date the Bus Co. honours the bill; the money is sent to London and used to clear up the acceptance credit opened for Engineering Ltd.

Table 18.1 Calculations — Value Added Tax (at 10%)

Business	Cost price free of tax	Sale price free of tax	Value added	Final charge to customer (incl. 10% tax)	Input tax	Output tax	Tax payable
	£	£	£	£	£	£	£
1 Farmer	0	200 (tree trunk)	200	220	0	20	20
2 Sawmill Co.	200	600 (sawn planks)	400	660	20	60	40
3 Furniture manufacturer	600	14 000 (coffee tables)	13 400	15 400	60	1 400	1 340
4 Retailer	14 000	20 000	6 000	22 000	1 400	2 000	600

Total tax levied £2 000

their suppliers of goods and services. The tax charged to them by these suppliers is called input tax.

(*d*) Complete a VAT Return (Form VAT 100) at intervals, and account for the tax due.

(*e*) Keep records and accounts that are adequate for these purposes.

An explanation of these items in greater detail is given below.

(*a*) *Registration Form VAT 1*. Everyone carrying on a business today whose taxable outputs, i.e. charges for goods and services supplied to customers, are likely to exceed £37 600 per annum must complete a form VAT 1. This makes the individual, firm or company a 'taxable person' under the regulations. They are then required to act virtually as the collecting agent of HM Customs and Excise Department, charging customers tax on goods and services supplied, and remitting it (less any tax they are entitled to recoup on inputs) to the Department. Persons whose businesses are so small that the turnover is not more than £37 600 need not be registered, and all their output will be exempt. They do not charge their customers tax but are not entitled to deduct the tax charged on goods and services received. They are therefore very much like a consumer, paying tax on all goods and services received. Such firms can register voluntarily if they wish to do so, in which case they must charge VAT on all outputs and may deduct VAT on all inputs.

(*b*) *Output records and the rate of tax*. Every 'taxable person' must keep records of the goods and services supplied to his/her customers, and must add to the charges made the correct rate of tax. Tax was originally chargeable at 10 per cent, but is now charged at $17\frac{1}{2}$ per cent (the standard rate) on all goods. There is no reason why the Chancellor of the Exchequer should not impose a multi-rate VAT system, e.g. some EC countries levy a 'luxury rate' tax on more expensive goods and services. In 1994 a lower rate tax of 8 per cent was levied on fuel, heating and lighting.

Certain goods and services are taxable, but at the zero rate. These include food, water, books and newspapers, items for the blind, building work, export services, transport and drugs supplied on prescriptions. It might seem pointless to say an item is taxable and then tax it at the zero rate, but in fact this enables a business that is not charging its customers tax on its outputs to reclaim the tax on its inputs, which it had paid to suppliers. There is a class of exempt goods and services that are not taxed at all. These include the leasing of land and buildings, insurance, banking, finance, postal services and lotteries. The suppliers of these services do not need to register or keep records, but they are unable to claim back any tax paid on inputs.

The final effect of keeping 'output records' is that the business is able to calculate the total tax that has been added to customers' statements, and which it must account for to the Customs and Excise authorities.

(*c*) *Input records.* A taxable person who is collecting tax from his/her customers as in (*b*) above does not have to pay the full amount over to the Customs and Excise. The proprietor is entitled to deduct from the sums collected as 'output tax', the total sums paid to his/her own suppliers. These are revealed by keeping 'input records', which show the value of goods and services supplied by other firms, and the tax that these firms have charged, i.e. the proprietor's 'input tax'.

(*d*) *The tax return (form VAT 100).* The taxable person must render a return of the tax outputs and inputs of the business and pay tax every 3 months. The 3-monthly intervals are known as 'tax periods', and the return and any tax due must be sent in within 1 month of the end of the tax period. A special tax period of only 1 month is allowed where a taxable person feels sure that the 'tax inputs' will exceed the 'tax outputs' in the usual course of events. For example, a grocer selling zero-rated goods would not collect any output tax from his/her customers but would pay input tax on many things purchased, such as shop fittings, wrapping paper, etc. Such a trader might be entitled to regular refunds of tax from the Customs and Excise. It would be hard on such small businessmen if they had to wait for 3 months to recover tax paid on inputs.

A typical extract from the return might look like this:

Output tax for period		26 323.10
Tax on imported goods		974.40
Tax on acquisitions from EC countries		797.20
Underpaid tax from previous period		196.70
Total tax due		£28 291.40
Less		
Input tax for period	23 649.60	
Tax overpaid previously	None	
Tax on acquisitions from EC countries	797.20	
		24 446.80
Net tax payable		£ 3 844.60

The reference to EC countries needs some explanation. Now that the EC is a single market area, goods purchased from EC countries are not called imports and goods sold to EC countries are not called exports. Instead they are called 'acquisitions'. Traders must account for VAT on all acquisitions that come in zero-rated, but as this VAT is a tax on inputs, they can immediately reclaim it as input tax.

The calculation shows the net tax payable, but where the input tax exceeded the output tax, the difference between the two figures would be 'net tax refundable by Customs and Excise' and not 'net tax payable'.

(*e*) *Accounting records*. The introduction of VAT required the redesign of many business forms and book-keeping rulings, which needed to take account of the new system. These rulings are improved from time to time, and the reader is urged to consult his/her supplier for appropriate rulings. VAT records must be kept for 6 years and are liable to inspection by VAT inspectors.

VAT fractions. One problem arising in VAT procedures is the question of VAT fractions. The tax is always specified in percentage terms, e.g. the two rates at present (apart from zero rate) are $17\frac{1}{2}$ per cent and 8 per cent. In the example given in Table 18.1 the rate used, for convenience, was 10 per cent. We will look at the concept of 'VAT fractions' for the three rates.

At the **10 per cent rate**, if we know the price of an item is £100 and the 10 per cent VAT is added, the calculation is:

	£
Price without VAT	100
VAT at 10 per cent	10
Price to customer	£110

Now what fraction of the £110 is VAT. We might feel inclined to say 1/10th, but 1/10th of £110 is £11, and clearly the VAT is only £10. The explanation is:

$$\text{Price without VAT is } 100\%$$
$$+ \text{ VAT } \quad 10\%$$
$$\text{Final price} = \quad \underline{110\%}$$

The VAT is $\frac{10}{110}$ of the final price, which cancels down to $\frac{1}{11}$.
So the VAT fraction for a 10 per cent rate is $\frac{1}{11}$, not $\frac{1}{10}$.

For example, a trader's total sales in a month are £37 965.40, and this includes output tax at the 10 per cent rate. How much must he pay to the VAT authorities?

$$Answer \quad \text{£37 965.40} \div 11 = \underline{\underline{\text{£3 451.40}}}$$

At the **8 per cent rate**:

$$\text{Price without VAT} = 100\%$$
$$\text{VAT at 8\% rate} = \quad 8\%$$
$$\text{Final price} = \quad \underline{108\%}$$

The VAT is $\frac{8}{108}$ of the final price $= \frac{2}{27}$

For example, a trader's sales of fuel oil in a month are £49 785.60 and this includes VAT at the 8 per cent rate. How much must he pay to the VAT authorities?

$$Answer \quad \text{£49 785.60} \times \frac{2}{27} = \underline{\underline{\text{£3 687.82}}}$$

At the **$17\frac{1}{2}$% rate**:

$$\text{Price without VAT} = 100\%$$
$$\text{VAT at } 17\frac{1}{2}\% = \quad 17\frac{1}{2}\%$$
$$\text{Final price} = \quad \underline{117\frac{1}{2}\%}$$

The VAT fraction is $\frac{17\frac{1}{2}}{117\frac{1}{2}}$ of the final price $= \frac{35}{2} \times \frac{2}{235}$

$$= \frac{7}{47}$$

For example, Wedding Gowns Ltd sells garments in a particular quarter worth £145 725. How much must Susan Green, the proprietor, pay to the Customs and Excise Department?

$$Answer \quad £145\,725 \times \frac{7}{47} = \underline{\underline{£21\,703.72}}$$

The reader will notice what large sums of VAT build up in even a 3-month period, and how necessary it is for the accountant to ensure that this money is banked safely in a special account to meet the tax bill as it falls due.

18.9 A firm's relationship with its bankers

Bankers offer a wide range of services to their customers. A full description of these services may be found in *Commerce Made Simple*. Here it is only necessary to touch upon these services, and the relationship that exists between the bank manager and the chief cashier. Since a firm always needs to anticipate its cash requirements, a close link should be established between the banker and the firm. This will simplify the day-to-day arrangements, ensuring courteous attention at all times. It will also enable the banker to know the firm's situation better, and judge its importance in the industry and the local community. Should the firm require financial assistance, this will be available more quickly and more willingly, since the bank manager is more likely to extend credit to an account he knows from personal experience to be fundamentally sound.

Current accounts

Banks extend current-account services to anyone whom they regard as reliable. A new customer will be asked for a reference, and if this proves satisfactory, the bank will accept an initial deposit, which will be entered in a current account. A chequebook will then be issued free of charge.

Once a customer has received a chequebook, it may be used to order the banker to pay out sums of money from the current account. The name 'current account' comes from the French word *courant*, which means 'running', and implies that money is being paid into, and paid out of, the account as often as the customer finds convenient. The balance of the account changes from day to day as the various transactions proceed. The usual method of paying money into an account is by means of a **paying-in slip**, while the **cheque** is the usual way of withdrawing money from the account.

Overdrafts are allowed, provided they are sanctioned by the branch manager, and loans are sometimes made. An **overdraft** permits the customer to draw out more money than has been paid in. A **loan** actually transfers a sum of money into the current account of the borrower, but a **loan account** is opened to record the debt that arises as a result. Usually a firm that has received a loan is not allowed to overdraw as well. Interest is charged, usually at 2—5 per cent above base rate, on both loans and overdrafts.

Deposit-account services

Deposit accounts are accounts in which individuals and firms deposit cash resources that are not needed at present. They bear interest at 2 per cent less than the bank's base rate. The bank lends these funds to borrowers at 2—5 per cent more than the base rate, the interest being shared therefore with the depositor. Since the bank is using these moneys, it cannot always regain them at short notice, and in theory the bank is supposed to be given 7 days' notice before money is withdrawn. In fact the bank usually waives this notice, but charges 7 days' interest instead on sums drawn out.

At the time of writing the arrangements between banks and their customers are very diverse. Heavy losses have made the banks offer less interest than in former times, yet competition is fierce and special terms are usually available to customers whom the banks do not wish to lose.

Bank statements

Every month at least the cashier will ask the bank for a bank statement. This is a copy of the bank's record of its transactions with the firm. The cashier will compare this record with the record in the firm's cash book. Usually they will disagree. The explanations for this failure to agree are as follows:

(*a*) *The bank often takes action without bothering to notify the firm.* For example, it deducts **bank charges** for operating the current account, or **bank interest** on overdrafts when they fall due. It also receives sums of money as credit transfers, or bank giro transfers, without notifying the firm of their arrival. The cashier is expected to sort out these matters when the bank statement is received. This is done by up-dating the cash book, recording the sums transferred to the firm and deducting those sums taken away for services rendered.

(*b*) *There are delays inevitable in the banking system.* Imagine that a cheque is paid out to a creditor, but he does not go to the bank and present it for several weeks. Clearly, the sum paid away will not in fact have left the bank. The bank will still think its customer has these funds in possession. Similarly, even when cheques have been presented, some delay arises as they are cleared. A cashier who banks fifty cheques at 9.30 am on the last day of the month, and collects his bank statement at the same time, cannot expect those fifty cheques to appear on the statement. They will appear in due course, when time enables them to be cleared. In order to explain these differences the cashier will draw up a **bank reconciliation statement**.

(*c*) *Mistakes often occur*. These may be made by the cashier or by the bank. If the two records cannot be 'reconciled' every figure must be scrutinized to find the mistake.

Preparation of a bank reconciliation statement

Consider the following information from Mr A. Dealer's cash book and bank statement (shown below).

Readers who are not very knowledgeable about accounts should note that the bank records appear to be the reverse of the records of A. Dealer. Since Dealer has deposited his money in the bank, he is a creditor for the sums deposited, although these appear as debits on his own cash book. This is quite logical – Dealer keeps the record according to *his* viewpoint; the bank keeps the record according to *its* viewpoint.

CASH BOOK (BANK COLUMN ONLY)

Dr 19..		£	19..		Cr £
Feb. 1	To Balance	1 225.00	Feb. 2	By Green	147.60
10	" Ambrose	450.75	14	" Howard	228.50
17	" Bloggs	162.62	19	" Ives	136.70
18	" Crayford	373.50			

A rough calculation shows that the balance on this Cash Book is £1 699.07 a debit balance.

BANK STATEMENT
A. Dealer in account with Barclay's Bank Limited

Date 19..	Details	Dr.	Cr.	Balance
Feb. 1	Balance forward		1 225.00	1 225.00
2	Green	147.60		1 077.40
12	Ambrose		450.75	1 528.15
16	Howard	228.50		1 299.65
16	Charges	15.25		1 284.40
17	Bloggs		162.62	1 447.02
28	Bank of England (bonds)		42.58	1 489.60

A careful look at these two accounts will show:

(*a*) The balances do not agree: £1 699.07 according to the cash book, £1 489.60 according to the bank statement.

(*b*) Both accounts did agree on 1 February, so the problem is quite recent. Sometimes we may find a time lag lasting months, usually because someone has failed to bank a cheque.

(*c*) Ives's cheque sent to him on 19 February has not yet been paid in by Ives. He may be a sole trader who bothers to go to the bank only once a week or so.

(*d*) Crayford's cheque received by 28 February, that is today, has been entered in A. Dealer's cash book and paid into the bank, but it is not recorded on the bank statement. This is another example of a time lag; the bank will probably credit it tomorrow to the account.

(*e*) The bank has charged Dealer £15.25 bank charges. Dealer did not know about this deduction from his funds, but now he has learned of it, he should deduct this amount from the bank account in his three-column cash book.

(*f*) The bank has received some interest from the Bank of England for Dealer. This is clearly interest on gilt-edged securities, and Dealer should record the money received on his bank account.

We must now proceed to reconcile the two records.

Procedure for drawing up a bank reconciliation statement
The procedure is as follows:

(*a*) Compare the two accounts and note all the items of disagreement, as we have done in (*a*) to (*f*) in the last section.

(*b*) Adjust all items that can be put right in the cash book — items that are wrong only because of our lack of knowledge of what our bankers have done.

(*c*) Reconcile the rest in a reasonable statement, starting with one balance and finishing with the other.

Our calculations then look like this:

REVISED CASH BOOK (BANK COLUMNS ONLY)

Dr			£				Cr £
Feb.	1	To Balance	1 225.00	Feb.	2	By Green	147.60
	10	" Ambrose	450.75		14	" Howard	228.50
	17	" Bloggs	162.62		19	" Ives	136.70
	28	" Crayford	373.50		28	" Bank Charges	15.25
	28	" Interest received	42.58		28	" Balance c/d	1 726.40
			£2 254.45				£2 254.45
Mar.	1	To Balance b/d	1 726.40				

BANK RECONCILIATION STATEMENT
(as at 28 February)

	£
Balance as per Cash Book	1 726.40
Add back the cheque not yet presented (because the bank has not yet been asked for the money)	136.70
	1 863.10
Deduct the Crayford cheque not yet cleared (because the bank is not yet crediting us with the money)	373.50
Balance as per bank statement	£1 489.60

Clearly, we have been able to explain the disagreement successfully. Bank reconciliation statements are typed out neatly and filed away for inspection when required.

18.10 Points to think about and discuss

(*a*) Two young men, who know nothing about accounting, are proposing to set up in business, making a technical product, which they are competent to produce. They ask you to advise them about a system of accounts. They believe the turnover will not exceed £30 000 in the first two years, and they have limited capital available. What alternative solutions are available to their accounting problems?

(*b*) The accountant has many responsibilities; to the management, to the creditors, to the employees. Consider these three responsibilities in detail, listing the headings under which these different parties will hold him accountable. Do their interests conflict?

(*c*) Thinking in the very widest terms of the security of cash, what measures would you recommend to prevent (i) the theft of petty cash by persons in the office, (ii) wage snatches by criminal gangs, (iii) burglaries after office hours?

(*d*) A businessman applies to a bank for permission to open a current account and to be issued with a chequebook. What measures do you consider the bank should take to ensure that he is a suitable person to have such an account?

(*e*) A cashier is devising a set of rules to be followed by the mail inwards department whenever letters are found to contain remittances from debtors. The firm has 56 000 mail-order accounts and many of these customers send cash, either registered or unregistered. They all send postal orders and cheques, many of which are not crossed. Suggest how these, and other methods of remitting funds, should be dealt with in the rules.

(*f*) The cashier of a supermarket has detected the following matters in recent months:

(i) Cashiers at tills have placed money received from customers in their own handbags instead of in the tills.

(ii) Cashiers have deliberately given change for a £50 note to customers related to them, who tendered only £10 for their purchases.

(iii) Cashiers have left a bag of goods (value £1) near the till. It has been added on to the bill of every customer and the total for the day has then been taken home in goods off the shelves, half by the cashier and half by the manager.

(iv) A cashier with a 'sprained ankle' was found to have slipped twenty-three 10p pieces into the bandage round the 'injured' foot.

How can such thefts be prevented? Is it desirable to prosecute employees in these cases?

18.11 Rapid revision — accounting and payment procedures

Cover the page with a sheet of paper and uncover one question at a time.

	Answers		Questions
	—	1	What system of book-keeping is used in an accounts department?
1	Double-entry book-keeping.	2	Who first devised this system?
2	The merchants of Lombardy, in northern Italy, who gave their name to Lombard Street in London.	3	Which is the most important book of account?
3	The ledger.	4	What is a trial balance?
4	It is a means of checking the accuracy of the book-keeping.	5	Why does book-keeping lend itself particularly to computerization?
5	Because (a) the book-keeping processes are logical and simple, (b) the work is repetitive and easy programmes can be devised, (c) the controls that can be built into the system are an enormous advantage to the accountant.	6	How can an accountant establish a good system of credit control?
6	By insisting upon (a) references being taken up on all new customers, (b) credit levels being set on all customers until they are well-known and respected clients, (c) overdue accounts being placed on a 'stop' list, (d) persistent follow-ups on overdue accounts, (e) careful control of new accounts with limited companies.	7	What is legal tender?

7 It is a means of payment recognized in law as satisfying debts.	8 What does 'legal tender' consist of?
8 Banknotes of various denominations and coin of the realm.	9 What other ways are often used to pay debts?
9 (*a*) Cheques, (*b*) standing orders, (*c*) credit transfers, (*d*) direct debits, (*e*) banker's drafts, (*f*) bills of exchange, (*g*) payments through the Post Office by Transcash or Girobank services.	10 Define a bill of exchange
10 See p. 425 for this (and then learn the definition by heart).	11 What methods are used to secure payment from overseas?
11 (*a*) Cash with order, (*b*) documentary letter of credit, (*c*) documents against payment, (*d*) documents against acceptance, (*e*) open account terms	12 Why does the record of our bank balance according to the business's books rarely agree with the bank balance shown on our monthly bank statement?
12 (*a*) Because the bank does things we don't know about, e.g. charging bank charges, paying direct debits and receiving direct credits; (*b*) because we do things the bank doesn't know about, such as using cheques that may not be paid in by the recipients; (*c*) because there are time lags for cheques to be cleared, etc.; (*d*) because both parties can make mistakes (especially us).	13 What do we do to sort out these differences?
13 (*a*) First get our cash book right by making entries in it for the things the bank has done which we now know about, (*b*) draw up a bank reconciliation statement to reconcile the bank's figure with our own (now corrected) figure.	14 Go over the page again until you are sure of all the answers.

18.12 Rapid revision − value added tax

Cover the following page with a sheet of paper and uncover one question at a time.

Answers	Questions
−	1 What is value added tax?
1 It is a tax that replaced purchase tax and selective employment tax.	2 What is the basis of the tax?
2 It is levied on the value added to goods at each stage of manufacture and distribution.	3 Who is liable to pay this tax?

3 The final consumer actually pays, but the tax is collected from any individual or firm which is a 'taxable person' under the regulations.	4 Who is a 'taxable person'?
4 Any individual, partnership or corporation that supplies goods and services worth more than £37 600 per year, or who voluntarily registers.	5 What are the duties of a 'taxable person'?
5 (*a*) To register on form VAT 1. (*b*) To record his/her 'outputs' and charge tax on them to customers. This gives the 'output tax' of the business. (*c*)To record his/her 'inputs' and hence calculate the 'input tax' of the business. (*d*) To render a return each quarter, and remit any tax payable. (*e*) To keep proper accounting records.	6 When is tax payable?
6 When 'output tax' exceeds 'input tax'.	7 When is tax refundable?
7 When 'input tax' exceeds 'output tax'.	8 What are the rates of tax?
8 (*a*) Standard rate = $17\frac{1}{2}$%; lower rate 8%; (*b*) Zero rate = 0%.	9 What fraction must be deducted from 'gross takings' to give the tax charged?
9 $17\frac{1}{2}$% rate $= \dfrac{17\frac{1}{2}}{117\frac{1}{2}} = \dfrac{7}{47}$ 8% rate $= \dfrac{8}{108} = \dfrac{2}{27}$	10 Go over the page again until you feel sure of the answers.

Exercises set 18

1 Select the correct word or phrase from the word list to complete the sentences given below.

   (*a*) All Accounts Departments keep records based upon a system of ...... book keeping.
   (*b*) Every transaction commences with the preparation of a business ......
   (*c*) A document made out when goods are returned is a ......
   (*d*) When documents arrive they are usually recorded in books of ......
   (*e*) The French word for 'day book' is ......
   (*f*) A Trial Balance checks up on the accuracy of the entries made in the ......
   (*g*) The accounts of real things the business owns, such as machinery, motor vehicles, etc., are called ......
   (*h*) The ...... are the accounts that record the losses of the business and the profits of the business, such as wages, rent and water rates (losses) or discount received, commission received, etc. (profits).

(*i*) If the two columns of a Trial Balance come to the same total, the Trial Balance is said to ......

(*j*) Professional firms such as doctors, dentists, etc., do not have a Profit and Loss Account, instead they have an ......

Word list: document, original entry, double-entry, nominal accounts, Income and Expenditure Account, agree, credit-note, Ledger, real accounts, Journal.

2   When accounting procedures are computerized, there are many changes. Explain how each of the following items would now be dealt with:

(*a*) The arrival of a number of invoices from different firms for purchases made, which would formerly have been entered in books of original entry and posted to the ledger.

(*b*) An invoice for a customer whom the computer has been instructed to regard as a bad debtor and no more goods are to be supplied.

(*c*) Cheques are to be made out and sent to suppliers; formerly they would have been handwritten by the chief cashier.

3   Write a few lines about each of these in computerization.

(*a*) Input validation.   (*b*) The CPU.
(*c*) The binary system.   (*d*) Data preparation.

4   Office accounting procedures have become increasingly computerized in recent years. Explain the advantages of such computerization and illustrate your answer by reference to one particular office routine.

5   Write a letter to T. Wall & Sons, 22 Long Line, Maidstone, Kent, ME2 5PQ telling them that, while in principle you do not supply goods on credit to customers in their first year of trading, you will in fact do so for orders in excess of £50, up to a limit of £500. Make it clear that your terms of trade are 'cash net, 30 days after invoice date', but a discount of 5 per cent can be taken if invoices are settled within 15 days. End the letter in a suitably courteous way.

6   Write a letter to M. Kimber & Sons, 2475 Hadrian's Way, Newcastle on Tyne NE3 7ST, requesting payment of the balance outstanding on their account, £520.75. Point out that the payment is already 2 weeks overdue, and if the bill is not paid within 7 days you will commence legal action. Point out also that if they lose their credit status by failing to comply with this request, even if the matter is finally resolved, you will be forced to deal with any future order on a pro-forma basis.

7   Write a letter to a customer who has a good record for placing orders over a 2-year period but who claims that his present position paying on pro-forma terms is inconvenient. He wishes to be allowed to pay on 'open account' terms, paying 30 days after a monthly statement has been received. State your willingness to agree to this, but only for a 1-year trial period. Further add that the credit limit you can allow is only £1 500 (because on one occasion he did place an order for goods worth £5 000). Don't say so, but while you were happy to supply him when he was paying the £5 000 in advance, you would not be quite so

happy to give him credit for such a large amount. Make it clear also that, while you value his custom greatly, if he does not abide by the terms of payment, no further goods will be supplied on open account, and he would have to revert to pro-forma trading.

8 What is meant by 'internal audit'? How can the expense of auditing accounts be justified?

9 You are asked to take charge of petty cash controlled by the *imprest system,* and to record receipts and payments in a petty cash book, *using analysis columns.* Explain clearly and fully what is meant by the words in italics.

10 Why is the Girobank system operated through post offices a useful addition to the methods of payment available in the United Kingdom? Refer in your answer to mail-order houses.

11 (*a*) Define a bill of exchange. (*b*) Explain how a bill of exchange can be used to obtain payment from a foreign customer under the 'documents against acceptance' procedure.

12 What are 'open account' terms in international trade? Explain the arrangements made, referring to (i) confidence in the overseas customer, (ii) time lags between the dispatch of the goods and the receipt of payment, (iii) finance during the time lag for an exporter short of funds.

13 The following shows the entries in T. Fitt's cash book in March:

19..		£	19..			£
Mar. 1	To Balance at bank brought forward	115.00	Mar. 5	By Drawings – self	20.00
			15	" Noah	80.00
16	" Brown	25.00		" Oliver	25.00
25	" Abel	185.00	29	" Rigg	95.00
31	" Warner	286.00		" Lee	15.00
			31	" Balance at bank carried forward	376.00
		£611.00			£611.00
Mar. 31	To Balance	376.00			

Early in April he received this statement from his bank:

T. FITT: IN ACCOUNT WITH LOANSHIRE BANK LIMITED

Date	Particulars	Debit £	Credit £	Balance £
Mar. 1	Balance forward			115.00
5	Self – T. Fitt	20.00		95.00
17	Sundries		25.00	120.00
18	Oliver	25.00		
18	Noah	80.00		15.00
26	Sundries		185.00	200.00
28	Cheque returned unpaid	25.00		175.00
31	Charges	4.00		171.00
31	Lee	15.00		156.00

Draw up a cash book, starting with the present balance of £376.00 and correct such differences as are caused by a lack of knowledge of the bank's activities. Then reconcile the revised cash balance with the balance at the bank in a bank reconciliation statement.

14 From the following prepare a bank reconciliation statement as at 30 June, after first bringing the cash book up to date if this is required:

J. JONES & CO.
CASH BOOK ON 30TH JUNE, 19..

19..			£	19..			£
June 4	To Bank Loan		500.00	June 1	By Balance		227.10
11	" R. Gee		3.20	8	" T. Smith		40.60
30	" L. Mitre		4.00	15	" R. Port		4.96
				29	" B. Lemon		62.10

BANK STATEMENT AS AT 30TH JUNE, 19..

Date	Particulars	Debit	Credit	Balance
		£	£	£
June 1			(Red) *Dr*	227.10
4	Loan		500.00	272.90
8	Sundries	40.60		232.30
11	"		3.20	235.50
16	Bank of America Div.		12.40	247.90
29	Sundries	62.10		185.80
30	Charges	0.50		185.30

15 A shopkeeper's takings (all his goods being charged to consumers with VAT at $17\frac{1}{2}$ per cent) were as follows: Monday £289.50, Tuesday £346.50, Wednesday £115.45, Thursday £186.60, Friday £376.70, Saturday £396.45. Calculate (*a*) his total takings, (*b*) his output tax, (*c*) his net-of-tax takings.

16 A small businessman is supplied with goods valued at £5 780 in a given tax period. This figure is increased by $17\frac{1}{2}$ per cent VAT. His sales during the same period totalled £11 285, according to his till rolls, and this figure included VAT at $17\frac{1}{2}$ per cent charged to customers. Calculate the tax payable to Customs and Excise.

17 A grocer only deals in goods charged at the zero rate, but pays VAT on many items supplied to him. During the tax month of July he pays tax on goods supplied to him worth £4 800, net of tax. What sum will pass between the grocer and the Customs and Excise in respect of this transaction and who will pay whom? (VAT $17\frac{1}{2}$ per cent.)

18 A professional man is told by the Customs and Excise authorities that his profession is exempt from VAT. What are the likely effects of this upon him? In your answer mention the following matters: (*a*) charges to be made for VAT to his customers, (*b*) registration on form VAT 1, (*c*) charges made to him by his suppliers.

19 Meetings

19.1 Types of meeting

Meetings can be held at all sorts of levels, and they may follow all sorts of procedures. They are held to assist communication and decision-making in the various fields of activity in which organizations engage. Some meetings are **formal** and others **informal**. A formal meeting follows clearly laid down procedures, as prescribed in the constitution of a club or society, or in the articles of association of a limited company. Notes will usually be taken, the **minutes** of the meeting, and the person responsible for keeping these notes is called the **secretary**. In large organizations a special **minuting secretary** may be appointed.

An informal meeting has no special procedures, and people are free to speak their minds without fear of being quoted on the matter later. The aim of an informal meeting is to clear the air and reduce tension by an open, unrestricted discussion.

We may list the common types of meeting as follows:

(*a*) Statutory meetings.
(*b*) Annual general meetings (AGMs).
(*c*) Extraordinary general meetings (EGMs).
(*d*) Board meetings.
(*e*) Committee meetings.
(*f*) Departmental meetings.

These may be explained as follows.

(*a*) *Statutory meetings*

A statutory meeting is one required by Act of Parliament, and in the case of limited companies it means the meeting designated as the annual general meeting (AGM) under S366 of the Companies Act, 1985.

(*b*) *Annual general meeting (AGM)*

Every company registered in the United Kingdom must hold an AGM within 18 months of the company's formation, and every 12 months thereafter. Similarly, most clubs and societies will hold an AGM. The purpose of the AGM is to afford the members an opportunity of reviewing the year's activities, of hearing a report from the chairman, or secretary, and of considering the financial situation of the company, or club, or society. They may also change the character of the board or committee (if they have the necessary voting power). In clubs and societies the usual rule is one member one vote, but in companies the rule is usually one share one vote, so that it is possible for a large group of members to be very dissatisfied but quite unable to change the composition of the board, because they cannot command enough votes. Those who control 51 per cent of the votes of a company (strictly speaking 50 per cent + 1 more vote) control the company.

(c) Extraordinary general meetings (EGM)

An EGM is a meeting called at the request of at least 10 per cent of the members of a company, i.e. 10 per cent of the voting shares, for a reason stated in their request. On receipt of such a request the directors must call a meeting within 21 days to discuss the matter raised. It is a way of drawing attention to some action on the part of the board, or of some member of the board, which gives serious cause for concern.

(d) Board meetings

Every limited company and many nationalized corporations are run by boards of directors. A board meeting is usually held monthly, but may be called at any time. The point is that not all the members of the board are full-time members, so a regular meeting, e.g. on the last Thursday of each month, is convenient. As Figure 19.1 shows, the board is divided roughly into two halves — the executive directors and the part-time non-executive directors. Executive directors have a full-time job to do for the company. The usual thing is for the managing director (MD) to lead the executive directors, who usually include the production (factory) manager, the marketing director, the chief accountant, the company secretary and the personnel officer. The non-executive directors are part-time outsiders, often with special knowledge of a technical, financial, legal or organizational nature.

Between the two groups, and taking charge of the meetings is the chairperson. Often a part-time director will be deputy chairperson, and take the chair should the chairperson be unable to attend. Other members of staff may be invited to sit in on a particular part of the board meeting, often to report about a particular item on the agenda. If a minuting secretary is appointed, he/she will usually sit a little apart, but where it is possible to hear all that is said.

(e) Committee meetings

Committees are of two kinds, standing committees and *ad hoc* committees. A standing committee is one that meets regularly and reports to the board periodically. Thus a works committee might

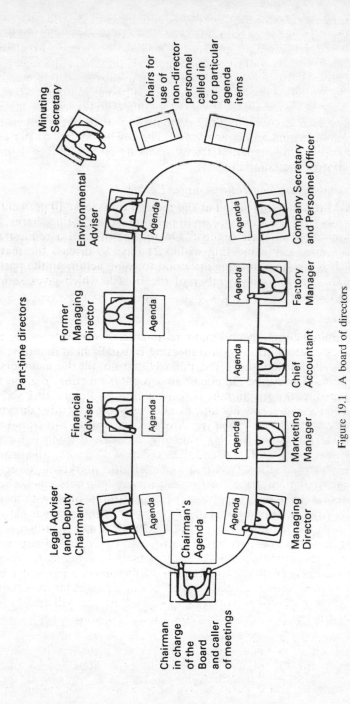

Figure 19.1 A board of directors

review all matters to do with the factory — safety, environmental matters, working conditions, etc. A welfare committee might consider such matters as bereavements, provisions for child-care, first-aid facilities, etc.

By contrast, an *ad hoc* committee is one that meets to deal with a specific situation. The Latin words mean 'for this particular purpose'. Thus a particular event — say a VIP visit — might call for a small *ad hoc* committee to make the arrangements and ensure that all was done that was necessary to make the event a success. After the occasion the committee would be disbanded, its purpose having been achieved.

(f) Departmental meetings

As the name implies, departmental meetings are held to bring a department together to develop an *esprit de corps* and improve communication between the management and the mass of people in the department. They tend to be less formal than other meetings, and give an opportunity for members of the department to discuss company and departmental affairs, to air grievances, to make announcements about events, and so on.

19.2 Organizing a meeting

The stages of organizing a meeting are as follows:

(a) The authorizing of the meeting

It is the duty of the chairperson to authorize the calling of the meeting, though someone else may actually do the work. This person will usually be called the secretary (in a club or society) but in a company the chairperson's personal assistant or secretary will do the work on behalf of the chairperson. At an early stage it will be usual to finalize the minutes of the previous meeting, which are often circulated with the 'notice of meeting'. This gives everyone a chance to read the minutes before the meeting begins. It will then be open to anyone present to propose 'That the minutes be taken as read' — a time-saving procedure, since the reading of minutes can be a tedious business.

(b) The finalizing of the minutes

Before a meeting can start, it is usual for the minutes of the previous meeting to be read (unless someone has proposed the time-saving procedure just referred to). The chairperson will then ask if all are agreed that the minutes do represent a true record of the previous meeting, and if this is agreed, the chairperson will sign the minutes. At this point the minutes become an accredited record of the committee's affairs. It is therefore essential to present a set of minutes to which no objection can be made. The chairperson and secretary will go carefully through the minutes, rephrasing any sentence that seems in any way to give a wrong impression, and arriving at a satisfactory summary of the various matters discussed. The secretary will then arrange to type the minutes and make enough copies for everyone.

(c) The agenda of the meeting

It is usual to send out an agenda with the notice of the meeting. An agenda is a detailed list of the items to be discussed at the meeting. It forms the basis for the conduct of the meeting. Anyone may submit an item for the agenda, provided he/she does so in good time, and it will be included unless pressure of business precludes it. In that case the chairperson might send a note of explanation to the member, expressing his/her regrets, but offering to deal with the matter under AOB, which is always the last item on the agenda, and stands for 'any other business'.

The first three items on any agenda are:

(i) *Apologies for absence.* As a matter of politeness those who cannot attend a meeting should send a note to the chairperson apologizing, and giving an explanation. If it is a question of acting as a representative of some group, it is permissible to send a substitute.

(ii) *Minutes of the previous meeting.* This has already been explained.

(iii) *Matters arising.* This refers to matters arising from the previous meeting. It may be that a short report is called for on some matter — say the welfare arrangements that followed some accident reported at the previous meeting. However, the chairperson would not allow any discussion of an item that was being treated as an agenda item later in the meeting. A full discussion will take place when that agenda item is reached.

The main agenda items. Some sort of priority must be decided upon in dealing with agenda items, and this order is at the chairperson's discretion. It is for the chair to deal with the items in the sequence laid down, but also to push on with the agenda so that later items are reached. In the next section (Section 19.3), which deals with the terminology of meetings, we shall find that some terms used are designed to push the meeting on by cutting down discussion that is not getting anywhere. Two of these terms are 'propose that the motion be now put' and 'move next business'.

The final agenda items. All agendae end with two items: AOB (any other business) and date of next meeting. These days everyone is busy, and liable to develop a full diary as the weeks pass. It is desirable to agree a date for the next meeting that everyone can attend, and, having found such a date, the members must resist attempts by other bodies to choose the same date and time for some other meeting. Inevitably clashes do occur, and the odd member who is forced to give greater priority to some other matter will send his/her apologies before the next meeting.

(*d*) *The 'notice of meeting'*
This is the covering letter sent to all members notifying them of the meeting. It must give:

  (i) The date, time and venue of the meeting.
 (ii) The purpose of the meeting, unless an agenda is enclosed, in which case it is only necessary to refer to 'the attached agenda'. In some cases where time is short the notice may read 'agenda to follow' or even worse 'agenda to be tabled'. This means that the agenda will be given to members when they get to the meeting, which is clearly a less than satisfactory situation.
(iii) The minutes of the previous meeting. Once again these may be sent later, 'minutes to follow' or even worse 'minutes to be tabled'.
 (iv) A circulation list, telling everyone who is going to be present.

The notice will be circulated to all those named, with the agenda and minutes, in good time for the meeting. Members should arrive at the meeting with these items, and the chairperson will usually take a poor view of failure to do so. The painstaking work of the secretary is totally defeated by such inefficiency.

(*e*) *The chairperson's agenda*
It is usual to give the chairperson an enlarged agenda on which he/she can make notes, both before and during the meeting. Thus a particular agenda item might call for a report from some 'outside' member of the firm, whom the chairperson will need to introduce and welcome to the meeting. A note of the person's name, position in the firm, etc., may be necessary. Sometimes official publications may need to be drawn to members' attention, or explanations given. On the right-hand side the chairperson may make notes of items to be followed up at a later date. He/she may also make a note of points that should appear in the minutes, although the minutes are probably being prepared by the minuting secretary. The need for accuracy in the minutes has already been referred to and it is the chairperson who is ultimately responsible for this.

(*f*) *The minutes*
The whole purpose of 'minutes' is to keep an accurate record of the salient features of a meeting — a brief account of the various points

raised as each agenda item was considered. We do not want a verbatim report. The eventual minute will record the general tone of the discussion, any resolutions discussed and so on.

A typical set of minutes is reproduced in Figure 19.2. Note that each item in the minutes is given a number in sequence, so that it can easily be referred to in future. In the entry 86/94, for example, there is a reference to item 79/94, which obviously refers to the previous set of minutes. No doubt the item 79/94 was a report to the welfare committee about the death of the R. Lambourne, and the decision taken to represent the committee at the funeral and to ensure that the bereaved family had been properly helped.

One final point about minutes is that they should be couched in temperate language, avoiding inflammatory accounts of events. For example, we would not say 'A violent argument then began ......' because when the minutes are actually read, several weeks later, it might be that such language offends the parties. Better to say 'a lively debate then took place'.

It is usual to pinpoint key persons and officials by using capital letters for such words as Chairperson, Secretary, Treasurer, etc. These are not common nouns but proper nouns (there is only one Chairperson in the little environment we are dealing with).

19.3 The conduct of meetings and the terminology used

The conduct of the meeting is in the hands of the Chairperson, who should be a person of recognized status. He/she must know all about procedure, and should keep readily available a reference book on the conduct of meetings. The meeting starts when the Chairperson calls those assembled to order. He/she will not usually do so until the appointed time, otherwise a person arriving in time for the meeting might find it had already started. The Chairperson will not call the meeting to order even at the appointed time if a **quorum** is not present. A quorum is the minimum number required to be present by the rules governing the meeting. As soon as the required number is present, the meeting will be called to order.

From that time on the meeting is subject to the rules laid down for it, perhaps in the articles of association of the company, or in the rules book of the association, society or club. The term 'standing orders' refers to this body of rules, as amended by motions passed in a proper manner over the previous years. At any moment a member who feels that the rules are not being followed may raise a point of order, which must be settled by the chair at once. The chair may rule a member out of order for speaking of a matter in an improper way, or at an incorrect time. A member may also be 'out of order' for using improper language or displaying any breach of good manners or good taste. Such occasions illustrate the need for a strong Chair-

Welfare Committee Meeting − XYZ Ltd.
Minutes of a meeting held at 10.30 am, Friday, 1 December 1994 in the Recreation Annexe

Members Present Mr R.T. Lucas, Director (Chairman)
Mr A. Jones (Welfare Officer)
Mrs J. Aylesford (Restaurant Manageress)
Mr R. Peterson (Works Representative)
Miss P. Jamieson (Office Representative)
Mr P. Whyte (Secretary, Entertainments Sub-Committee)
Miss J. Lee (Minuting Secretary)
Messrs J. White, P. Tripp, C. Lea and B. Lucas (Departmental Representatives − Sales)

Apologies   All were present on this occasion.

85/94 *Minutes of previous meeting*
The minutes of the meeting held on Friday, 29 September 1994 were taken as read, adopted and signed by the Chairman.

86/94 *Matters arising*
79/94 Mr Lucas reported that he and Mr Jones attended the funeral of R. Lamborne who was killed in a machine shop accident. The widow's welfare had been properly cared for.

87/94 *Restaurant report*
The accounts of the restaurant for the half year were adopted. Three complaints about restaurant matters had been investigated and the details were explained. All three had been resolved satisfactorily.

88/94 *Christmas activities*
Mr Whyte reported that the Social on Christmas Eve was fully planned and promised to be successful. The children's party had been arranged for 7 January and a full programme had been arranged. A grant of £100 was approved.

89/94 *Letter of complaint*
A matter raised concerning toilet facilities in the firm's motor transport department was agreed to need thorough investigation.

It was *RESOLVED* that a sub-committee be formed (Messrs R.T. Lucas, A. Jones, R. Peterson to serve).

90/94 *Technical training*
A complaint about inadequate pre-examination study leave was received from the works representative.

It was *RESOLVED* that this matter be raised at boardroom level and the Chairman arrange its inclusion in the board meeting agenda. Mr R. Peterson be proposed to attend and explain the matter.

91/94 *AOB*
There being no other business, the meeting adjourned at 12.50 pm.

Date of next meeting
Friday, 2 March 1995 at 10.30 am in the recreation annexe.

Chairman: 2 March 1995 _____

Figure 19.2   Minutes of a welfare-committee meeting

person, who must listen attentively to everything said and keep the atmosphere friendly, and attitudes positive.

During the meeting all remarks should be addressed to the chair, and not to individuals. This tends to reduce the personal impact of the statements being made, which are addressed to the whole meeting and not to any individual. It also prevents the meeting breaking down into a number of separate discussions, which the secretary would find impossible to minute, since they are all taking place at once. The phrase 'through the chair, please' is often used by the Chairperson, or indeed anyone attending the meeting, to stop people talking while other people are talking. Only one person can be heard by the Chairperson, so those who are voicing private points to their neighbours must be quiet until they 'have the floor'.

The following terms are used about various aspects of meetings.

(*a*) *Quorum*. The minimum number of members that must be present at a meeting, under the rules, if the proceedings are to be valid.

(*b*) *Ex officio*. 'By virtue of office.' An official may automatically qualify for a position because of the office he/she holds. Thus the mayor of a borough was until recently *ex officio* a justice of the peace during his/her tenure of office. Similarly, a personnel officer may be *ex officio* a member of the industrial relations committee of a company.

(*c*) *To co-opt*. Co-option is the power of a committee to ask others to serve on the committee if it seems that their expertise will be helpful. Usually a person may be co-opted by a simple majority vote of the committee.

(*d*) *Motion*. A motion is a proposition for consideration at a meeting. It should normally be written out and handed to the chairperson or secretary in advance, so that it can be included in the agenda, but as a matter of urgency a motion may be introduced at a meeting, if the meeting agrees.

(*e*) *Proposer and seconder*. The proposer is the person who speaks to the motion, explaining why it is being proposed. He/she is followed by the seconder. A discussion then follows and the proposer has the right to reply to the discussion.

(*f*) *Amendment*. An amendment is a suggestion to alter the wording of a motion during discussion to make it more acceptable to the meeting, or cover some point omitted in the original motion. It must be proposed and seconded. If there is no seconder, it is not proceeded with. If the amendment is carried, the motion is forthwith amended.

(*g*) *Resolution*. A resolution is a formal decision carried at a meeting. It is proposed, seconded and carried, i.e. passed by a majority vote.

(*h*) *Ways of carrying a resolution*. (*a*) *Unanimously* − everyone in agreement. (*b*) *Nem.con.* − no one contradicting. Some people voted in favour, and no one against, but some people did not vote. (*c*) *By a majority* − say 8:3 or 7:5. The majority required may be specified in the rules. (*d*) *By the chairperson's casting vote* − if voting is exactly equal, the chairperson is allowed a second vote to resolve the difficulty.

(*i*) *'Through the chair.'* As explained, this term is used when people are talking to one another when others are trying to speak. At a meeting all remarks are made to the chair. You begin your contribution with the words 'Mr Chairman' or 'Madam Chairman'. You may not speak across the table direct to another person, or engage in side discussions while someone else is speaking to the chair.

(*j*) *'Lie on the table.'* This phrase is used when no further action will be taken on a letter, document or motion at this particular meeting. The matter will then be given time for developments to take place, and may be raised at the next meeting if anyone is interested.

(*k*) *'Move next business.'* It means that the matter under discussion shall be left for the present, it having been well and truly aired and no agreement seeming likely, and that the next item on the agenda should be discussed.

(*l*) *'Move that the motion be now put.'* It means that the discussion in the view of the proposer has gone on long enough and that the chairperson should put it to the vote. If this is carried, the proposer of the original motion is allowed to reply to the discussion and then the motion is voted upon.

(*m*) *Adjournment*. It is the breaking-off of a meeting, to postpone further discussion or because of shortage of time. The chairperson proposes an adjournment, and if the meeting agrees, discussion will proceed at a later meeting, for which adequate notice will be given.

19.4 Secretarial duties after the meeting

The chairperson will often be a senior member of staff, who will have other duties to attend to after a meeting. It is the usual thing for the secretary to round off the work of the committee in the following way.

(*a*) Ensure that the room that has been used is left tidy and that all the surplus materials, copies of the agendae, copies of the minutes, pencils supplied, etc., are collected and taken away.

(*b*) If coffee or snacks have been served, it is usual to see that the cups, etc., are collected and left available for clearance by canteen staff, if not actually returned to the canteen. It is courteous to send a note of thanks to the person in charge, and if any chit needs to be signed, the secretary will either sign it personally or present it to the chairperson for signature before sending it to the canteen supervisor.

(*c*) The secretary, with the minuting secretary, if present, will then go through the notes of the meeting, to draw up draft minutes for presentation to the chairperson at an early date — before ideas of what was actually said grow hazy. An approved set of minutes should be agreed with the chairperson within, at most, a couple of days of the meeting. In the course of doing this the following points may be dealt with:

(i) The chairperson may send a brief note of thanks to any outsider who attended the meeting to deal with an agenda item.

(ii) Where any member was asked to take on some responsibility and report back at the next meeting, or where a sub-committee was set up to deal with some problem, a short note reminding the members concerned about the matters and formally giving the terms of reference will ensure that they are clear about them, and know what is expected.

(iii) The committee file should be up-dated by the secretary, and a copy of the minutes of the meeting just ended should be inserted. Enough copies of the minutes should be run off to supply every member when the next 'notice of meeting' is sent out. If for some reason this cannot be done at once, the secretary should put a reminder notice in his/her diary to ensure it is not overlooked.

(iv) It is a good idea to start drawing up the next agenda, by entering on it any 'carry-forward' items that appear to be necessary if the meeting that has just ended is to be followed up properly at the next meeting.

(*d*) Finally, the secretary should ensure that the date and time of the next meeting are added to the diaries and year planners of those affected (top level staff who need to know about such matters even if they are not members of the committee). A note of the date and time should also be sent at once to those who sent 'letters of apology'. If the minutes are already available, they could be sent to the absentees at the same time, to keep them informed of the matters discussed.

19.5 Rapid revision − meetings

Answers		Questions
−	1	What is meant by a formal meeting?
1 One conducted according to the normal rules for a meeting of that type, presided over by a chairperson, and with a secretary keeping notes from which normal minutes will be prepared.	2	What are the rules for the conduct of such a meeting?
2 (*a*) The meeting will start at a prescribed time, provided a quorum is present. (*b*) If a quorum is not present, a short delay may be allowed for late arrivals. (*c*) Once started, the meeting begins with apologies for absence, and the approval of the minutes of the previous meeting. (*d*) It then follows an agreed agenda. (*e*) All remarks are made 'through the chair'.	3	List the most important meetings of companies and similar bodies.
3 (*a*) AGMs, (*b*) EGMs, (*c*) board meetings, (*d*) committee meetings, (*e*) departmental meetings.	4	Who are the members of a 'board' of a company?
4 (*a*) The chairperson, (*b*) the executive directors, chief of whom is the managing director, (*c*) the non-executive (part-time) directors, (*d*) the company secretary.	5	What are the stages in organizing a meeting?
5 (*a*) The meeting is authorized, (*b*) the room is booked and other arrangements made (coffee, etc.), (*c*) the minutes of the last meeting are finalized and duplicated, (*d*) the agenda is drawn up, (*e*) the notice is prepared and duplicated, (*f*) the	6	When can a meeting begin?

notice, agenda, and the minutes of
the previous meeting are circulated
to members.

6	At the agreed time, provided a quorum is present.	7	What is a quorum?
7	The minimum number for a meeting to be a valid meeting, capable of passing resolutions that will bind the committee at future sessions.	8	How does the meeting proceed?
8	With the agenda items, in the order listed on the agenda.	9	What do we call a matter for discussion at a meeting?
9	It is called a motion. It is proposed by A, seconded by B, thrown open to general discussion, to which the proposer may reply, and is finally put to the meeting as a formal resolution, which is voted upon.	10	When the meeting supports a resolution, we say it has been 'carried'. In what ways may it be carried?
10	(*a*) Unanimously, (*b*) *nem. con* (no-one contradicting it), (*c*) by a majority, (*d*) by the chairperson's casting vote.	11	If a resolution is not carried, we say it is ......?
11	Defeated	12	Go over the list again until you are sure of all the answers.

Exercises set 19

1 Write down the letters (*a*)–(*j*) one under the other. Then write next to each letter the word or phrase from the word list below that is most appropriate to each of the sentences (*a*)–(*j*) below.

(*a*) In view of the changes in VAT regulations I suggest we set up a small ...... to consider whether our accounting systems need modifying.

(*b*) The chairperson said 'In view of the lateness of the hour I propose we ...... this discussion until 2 pm tomorrow, in this venue'.

(*c*) 'I ...... that proposal' said the personnel officer.

(*d*) A ...... meeting is one required by Act of Parliament.

(*e*) Apart from the independent chairperson, Mrs Groves, the balance of the Enquiry Committee will be preserved by having three staff representatives and three ...... members, led by the chief accountant.

(*f*) To save time, Madam Chairman, I propose that the minutes ......

(*g*) A minuting secretary should always couch the minutes in ...... language.

(*h*) At an annual general meeting of a club or society the ...... will give a report on the organization's finances.

(*i*) Under the rules of this standing committee the chairperson may ...... on to the committee any person who has special knowledge about a particular agenda item.

(*j*) 'I must remind members that all remarks should be made ......'
said the Chairman.

Word list: *ex officio*, adjourn, treasurer, co-opt, *ad hoc* committee,
statutory, second, through the chair, temperate, be taken as read.

2   What are the duties of a minuting secretary? With whom would he/she
liaise about the minutes of a meeting?

3   Draft an agenda and a 'notice of meeting' for a health and safety at
work meeting. The three chief items for discussion are (*a*) no-smoking
areas in office premises, (*b*) fork-lift problems in the warehouse (fumes
and drive-thru doors), and (*c*) conveyor systems in the factory. A
special item concerns the death of Ivor Waywivem, a garage mechanic,
crushed by a vehicle in the loading bay. Invent names for the chairperson, the secretary, the minuting secretary and eight departmental
representatives.

4   You are to oppose the motion in a debate. The motion reads 'The
employees of Techno-Cranes Ltd find no merit in the formal procedures
used in the Industrial Relations Committee chaired by the Personnel
Officer'.

5   Draw up a short constitution for the 'Bulls-eye Club', a central recreational
area in a factory complex, staffed by a manager and a secretary, and
presided over by the managing director. Mention the rights and responsibilities of members, the membership of the club committee, the frequency and conduct of meetings and an appeals committee (to whom
barred members may apply for reinstatement).

6   Write a short report as chairperson of a small *ad hoc* committee appointed
to investigate the theft of canteen linen. The control of such linen has
been lax, but has been made worse by the employment of homeless
persons as part-time workers in the lowest grades of work. Suggest some
possible solutions.

20   Travel arrangements

20.1   Patterns of business travel

Business travel takes place at several levels, and it is important for office staff to understand the sort of arrangements that are necessary at each level. The basic requirements are 'safe arrival' and 'safe return'. Sandwiched in between these obviously desirable require- ments is 'successful completion of the business to be undertaken'.

We may divide travel into three chief levels:

(*a*) Routine journeying.
(*b*) Home market travel.
(*c*) Executive travel overseas.

Now that the European Community is a single market, it is most convenient to treat the EC as the 'home' market and include travel in the Community as part of the second group above. This leaves executive travel overseas as an essentially 'long-haul' activity.

20.2   Routine journeying

It is often necessary to make short journeys on behalf of the firms and companies for which we work. It is a common thing to use young and inexperienced people for such 'messenger' services, and it is certainly a way of varying their daily work, helping them to gain confidence and experience and perhaps display resourcefulness. For a new and untried junior member of staff even a trip to deliver a parcel or collect some artwork is an adventure, and it is also only too easy for them to get lost, get injured and even get 'mugged'. The days have gone when a child could walk the length and breadth of the United Kingdom and never think of harm. We must, under the Health and Safety at Work Act, 1974, provide a safe system of work, and that includes careful induction of the new employee into these sorts of activities.

Some of the important aspects may be listed and described as follows:

(*a*) *Where is the messenger going?* Make it quite clear where he/ she is to go, and give the information in writing.

(*b*) *What is he/she to do?* Here again, it is not good enough to say a thing once and bundle the messenger out of the front door. Put it in writing. 'To take the parcel to Brown and Jones, at the address given and ask for Miss Hawkins. Miss Hawkins should then give you an envelope, with a banker's draft in it for £284.00. She will show you the cheque before she seals the envelope in your presence, and in the presence of another person from her own firm. Bring the cheque back safely and take it straight to the cashier, Mr Jackson. Then report to the duty receptionist to say you are safely back'.

(*c*) *Does he/she know the way?* It is always desirable to have local maps in the office to which messengers can turn to find their way. Induct a new member of staff into the correct way to use such a map. The A–Z maps are good, and there are several other famous names, e.g. Geographia. Have two or three copies available and let the messenger take one with him/her if it makes them feel safer. If they have to use public transport, explain carefully, and put in writing, which buses, tube stations, etc., are to be used.

(*d*) *Have they got money?* Most young people have little enough money, and can't afford to subsidize firms whose proprietors are millionaires. Make sure they have money, and tell them to bring back any tickets or petty cash vouchers they can to prove what expenses they have had to bear. Make it clear that in an emergency they may call a taxi, and you will pay the cost on arrival. Similarly, in an emergency they may phone for help, or reverse the charges if necessary. It is even a good idea to keep one or two phonecards in the office, and give a messenger one before he/she sets off, collecting it again on return. Some phone boxes will not accept money, only cards.

(*e*) *Is he/she adequately clothed?* Staff should be encouraged to dress sensibly, and not go off thoughtlessly if weather is likely to turn bad. The odd cagoule, or umbrella, in the receptionist's cupboard can mean safe delivery of vital packages through the heaviest rainstorms.

(*f*) *Is he/she insured?* All firms must by law be covered by an insurance policy called 'employer's liability insurance'. It is advisable when negotiating such cover to make it clear that the firm requires cover for accidents, etc., which happen off the premises, on these types of routine journey.

20.3 'Home market' travel

The chief causes of 'home market' travel are the needs to seek supplies and to find markets for our products. An increasing share of United Kingdom trade these days is import trade. We must visit suppliers to ensure that the products we need are being grown or manufactured in conditions of which we approve, using safe materials, good quality labour, environmentally friendly packaging, etc. Equally, when we market our own products, it is helpful to meet the agents and merchants who are handling the product as intermediaries between us and the final customer. We need to see the situation from the customer's end.

All such travel arrangements need careful planning, and have to be 'thought through' from start to finish. Why is the visit being made? Who is likely to be visited and what is it hoped to achieve? What arrangements need to be made for the travel itself, including hotel accommodation, meeting places, car hire, etc.? What will the executive need on each day of the journey? Sometimes it helps to pack a box with each day's needs and check it through carefully to see nothing has been overlooked. Make arrangements to cover the executive's own work while he/she is away; also make arrangements to liaise with him/her every day, and provide the back-up needed.

Emergencies always arise, e.g. a customer may want information on a product it was not anticipated would interest him/her. Promises to make brochures, etc., available must be honoured by the back-up staff. Extra data may be faxed through to the executive's hotel, etc. The executive wants to off-load the day's completed work and move on to the next day's itinerary. An itinerary is a plan for a journey showing the dates and times of each stage, the transport to be used, the time and place of meetings, who one is likely to meet, and the detailed aim of each meeting.

EC travel

Although the EC must now be regarded as a single market and viewed as a 'home' rather than a 'foreign' trading area, it does still present some difficulties. There are language problems to be overcome, and it may be necessary to arrange for an interpreter. Many foreign nationals do speak English, but not all, and some important people with whom executives need to converse may have less reason to master English than others. For example, sales staff have a greater incentive to study English than engineers, but a clear understanding between an exporter and the engineer handling the assembly of the exporter's product may be essential.

It is also essential to make arrangements that suit the country to be visited. For example, we do not want to arrive on a day that is a public holiday, and we need to know what are the usual business hours. We need to know the currency and the breakdown of the coinage. All this sort of information is available in handbook form from specialist publishers. The best of all is Croner Publications Ltd, Croner House, London Rd, Kingston upon Thames, Surrey, RT2 6SR Tel 081 547 3333. Its *Office Companion*, *Reference Book for Exporters*, and *Reference Book for Importers* have 'country pages' that give a host of details about every country in the world. These handbooks are up-dated monthly, new pages being sent out whenever details change, and they are therefore very reliable. Most offices will have at least one handbook from the Croner range, and heads of department will usually obtain the most appropriate one for their use. A typical 'country page' gives details of the capital city, major business centres, languages spoken, whether English-speakers are commonly found, business hours, public holidays, religions, currency, exchange rates, weights and measures, voltages, climate, vaccinations required, embassy addresses, chambers of commerce addresses, major banks, airlines, and lots, lots more.

Since the detailed arrangements for visits to EC countries are very similar to those for longer-range overseas travel, the discussion of arrangements is made in the next section.

20.4 Executive travel overseas

Generally speaking, the arrangements for overseas travel are divided between the executive who is making the visit, possibly with support staff as companions, and the secretarial and clerical staff who will be handling the routine arrangements, ensuring everything is in order and providing the back-up for the visit from the home base.

The executive's viewpoint. From this point of view the chief pre-occupation of the executive is the purpose of the visit, what it is hoped to achieve and what preparations must be made. Overseas visits are not made every day, so they generally call for a review of the activities in the country or countries concerned. It may be necessary to call for reports on the sales, servicing facilities, agents, factories, depots and other installations. It may call for a review of personnel — their skills, productivity, strengths and weaknesses. There may be problems with government officials, trade unions, bankers, customs authorities, etc. The executive must collect data and opinions from advisers, must be briefed on the problem areas, must know what products are of interest and the degree of progress made on outstanding contracts. The costs of the visit must be estimated and arrangements made to obtain funds from banks along the way. The aim will be to draw up a list of precise objectives, and to provide all the knowledge and equipment that will enable the executive and his/her team to achieve them.

The secretary's viewpoint. While the executive is busy with the actual subject matter of the various meetings, the secretary is concerned with the detailed arrangements for the trip. The itinerary must be agreed before the travel arrangements can go ahead. It will decide what towns or cities are to be visited and in what order. It will decide which agents, branches, depots and sites are to be visited and inspected. Protocol may enter into the arrangements, with various officials to be met and perhaps entertained. Public relations work is often of crucial importance, and the proper courtesies must be exchanged. Matters of etiquette, dress, etc., may need to be borne in mind, and a secretary will seek to forewarn the executive about any such matters drawn to his/her attention.

The itinerary has to be carefully timed. There may be many meetings to arrange, many customers to see, and staff who will hope to take part in at least some of the functions. It may be necessary to bring less important members of staff in to a general meeting, cocktail party or similar function, just to include as many people as possible. It is easy to fit too much into the schedule, especially if the odd snag occurs and rearrangements are necessary. The odd clear half-day here and there gives some chance of making a rearrangement without it becoming a nightmare scenario for the secretarial staff.

20.5 Travel arrangements

The outline plan of the visit should now be clear and it is advisable to hand over the actual travel arrangements to an expert in the field. There are so many outside agencies that can assist in travel and hotel arrangements that there is little point in trying to do these things oneself. The charges are not high in a competitive field like this, and the specialist agencies have established links which can be made cheaply and effectively with a guarantee that the standard of facility will be adequate in relation to the price range used. Such arrangements can include car hire for the period required, and the reservation of rail travel and internal flights. It is desirable to use the car and public transport in any country visited, for both give real experience of the country concerned and broaden the executive's background.

While the travel agents are busy with these arrangements, the secretary must turn to filling in the detailed programme on the outline itinerary. This may require the booking of actual appointments with customers, the calling of meetings and conferences to be attended by overseas staff, the delegation of arrangements to managers overseas so that all will go well on the day, and the allocation of budgeted funds to ensure that an adequate sum is available without exceeding the budget.

The whole itinerary must then be examined in detail so that every event, visit or function has been properly thought through. The following list of items that may be required to meet the needs of every event illustrates the diversity of requirements.

(*a*) *Visiting cards*. These should be as high-powered as possible, conferring a suitable degree of status on the executive.

(*b*) *Customer records*. These should be as detailed as possible and should highlight lines the customer does not at present handle, new lines becoming available, quantity discounts to be offered as inducements for larger orders and suggestions for limits to which the executive may go in offering credit extensions on larger orders.

(*c*) *Sales literature*. Sales literature must of course be in the local language, and should cover the full range of products. Since only one or two copies of each can be carried, it is necessary to have a back-up stock from which the executive's case can be replenished each day. Making this back-up stock into 'daily' packs so that a new pack can be slipped into the case without any waste of time is a useful idea.

(*d*) *Display equipment*. Today relatively light travel packs, which include slide projectors, video presentations tape-recorded sales patter and even films, can be made up quite cheaply. This type of audio-visual package, if well prepared, takes a great deal of strain off the marketing executive, and is interesting to the customer.

(*e*) *Visit briefs*. A 'visit brief' is a short account of the chief objectives of each visit, together with pertinent data based upon the customer's record. It may include details of the particular market area covered by the customer and information about the customer's special needs. Even his/her personality and general attitude may be hinted at, and any particular problems of finance, transport, ware-housing or marketing may be analysed. Before departure each brief should be gone through, perhaps with a mini-conference of all who know the customers and their problems, so that the executive really understands the brief. Before making the actual call, the executive reads through the 'visit brief' and recalls the relevant points. He/she then enters the interview knowledgeable about the needs of the particular customer, and makes a more impressive impact as a result.

(*f*) *Speeches*. If the purposes of the visit include the holding of conferences and displays, it will be necessary to plan these in detail or delegate their planning to senior staff abroad. The executive will certainly need speeches to be prepared; speeches which make the points that head office considers necessary. Such speeches will be based on reports already in existence or specially prepared, and this background material may need to travel with the speeches to give the executive a full package of background information.

(*g*) *Procedural routines*. It is important to plan in advance the routine procedures the executive is to follow so that his/her secretary and other members of the back-up team can give the fullest possible support. Thus an 'immediate action' routine for any sales made should be devised so that they are followed up while the trail is still warm. Similarly, the executive may wish to dictate reports on the views expressed at any conference or meeting, as feedback to head office. Arrangements for tapes to be flown back for transcription, or for facsimile copies of reports typed abroad to be transmitted to head office, may be finalized, including detailed arrangements for their appraisal at head office in his/her absence.

One routine that must be established is how the executive can be contacted for certain. Where the time lag is not too great, e.g. when visiting European countries, it may be sound policy to fix a time, or perhaps two times, every day when the executive will try to ensure that he/she is in the hotel room. This will enable direct links to be established should they be required. If there is nothing to report either way, the call can be terminated at once to save expense. With countries where the time lag is great, it may be quite impossible to establish a link in office hours. Arrangements to have a telex or fax link with one of the firm's agents may then be the most satisfactory method of contacting the executive, while the willingness of the secretary or some senior executive to accept calls at any time of the night will cater for real emergencies. The greater accuracy of a telex or fax link compared with a conversation on a poor line is also an advantage.

(*h*) *Address and telephone lists*. A full list of all the business contacts in each itinerary area should be built up, with addresses and telephone numbers. It is convenient if they are in itinerary order, and it may be sound policy to prepare postcards in advance announcing arrival and confirming visit dates and times. These can be posted as soon as the executive arrives, although early appointments are better confirmed by telephone.

Friends and relatives (if any) should also be contacted, since they are often most helpful in assisting the visitor, and in addition enable him/her to relax by reducing the endless round of business that otherwise develops.

20.6 Practical travel details and documents

Although travel agents or hotel agencies are to be used for the actual travel arrangements, the executive's secretary must attend to many details personally. The secretary should ensure that nothing is forgotten. Most of the points listed below are important.

(*a*) *Passport*. It is essential to have a valid passport with plenty of spare pages. It is taking longer these days to secure a new passport, except for the simplified 'British visitors' type, which only lasts 1 year and is inappropriate for business staff who have to secure visas and entry permits. Order a new passport in good time if the pages are nearly all used up. It is wise for the executive to learn the number of the passport by heart, although it should also be recorded in several places. A few extra passport photographs may be helpful, and can be given up if required on entry to plants or depots where security is tight.

(*b*) *International driving licences*. The Automobile Association and the Royal Automobile Club are authorized to issue international driving licences at a relatively modest fee to those people travelling abroad who may find an ordinary United Kingdom Driving Licence unacceptable. The charge is quite small (£3.00 at the time of writing) and they are only issued to persons who possess already a valid

United Kingdom licence. A passport-type photograph must be attached.

(*c*) *Insurance*. Most business staff who represent their firms abroad enjoy a high salary and have mortgages and family commitments to meet. It follows that they should insist on adequate insurance when travelling on their firm's business, for the risks of air travel and foreign travel generally are considerable. A policy for a realistic sum, say £50000, for a short period is not very expensive, and may mean a great deal to a spouse and children deprived of their breadwinner. Insurance against sickness, loss of property, etc., is usually taken out without hesitation by any traveller; life insurance at a sensible figure is not so frequently considered.

(*d*) *Credit cards*. While the major United Kingdom banks issue credit cards that have a very wide acceptability, it is regrettably true that not everyone will accept them abroad. This is partly due to the ways in which currencies are allowed to 'float' these days, so that a foreigner supplying goods and services to a UK visitor may find that the exchange rate has moved against him/her before payment is received under the credit card. 'Bank of America' and 'American Express' cards are acceptable almost anywhere, and may be obtained relatively easily by business personnel. It is therefore desirable to carry one of these cards when travelling abroad.

(*e*) *Foreign exchange*. Adequate supplies of foreign exchange should be obtained before departure, and travellers' cheques or letters of credit, which will enable cash to be obtained abroad should also be carried. Some of the earliest contacts with foreigners on arrival require small notes or coins. For example, one does not wish to give a 100 franc tip to the porter. It is therefore helpful to bring back from each trip a small amount of loose change and small denomination notes. Stored away in an envelope in the filing cabinet, these small amounts will be useful on the next visit abroad.

(*f*) *Health aids*. While in many foreign countries it is possible to buy products like antibiotics over the counter without a doctor's prescription, it often happens that ordinary medicaments like aspirin, ointments, etc., are difficult to obtain when required. A reasonable selection of health aids should be taken out. Such items as salt tablets and anti-malaria tablets may be necessary and a doctor's assistance should be sought in any difficulty. A full range of injections should be arranged against such diseases as yellow fever, bubonic plague, typhoid, etc., where embassies require or advise such precautions. A World Health Certificate certifying details of the inoculations obtained is essential in many countries. A doctor will supply prescriptions for any drugs required for the duration of the trip, or a letter advising foreign doctors of treatment being given.

Notice also that in these days, when drug-smuggling is all too common, Customs authorities will often seize all tablets taken into a country, to the great disadvantage of some travellers with medical problems. In case of such eventualities it is wise to carry an open letter to Customs authorities, in the correct language, explaining the nature of the medical problem, the drug prescribed and the duration of the visit. A reference point (such as the consular address and telephone number) might be helpful in this situation.

One of the worst calamities of all is to break one's spectacles in a foreign country where it may be difficult to replace them. A second pair should be taken along, and also a prescription for their replacement if necessary. In some countries sunglasses are essential, and a spare pair is also advisable.

(g) *Electrical equipment.* Variations in voltage, etc., sometimes render equipment such as display matter, portable electric typewriters, electric razors, etc., unsuitable in some countries. Alternatively, it may be necessary to change over a switch from one voltage to another. Adaptors may be necessary and advice can often be obtained from travel agents or embassies.

(h) *Climatic aspects of the journey.* The secretary should check the climatic aspects to ensure that the executive has appropriate weights of clothing and sufficient changes to meet all likely needs. Books such as Croner's *Reference Book for Exporters* give such details for all countries in the world.

20.7 Accompanying staff

It is frequently the case that top executives are accompanied by other staff, often of personal assistant (PA) status, but also of lower status. Such people usually require support, particularly with dress, since they may have hostess or reception duties to perform, and as such represent the firm just as much as the executive. An adequate dress allowance must be built into the budget so that all such people have appropriate clothing to suit the climate, and are adequately provided with items for grooming, evening dress, etc.

20.8 Departure day minus one

It is of considerable help to the executive if a final review of everything affecting the trip is held on the day before departure. The secretary should go through the contents of his/her briefcase with the executives explaining what has been provided and where it is packed. The location of the travel documents, itinerary, visit briefings, sales literature, etc., should be clarified and related to the checklist for the visit to ensure that nothing has been forgotten.

Finally the secretary should give the executive a checklist to use before leaving for the airport. It should list all those items which are to be taken as separate units. Thus if the airline tickets are already in the briefcase, the word 'briefcase' on the checklist should be enough, but if they are to be carried separately, in a wallet or handbag, they should appear as a separate unit on the checklist. A typical list is shown in Figure 20.1.

20.9   Covering the executive's absence

If an executive is away from the office, for whatever reason, his/her work does not stop and must be adequately covered by someone else. If the reason for absence is an overseas visit, the work will almost certainly be intensified as he/she calls in for back-up support, reports on progress or requests data and information not anticipated in the planning period.

If the executive has a personal assistant or secretary who has not travelled with the visiting party, he/she is obviously best placed to cover the executive's absence. He/she will know all about the arrangements, who to contact for further information and who needs to receive the information arriving from abroad. This period of time requires a very responsible attitude on the part of the secretary or PA. The mail has to be opened; faxes and telexes arriving must be acted upon, and if necessary replied to; ordinary calls have to be answered; and if the executive is likely to ring the office, it must be manned.

Final check list

Passport
Visa
International driving licence
World Health Certificate
Airline tickets
Foreign currency
Sterling
Credit cards
Traveller's cheques
House keys
Car keys
Medical pack (including spectacles)
Itinerary (briefcase)
Audio-visual pack
Back-up stock pack
Visiting cards (briefcase)
Spectacles
Briefcase
Personal suitcase
Hand luggage

Figure 20.1   A final checklist

If the personal assistant is travelling with the party, the arrangements for covering the executive's work are more difficult. If a PA
of equal stature can be 'borrowed' from another executive, this will
be a sound arrangement. More usually a younger secretary is inducted
into the department's work during the visit-planning period, and is
then left to deal with problems as they arise, in liaison with a senior
secretary if difficulties arise. It is very important that this senior aide
should be sympathetic and knowledgeable, and realize the importance of smooth handling of any problems that develop.

The office will usually be in contact with the executive much more
regularly and directly than the executive's own family. The back-up
staff should ensure that the family is told of his/her safe arrival at
destination, and that any personal messages that come through are
passed on accurately. If the secretary is accompanying the executive,
his/her own family should similarly be kept in touch with the progress
of the visit.

20.10 Points to think about and discuss

(*a*) An executive, his personal assistant, a chauffeur and a general
handyman are to travel to Holland to make a series of visits to
possible customers for the firm's engineering products.

What sort of things might each of them be doing in the weeks'
leading up to the visit? Before the subject is thrown open for
discussion, appoint one member of your group for each of the four
travellers to draw up a list of points that arise during the discussion
and which will be useful to that particular member of the team.

(*b*) You are appointed to a team of three people to investigate
the circumstances that led to a young female member of staff being
assaulted while on an errand to take drugs to a West London
hospital. The attack occurred in the corridor of an East London
hospital miles from her true destination. Police dealing with the
crime intend to visit the office later this day and the chief administration officer has called for a report by lunch-time. What points
call for investigation?

20.11 Rapid revision − executive travel

Answers		Questions
−	1	Why do executives need to travel?
1 To obtain the supplies we need, and to find markets for the products we make.	2	What are the important points in planning executive travel?
2 (*a*) Know why the visit is being made, (*b*) know what it is hoped to achieve, (*c*) know who is likely to be visited,	3	Where does the planning begin?

(*d*) establish linking arrangements so both the executive and the secretary can always get in touch, (*e*) think the whole process through and arrange the practical details at every stage, (*f*) make arrangements to cover for the executive while he/she is away.

3	With preliminary discussions about the purpose of the visit, the places to be visited, the people to be interviewed and the aims to be achieved in each section of the journey.	4	What is an itinerary?
4	It is a plan for a journey, showing the dates and times of each stage of the journey – the meetings to be held, the travel necessary, the factories or depots or offices to be visited, etc.	5	Why is it important not to have too tight a schedule?
5	(*a*) Because foreign travel is always unreliable (weather may be unfavourable, etc.) (*b*) Because customers or suppliers hope to make friends and show off their country, its sights and special features. These events cannot be rushed. (*c*) Because the pace of life may be slower, and it is best to 'flow with the rest' rather than battle your way through a series of obstructions and difficulties	6	Name some of the problems of foreign visits
6	(*a*) Public holidays are different and should be checked out by reference to the 'country pages' of such handbooks as *Croner's Handbook for Exporters*. (*b*) Visas may be required and must be arranged well beforehand. (*c*) Foreign currency has to be obtained, as well as acceptable traveller's cheques, credit cards, etc.	7	Why is it best to leave all the actual travel arrangements to travel agents?
7	Because they have links and computerized connections all over the world.	8	List the supplies an executive might need on his/her journey.
8	(*a*) Visiting cards; (*b*) sales or other promotional literature; (*c*) customers' records or records of output at factories, plantations, etc., and possibly accountants' reports, etc.; (*d*) visit briefs; (*e*) prepared speeches for various occasions; (*f*) Lists of names, addresses, telephone numbers, etc.; (*g*) prepared postcards or letters to be posted ahead to the next stage of the journey, reminding people of one's arrival, etc.	9	How should these materials be made available to the executive?

9 Preferably in packs in itinerary order, so that each set is not muddled with other materials but is only opened when the executive reaches that stage of the journey.	10 What is a visit brief?
10 A package of information referring to a particular part of an itinerary — a special visit or event.	11 How is it used?
11 He/she reads it all through before setting off and discusses it with anyone on the staff who knows the place, its problems and potential. Then it is read again the night before the actual visit, and any more recent developments notified are incorporated into the package. A prepared report might be included, one enabling the executive to complete a full account of the current position by completing boxes or spaces on the report after the visit. This can then be airmailed or faxed home for action by the back-up team.	12 Go over the page again until you are sure of all the answers.

Exercises set 20

1 Write down the letters (*a*−*j*) on separate lines in your exercise book. Against each letter write a word from the word list below that is most appropriate for each sentence below.

(*a*) Young members of staff must be carefully ...... into safe procedures when sent on errands for the firm or company.

(*b*) ...... should be clear, and addresses and names of persons, railway stations, etc., should preferably be in writing.

(*c*) All firms should make sure that their ...... covers young employees going on essential errands out of the firm's own premises.

(*d*) The essential thing for all visits, home or overseas, is to ..... from start to finish.

(*e*) Croner's reference books, and similar publications have '...... pages' giving complete details of every place we might need to visit abroad.

(*f*) The executive's chief preoccupation is with the ...... of the visit, and what it is hoped to ......

(*g*) The detailed plan of a journey is called the ......

(*h*) The simplest of all reminders of a visit, and the one most likely to bring in orders, is the ......

(*i*) Executive absence is not a time to slack off; on the contrary the back-up team must behave ...... and offer immediate ...... by fax, telex, etc.

(*j*) Executives should obtain ...... advice in good time before departure, and should obtain such ...... as the doctors advise for the countries they are about to visit.

Word list: liability insurance, achieve, itinerary, responsibly, inducted, support, inoculations, medical, instructions, purpose, country, visiting card, think-them-through.

2 You are proposing to visit Singapore and Malaya, where your firm has widespread interests. Refer to a map of the area and list five main centres that can be used as meeting places. Then use a gazetteer to find out background information on the towns concerned.

3 You are about to go on a journey for your firm, leaving your secretary to keep general control of your work while you are away. Suggest the arrangements you should make about (*a*) very important matters, which the secretary could not be expected to deal with, (*b*) routine matters of an everyday nature, (*c*) a daily contact between the secretary and yourself, (*d*) what to do in the event of your death abroad.

4 What arrangements should be made for passports for an executive who is to tour the 'Pacific Fringe' area?

5 An overseas visit is to take in calls in Greece, Cairo, Bahrain Island, Karachi, New Delhi and Singapore. How would you ensure that the executive was adequately provided with visas, foreign currency and finance and medical cover throughout the visit?

6 You are planning a series of exhibitions in the foyers of colleges and universities in Scotland on behalf of your publishers, who produce musical scores, sheet music and books with a 'musical' interest, and which also act as agents for a well-known producer of woodwind and brass instruments.

(*a*) Draw up a list of colleges and universities that might be interested in such an exhibition.
(*b*) Draw up a letter to be sent to all such bodies seeking to know whether they would be interested, what space, etc., would be available for the 3-day event, possible dates; whether accommodation could be offered for three staff during the display, and two other points you think might be helpful. You may promise a contribution of £500 to university funds in return for these facilities.

7 Your head scientist is to visit Katmandu to set up a water-monitoring project that will use telemetry units at key points in rivers to test for oxygen, and heavy metals and other pollutants. You are to be one of the party, assisting in any way you can. Draw up a list of the matters that need to be arranged under the following headings:

(*a*) Technical matters.
(*b*) Routine travel arrangements.
(*c*) Back-up systems.
(*d*) Cover for both the executive and yourself in your absence.

21 Sources of information

21.1 Introduction

One cannot possibly know all the information that is needed to carry out even the simpler jobs in a modern office. It is necessary at times to turn to a reference book, and the range of books that will be helpful is very great. Many are specialist books, serving a particular aspect of the work of an office. Good examples are the sorts of reference books published by Croner Publications Ltd, such as:

The Reference Book for Exporters.
The Reference Book for Importers.
The Reference Book for Employers.
The Reference Book for the Self-employed and Smaller Businesses.

These books are all invaluable, and are kept up to date by monthly revision pages that are easily slipped into place, the obsolete pages being discarded. Croner Publications Ltd's address is Croner House, London Rd, Kingston upon Thames, Surrey, KT2 6SR.

Other books are general works of reference, such as *Pears Cyclopaedia*, offering information on a large range of matters that may arise over the course of the year. The most useful person in an office is often not the person who professes to know everything but the person who is surrounded by a selection of suitable reference books. The quick use of such books comes only with practice, and the reader is urged to build up a selection of such books for personal use in the office.

On a point of good office discipline, it is desirable that junior staff should be encouraged to use reference books rather than ask unnecessary questions. Although modern offices are less strict than in former times about staff talking in working hours, it is a great nuisance if a junior member of staff interrupts the train of thought of senior personnel to ask routine questions that can be answered by reference to the calendar, a dictionary or a *Pears Cyclopaedia*.

An office that is poorly supplied with reference books will be a less satisfactory place to work in for that reason. Suggestions of necessary reference books are usually welcome, and senior staff should regularly review, up-date and improve the supply available.

Today the provision of information by electronic means is widespread, and enormous libraries of information are available and accessible by telephone link or on CD ROM discs. The term CD ROM stands for 'compact disc – read only memory'. The discs have the entire body of information on any particular subject recorded on them, and anyone who purchases the disc can play the information to themselves as often as they like. However, while they can read everything that is in the memory, they cannot 'write to' the disc and change it in any way, because it is very unlikely that most of us have anything to contribute to the compact disc's memory. Anyone who is knowledgeable in the field and wishes to amend or extend the memory must contact the learned body concerned and make representations to them. Those interested in CD ROM information services might like to approach Microinfo Ltd, PO Box 3, Omega Park, Alton, Hampshire, GU34 2PG, England.

Reference books may be conveniently divided up as shown in Section 21.2 below.

21.2 A list of reference books

(a) Correspondence and the use of the English language

   (i) A good dictionary, e.g., the *Concise Oxford Dictionary* or *Chambers's Twentieth Century Dictionary*.
   (ii) *Fowler's Modern English Usage*.
   (iii) *Roget's Thesaurus of English Words and Phrases*.
   (iv) *Black's Titles and Forms of Address*.
   (v) *Pitman 2000 Dictionary of English Shorthand*.
   (vi) *Pitman New Era English Shorthand Dictionary*.

(b) Post Office and telecommunication services

   (i) *Mailguide*.
   (ii) *Index to postcode directories*.
   (iii) Telephone directories.
   (iv) BT Business Catalogue.
   (v) *UK Telex Directory*.

(c) People

   (i) *Who's Who*.
   (ii) *Debrett's Peerage or Burke's Peerage*.
   (iii) Professional lists, according to the needs of the office, e.g. *Medical Register* or *Medical Directory*, *Law List*, *Crockford's Clerical Directory*.
   (iv) Service lists: *Army List*, *Navy List*, and *Air Force List*.
   (v) A local street directory or electoral roll, where appropriate.
   (vi) *Vacher's Parliamentary Companion* (pronounced *Vasher's*).
   (vii) *Vacher's European Companion*.
   (viii) *Vacher's Biographical Guide*.

(*d*) **Trade and industry**
- (i) *UK Kompass.*
- (ii) *Kelly's Directories.*
- (iii) World Bank publications.
- (iv) *Yellow Pages* as appropriate.
- (v) *Stock Exchange Official Year-Book.*
- (vi) *Directory of Directors.*
- (vii) Individual specialist directories as required, e.g. *Benn's Hardware Guide, Food Trades Directory*, etc.

(*e*) **Travel and leisure**
- (i) *ABC Rail Guide.*
- (ii) *ABC World Airways Guide.*
- (iii) *AA and RAC Handbooks.*
- (iv) A good world atlas and gazetteer.
- (v) An atlas and gazetteer of London and/or the local area, as appropriate.
- (vi) *Hotels and Restaurants in Great Britain.*
- (vii) *Good Food Guide.*
- (viii) *Historic Houses, Castles and Gardens.*
- (ix) *Museums and Galleries in Great Britain and Ireland.*

(*f*) **General and current information**
- (i) *Whitaker's Almanack.*
- (ii) *Pears Cyclopaedia.*
- (iii) *Annual Abstract of Statistics* and the *Monthly Digest of Statistics.*
- (iv) *Britain: an Official Handbook.*
- (v) *Croner's Office Companion.*

(*g*) **Miscellaneous**
- (i) *Writers' and Artists' Year Book.*
- (ii) *Willing's Press Guide.*
- (iii) *Municipal Year Book.*

Finally, since an enormous range of reference works is available, most libraries have a copy of *British Sources of Reference and Information*, edited by T. Besterman, which is a major reference book about reference books.

21.3 A brief description of some of the more important reference books

Dictionaries
While many dictionaries offer roughly the same information, the

Concise Oxford Dictionary is a particularly reliable reference work. It tells you the following things:

  (i) How to spell the word.

  (ii) How to pronounce the word.

  (iii) What part of speech it is (i.e. noun, verb, adjective, etc.).

  (iv) What the word means.

  (v) The derivation of the word, i.e. where it originated, from Latin, Greek or a foreign language.

  (vi) Derivatives of the word (what other words have been formed from it).

  (vii) Cross-references to other words that are related.

(viii) How to form the plural of the word.

Fowler's Modern English Usage

A guide to the normally accepted 'correct' use of the English Language. It includes points of grammar, punctuation, idioms, etc. – for example, the difference between inquiry and *e*nquiry.

Roget's Thesaurus

The word *Thesaurus* comes from the Greek for 'treasury'. This book is a treasury of English words and phrases, listing all words of similar meaning, or related meaning. The clerk or executive who is 'stuck for the best word' to explain his meaning will always find it in the thousands of words classified in the *Thesaurus*. For example, under the heading 'probity' or 'honesty', appear twenty-four groups of words, totalling altogether over 500 words or phrases about upright behaviour.

Black's Titles and Forms of Address

A guide to the correct way of addressing people of rank, or holding official positions, both in writing and in speech. It also includes a guide to the pronunciation of certain surnames.

Mailguide

A guide to the services available from the Post Office, in a loose-leaf form, with replacement pages provided from time to time.

Telephone directories

These are issued free to all subscribers for their own locality and give names and addresses of most of the people who are on the telephone. A few people who, perhaps because they are particularly famous, or for some other reason, prefer not to have their telephone number widely known have what are called 'ex-directory' numbers. Such subscribers can be contacted by telephone only if they give their ex-directory number to personal friends. Telephone directories for other areas may be purchased by subscribers for a modest charge.

Classified trade lists are also issued, in what are called the 'yellow-page' directories. This idea proved to be such good business for the telephone service that 'yellow pages' have been bound into many ordinary alphabetical directories as a separate section at the end. This enables housewives or businessmen who want a particular service − say, the plumber − to find a list of all the plumbers in the area. A quick rundown the list will enable the housewife to find a plumber near her home, whom she can phone for assistance in any emergency.

Now that STD services (subscriber trunk dialling) have spread to all areas around the world, the codes required are provided in special sections at the front of all telephone directories.

A *Telex Directory*, also available, gives details of telex subscribers throughout the world.

The ABC Guides

The ABC Guides are published by Reed's Travel Services, Church St, Dunstable, Bedfordshire, LU5 4HB, United Kingdom. The full list is:

ABC World Airways Guide
Hotel & Travel Index/ABC International Edition
ABC Travel Disc
ABC Executive Flight Planners
Official Hotel Guide
ABC Holiday Guides
ABC Travel Directory
ABC Agents' Hotel Gazetteers
ABC Star Service
ABC World Airways Guide Fares Supplement
ABC Guide To International Travel
ABC Air Travel Atlas
ABC Cruise and Ferry Guide
ABC Railway Guide
ABC Air Cargo Guide

In more detail, for example:

The ABC Railway Guide

This is published monthly and lists all railway services to and from London, alphabetically, according to the destination from London, as well as the major provincial Inter-City services. It gives details about towns such as the early closing day, the population and the name of the chief hotels. It can also indicate how to travel to places without a direct rail connection by showing bus connections to the nearest rail service. In some offices regional and Continental railway guides may also be useful.

The ABC World Airways Guide

This is a similar volume, on a worldwide scale, giving details of scheduled air services throughout the world, fares, freight rates, principal travel agents and details of visa and health requirements. *Airport Times* is an inexpensive publication, appearing monthly, with sufficient detail about flight schedules for most offices.

The AA Handbook and RAC Handbook.

These handbooks are available to members of these motoring organizations. Many motorists have back copies they are prepared to give away. The maps and gazetteer section are very useful for planning convenient routes from place to place, and there is much useful information on hotels, garage facilities and apartments in every town in the country.

An atlas

This is a volume of maps showing the world, continents and countries. Generally speaking each map is repeated twice: once to show the political features, i.e. which areas are under different governments, and the second time to show the physical features — the mountain systems, river systems, low-lying areas, etc. The index is helpful to locate towns and cities which you wish to check up on. A rather similar book, called a 'gazetteer', is a geographical dictionary which gives details of countries and towns, their populations, chief products, national incomes, etc. This can be a very useful reference book, especially to a secretary asked to provide an executive with a mass of background information on a country or place which is to be visited shortly.

Hotels and Restaurants in Great Britain

This includes a useful section on London's specialist restaurants such as Chinese, Greek and seafood restaurants.

The Good Food Guide

Published by the Consumers' Association, this book aims to provide unbiased reports on restaurants.

A-Z maps

These maps are prepared by the Geographers' Map Co. Ltd, of Sevenoaks in Kent. Based on the official Ordnance Survey Maps, they include, besides a detailed street map of major towns, an index to all street names and references to places of public interest and entertainment. By showing the house numbering along the streets they enable you to judge where to leave public transport services for easiest access to the address you wish to reach.

Whitaker's Almanack

This is an annual publication that contains a vast collection of information on the countries of the world, their rulers, political organization, population, production, etc. Originally an almanack was a list of months and days, astronomical facts for the year, tidal information, etc. This is still to be found in Whitaker's, but sections on the monarchy, the Houses of Parliament, the law courts, societies and associations and many other topics make it an invaluable reference work on all aspects of British life.

Who's Who

This provides information on prominent people in this country, MPs, people with titles, honours and sporting and entertainment personalities. A biographical dictionary, or the various volumes of *Who Was Who*, will give information of people no longer living. There are also Who's Who publications for specialist fields, such as *The Authors' and Writers' Who's Who*.

The Medical Register

This is the official list of qualified doctors. There is also a *Dentists' Register* and similar lists for opticians, chiropodists, etc. The *Medical Directory* also lists medical practitioners, but in slightly more detail. Information on hospitals and their medical staff is included as well. Similar directories are issued in most other professional fields; for example, *Crockford's Clerical Directory* is the official guide to clergy of the Church of England.

Vacher's Parliamentary and European Companions

These books are updated every 3 months and give the names and departments of all parliamentary and government personalities in the United Kingdom and Europe. They enable office staff to pinpoint officials with responsibilities in particular fields, and enable them to address correspondence to the person most interested in it.

UK Kompass Register

This is published by Reed Information Services, East Grinstead, West Sussex, RH19 1ZB, and produced in association with the CBI; it is recommended by both the Chartered Institute of Marketing and the Institute of Purchasing and Supply. *Kompass* comes in four volumes to provide a complete industrial information system.

Volume 1 identifies the suppliers of over 44 000 products and services within eighty-nine industrial groups. Volume 2 provides detailed company profiles on these suppliers, backed up by the full financial information to be found in Volume 3. The new Volume 4, *Parents and Subsidiaries*, identifies a company's position within its corporate structure.

Kompass Online

A major database of business and commercial information, *Kompass Online* has an active file of over 155 000 UK companies and their products and services, plus over 300 000 named directors and managers. The system also enables users to gain access to information on the 1.2 million companies registered at Companies House as well as 300 000 European and 230 000 US companies. Up-dated daily, *Kompass Online* provides direct access by telephone, using a microcomputer or Prestel terminal. A CD-Rom containing all the data is also available.

Kelly's Directories

These are also available from Reed Information Services (see *UK Kompass Register*. above). The full list is:

Kelly's Business Directory. Published for over 100 years, this comprehensive and commercial directory contains details of over 84 000 businesses throughout the UK, classified under 15 000 product and service headings.

Kelly's Business Link. With its 100 000 free controlled circulation, the UK's most widely used one-stop purchasing guide is targeted at individuals with buying influence in major companies across a broad range of industries.

Kelly's Oil and Gas Industry Directory. This specialist guide gives details on more than 9 000 companies connected with the oil industry, and 8 000 copies are distributed on free controlled circulation.

Kelly's Export Services Directory. Distributed free of charge to major exporting organizations, this publication provides a guide to export support services, including bankers, insurance, transport, packaging and freight forwarding companies.

Kelly's Post Office London Professional Services Directory. This new publication covers, in one volume, all the professional services in the London area, including legal, financial and property. Its 15 000 free controlled circulation is targeted at key users in the capital.

Stock Exchange Official Year-Book

This gives financial information on firms, and is also a useful source for general information on companies.

The Directory of Directors

An alphabetical list of directors indicating the various companies with which they are associated, as well as a little biographical information.

Pears Cyclopaedia

This is a useful small encyclopaedia with many references about the world, everyday information and home and personal matters. It is inexpensive and covers many of the points an office junior may need to look up.

Annual Abstract of Statistics and Monthly Digest of Statistics

Official statistics for Britain in the past year, covering trade, population, weather, crime, etc.

Britain – An Official Handbook

A general description of Britain and its institutions, with some facts and figures.

Willing's Press Guide

A guide to newspapers, national and provincial, and magazines published in Britain. Some overseas newspapers and magazines are also indicated.

The Municipal Year Book

The guide to local councils and their services.

Business Equipment Digest

This is a controlled-circulation monthly magazine distributed free to office managers responsible for the purchase of office equipment and supplies. By regularly reviewing each field of office activity and evaluating new equipment, systems, etc., it helps keep senior staff up to date and alert to developments in every field.

Croner's Office Companion

A loose-leaf handbook in the Croner tradition, up-dated quarterly, which provides the secretary with a wide back-up of information on the following subject areas: general information, sources of information, travel, office management, health and safety, entertainment, employment, financial information, politics and communications.

21.4 Other sources of information

While reference books are the most useful source of information, other sources are available. The following are of interest:

(*a*) The **time** can be discovered by telephoning the talking clock, on the code number given in every telephone directory.

(*b*) The **weather** in any area may be discovered by telephoning an appropriate 'weather' telephone number. This is often very useful to travellers wishing to arrive suitably clad for functions.

(*c*) *Trade associations*. Nearly all the trades have a trade association or professional body, which acts as a source of valuable information for its members. Membership is usually relatively cheap, and a great deal of useful information is provided in the handbook produced for members each year. More specialized enquiries will usually be dealt with by a research department, whose staff are available to answer telephone enquiries, or to assist callers.

Appendix: Professional bodies

Those studying Office Procedures may take employment in many walks of life and in the course of time achieve promotion to middle management level, from which higher posts follow. Ideally once a student has found an area of commerce or industry which is appealing and interesting it is advisable to seek the fullest qualifications possible. In many vocations the fullest recognition is only accorded to those who have gone through various levels of education and then become members of the professional organization representing the industry or profession in which they actually put their skills and expertise to work. It is essential to enrol at the appropriate point as a student of whichever professional body is best for you, and to 'qualify' with them. The word 'qualify' is quoted because it means not only that you must pass the necessary examinations, but that you must acquire the necessary practical experience by working in the industry or profession. Thus, it is possible to acquire academic qualifications that bear upon transport and distribution, for example, but still be hopelessly lost when faced with a practical freight-forwarding problem. Only membership of the Institute of Freight Forwarders or the Chartered Institute of Transport, or some similar professional body, will give the necessary knowledge and status in the industry or profession of your choice.

Whatever level you enter an industry at it is advisable to register as soon as possible as a student member of the appropriate institute. It is possible to enter at all levels and to take exemption from any subjects you have already studied in the professional examinations, pursuing the rest to achieve full qualification. At the same time your registration gives you credit for your experience in the industry itself, which accumulates over the years to combine practical skills with the theory studied in the professional study courses.

It is hoped that the following list will help readers locate the professional body most appropriate to their field of activity. The list is up to date at the time of going to press, but addresses and telephone numbers of course may change.

Your aim should be to obtain full qualifications in the professional body of your choice, after concluding any academic course you are presently embarked on. For those in employment already, and not possessing the necessary qualifications for entry to a professional body, guidance will usually be given about subjects to study. The Made Simple series contains most of the books you will need, and 6–12 months' study is usually enough to qualify for student entry. Write well in advance to educational bodies whose examinations you wish to sit, so as not to miss vital deadlines for entry.

A businesslike approach to such studies is essential. Buy the books, and enroll on courses in your own locality if you can; if not, study hard on your own and work systematically.

Professional bodies whose names and addresses are not included in the list are invited to submit details for inclusion in the next edition. The author apologizes in advance for any such omissions. Mention of this textbook as a set book for students, or as a 'recommended-reading' book, would be appreciated.

Professional bodies

Acronym	Name of institution	Address and telephone number
AAT	Association of Accounting Technicians	154 Clerkenwell Road, London EC1R 5AD Tel: (071) 837 8600
ABE	Association of Business Executives	William House, Worple Rd, London SW19 4DD Tel: (081) 879 1973
ACCA	Chartered Association of Certified Accountants	29 Lincoln's Inn Fields, London WC2A 3EE Tel: (071) 242 6855
BIFA and IFF	British International Freight Association and Institute of Freight Forwarders Ltd	Redfern House, Browells Lane, Feltham, Middlesex TW13 7EP Tel: (081) 844 2266
CA	Institute of Chartered Accountants in England and Wales	Moorgate Place, London EC2P 2BJ Tel: (071) 628 7060
CAM	The Communication, Advertising and Marketing Educational Foundation	Abford House, 15 Wilton Road, London SW1 1NJ Tel: (071) 828 7506
CBSI	Chartered Building Society Institute	*See address for Chartered Institute of Bankers*
CIB	Chartered Institute of Bankers	Emmanuel House, 4–9 Burgate Lane, Canterbury, Kent CT1 2XJ Tel: (0227) 762600
CII	Chartered Insurance Institute	31 Hillcrest Road, London E18 2JP Tel: (081) 989 8464

CIMA	Chartered Institute of Management Accountants	63 Portland Place, London W1N 4AB Tel: (071) 637 2311
CIM	Chartered Institute of Marketing	Moor Hall, Cookham, Maidenhead, Berkshire SL6 9QH Tel: (06285) 24922
CIPFA	Chartered Institute of Public Finance and Accountancy	3 Robert Street, London WC2N 6BH Tel: (071) 895 8823
CIPS	Chartered Institute of Purchasing & Supply	Easton House, Easton on the Hill, Stamford, Lincs PE9 3NZ Tel: (0780) 56777
CIT	Chartered Institute of Transport	80 Portland Place, London W1N 4DP Tel: (071) 636 9952
CLE	Council of Legal Education	Inns of Court School of Law, 4 Gray's Inn Road London WC1R 4AJ Tel: (071) 404 5787
FOA	Faculty of Actuaries	23 St Andrews Square, Edinburgh, EH2 1AQ Tel: (031) 557 1575
HCIMA	Hotel, Catering and Institutional Management Association	191 Trinity Road, London SW17 7HN Tel: (081) 672 4251
IAM	Institute of Administrative Management	40 Chatsworth Parade, Petts Wood, Orpington, Kent Tel: (0689) 875555
IAS	Institute of Agricultural Secretaries	NAC Stoneleigh, Kenilworth, Warwickshire CV8 2LZ Tel: (0203) 696592
ICM	Institute of Commercial Management	PO Box 125, Bournemouth, Dorset BH1 1XF Tel: (0202) 290999
ICOMA	The Institute of Company Accountants	40 Tyndalls Park Road, Bristol BS8 1PL Tel: (0272) 738 261
ICS	Institute of Chartered Shipbrokers	3 Gracechurch St, London EC3V OAT Tel: (071) 283 1361
ICSA	Institute of Chartered Secretaries and Administrators	16 Park Crescent, London W1N 4AH Tel: (071) 580 4741

IHSM	Institute of Health Service Management	75 Portland Place, London W1N 4AN Tel: (071) 580 5041
IMS	Institute of Management Services	1 Cecil Court, London Road, Enfield, Middlesex EN2 6DD Tel: (081) 363 7452
IOA	Institute of Actuaries	Staple Inn Hall, High Holborn, London WC1V 7QJ Tel: (071) 242 0106
IOTA	Institute of Transport Administration	32 Palmerston Road, Southampton SO1 1LL Tel: (0703) 631380
IOX	Institute of Export	Export House, 64 Clifton Street London, EC2A 4HB Tel: (071) 247 9812
IPM	Institute of Personnel Management	IPM House, Camp Road, Wimbledon, London SW19 4UX Tel: (081) 946 9100
IQPS	Institute of Qualified Private Secretaries	126 Farnham Road, Slough, Bucks SL1 4XA Tel: (0753) 522395
IRTE	Institute of Road Transport Engineers	1 Cromwell Place, Kensington, London SW7 2JF Tel: (071) 589 3744
MRS	Market Research Society	15 Northbury St, London EC1V OAH Tel: (071) 490 4911
NEBSM	National Examining Board in Supervisory Management	76 Portland Place, London, W1N 4AA Tel: (071) 278 2468

Index